An Introduction to Computational Macroeconomics

Anelí Bongers
Universidad de Málaga, Spain
Trinidad Gómez
Universidad de Málaga, Spain
José L. Torres
Universidad de Málaga, Spain

 Bridging Languages and Scholarship

Series in Economic Methodology
VERNON PRESS

www.vernonpress.com

In the Americas:	In the rest of the world:
Vernon Press	Vernon Press
1000 N West Street,	C/Sancti Espiritu 17,
Suite 1200, Wilmington,	Malaga, 29006
Delaware 19801	Spain
United States	

 Bridging Languages and Scholarship

Series in Economic Methodology

Library of Congress Control Number: 2019944475

ISBN: 978-1-62273-943-1

Also available: 978-1-62273-654-6 [Hardback]; 978-1-62273-940-0 [PDF, E-Book]

Book is also available in Spanish as *Introducción a la Macroeconomía Computacional* (Vernon Press, 2019): 978-1-62273-600-3 [Hardback, US]; 978-84-17332-02-0 [Paperback, Spain Edition]; 978-1-62273-811-3 [PDF, E-Book].

The accompanying files for this title can be downloaded here: https://vernonpress.com/book/714

Cover design by Vernon Press, using elements created by Starline / Freepik.

Table of Contents

Preface

Dynamic General Equilibrium (DGE) models, either stochastic or deterministic, have become a fundamental tool in current macroeconomic analysis. Modern macroeconomic analysis is increasingly concerned with the construction, calibration and/or estimation, and simulation of Dynamic Stochastic General Equilibrium (DSGE) models. Notwithstanding the approach's important shortcomings, DSGE models are now in common use everywhere, spreading from academic research to Central Banks and other public and private economic institutions. This typology of models, which are based on the micro-foundation of the decisions taken by the different economic agents that are assumed to be rational, constitutes the reference theoretical framework of current macroeconomic analysis, and has two main characteristics. Firstly, these are dynamic models incorporating forward-looking variables, i.e., future variables in expected terms that are supposed to be determined in a context of rational expectations. Secondly, they are models in which the determination of macroeconomic variables is based on microeconomic analysis (microfoundation) and in a general equilibrium environment. In parallel, there is another typology of dynamic macroeconomic models, also in a context of rational expectations, which are non-micro-based, but are in turn based on the traditional IS-LM approach and the Phillips curve, or on more recent developments that incorporate monetary policy rules and a micro-based aggregate demand. Both types of models can be represented through a system of dynamic equations, which is composed of a set of equations that can be calculated numerically in a relatively simple way. However, apart from the greater or lesser complexity of this type of dynamic models at a theoretical level, the main problem that we find when teaching macroeconomics to undergraduate students or for those who want to get into this branch of macroeconomic modeling, is that they do not have an explicit solution, so they can only be solved numerically or by resorting to graphical analysis, mainly through phase diagrams, which is an important barrier to their incorporation into the teaching of advanced macroeconomics at the undergraduate level. This dynamic theoretical modeling approach makes the interrelation between current macroeconomics and numerical computing tools very tight, thus making it necessary to introduce a new approach that includes both elements in the learning of macroeconomics. Even the teaching of non-micro-based, simple dynamic models, requires the use of relatively complex analytical tools in order to work with systems of difference equations or differential equations. In all these cases, the usual strategy at introductory levels is to apply graphical analysis, through the construction of the phase diagram, as a basic instrument for carrying out macroeconomic analysis. However, even the use of the phase diagram assumes a certain level of difficulty while also presenting a number of limitations. All these elements result that the macroeconomic analysis scheme that is used by the majority of economic authorities, from governments to central banks, international organizations, and research centers, is not known by economics graduates, which is very striking, as the teaching of macroeconomics in universities at an undergraduate level is one step behind its use at academic level and its practical application in the real world.

However, it is feasible to introduce dynamic macroeconomic models in a relatively understandable way, as well as their numerical solution at a basic level. In fact, the contents of this book are based on the idea of introducing a new approach to the teaching of macroeconomics, which allows, through techniques that are relatively easy to implement and comprehensible at introductory levels, the numerical solution of these models and their use for macroeconomic analysis. Although current macroeconomic analysis need knowledge of some complex computer tools and mathematical techniques, in practice, these models can be solved with simple computer software as it is the case of a spreadsheet. A spreadsheet contains a set of tools that can be used for the numerical solution of any type of dynamic macroeconomic models. The proposed approach offers a new perspective for the teaching of macroeconomics at an undergraduate level, since it allows the flexible use of dynamic models for its application to macroeconomic analysis, being at the same time an introduction to numerical solution methods. All this can be done with accessible computational software that is easy to learn and is already well known, at least to some degree, by undergraduate students. This is the strategy pursued in this book.

As we have indicated previously, in general terms, we can distinguish two types of models used in current macroeconomic analysis. Firstly, simple dynamic models that do not have a microeconomic foundation, but that use rational expectations. An example of these models is the overreaction or overshooting of the exchange rate, or the IS-LM traditional Phillips Curve model. Secondly, the models based on the so-called Dynamic General Equilibrium model, both stochastic and deterministic, or Ramsey's optimal growth model, which constitute the theoretical framework of reference used in current macroeconomic analysis. These macroeconomic models do not have, in general, a closed-form solution and, therefore, can only be solved using numerical methods. This makes computational macroeconomics a key element in current macroeconomic analysis and the introduction of a necessary change in the way in which students are introduced to macroeconomic analysis.

The objective of this book is to make an introduction, at the most basic level, to computational macroeconomics and to the resolution of micro-based macroeconomic dynamic general equilibrium models. The fundamental idea is to show that it is relatively achievable task to solve a dynamic macroeconomic model, whether micro-based or not, using tools that are available to everyone, without the need to learn computer programs and languages of a certain complexity, which limit their practical application. This book includes a series of computer exercises with alternative macroeconomic models, divided into three parts: Basic Dynamic Models, Introduction to Dynamic General Equilibrium, and Economic Growth. The objective is to solve different and simple models by using numerical and computational methods. Computation in this context means we will use a computer to solve these models and that their solution will be done numerically. All the models that we study are solved and computed in a deterministic environment, although their resolution in a stochastic environment does not pose major problems since a spreadsheet contains tools for the incorporation of random variables. However, we consider that the deterministic environment is much more illustrative for learning purposes than a stochastic environment, so we have not considered it relevant to introduce the stochastic component in the studied models.

The first part of the book includes a series of numerical exercises using simple linear dynamic models. In Chapter 1, an exercise of a general model, not representing any specific macroeconomic model, is carried out, based on a dynamical system composed of two difference equations. The objective of this exercise is to introduce the fundamental concepts to be use next, as well as to present the analytical framework to be use for the numerical solution of these types of models. Next, in Chapter 2, we present a dynamic version of the IS-LM model. The IS-LM model constitutes the basic theoretical framework used in the teaching of macroeconomics at intermediate levels. The model considered here is a dynamic version, where there is a process of adjustment in the price level over time (the Phillips curve). To close this first part, Chapter 3 presents Dornbusch's overshooting model of the exchange rate. This is a model for a small open economy that allows explaining the response of the nominal exchange rate to different shocks.

The second part of the book is composed of five chapters. In Chapter 4, we present the basic household problem in terms of the consumption-savings decision. This analysis constitutes a fundamental piece in the dynamic models of general equilibrium that are used in the current macroeconomic analysis. Chapter 5 introduces the consumption-leisure decision in the household problem, including leisure as an additional argument in the utility function, from which the labor supply is derived. Chapter 6 analyzes the consumption-savings decisions by households, but also considering the role of the government, with the objective of studying how households' decisions change according to tax rates and social security contributions. Chapter 7 studies the investment decision through Tobin's Q model. To close this second part, Chapter 8 presents a very simple version of the dynamic general equilibrium model.

The last part of the book focuses on the analysis of economic growth models. We study two different models. First, in Chapter 9, we conduct a numerical solution of Solow's exogenous growth model, which is the basic framework for studying the long-term behavior of an economy. Finally, in Chapter 10, we present Ramsey's optimal growth model. In this case, the analysis is similar to the dynamic general equilibrium model presented above, but considering population growth.

The software used in this book is Excel® from Microsoft®. Excel is a spreadsheet, similar to others such as Open Office Calc. The advantages of spreadsheets are that they are easy to handle, widely used and known by a large number of users, while having a high capacity to perform a wide variety of numerical operations. Barreto (2015) presents a series of arguments about why Excel is an adequate tool for the teaching of macroeconomics, indicating that spreadsheets have important advantages when communicating ideas and presenting statistical data to students.[1] In fact, spreadsheets are a resource that is increasingly used in the teaching of economics, Strulik (2004)[2], and Gilbert and Oladi (2011)[3] being examples. More recently, Barreto (2016) proposes a set of spreadsheets for the teaching of macroeconomics at introductory and intermediate levels[4]. Another macroeconomics manual with simulations in Excel is that of Carlin and Soskice (2015)[5]. A book with different examples of computational economy where other computer programs are also used, apart from spreadsheets, is Kendrick, Mercado and Amman (2006).[6]

This book shows that the numerical solution of dynamic general equilibrium models is a relatively simple task that can be done in a spreadsheet. Micro-

---

[1] Barreto, H. (2015). Why Excel?, Journal of Economic Education, 46(3), 300-309.

[2] Strulik, H. (2004). Solving Rational Expectations Models Using Excel, Journal of Economic Education, 35(3): 269-283.

[3] Gilbert, J. y Oladi, R. (2011). Excel Models for International Trade Theory and Policy: An Online Resource, Journal of Economic Education, 42(1): 95.

[4] Barreto, H. (2016). Teaching Macroeconomics with Microsoft Excel. Cambridge University Press.

[5] Carlin, W. y Soskice, D. (2015). Macroeconomics: Institutions, Instability, and the Financial System. Oxford University Press.

[6] Kendrick, D. M., Mercado, P. R. y Amman, H. M. (2006). Computational Economics. Princeton University Press.

based macroeconomic models can be solved by following two alternative approaches. First, they can be solved using Excel's Solver tool, which allows the maximization of an objective function subject to certain restrictions. Secondly, these models can be solved directly using a linear approximation to the non-linear equations of the model in terms of the deviations from the steady state. This allows us to calculate in a simple way the eigenvalues associated with the system and use them to calculate numerically the readjustment in the forward-looking variables facing a disturbance when the solution is a saddle-point, in a similar way to the procedure that we would use for solving more traditional non-micro-based dynamic models.

Finally, the book includes a series of appendices with some basic mathematical concepts that are necessary for the performed analysis. These appendices also include a series of computer code, where the different models are solved in both MATLAB® and DYNARE, which are computational tools commonly used in current macroeconomic analysis. For those who want to use their smartphone or tablet for the solution of stochastic dynamic general equilibrium models, see Blake (2012).[7]

Anelí, Trinidad and José Luis
Málaga, December 2019

---

[7] Blake, A. P. (2012). DSGE modeling on iPhone/iPad using SpaceTime. Computational Economics, 40(4): 313-332.

Part I: Basic Dynamic Systems

1. An introduction to computational dynamic systems

1.1. Introduction

$$f(x) = f(x-1)$$

Dynamic macroeconomic model can be written as a system of dynamic equations: a system of differential equations if the model is defined in continuous time or a system of difference equations if we define it in discrete time. The used temporal approach depends on the type of analysis to be carried out. At a theoretical level, it is usual to develop macroeconomic models in continuous time, which allows the application of certain analytical instruments, such as the phase diagram, in order to obtain a graphical representation of the model to be used for shock analysis. However, if our objective is the numerical resolution of the model, then the approach to be used would be the discrete-time approach. In this case, the macroeconomic model is defined as a system of difference equations. In any case, both specifications are equivalent and lead to similar results, although the exact specification of each equation may be different in both temporal contexts. The set of equations that make up a model includes three elements: endogenous variables (unknowns), exogenous variables and parameters. Given some values for the parameters, which have to be calibrated or estimated, and given some values for the exogenous variables, which are supposed to be given, we can numerically calculate the corresponding value of the endogenous variables. On the other hand, the numerical resolution requires the use of specific functional forms that determine the relationship between these elements, so it is necessary to have a specific functional form for each equation.

In this first chapter, we carry out a simple computational exercise with the aim of illustrating how a computer can be used to perform numerical simulations of dynamical models. For this, we will use a relatively easy-to-use tool widely known as a spreadsheet. In particular, we will use the Microsoft Office Excel spreadsheet, although we could also use other similar spreadsheets, such as Open Office Calc. In various appendices, we include similar exercises but using other tools commonly used in macroeconomic analysis, such as MATLAB, or based in a software designed specifically for the resolution of dynamic macroeconomic models with rational expectations, such as DYNARE. The fundamental idea of this first chapter is not to solve a particular macroeconomic model but to show how to solve and numerically simulate a dynamic system in discrete time and show that it is a relatively simple task.

Solving this type of dynamic systems numerically has important advantages when carrying out different analyses to study the effects of different disturbances on the economy. In the first place, it allows the obtaining of the temporary paths of the endogenous variables in response to a shock, that is, it allows one to know how each macroeconomic variable reacts to a disturbance represented by a change in the exogenous variables. This is what is known as impulse-response function or transition dynamics, an instrument widely used in macroeconomic analysis. For that, it is enough to make a plot of the value of each variable as a function of time to appreciate its dynamic behavior in response to a change in the economic environment. Secondly, it allows one to carry out sensitivity experiments, studying the behavior of the model according to the value of the different parameters. Thus, once the model is solved and computed numerically, it is only necessary to change the value of a parameter to observe how the economy reacts, both in terms of its equilibrium and its dynamics. This means that we can simulate the different trajectories of the endogenous variables in response to a change in the exogenous variables, conditioned to a given value of the parameters of the model.

In this first chapter, we numerically simulate Richardson's model of arms race. This is a model composed of two linear difference equations that represent the behavior over time of two countries, potentially enemies, and their decisions on the stock of weapons of each of them in relation to the stock of weapons of the other country. The choice of this particular model as the starting point obeys several factors. First, it is a very popular model in both political science and economics (used, for example, in microeconomics to analyze the behavior of a duopoly in a dynamic context where the endogenous variables are the market shares of the firms). Secondly, it is a model with a very simple structure, so it is easy to understand. Finally, it is a model in which, depending on the value of the parameters, we obtain the two types of solutions we can obtain in a macroeconomic model: global stability (when all trajectories bring us to equilibrium) or saddle point (when only a few trajectories take us to the steady state, while the rest take us away from it). In Section 2, we present a brief description of the difference equations as well as the notation of the dynamic system that we will solve in discrete time. In Section 3, we present an example of a dynamic system, and how to simulate it numerically. Section 4 shows the numerical resolution of the dynamic system in Excel, describing all the elements that must be entered in the spreadsheet to obtain the numerical solution. Section 5 uses the previously constructed spreadsheet to analyze the effects of a given disturbance, that is, a change in the exogenous variables. Finally, in Section 6, a similar analysis is carried out but in terms of a change in the value of the parameters. This is what is called sensitivity analysis. In the particular case of the model that we are analyzing, the sensitivity analysis has special relevance, since the system stability can change from a solution with global stability to a saddle point solution.

1.2. A simple dynamic model

In general, we can write a macroeconomic model as a dynamic system that is composed of a set of difference equations:

$$\Delta X_t = F(X_t, Z_t) \tag{1.1}$$

where X_t is a vector of endogenous variables of dimension n, Z_t is a vector of exogenous variables of dimension m, and $F(\cdot)$ is a particular mathematical function. The symbol Δ indicates variation with respect to time, such that:

$$\Delta X_t = X_{t+1} - X_t \tag{1.2}$$

that is, the variation at the moment t is defined as the difference between the value of the variable at the moment $t + 1$ and its value in the previous period, t.[1] In this way, the value of the endogenous variables at the moment t is equal to their value in the previous period plus their rate of variation during that period, so we could define:

$$X_t = X_{t-1} + \Delta X_{t-1} \tag{1.3}$$

Expression (1.1) indicates that the variation with respect to the time of the vector of endogenous variables is a function of the value of these endogenous variables and the value of the exogenous variables. In this way, what this system of equations indicates is how the endogenous variables move along time as a function of the changes that occur in the exogenous variables.[2]

---

[1] Another way also used to define the variations of the variables at the moment t is:

$$\Delta X_t = X_t - X_{t-1}$$

The use of one specification or another depends on whether the value of the variable is defined at the beginning of the period or at the end of it. Both specifications are not equivalent, resulting in different results.

[2] Alternatively, the system of equations can be written as:

$$X_t = G(X_t, Z_t)$$

that is known as normal form (see Appendix A). However, to make the analysis equivalent to the one carried out in continuous time, in which the equations are specified in terms of the derivative with respect to the time of the endogenous variables, which is the form usually adopted in macroeconomic analysis, we have opted to carry out all the analyzes with the representation given by the specification (1.1).

As a previous step, we will proceed to apply logarithms to all variables (except those that are defined in percentage terms, such as the interest rate), denoted by a lowercase letter. Therefore, we define:

$$x_t = \ln X_t \tag{1.4}$$

Hence, the growth rate for each variable, can be defined as:

$$\Delta x_t = x_{t+1} - x_t = \ln X_{t+1} - \ln X_t = \ln \left(\frac{X_{t+1}}{X_t} \right)$$

$$= \ln \left(1 + \frac{X_{t+1} - X_t}{X_t} \right) \cong \frac{X_{t+1} - X_t}{X_t} \tag{1.5}$$

that is, the variation with respect to time in logarithmic terms is approximately equivalent to the growth rate of the variables, which is very useful, since in most cases, our interest will focus on knowing how the growth rate of macroeconomic variables is. Indeed, the rate of growth of the output level is named economic growth, the rate of growth of prices is named inflation, etc.

Initially, we will work with systems of linear difference equations. In practice, many of the equations that make up a macroeconomic model, mainly micro-based macroeconomic models, are non-linear equations. We can suppose that the system of difference equations is linear or construct a linear approximation of the same in the case that the initial equations are non-linear and write it as:

$$\Delta x_t = A x_t + B z_t \tag{1.6}$$

where A is a matrix $n \times n$, B is a matrix $n \times m$ and z_t is the vector of exogenous variables $m \times 1$. Although we specify the vector of exogenous variables as a function of time, in practice it is a constant, except when an exogenously determined disturbance that affects its value occurs. The fact of defining the exogenous variables as a function of time is only intended to differentiate them from the parameters of the model, which are also constant.

For illustrative purposes, we assume that $n = 2$, that is, our model would be composed of two difference equations and two endogenous variables. The analysis would be similar if the number of equations in the system is greater. In particular, the typical dynamic system with which we will work is the following:

$$\begin{bmatrix} \Delta x_{1,t} \\ \Delta x_{2,t} \end{bmatrix} = A \begin{bmatrix} x_{1,t} \\ x_{2,t} \end{bmatrix} + B z_t \tag{1.7}$$

being

$$A = \begin{bmatrix} a_{11} & a_{12} \\ a_{21} & a_{22} \end{bmatrix} \tag{1.8}$$

and where the dimension of the matrix B will depend on the number of exogenous variables included in the vector z_t.

1.3. An example of dynamic system: Richardson's model of arms race

Before proceeding with the numerical resolution of different macroeconomic models, we begin by solving a general dynamic system that does not correspond to any specific macroeconomic model. This is the arms race model, developed by Lewis Fry Richardson (1881-1953) in 1919.[3] This model represents two countries, which are potentially enemies, and where the endogenous variable is the armament stock of each of them. This simple set-up is very intuitive to understand the dynamic behavior of the endogenous variables. Depending on the value of the parameters, the solution of the model is determined by the existence of global stability or by a saddle point, two different solutions that we can find in macroeconomic models to be study later.

Richardson's model of arms race can be defined through the following linear dynamic system, in which we have two endogenous variables $(x_{1,t}, x_{2,t})$ and two exogenous variables $(z_{1,t}, z_{2,t})$, where the stock of armament of each country depends positively on the stock of armament of the other country and negative on our own stock of armament. In matrix notation:

$$\begin{bmatrix} \Delta x_{1,t} \\ \Delta x_{2,t} \end{bmatrix} = \underbrace{\begin{bmatrix} -\alpha & \beta \\ \gamma & -\delta \end{bmatrix}}_{A} \begin{bmatrix} x_{1,t} \\ x_{2,t} \end{bmatrix} + \underbrace{\begin{bmatrix} \theta & 0 \\ 0 & \eta \end{bmatrix}}_{B} \begin{bmatrix} z_{1,t} \\ z_{2,t} \end{bmatrix} \tag{1.9}$$

where the matrix A represents the matrix of coefficients associated with the endogenous variables and the matrix B the coefficients associated with the exogenous variables. The endogenous variables represent the armament stock of each country (countries 1 and 2), while the exogenous variables represent any factor that affects the decision on the armament stock in each of the countries. All parameters, represented by Greek letters, are defined in positive terms.

Therefore, the equations that define the behavior over time of the two endogenous variables are the following:

---

[3] Richardson, L. F. (1919). The mathematical psychology of war. W. Hunt: Oxford. Richardson, L. F. (1935a). Mathematical psychology of war. Nature, 135: 830-831. Richardson, L. F (1935b). Mathematical psychology of war. Letter to the Editor. Nature, 136: 1025.

$$\Delta x_{1,t} = -\alpha x_{1,t} + \beta x_{2,t} + \theta z_{1,t} \tag{1.10}$$

$$\Delta x_{2,t} = \gamma x_{1,t} - \delta x_{2,t} + \eta z_{2,t} \tag{1.11}$$

This model describes the reaction functions of each country with respect to the decision on armament of the other. Thus, observing the sign of the parameters of the matrix A, we find that the dynamics of the armament stock in a country depends negatively on its own armament stock and positively on the armament stock of the other country. The parameter β represents how country 1 reacts to the stock of weapons in country 2, while the parameter γ indicates how country 2 reacts to the stock of weapons in country 1.

Structure of the model of arms race	
Reaction function of country 1	$\Delta x_{1,t} = -\alpha x_{1,t} + \beta x_{2,t} + \theta z_{1,t}$
Reaction function of country 2	$\Delta x_{2,t} = \gamma x_{1,t} - \delta x_{2,t} + \eta z_{2,t}$
Variation of the armament stock country 1	$\Delta x_{1,t} = x_{1,t+1} - x_{1,t}$
Variation of the armament stock country 2	$\Delta x_{2,t} = x_{2,t+1} - x_{2,t}$

Next, we will study two concepts that are fundamental for the analysis to be done later: first, the concept of equilibrium, which we define as the steady state, and second, the concept of stability of the system, which will indicate how the trajectories of the variables are with respect to the steady state.

1.3.1 Definition of equilibrium: The Steady State

The concept of equilibrium used in dynamic analysis is the so-called Steady State. While in a static analysis the concept of equilibrium typically relates to a situation in which the supply of a certain variable is equal to its demand (market clearing), in the dynamic analysis, the concept of equilibrium relates to a situation in which economic variables remain constant over time (their time variation is zero, so they take the same value period by period). The value of the variables in steady-state, denoted by a horizontal bar on the variable, therefore, would be defined by that situation in which the variation with respect to the time is equal to zero.

$$\bar{x} \Rightarrow \Delta x_t = f(x_t, z_t) = 0 \Rightarrow x_t = \bar{x} \tag{1.12}$$

This means that the steady state of a dynamic system is given by a vector of n-dimension zeros, for each of the difference equations of the system presenting the temporal variation of the endogenous variables ($\Delta x_t = 0$).

To obtain the steady state of our system given by (1.9), we calculate the vector of zeros for the vector of variations with respect to time. This means that the matrix A multiplied by the vector of endogenous variables has to be equal to the negative of the matrix B times the vector of exogenous variables. In this situation, the vector of endogenous variables would correspond to its steady-state value, such that:

$$\begin{bmatrix} \Delta x_{1,t} \\ \Delta x_{2,t} \end{bmatrix} = \begin{bmatrix} 0 \\ 0 \end{bmatrix} \Rightarrow A \begin{bmatrix} x_{1,t} \\ x_{2,t} \end{bmatrix} = -B z_t \tag{1.13}$$

By solving for the vector of variables in steady state, we obtain the following expression that allows us to calculate the value of each endogenous variable in equilibrium (steady state values):

$$\begin{bmatrix} \bar{x}_{1,t} \\ \bar{x}_{2,t} \end{bmatrix} = -A^{-1} B z_t \tag{1.14}$$

under the assumption that the matrix A is non-singular, that is, $Det(A) \neq 0$, so that its inverse exists (that is, we assume that $rank(A) = 2$). As we can verify, the steady state of each variable is a number, i.e., it is a constant, which depends on the parameters of the matrices A and B, and the value of the exogenous variables. Therefore, alterations of the exogenous variables or of the parameters contained in the matrices A and B cause changes in the steady-state value of the endogenous variables. In the particular example that we are analyzing, we have:

$$A = \begin{bmatrix} -\alpha & \beta \\ \gamma & -\delta \end{bmatrix}, B = \begin{bmatrix} \theta & 0 \\ 0 & \eta \end{bmatrix}, z_t = \begin{bmatrix} z_{1,t} \\ z_{2,t} \end{bmatrix} \tag{1.15}$$

Calculating the inverse of the matrix A results in:

$$A^{-1} = \frac{1}{\alpha\delta - \gamma\delta} \begin{bmatrix} -\delta & -\beta \\ -\gamma & -\alpha \end{bmatrix} \tag{1.16}$$

and therefore, the steady state, using the definition given in (1.14), is given by:

$$\begin{bmatrix} \bar{x}_1 \\ \bar{x}_2 \end{bmatrix} = -\frac{1}{\alpha\delta - \gamma\delta} \begin{bmatrix} -\delta & -\beta \\ -\gamma & -\alpha \end{bmatrix} \begin{bmatrix} \theta & 0 \\ 0 & \eta \end{bmatrix} \begin{bmatrix} z_{1,t} \\ z_{2,t} \end{bmatrix} \tag{1.17}$$

By operating in the previous expression, it turns out that the value of the variables in steady state is given by:

$$\bar{x}_1 = \frac{\delta\theta}{\alpha\delta - \gamma\beta} z_{1,t} + \frac{\beta\eta}{\alpha\delta - \gamma\beta} z_{2,t} \tag{1.18}$$

$$\bar{x}_2 = \frac{\gamma\theta}{\alpha\delta - \gamma\beta} z_{1,t} + \frac{\alpha\eta}{\alpha\delta - \gamma\beta} z_{2,t} \tag{1.19}$$

As we can see, the resulting value is a number, given that it only depends on the exogenous variables and the parameters of the model, which in turn are all numbers. Obviously, if the value of the exogenous variables changes, the steady-state value of the endogenous variables will also change. The same would happen if the value of the parameters is altered. Finally, note that to obtain a steady state in this model, it must be fulfilled that $\alpha\delta - \gamma\beta \neq 0$, since otherwise, the determinant of the matrix A would be 0.

1.3.2 Stability of the System

The dynamic properties of the system of equations are fundamental when determining how the trajectories of the different endogenous variables are when a shock occurs that affects the values of the exogenous variables. These trajectories may be convergent or divergent with respect to the steady state. Next, we indicate the procedure we will use to study the stability of the system. To perform the stability analysis of the system and know how the trajectories of the variables will be related to the steady state, we must calculate the roots (eigenvalues, which we call λ) associated with the matrix of the endogenous variables. Stability is an important property of the system because it tells us, given a disturbance that leads to a certain situation of imbalance, what are the time trajectories to be followed by the different endogenous variables to reach the new steady state.

To perform the stability analysis of our system of two differential equations, we have to solve a second-degree equation that we obtain from equalizing to zero the determinant of the coefficients matrix associated with the endogenous variables minus the identity matrix multiplied by λ. That is, we would calculate:

$$Det[A - \lambda I] = 0 \tag{1.20}$$

where I is the identity matrix, being:

$$I = \begin{bmatrix} 1 & 0 \\ 0 & 1 \end{bmatrix} \tag{1.21}$$

Therefore, returning to the system defined in (1.9), given the matrix A and using expression (1.20), we have

$$Det\begin{bmatrix} -\alpha & \beta \\ \gamma & -\delta \end{bmatrix} - \lambda\begin{bmatrix} 1 & 0 \\ 0 & 1 \end{bmatrix} = Det\begin{bmatrix} -\alpha - \lambda & \beta \\ \gamma & -\delta - \lambda \end{bmatrix} = 0 \tag{1.22}$$

By calculating the determinant, grouping the terms and equalizing to zero, we arrive at the following second-degree equation:

$$\lambda^2 + (\alpha + \delta)\lambda + (\alpha\delta - \gamma\beta) = 0 \tag{1.23}$$

or equivalently

$$\lambda^2 - tr(A)\lambda + Det(A) = 0 \tag{1.24}$$

where $tr(A)$ is the trace of the matrix A. By solving, we obtain that the roots (eigenvalues) are the following:

$$\lambda_1, \lambda_2 = \frac{-(\alpha+\delta)\pm\sqrt{(\alpha+\delta)^2-4(\alpha\delta-\gamma\beta)}}{2} \tag{1.25}$$

The stability of the system will depend on the resulting values for the eigenvalues, λ_1, λ_2. In particular, the stability of the system will depend on the value of the module of the eigenvalues plus the unit, depending on whether it is greater or lesser than the unit (see Appendix A for a description of the necessary stability conditions). These eigenvalues can be real or complex, depending on the sign of $(\alpha + \delta)^2 - 4(\alpha\delta - \gamma\beta)$. If its value is positive, then the eigenvalues are real numbers. On the contrary, if its value is negative, then we obtain complex numbers. However, in this particular model, this last case is not possible given that $(\alpha + \delta)^2 - 4(\alpha\delta - \gamma\beta) = \alpha^2 + \delta^2 + 2\alpha\delta - 4\alpha\delta + 4\gamma\beta = (\alpha - \delta)^2 + 4\gamma\beta$ is always greater than or equal to 0.

In the case that the roots are real, the modulus, that is, the absolute value of the eigenvalues plus one, is defined as:

$$Modulus(\lambda + 1) = |\lambda + 1| \tag{1.26}$$

In the case where the roots are complex, that is when $\lambda = a \pm bi$, then the modulus would be defined as:[4]

$$Modulus(\lambda + 1) = \sqrt{(a + 1)^2 + b^2} \tag{1.27}$$

The system would show global stability, that is, all the trajectories converge to the steady state, if $|\lambda_1 + 1| < 1$ and $|\lambda_2 + 1| < 1$, in the case that the eigenvalues are real numbers. If the eigenvalues are complex numbers, $\lambda = a \pm bi$, then $\sqrt{(a + 1)^2 + b^2} < 1$ would have to be fulfilled. If, on the other hand, the module of one of the roots plus one is greater than the unit, for example, $|\lambda_1 + 1| < 1$ and $|\lambda_2 + 1| > 1$, then the solution would present a saddle point, where there would be both convergent and divergent trajectories. Finally, if it turns out that $|\lambda_1 + 1| > 1$ and $|\lambda_2 + 1| > 1$, for the case of real roots, or else $\sqrt{(a + 1)^2 + b^2} > 1$, for the case of complex roots, then the system would present global instability, where all the trajectories would be divergent with respect to the steady state.

1.4. Numeric solution

Next, we will proceed to solve numerically the system of difference equations defined previously by using a spreadsheet (in particular, Excel). The procedure is relatively simple, since we only have to numerically simulate the value of

---

[4] If we move the complex number $\lambda = a \pm bi$ to a point on a Cartesian plane, we can verify, using the Pythagorean theorem, that the absolute value of this complex number is equal to the Euclidean distance from the origin of the plane to that point.

the dynamic equations that make up the model for a certain number of periods. For this, we need to previously give values both to the system parameters and the exogenous variables. Usually, we have statistical information about the value of exogenous variables. Regarding the parameters, these have to be either estimated or calibrated. The Excel's file we are going to use first is called "**ICM-1-1.xls**" and its structure is shown in Figure 1.1. We will now describe how we build this spreadsheet.

	A	B	C	D	E	F	G	H	I
1	EXERCISE 1: An example of dynamical system								
2					Time	x_1	x_2	Δx_1	Δx_2
3	*Endogenous variables*	*Variation over time*			0	4.000	4.000	0.000	0.000
4	x_1	Δx_1			1	4.000	4.000	0.000	0.000
5	x_2	Δx_2			2	4.000	4.000	0.000	0.000
6					3	4.000	4.000	0.000	0.000
7	*Parameters*				4	4.000	4.000	0.000	0.000
8	Alpha	0.50			5	4.000	4.000	0.000	0.000
9	Beta	0.25			6	4.000	4.000	0.000	0.000
10	Gamma	0.25			7	4.000	4.000	0.000	0.000
11	Delta	0.50			8	4.000	4.000	0.000	0.000
12	Theta	1.00			9	4.000	4.000	0.000	0.000
13	Ita	1.00			10	4.000	4.000	0.000	0.000
14					11	4.000	4.000	0.000	0.000
15	*Exogenous variables*	*Initial*	*Final*		12	4.000	4.000	0.000	0.000
16	z_1	1	1		13	4.000	4.000	0.000	0.000
17	z_2	1	1		14	4.000	4.000	0.000	0.000
18					15	4.000	4.000	0.000	0.000
19	*Steady State (SS)*	*Initial SS*	*Final SS*		16	4.000	4.000	0.000	0.000
20	Steady State x_1	4.00	4.00		17	4.000	4.000	0.000	0.000
21	Steady State x_2	4.00	4.00		18	4.000	4.000	0.000	0.000
22					19	4.000	4.000	0.000	0.000
23	*Eigenvalues*	*Real*	*Imaginary*		20	4.000	4.000	0.000	0.000
24	λ_1	-0.25	0.00		21	4.000	4.000	0.000	0.000
25	λ_2	-0.75	0.00		22	4.000	4.000	0.000	0.000
26					23	4.000	4.000	0.000	0.000
27	*Stability condition*				24	4.000	4.000	0.000	0.000
28	Modulus $(1+\lambda_1)$	0.750			25	4.000	4.000	0.000	0.000
29	Modulus $(1+\lambda_2)$	0.250			26	4.000	4.000	0.000	0.000
30					27	4.000	4.000	0.000	0.000
31					28	4.000	4.000	0.000	0.000
32					29	4.000	4.000	0.000	0.000
33					30	4.000	4.000	0.000	0.000

Figure 1.1: Structure of the spreadsheet ICM-1-1.xls.

First, for the numerical resolution of the model, we need two blocks of numerical information: the value of the parameters and the initial value of the exogenous variables. If we want to perform disturbance analysis, it would also be necessary to indicate the final value (the new value) of the exogenous variables. The first step consist in assigning values to the parameters of the model (indicated by lowercase Greek letters). Obviously, the dynamics of the system will depend on these values, so in later sections, we will proceed to analyze the effects of the changes in them, which is what we call sensitivity analysis. When choosing the values of the parameters, we must consider both their meaning and the restrictions on them that can be derived from the stability of the system. In fact, as we will verify later, the dynamic properties and stability of this model depend on the value of these parameters. Table 1.1 shows the selected values for the different parameters arbitrarily (however, it is worth noting that these values have been selected so that the system has global stability).

Table 1.1: Calibration of model parameters

Symbol	Definition	Value
α	Elasticity of $\Delta x_{1,t}$ with respect to $x_{1,t}$	0.50
β	Elasticity of $\Delta x_{1,t}$ with respect to $x_{2,t}$	0.25
γ	Elasticity of $\Delta x_{2,t}$ with respect to $x_{1,t}$	0.25
δ	Elasticity of $\Delta x_{2,t}$ with respect to $x_{2,t}$	0.50
θ	Elasticity of $\Delta x_{1,t}$ with respect to $z_{1,t}$	1.00
η	Elasticity of $\Delta x_{2,t}$ with respect to $x_{2,t}$	1.00

Next, it is necessary to have the values for the exogenous variables. In this case, we have two exogenous variables and we will also set their values (Table 1.2) arbitrarily.

Table 1.2: Calibration of exogenous variables

Variable	Definition	Value
z_1	Variable that positively affects $x_{1,t}$	1
z_2	Variable that positively affects $x_{2,t}$	1

Once these values are determined, we can proceed to calculate the numerical value of the endogenous variables in steady state and calculate the eigenvalues associated with this system. Using the expressions (1.18) and (1.19) calculated above and substituting the values given in Tables 1.1 and 1.2, it appears that:

$$\bar{x}_1 = \frac{0.5 \times 1}{0.5 \times 0.5 - 0.25 \times 0.25} \times 1 - \frac{0.25 \times 1}{0.5 \times 0.5 - 0.25 \times 0.25} \times 1 = 4$$

$$\bar{x}_2 = \frac{0.25 \times 1}{0.5 \times 0.5 - 0.25 \times 0.25} \times 1 - \frac{0.5 \times 1}{0.5 \times 0.5 - 0.25 \times 0.25} \times 1 = 4$$

Figure 1.1 shows the structure of the spreadsheet that we have constructed for the numerical solution of this dynamic system, in which different blocks of necessary information appear. As we can verify, the value of the parameter α, which we have named "Alpha", appears in cell "B8". The value of the parameter β, which we have named "Beta", appears in cell "B9". The value assigned to γ, which we have called "Gamma", is given in cell "B10". The value of the parameter δ, which we have named "Delta", appears in cell "B11". The parameter θ, which we have called "Theta", is defined in cell "B12". Finally, the value of the parameter η, which we have named "Ita", appears in cell "B13".

A very useful Excel resource is to redefine the name of the cells, so that the value we assign to each parameter is defined in terms of its own name. So, for example, if we place the cursor in cell "B8", we see that this cell takes "Alpha" as its reference name. To enter a cell name, we simply have to place the cursor in the window at the top left where the cell pointer appears and enter in it the name we want. With this, we achieve several things: the formulas that we have to introduce are going to be clearer and easier to interpret, we avoid the continuous use of the "$" symbol to fix the value of a certain cell and, most importantly, we avoid making mistakes. Alternatively, Excel has an option to manage the names of the cells. Within "Formulas", we have the option "Define Name", in which we can introduce new names, modify them or delete them.

Next, we define the value of the exogenous variables. In this case, we define the initial value, corresponding to the period 0 and determining the initial steady state, and the final value, corresponding to period 1 and determining the new steady state. A disturbance (occurring at period 1) to these variables would be represented by a final value different from the initial one. These values appear in columns "B" and "C", in rows 16 and 17. In the case that there is no disturbance, the values in column "B" will be the same as those in column "C". As we can see, the value given to the exogenous variable, at the initial moment, is 1, which appears in cell "B16". On the other hand, the value given to the exogenous variable at the initial moment is 1 and it is reflected in cell "B17". Initially, these same values also appear in cells "C16" and "C17", which would correspond to their final value. Thus, if we want to perform a disturbance analysis, we would only have to change some of these values in column "C".

The information referring to the eigenvalues of the system and its stability condition appear in rows "24", "25", "28" and "29". Rows "24" and "25" show the values of the roots (eigenvalues) of the system. In column "B" the real part of the eigenvalues appears, while in column "C", the imaginary part is shown. If we place the cursor in cell "B24", the following expression appears:

=IF((Alpha+Delta)^2-4*(Alpha*Delta-Gamma*Beta)>0;

(-(Alpha+Delta)+ROOT((Alpha+Delta)^2-

4*(Alpha*Delta+Gamma*Beta)))/2;(-(Alpha+Delta))/2)

which is a conditional in terms of whether the value of the coefficient that is within the square root is positive or not, an expression that is derived from (1.25). If this value is positive, then the roots are real, and their values appear in the real part. In the case where the coefficient is negative, then the root will have an imaginary part, and the real part is simply obtained as a result of dividing by 2 the negative of the coefficient associated with λ in the expression (1.23). On the other hand, if we place the cursor in cell "C24", the expression that appears is:

=IF((Alpha+Delta)^2-4*(Alpha*Delta-Gamma*Beta)>0; 0;

+ROOT(-((Alpha+Delta)^2-4*(Alpha*Delta-Gamma*Beta)))/2)

Again, we use a conditional in terms of the sign of the coefficient that is inside the square root. In the case where the coefficient is positive, then the imaginary part is zero. Otherwise, we would calculate the square root of the negative of the coefficient. In cell "B25" the equivalent expression appears for the real part of the other eigenvalue, while in cell "C25", its imaginary part appears.

Finally, cells "B28" and "B29" show the steady condition of the system. As defined in Appendix A, the system would be steady if the value of the eigenvalue plus one is within the unit circle. If we place the cursor in cell "B28", the expression that appears is the following:

=IF(C24=0;ABS(1+B24);ROOT((1+B24)^2+C24^2))

This expression is another conditional that indicates that if the root has no imaginary part, that is, (C24=0), then the module is the absolute value of its real part plus the unit, (ABS(1+B24)). In the contrary case, that is, when the root is imaginary, the module would be calculated as (ROOT((1+B24)^2+C24^2)). As we can see, the value that appears in cell "B28" is 0.75, which is the real part of the first eigenvalue plus the unit, while in cell "B29", the value that appears is 0.25, that is, the real part of the second eigenvalue plus the unit. In effect, if we substitute the values of the parameters that appear in Table 1.1 in the expression (1.25), we obtain:

$$\lambda_1 = \frac{-1+\sqrt{1^2-1.75}}{2} = -0.25$$

$$\lambda_1 = \frac{-1-\sqrt{1^2-1.75}}{2} = -0.75$$

that is, the two roots are real and negative. If we add one to both roots, the result we obtain is 0.75 and 0.25, values both lower than the unit, which indicates that the system shows global stability, that is, all trajectories tend to the steady state.

Next, we define the block that allows us to obtain the numerical solution of the model for the endogenous variables at each moment of time. In column "E", we have represented the time, starting with 0, which would be the initial steady-state situation. Temporal index 1 is the one that we are going to use as a referent of the moment in which a certain disturbance occurs. To build this column, we simply have to enter a number and add 1 to the value of the cell corresponding to the previous row. So, for example, if we place the cursor in cell "E5" we see that the following formula appears, "=E4+1", which indicates the value of the previous row plus one unit.

Next, columns "F" and "G" present the value of the variables at each moment of time, while columns "H" and "I" show their variation over time. We have obtained the first values of the variables by calculating their value in steady state, given the values of the exogenous variables and the value of the parameters. These values are calculated in cells "B20" and "B21", respectively. In effect, if we place the cursor in cell "B20", we see that in the upper window the following expression appears:

=Theta*Delta/(Alpha*Delta-Gamma*Beta)*z1_0

+Beta*Ita/(Alpha*Delta-Gamma*Beta)*z2_0

which corresponds to the expression (1.18). On the other hand, if we place the cursor on cell "B21", we see that the formula that contains this cell is:

=Theta*Gamma/(Alpha*Delta-Gamma*Beta))*z1_0

+Alpha*Ita/(Alpha*Delta-Gamma*Beta))*z2_0

which corresponds to the expression (1.19). We have named these values "x1bar_0" and "x2bar_0", respectively. Cells "F3" and "G3" are precisely these values, which correspond to the equilibrium (initial steady state) of the system. The following cells in columns "F" and "G" are obtained simply by adding the corresponding variation to the value of the variable in the previous period, given that $x_t = x_{t-1} + \Delta x_{t-1}$. Thus, cell "F4" contains the expression "=F3+H3". This formula applies to the entire "F" column. Thus, for example, after copying the previous expression, cell "F5" must contain the expression "=F4+H4". The same structure has the column "G" corresponding to the second endogenous variable. In this case, cell "G4" contains the expression "=G3+I3" and so on in the following rows of this column.

Finally, the rows "H" and "I" indicate the variations of the endogenous variables at each moment of time, which are given by the difference equations that define the proposed dynamic system. Row "H" calculates the variations of the endogenous variable 1. If we place the cursor on cell "H3" we see that it contains the expression:

=-Alpha*F3+Beta*G3+Theta*z1_0

where "F3" refers to the value of the first endogenous variable, "G3" refers to the value of the second endogenous variable and "z1_0" is the value of the exogenous variable 1 at the initial moment (period 0), which is equivalent to the difference equation for the first exogenous variable:

$$\Delta x_{1,t} = -\alpha x_{1,t} + \beta x_{2,t} + \theta z_{1,t} \tag{1.28}$$

On the other hand, cell "H4", contains the following expression:

=-Alpha*F4+Beta*G4+Theta*z1_1

in which the exogenous variable 1, "z1_1", is the one corresponding to the moment in which the disturbance occurs (period 1). This expression is what we would copy in the following cells in this column. In an equivalent way, column "I" calculates the variations of the endogenous variable 2, having the same structure. The difference equation corresponding to this variable is:

$$\Delta x_{2,t} = \gamma x_{1,t} - \delta x_{2,t} + \eta z_{2,t} \tag{1.29}$$

If we place the cursor in cell "I3", we see that the expression that appears is:

=Gamma*F3-Delta*G3+Ita*z2_0

which is exactly the previous equation at period $t = 0$. On the other hand, if we place the cursor in cell "I4", the expression that appears is:

=Gamma*F4-Delta*G4+Ita*z2_1

in which the exogenous variable 2 is the one corresponding to the new situation once the disturbance has occurred at the moment. This expression is what we would copy into the following cells in column "I".

Finally, we build graphs in the spreadsheet that represent the value of each of the endogenous variables as a function of time. In the spreadsheet that we have built, we consider 30 periods (a number of periods large enough to permit the endogenous varibles to adjust to the new steady state when a shock occurs). When there is no change in the exogenous variables, we obtain a constant value for the two endogenous variables, given that the system is in steady state. This graphical representation can be used to verify that all the calculations we have made in the Excel sheet are correct, since in steady state each endogenous variable takes the same value for all the periods. Appendix B shows what the simulation of this model would look like in MATLAB, while in Appendix C, we present the corresponding code in DYNARE.

1.5. Change in the value of exogenous variables: Shock Analysis

One interesting exercise that we can do with the numerical solution of the model is to study the behavior of endogenous variables over time in the face of a change in some of the exogenous variables. This is what is called shock analysis, which consists of introducing a change in the system's environment, represented by the exogenous variables, starting from an initial equilibrium situation, and studying how the endogenous variables behave over time in response to the shock, as well as determining the new steady state. Once the previous system is solved numerically, we proceed to analyze the effects of a disturbance consisting of the change in the value of an exogenous variable. In the computational context we are developing, this analysis is very easy to perform since we only have to change the value of the selected exogenous variable in the desired direction and the spreadsheet will be automatically updated with the new values for the endogenous variables, the new steady state and the graphic representation of the dynamics. In fact, this is the main advantage of numerically solving this type of dynamic systems in a spreadsheet. Once we have the numerical simulation of the model, it is enough to make the desired change and the spreadsheet is automatically updated, calculating the new solution in terms of the steady state as well as the path of adjustment of the variables with respect to it.

In particular, let's suppose that the exogenous variable 1 increases from an initial value of 1 to a new value of 2. To perform this analysis, we only have to change the value of cell "C16" in the spreadsheet "**ICM-1-1.xls**". If, instead of putting a value of 1, we enter a value of 2, we can see that numbers in the sheet change automatically, representing the effects of this disturbance. If we want to study the effects of a change in the exogenous variable 2, then we would change the value of cell "C17". We can also analyze the effects of two simultaneous disturbances, changing the values of both the exogenous variable 1 and the exogenous variable 2, that is, simultaneously changing the values of cells "C16" and "C17".

Following that shock, we can see that now the steady state is different. Before any change in the exogenous variables, the steady-state value was 4 for the two endogenous variables. Now, we can verify that the values of the endogenous variables in the new steady state are 6.67 and 5.33, respectively. In this way, we obtain a direct estimate of the effects of this disturbance in the long term, resulting in an increase of the armament stock for the two countries, although to a greater extent for country 1. The disturbance is representing an increase in the exogenous variable that affects the dynamics of the first equation. In the context of this model, this can be interpreted as the existence of a more warlike government or an increase in preferences regarding national security. This change sets in motion an arms race between the two countries, since the disturbance causes country 1 to increase its armament stock, to which country 2 also responds with an increase in its armament stock, leading to a new response from country 1, and so on.

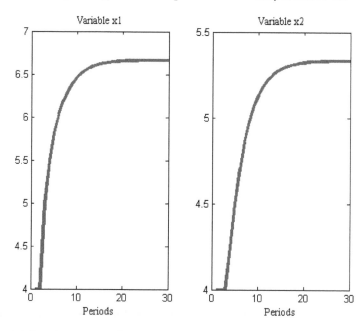

Figure 1.2: Impulse-response functions (transition dynamics) to a change in exogenous variable 1.

The transition dynamics from the initial steady state to the final steady state for each country are represented in Figure 1.2. The initial increase in the armament stock of country 1 also entails an increase in the stock in country 2, and this process repeats until the new equilibrium value in the long term is reached. At first, the response is very high, decreasing the rate at which both variables increase as they approach the new steady state. As we can see, variable 1 begins to increase in response to the disturbance. Given the initial increase in variable 1, variable 2 also begins to increase, given that the dynamics of this second variable depend positively on the value of the first variable. However, the increase in variable 1 causes the increase in this variable to be smaller over time, given the negative relationship between the dynamics of the first variable and its value (similar for the other endogenous variable). As we can see, both variables are converging gradually to the new steady state, which is higher in values than the initial ones, given the positive effect of the shock on both variables in the long-run. The new steady state is reached approximately around period 15, from which the variables return to remain practically constant and close to their new steady state. The main characteristic of these trajectories is that they are monotonous, moving the variables gradually towards the new steady state and decreasing their speed of adjustment as they approach it. This is an example of a permanent shock, resulting in a new steady state for both endogenous variables, where the transition dynamics from the initial to the new steady state are driven by the response of each endogenous variable to the other. In this particular example, these trajectories represent an arm race between the two countries.

1.6. Change in the value of the parameters: Sensitivity analysis

Another exercise of interest that we can perform directly with the numerical resolution of the dynamic system is to study the effects of the values of the parameters on the dynamics of the system and the equilibrium of the model. This exercise is called sensitivity analysis, since it tells us how the system reacts depending on the value of the parameters of the system. In macroeconomic models, a large number of preference, technological, adjustment, or elasticity parameters appear. In this context, analyzing the properties of the model with respect to different possible values of these parameters is of great interest for its validation as a useful tool for macroeconomic analysis.

In the dynamic system we are studying, we find two groups of parameters: those associated with the exogenous variables and those associated with the endogenous variables. The value of the parameters associated with the exogenous variables (those that make up the matrix B) will determine the effect of the impact of the disturbance, that is, how the endogenous variables are affected initially in the face of a change in some of the exogenous variables. On the contrary, the dynamics of the system, that is, how the endogenous variables change over time once the impact effect of the disturbance has taken place, is determined by the value of the parameters associated with these variables (the parameters of the matrix A). As indicated above, the macroeconomic models that are used in the current macroeconomic analysis can only be solved in numerical terms, so the results are conditioned by the values used for the set of parameters. These values can be determined either through a calibration process, or through the econometric estimation, or a combination of both methods. Although many of these parameters can be calibrated or estimated in a relatively accurate way, the calibration or estimation of some parameters could be more difficult, so it is compulsory to perform a sensitivity analysis to study the behavior of the model at different values of these parameters.

The exercise of changes in the parameters will also serve to illustrate an important property of this model. With the previously calibrated parameters, the system presented global stability, with all the trajectories being convergent to the steady state. However, for another value of parameters, this model can result in a saddle-point solution. Specifically, we will perform both exercises, which will allow us to introduce certain differentiating elements in the analysis that we have to apply depending on whether the solution of the model is a saddle point or global stability.

1.6.1 Change in parameters: Global stability

To carry out this first sensitivity analysis, we assume that the same disturbance that we have analyzed previously occurs, but now for a different value of the parameter α. To do this, we only have to change the value of cell "B8", in the spreadsheet "**ICM-1-1.xls**". Instead of assuming that its value is 0.5, as we have done previously, let's assume that its value is 0.7. This change makes both countries asymmetric, both now having a different steady state, given that country 1 responds more to the armament stock in country 2, than country 2 does to country 1. This change will affect both the value of the variables in the steady state and the dynamics that the endogenous variables will follow to a disturbance, given that it is a parameter associated with the set of endogenous variables (belonging to the matrix *A*). In this case, we have to take into account how the variation in this parameter affects the stability of the system, since we can find situations in which the new value leads to an explosive situation.

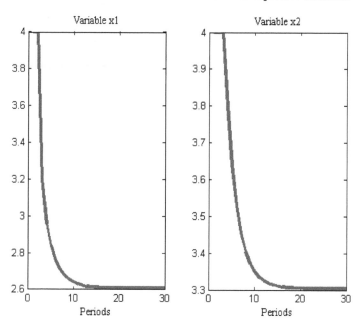

Figure 1.3. Sensitivity analysis: Effects of an increase in the value of the parameter α.

If we calculate the new eigenvalues associated with this system, we obtain:

$$\lambda_1 = \frac{-1.3 + \sqrt{1.3^2 - 4 \times (1.3 - 0.0625)}}{2} = -0.33$$

$$\lambda_2 = \frac{-1.3 - \sqrt{1.3^2 - 4 \times (1.3 - 0.0625)}}{2} = -0.87$$

Since the modules of the roots plus one are less than unity in both cases (they would take values of 0.67 and 0.13, respectively), the system continues to show global stability. This change in the parameter α assumes a different behavior of the model. First, as we can see, the value of the variables in the steady state changes with respect to the previous situation. In effect, the value of the variables in steady state depends on the value of the parameters (and the value of the exogenous variables), so if we alter their value, we obtain a different steady state value for the endogenous variables. Thus, now the initial steady state takes a value of 2.61 for the endogenous variable 1 and of 3.30 for the endogenous variable 2. That is, the steady state stock of armament for both countries decreases as a consequence of altering the value of this parameter.

The parameter α represents the sensitivity that country 1 has regarding its own stock of armaments. The higher its value, the smaller the armament stock of country 1, since the variation in the stock depends negatively on its level. Therefore, as a sequence of the increase in this value, we must expect that the stock of weapons in country 1 is smaller than in the initial situation. On the other hand, given the reduction in the armament stock in country 1, country 2 will also reduce its own stock. However, the new equilibrium is asymmetric, given that the parameters are no longer the same for both countries. The new steady state will take us to a situation where the stock of armament of country 2 is superior to that of country 1. Figure 1.3 shows the transitional dynamics of the endogenous variables from the initial steady state to the new steady state.

1.6.2 Change in parameters: Saddle point

Finally, we will propose alternative values for the parameters, for which the system shows a saddle point solution. In such a case, there will be both convergent and divergent (explosive) trajectories with respect to the steady state. The main differential element with respect to the previous case of global stability is the existence of a unique trajectory, called the stable saddle path, that takes us directly to the steady state and to which any other trajectory that is stable converges. In fact, each steady state is in this case associated with a stable saddle path, so that before a disturbance that gives rise to the existence of a new steady state, the stability of the system is only guaranteed if the endogenous variables move to reach this new stable path. Specifically, we are going to assume that one of the endogenous variables suffers an instantaneous readjustment in its value when a disturbance occurs, until reaching the new stable saddle path, moment from which all the endogenous variables are readjusted following this stable path until reaching the new steady state.

Tables 1.3 and 1.4 show the new values for the parameters and the exogenous variables of the model that we have selected for the realization of this exercise. As we can see in Table 1.3, now the parameters β and γ, are greater than the parameters α and δ. On the other hand, and given these new values of the parameters, for the value of the endogenous variables in steady state to be positive, it is necessary that the exogenous variables take a negative value. Specifically, we have assumed that both exogenous variables take a value of -1.

Table 1.3: Alternative calibration of the model's parameters

Symbol	Definition	Value
α	Elasticity of $\Delta x_{1,t}$ respect to $x_{1,t}$	0.25
β	Elasticity of $\Delta x_{1,t}$ respect to $x_{2,t}$	0.50
γ	Elasticity of $\Delta x_{2,t}$ respect to $x_{1,t}$	0.50
δ	Elasticity of $\Delta x_{2,t}$ respect to $x_{2,t}$	0.25
θ	Elasticity of $\Delta x_{1,t}$ respect to $z_{1,t}$	1.00
η	Elasticity of $\Delta x_{2,t}$ respect to $z_{2,t}$	1.00

Table 1.4: Alternative calibration of exogenous variables

Variable	Definition	Value
z_1	Variable that directly affects $x_{1,t}$	-1
z_2	Variable that directly affects $x_{2,t}$	-1

Again, by using the expressions (1.18) and (1.19) and substituting the values given in Tables 1.3 and 1.4, it turns out that the new steady state would be given by:

$$\bar{x}_1 = \frac{0.25}{0.5\times0.5-0.25\times0.25} \times (-1) - \frac{0.5}{0.5\times0.5-0.25\times0.25} \times (-1) = 4$$

$$\bar{x}_2 = \frac{0.5}{0.5\times0.5-0.25\times0.25} \times (-1) - \frac{0.1\times2}{0.5\times0.5-0.25\times0.25} \times (-1) = 4$$

The file that we are going to use to perform this numerical exercise is called "**ICM-1-2.xls**" and its structure is similar to the one used previously, "**ICM-1-1.xls**", except for the fact that we have to calculate the jump that occurs in the variables to reach the stable path, as a consequence of the existence of a saddle point. In this case, we can see that the system has eigenvalues values of -0.75 (cell "B24") and 0.25 (cell "B25"). In effect, if we substitute the values of the parameters that appear in Table 1.3 in the expression (1.25), we obtain:

$$\lambda_1 = \frac{-0.5-\sqrt{0.5^2-4\times(0.0625-0.25)}}{2} = -0.75$$

$$\lambda_2 = \frac{-0.5+\sqrt{0.5^2-4\times(0.0625-0.25)}}{2} = 0.25$$

and if we add one to both roots, the result is 0.25 and 1.25 (cells "B28" and "B29"), respectively, with which the result is less than 1, in one case, and greater than 1 in the other, resulting in the steady state of the system being a saddle point, that is, there are divergent trajectories and convergent trajectories with respect to the steady state (see Case I.c of Appendix A).

The solution of the system of linear equations can be expressed in the following way:

$$\begin{bmatrix} x_{1,t} \\ x_{2,t} \end{bmatrix} = v_1(\lambda_1 + 1)^t a_1 + v_2(\lambda_2 + 1)^t a_2 + \begin{bmatrix} \bar{x}_1 \\ \bar{x}_2 \end{bmatrix} \qquad (1.30)$$

where v_1 and v_2 are the eigenvectors associated with λ_1 and λ_2, respectively. In addition, a_1 and a_2 are constants whose values depend on the initial conditions of the system. Substituting the values corresponding to the eigenvalues and the steady-state values calculated above results in:

$$\begin{bmatrix} x_{1,t} \\ x_{2,t} \end{bmatrix} = v_1(0.25)^t a_1 + v_2(1.25)^t a_2 + \begin{bmatrix} 4 \\ 4 \end{bmatrix}$$

According to the previous expression, for any value of a_1 and $a_2 = 0$, we have

$$\begin{bmatrix} x_{1,t} \\ x_{2,t} \end{bmatrix} = v_1(0.25)^t a_1 + \begin{bmatrix} 4 \\ 4 \end{bmatrix}$$

with which the variables will tend towards the stationary point, as the time increases since the term $v_1(0.25)^t a_1$ will tend to zero. These will be the only convergent trajectories (for the different values of a_1) to the stationary point, and it constitutes the so-called stable path, which is unique.

On the other hand, if we consider $a_1 = 0$ and any value of a_2 we have

$$\begin{bmatrix} x_{1,t} \\ x_{2,t} \end{bmatrix} = v_2(1.25)^t a_2 + \begin{bmatrix} 4 \\ 4 \end{bmatrix}$$

that tends to infinity as time grows. In general, and whenever $a_2 \neq 0$, the solution system trajectories will move away from the stationary point.

The stable saddle path

Given the eigenvalues calculated above, the steady state of this model turns out to be a saddle point. As we have already indicated, this implies the existence of trajectories both convergent and divergent to the steady state. In this case, we have seen that there is a single stable path given, in general terms, by:

$$\begin{bmatrix} x_{1,t} \\ x_{2,t} \end{bmatrix} = v_1(\lambda_1 + 1)^t a_1 + \begin{bmatrix} \bar{x}_1 \\ \bar{x}_2 \end{bmatrix} \qquad (1.31)$$

being λ_1 the eigenvalue for which $\lambda_1 + 1$ is less than 1, and v_1 an eigenvector associated with it. From this expression, we have that in the next period, $t + 1$, the solution of the system can be defined as:

$$\begin{bmatrix} x_{1,t+1} \\ x_{2,t+1} \end{bmatrix} = v_1(\lambda_1 + 1)(\lambda_1 + 1)^t a_1 + \begin{bmatrix} \bar{x}_1 \\ \bar{x}_2 \end{bmatrix} \qquad (1.32)$$

whereby, subtracting both expressions (1.31 and 1.32) results in,

$$\begin{bmatrix} \Delta x_{1,t} \\ \Delta x_{2,t} \end{bmatrix} = \lambda_1 v_1(\lambda_1 + 1)^t a_1 \qquad (1.33)$$

being $\Delta x_{1,t} = x_{1,t+1} - x_{1,t}$, and $\Delta x_{2,t} = x_{2,t+1} - x_{2,t}$. On the other hand, from expression (1.31), we obtain:

$$v_1(\lambda_1 + 1)^t a_1 = \begin{bmatrix} x_{1,t} - \bar{x}_1 \\ x_{2,t} - \bar{x}_2 \end{bmatrix} \qquad (1.34)$$

and, by substituting in the expression (1.33), we finally arrive at:

$$\begin{bmatrix} \Delta x_{1,t} \\ \Delta x_{2,t} \end{bmatrix} = \lambda_1 \begin{bmatrix} x_{1,t} - \bar{x}_1 \\ x_{2,t} - \bar{x}_2 \end{bmatrix} \qquad (1.35)$$

which indicates the trajectories of the variables according to their deviations with respect to the steady-state and the stable eigenvalue (with a value plus one is less than the unit). The eigenvalue λ_1 is known as the convergence rate since it represents the rate at which the solution trajectories converge toward the steady state on the stable path.

Adjustment to the stable saddle path

The instantaneous adjustment to a disturbance is determined by the degree of flexibility to the adjustment of the different variables. In the particular case of the model that we are studying, both variables can be assumed to be flexible, since they represent the expenditure on armaments of a country which is a variable that the government decides and it can change its value instantaneously. Suppose that the exogenous variable increases to a new value of -0.5. To carry out the analysis, we introduce this value in cell "C16" of the spreadsheet "**ICM-1-2.xls**".

In the first place, we can observe that now the steady state is different, being the steady state value of the endogenous variables 3.33 and 2.67, respectively (cells "C20" and "C21"). Secondly, columns "H" and "I" are now no longer zero from period 1, which indicates that the system is in motion as a result of the disturbance. We are going to assume that before any disturbance, the variable $x_{1,t}$ is the one that will react most quickly (the analysis could be done analogously if it is supposed to be the other variable). From expression (1.35), we obtain that the stable path is defined by the following trajectory:

$$\Delta x_{1,t} = \lambda_1(x_{1,t} - \bar{x}_1)$$ (1.36)

On the other hands, the dynamic equation of the model for the variations of this endogenous variable is:

$$\Delta x_{1,t} = -\alpha x_{1,t} + \beta x_{2,t} + \theta z_{1,t}$$ (1.37)

The short-term effect (readjustment to the stable saddle path) of this disturbance can be quantified by equating both expressions, such that:

$$-\alpha x_{1,t} + \beta x_{2,t} + \theta z_{1,t} = \lambda_1(x_{1,t} - \bar{x}_1)$$ (1.38)

and solving for $x_{1,t}$, results in,

$$x_{1,t} = \frac{\beta}{\alpha+\lambda_1}x_{2,t} + \frac{\theta}{\alpha+\lambda_1}z_{1,t} + \frac{\lambda_1}{\alpha+\lambda_1}\bar{x}_1$$ (1.39)

indicating the new value of the endogenous variable 1, at the moment of the disturbance, so that the system is on the stable saddle path. This expression is the one that has been introduced in cell "F4" to obtain $x_{1,1}$ (resulting equal to 2) and thus takes the system to the stable saddle path so that steady state is reached. In effect, if we place the cursor in cell "H4", the expression that appears is:

=(Beta/(Alpha+Lambda1))*G4+(1/(Alpha+Lambda1))*z1_1

+(Lambda1/(Alpha+Lambda1))*x1bar_1

which is exactly the expression (1.42). Analogously, it could be done if the disturbance affected $z_{2,1}$ or both, $z_{1,1}$ and $z_{2,1}$, and considering that the variable $x_{1,t}$ is the most flexible and, therefore, quantifying the instantaneous variation in that variable, according to the previous expression.

Figure 1.4 shows the dynamic trajectory of the model in response to the shock. As we can see, the armament stock in country 1 decreases instantaneously at the moment in which this disturbance occurs, in order to reach the new stable path associated with the new steady state. Subsequently, the stock of armament increases, producing a rebound effect (an overreaction), until reaching its new steady state, at the same time that country 2 is also progressively decreasing its armament stock. The main element in this response is given by the instantaneous readjustment of variable 1, a setting that leads the system to the stable path. Then, both variables change (1 increasing and 2 decreasing) along the stable saddle path, until ending in the new steady state. Only if this initial adjustment occurs in variable 1, the system converges to the new steady state.

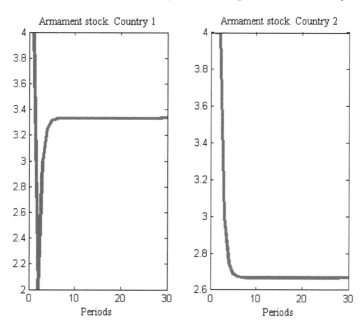

Figure 1.4. Effects of an increase in z_1 (saddle point solution).

Exercises

1. Using the "**ICM-1-1.xls**" spreadsheet, analyze the effects of a decrease in the exogenous variable $z_{2,t}$. Specify the dynamic effects on the endogenous variables, as well as their long-term effects (new steady state).

2. What conditions have to be met in order for the armament stock in each country to converge to zero.

3. Analyze the effects of a simultaneous decrease in the same amount of exogenous variables $z_{1,t}$ and $z_{2,t}$, using the spreadsheet "**ICM-1-1.xls**". What effects does it have in the long term as well as in the transition to the new steady state?

4. Using the spreadsheet "**ICM-1-2.xls**", check what happens if $\alpha = 1$. Why do we obtain this result?

5. Using the "**ICM-1-2.xls**" spreadsheet, analyze the effects of a decrease in the exogenous variable $z_{2,t}$. Specify the dynamic effects on the endogenous variables, as well as their long-term effects (new steady state). Replicate the

same analysis performed previously but now suppose that the variable that adjusts instantaneously to the stable path is the variable x_2. Build the new spreadsheet corresponding to this exercise.

2. The dynamic IS-LM model

2.1. Introduction

In this chapter, we will numerically solve a dynamic version of the standard IS-LM (Investment-Saving-Liquidity-Money) or Aggregate Demand model and use that theoretical framework to study the effects of different shocks that affect the economy. The static IS-LM model, also known as the Hicks-Hansen model (John Richard Hicks, 1904-1989, Alvin Hansen, 1887-1975), continues to be the central core of the teaching of macroeconomics at the introductory/intermediate level. Although, at present, it would be more appropriate to use an IS-MP type model, with a monetary policy rule instead of a standard LM function, which is better adapted to the modeling of the money market, this specification is still little used in the practice of teaching of macroeconomics, so we have chosen to use the more traditional and widely-known version.

Although the original IS-LM model presents a large number of limitations since it is a static and non-microfounded model (even if the micro-foundation of the IS curve and the monetary policy rule can be carried out very simply), it also produces results of interest as a macroeconomic teaching tool. However, the model to be solved here is a dynamic version, with very different properties from the traditional static IS-LM with fixed prices. Moving from a static to a dynamic environment in terms of Aggregate-Supply/Aggregate-Demand is relatively simple, for which we need to specify the dynamics that both the price level and output level will follow. Thus, in this theoretical framework, prices are not fixed, but vary in time, although showing some rigidity (price stickiness), so that its adjustment is not instantaneous when a shock hits the economy. In this framework monetary neutrality holds in the long-run, whereas in the short and medium term a nominal shock has real effects on the economy, as a result derived from price rigidities. In sum, this model would be similar to the model of the New Consensus Macroeconomics (NCM), although in our case we specify an LM function to define the money market equilibrium through the consideration of a money supply, instead of specifying a rule of monetary policy based on the determination of the interest rate, as it is standard in the NCM model.

The dynamic IS-LM model starts, similar to the traditional static version, from the existence of two markets: the money market and the goods and services market. Macroeconomic equilibrium would be represented by the existence of equilibrium in both markets simultaneously. We also assume that both the price level and the production level are rigid variables, which adjust gradually to an imbalance. The model assumes that the variations in prices depend on the difference in the level of production with respect to its potential level, which would be equivalent to the Phillips curve, while the variations in the level of production depend on the differences between the aggregate demand and the level of output. That is, inflation depends on overproduction in the economy, while production is adjusted according to the level of aggregate demand. These new elements give rise to a model that, while maintaining the fundamental elements of the traditional static IS-LM model, will generate more realistic and interesting results.

The analytical approach to solve this model is the same as the one developed in the previous chapter, but now applied to a dynamic system that has economic content. To computationally solve these models, we will continue using the Excel spreadsheet. As alternatives, in appendix D, the code to perform this same exercise is shown in MATLAB, while the corresponding code in DYNARE is shown in appendix E. Our objective is to obtain a numerical solution for the endogenous variables of the model and the steady state, and to calculate the time path of the different endogenous variables of the economy when a disturbance occurs, consisting of a change in the exogenous variables, and how the dynamic of the economy changes depending on the calibratrated value of the parameters. As we will see below, this model presents a solution with global stability, but where eigenvalues can be real or imaginary, resulting in direct or asymptotic trajectories to the steady state, respectively.   *where* $\dot{dt} = 0$

The structure of the rest of the chapter is as follows. In Section 2, we present the resolution of the model in analytical terms. In Section 3, we present the calibration of the model and the description of the model's spreadsheet, together with the calculation of the value of the variables in steady state and the corresponding stability analysis. Section 4 presents a shock analysis carried out with the numerically-solved model. In particular, we study the effects over time of an increase in the quantity of money (a nominal shock), calculating the impulse-response functions for each of the variables. Finally, Section 5 presents a sensitivity analysis of the model in response to an alteration in the value of one of the parameters. In particular, we consider a change in the value of one of the parameters such that the eigenvalues are imaginary, in order to obtain asymptotic trajectories of the variables towards the steady state.

2.2. The dynamic IS-LM model

The IS-LM model or Hicks-Hansen model constitutes a standard theoretical framework for macroeconomic analysis in a static context. It starts by defining the macroeconomic equilibrium in a closed economy based on the existence of two markets: the market for goods and services, and the money market. The equilibrium in the market of goods and services is defined through the equality between investment, I, and savings, S, (I=S), hence the name of IS curve to define the function that represents the combinations of output and interest rate that determine the equilibrium in this market. In the case of the money market, the condition is that the demand for money or liquidity, L, is equal to the quantity of money, M, (L=M), resulting in the function called LM, which tells us the combinations of output and interest rate that determine the equilibrium in the money market. Although the model that we develop here is a dynamic version of the IS-LM model, it presents important differences with respect to its static version. The standard IS-LM model is a static model, where the fundamental assumption is that prices are constant. This is not the case in the model we study here, in which the dynamics of prices, that is, their variability over time, play a fundamental role in determining the behavior of the economy. To do this, we just have to incorporate an equation representing the Phillips curve to the traditional static specification. On the other hand, in this dynamic version, aggregate demand is a function of inflation expectations, expectations that are not present in the standard IS-LM model either. These two elements, together with the consideration of time, make this model, despite its simplicity, much more powerful than the static IS-LM model to explaining the behavior of an economy.

Let's suppose that the structure of our economy is given by the following system of equations:

$$m_t - p_t = \psi y_t - \theta i_t \tag{2.1}$$

$$y_t^d = \beta_0 - \beta_1(i_t - \Delta p_t^e) \tag{2.2}$$

$$\Delta p_t = \mu(y_t - y_t^n) \tag{2.3}$$

$$\Delta y_t = \upsilon(y_t^d - y_t) \tag{2.4}$$

where m is the logarithm of the amount of money, p the logarithm of the price level, y^d the logarithm of the level of demand, y the logarithm of the level of production, y^n the logarithm of the level of potential output, and i the nominal interest rate. The symbol Δ defines the variation of the corresponding variable between two periods, being:

$$\Delta p_t = p_{t+1} - p_t \tag{2.5}$$

$$\Delta y_t = y_{t+1} - y_t \tag{2.6}$$

As we can see, the model is defined in discrete time, since the solution approach is numerical. However, its structure is exactly equivalent to the corresponding one in continuous time.[1] Note that assuming that all variables are defined in logarithmic terms (except the nominal interest rate), Δy_t is what we call GDP growth and Δp_t is what we call inflation.

The equation (2.1) is the equilibrium condition in the money market, where the real balances, $m_t - p_t$ (remember again that the variables are defined in logarithmic terms, and hence, $\ln(M_t/P_t) = \ln M_t - \ln P_t = m_t - p_t$), depend positively on the level of production and negatively on the nominal interest rate. The equation (2.2) represents the aggregate demand of the economy, which depends positively on public spending (or the autonomous component of it), which we assume is an exogenous variable, and negatively of the real interest rate. The real interest rate is represented by the approximation to the Fischer equation and is obtained as the difference between the nominal interest rate and the expected inflation rate.

Apart from the two equilibrium equations for the two markets, the model is also composed of two dynamic equations that indicate the behavior of two endogenous variables (price level and production level) over time. Equation (2.3) indicates how prices move over time based on the differences between the level of output and potential output. This equation can be interpreted as a version of the Phillips curve. If the production level is greater than the potential, then this equation is positive, so that prices increase (positive inflation). On the contrary, if the production level is below the potential, the equation would have a negative sign, indicating that prices would decrease (deflation). Finally, equation (2.4) is similar but representing the dynamics of the production level. This expression indicates how changes in the level of output (the growth rate of the economy) moves depending on the differences between aggregate supply and demand. If the aggregate-demand level is higher than the production level, the expression would take a positive value, indicating that the level of production increases. On the contrary, if the production level is higher than the demand, then the expression would take a negative value, so that the production level of the economy would decrease.

All parameters are defined in positive terms. The parameter ψ represents the elasticity of the real balances with respect to the level of production. θ is the semi-elasticity of the demand for money with respect to the nominal interest

---

[1] This does not always have to be the case, since there are cases, for instance when the variables are defined in per capita terms, in which the equations of a discrete-time model differ from the continuous-time equivalents.

rate. It is a semi-elasticity because all the variables of the model are defined in logarithmic terms, except the interest rate, which, as it is a percentage, logarithms cannot be applied to it, since it is as if it were in that term. The parameter β_1 represents the elasticity of the level of aggregate demand with respect to the real interest rate, while β_0 is the autonomous component of aggregate demand, which we assume reflects public spending (public consumption). The parameter μ is the speed of adjustment of prices to differences between the level of production and the level of potential production. Finally, the parameter v indicates the speed of adjustment of the level of output in response to differences between the level of aggregate demand and the production level of the economy.

Structure of the dynamic IS-LM model	
Money market	$m_t - p_t = \psi y_t - \theta i_t$
Goods and services market	$y_t^d = \beta_0 - \beta_1 (i_t - \Delta p_t^e)$
Prices adjustment	$\Delta p_t = \mu(y_t - y_t^n)$
Production adjustment	$\Delta y_t = v(y_t^d - y_t)$
Inflation	$\Delta p_t = p_{t+1} - p_t$
Output growth	$\Delta y_t = y_{t+1} - y_t$

As we can see, the model is identified for a total of four equations, since we have four endogenous variables (output, prices, aggregate demand and nominal interest rate). On the other hand, the model includes a total of three exogenous variables (autonomous component of aggregate demand that we interpret as public expenditure, β_0, quantity of money, m, and level of potential output, y^n). To solve this model analytically, as a previous step to its numerical resolution, we will proceed in a similar way as we would do in the case that our objective was its graphical representation through the phase diagram, that is, reducing the model to a system of two difference equations, in terms of the price level and output. To obtain these two equations for inflation and output growth, we must first solve for the rest of the endogenous variables, that is, nominal interest rate and aggregate demand. For this, we use the expressions (2.1) and (2.2). To obtain the nominal interest rate, we solve equation (2.1):

$$i_t = -\frac{1}{\theta}(m_t - p_t - \psi y_t) \tag{2.7}$$

to obtain the value of the nominal interest rate as a function of the endogenous variables to calculate (prices and output) and the exogenous variables (quantity of money).

Next, we will solve for the aggregate demand level. As we can see in equation (2.2), the nominal interest rate appears as a variable driving aggregate demand. Since we already have it calculated, what we do is replace (2.6) in (2.2), so that we obtain:

$$y_t = \beta_0 - \frac{\beta_1 \psi}{\theta} y_t + \frac{\beta_1}{\theta} (m_t - p_t) + \beta_1 \Delta p_t^e \tag{2.8}$$

The above expression is not a solution, since at this step we cannot calculate yet the value of the aggregate demand. Indeed, in the right part of the equation appears a term that, a priori, is unknown: expected future inflation. This term appears as a consequence of the definition of the real interest rate. The real interest rate is an unknown variable, since it depends on the inflation that will exist at the end of the maturity period to which the corresponding nominal interest rate is referred. This means that aggregate demand is not known except in expected terms, since it will depend on inflation expectations.

Therefore, we have to resolve the expectations terms. We assume that expectations are rational. That means that the mathematical expectation of inflation is equal to inflation plus a white noise. On the other hand, we will assume that there is no uncertainty, so we would be in a context of perfect foresight. This means that the white noise, the error term of rational expectations is always zero, so the expected value of a variable in the future is the current value. In this case, the expected inflation is simply the current inflation ($\Delta p_t = \Delta p_t^e$). Therefore, the equation that determines the aggregate demand of the economy would be:

$$y_t = \beta_0 - \frac{\beta_1 \psi}{\theta} y_t + \frac{\beta_1}{\theta} (m_t - p_t) + \beta_1 \Delta p_t \tag{2.9}$$

To obtain the two dynamic equations that will determine the behavior of our economy, we have to replace these two endogenous variables (nominal interest rate and aggregate demand) in the adjustment equations of the endogenous reference variables (price level and production level). In the case of the dynamic equation for the price level, these variables do not appear, so this first equation is exactly the same as that provided by the model (equation 2.3):

$$\Delta p_t = \mu(y_t - y_t^n) \tag{2.10}$$

Next, we obtain the dynamic equation for output. For this, we substitute the value obtained for the aggregate demand in the dynamic equation for output, such as:

$$\Delta y_t = v \left[\beta_0 - \left(\frac{\beta_1 \psi}{\theta} + 1 \right) y_t + \frac{\beta_1}{\theta} (m_t - p_t) + \beta_1 \Delta p_t \right] \tag{2.11}$$

As we can see, inflation appears in the previous equation as an additional variable driving the dynamics of output. Therefore, we have to substitute the equation (2.3) in the previous expression, resulting in:

$$\Delta y_t = v\left[\beta_0 - \left(\frac{\beta_1\psi}{\theta} + 1\right)y_t + \frac{\beta_1}{\theta}(m_t - p_t) + \beta_1\mu(y_t - y_t^n)\right] \tag{2.12}$$

Operating to group terms and calculate the parameter associated with each of the endogenous reference variables and the exogenous variables results in:

$$\Delta y_t = v\left[\beta_0 - \left(\beta_1 - \frac{\beta_1\psi}{\theta} + 1\right)y_t + \frac{\beta_1}{\theta}(m_t - p_t) - \beta_1\mu y_t^n\right] \tag{2.13}$$

In summary, the dynamic IS-LM model can be defined in terms of the following two (log-)linear difference equations:

$$\Delta p_t = \mu(y_t - y_t^n) \tag{2.14}$$

$$\Delta y_t = v\left[\beta_0 - \left(\beta_1 - \frac{\beta_1\psi}{\theta} + 1\right)y_t + \frac{\beta_1}{\theta}(m_t - p_t) - \beta_1\mu y_t^n\right] \tag{2.15}$$

In matrix notation, we have:

$$\begin{bmatrix}\Delta p_t \\ \Delta y_t\end{bmatrix} = \underbrace{\begin{bmatrix} 0 & \mu \\ \frac{-v\beta_1}{\theta} & v\left(\beta_1 - \frac{\beta_1\psi}{\theta} + 1\right)\end{bmatrix}}_{A}\begin{bmatrix}p_t \\ y_t\end{bmatrix} + \underbrace{\begin{bmatrix} 0 & 0 & -\mu \\ v & \frac{v\beta_1}{\theta} & -v\beta_1\mu\end{bmatrix}}_{B}\begin{bmatrix}\beta_0 \\ m_t \\ y_t^n\end{bmatrix} \tag{2.16}$$

where A is the matrix of parameters associated with the vector of endogenous variables and B the matrix of parameters associated with the vector of exogenous variables.

2.3. Calibration of the model

As we have seen in the previous chapter, in order to numerically solve a model, previously we need the value of the parameters and the exogenous variables, as well as have a specific functional form of the different functions that make up the model's equations. This is what is known as calibration or estimation of the model. On the other hand, we have already started by assuming specific functional forms, both for the demand for money and aggregate demand, and for the adjustment in prices and production level. For the numerical resolution of this exercise, we will assume the values for the parameters that are reflected in Table 2.1. These values are obtained either from the realization of econometric estimations or from their calibration based on observed data. For example, to estimate the semi-elasticity of the interest rate and the elasticity of money demand, we can econometrically estimate the money demand equation by taking the real balances as the variable to be explained and as explanatory variables the level of production and the nominal interest rate. The estimated coefficients of that equation for a given economy would be the values corresponding to θ and ψ. Another way to calculate the parameters of the model is to calibrate them so that the theoretical structure adapts to the statistical observed data. Thus, we would try to use the observed macroeconomic variables to determine some important ratios that allow us to infer the value of the parameters using the different equations of the model. In practice, the most used approach is the calibration of the parameters or a combination of calibration/econometric estimation methods. The values of the parameters can be very different from one economy to another, reflecting the particular characteristics of each economy in terms of the speed of adjustment of the different variables, technology, or preferences.

Table 2.1: Calibration of the parameters

Symbol	Definition	Value
ψ	Elasticity of real balances to output	0.05
θ	Interest rate semi-elasticity	0.5
β_1	Elasticity of aggregate demand to the interest rate	50
μ	Speed of adjustment of prices	0.01
ν	Speed of adjustment of production level	0.2

Next, we must determine the initial value of the model exogenous variables, which combined with the values of the parameters will determine the starting steady-state of the economy. First, we determine the value of the exogenous variables at the initial period, which are shown in Table 2.2. These values are completely arbitrary, but we have to take into account in some way the economic meaning of each variable.

Table 2.2: Values of exogenous variables

Variable	Definition	Value
m_0	Money supply	100
β_0	Autonomous component of aggregate demand	2,100
y_0^n	Potential output	2,000

Given the values of the parameters and of the exogenous variables, the numerical solution for the two difference equations for inflation and output growth would be:

$$\Delta p_t = 0.01 \times (y_t - 2{,}000)$$

$$\Delta y_t = 0.2 \times [2{,}100 - 5.5 \times y_t + 100 \times (100 - p_t) - 0.5 \times 2{,}000]$$

In matrix terms, the resulting system would be:

$$\begin{bmatrix} \Delta p_t \\ \Delta y_t \end{bmatrix} = \begin{bmatrix} 0 & 0.01 \\ -20 & -1.1 \end{bmatrix} \begin{bmatrix} p_t \\ y_t \end{bmatrix} + \begin{bmatrix} 0 & 0 & -0.01 \\ 0.2 & 20 & -0.1 \end{bmatrix} \begin{bmatrix} 2{,}100 \\ 100 \\ 2{,}000 \end{bmatrix}$$

Once the values of the parameters and the exogenous variables are determined, we proceed to determine the value of the endogenous variables at the initial period, such that the variation of each variable is zero, so the value of the endogenous variables will coincide with its steady-state value. Therefore, to calculate this value, we resort to the definition of steady state.

2.3.1. Steady state

To calculate the initial equilibrium value (the steady state) of the endogenous variables of our economy, we can directly use the dynamic system obtained previously for the two endogenous reference variables, which in this case are the price level and the production level. Remember that this is calculated by simply equating the dynamic equations of the system to zero, indicating that the variation over time of the endogenous variables is zero, so the variables are constant period to period. Using the model in matrix notation, the vector variables in steady state would be defined as:

$$\begin{bmatrix} \bar{p}_t \\ \bar{y}_t \end{bmatrix} = -A^{-1} B z_t \tag{2.17}$$

where, for the model we are solving, it results:

$$A = \begin{bmatrix} 0 & \mu \\ \frac{-\upsilon\beta_1}{\theta} & \upsilon(\beta_1\mu - \frac{\beta_1}{\theta} - 1) \end{bmatrix}, B = \begin{bmatrix} 0 & 0 & -\mu \\ \upsilon & \frac{\upsilon\beta_1}{\theta} & -\upsilon\beta_1\mu \end{bmatrix}, z_t = \begin{bmatrix} \beta_0 \\ m_t \\ y_t^n \end{bmatrix} \tag{2.18}$$

We start by inverting the matrix A. To do this, first calculate the adjugate of matrix A, $adj(A)$, i.e., being:

$$adj(A) = \begin{bmatrix} \upsilon(\beta_1\mu - \frac{\beta_1\psi}{\theta} - 1) & -\mu \\ \frac{\upsilon\beta_1}{\theta} & 0 \end{bmatrix} \tag{2.19}$$

where the determinant is:

$$|A| = \frac{\upsilon\beta_1\mu}{\theta} \tag{2.20}$$

so the negative of the inverse of matrix A is:

$$-A^{-1} = -\frac{\theta}{\upsilon\beta_1\mu} \begin{bmatrix} \upsilon(\beta_1\mu - \frac{\beta_1\psi}{\theta} - 1) & -\mu \\ \frac{\upsilon\beta_1}{\theta} & 0 \end{bmatrix} \tag{2.21}$$

or:

$$-A^{-1} = \begin{bmatrix} -\theta + \frac{\psi}{\mu} + \frac{\theta}{\beta_1 \mu} & \frac{\theta}{\upsilon \beta_1} \\ -\frac{1}{\mu} & 0 \end{bmatrix} \tag{2.22}$$

Therefore, we obtain:

$$\begin{bmatrix} \bar{p}_t \\ \bar{y}_t \end{bmatrix} = -A^{-1}B\mathbf{z}_t = \begin{bmatrix} -\theta + \frac{\psi}{\mu} + \frac{\theta}{\beta_1 \mu} & \frac{\theta}{\upsilon \beta_1} \\ -\frac{1}{\mu} & 0 \end{bmatrix} \begin{bmatrix} 0 & 0 & -\mu \\ \upsilon & \frac{\upsilon \beta_1}{\theta} & -\upsilon\beta_1\mu \end{bmatrix} \begin{bmatrix} \beta_0 \\ m_t \\ y_t^n \end{bmatrix} \tag{2.23}$$

and by multiplying the matrices $-A^{-1}B$ we get:

$$\begin{bmatrix} \bar{p}_t \\ \bar{y}_t \end{bmatrix} = \begin{bmatrix} \frac{\theta}{\beta_1} & 1 & -\psi - \frac{\theta}{\beta_1} \\ 0 & 0 & 1 \end{bmatrix} \begin{bmatrix} \beta_0 \\ m_t \\ y_t^n \end{bmatrix} \tag{2.24}$$

Operating, we obtain the following expressions that define the steady state of the economy:

$$\bar{p}_t = \frac{\theta \beta_0}{\beta_1} + m_t - \left(\psi + \frac{\theta}{\beta_1}\right) y_t^n \tag{2.25}$$

$$\bar{y}_t = y_t^n \tag{2.26}$$

As we can see, the steady-state value of the price level depends positively on public spending and the quantity of money, while it depends negatively on the level of potential output. On the other hand, the level of production in steady state turns out to be equal to the level of potential output. Therefore, in our case, using the calibration of the model, it turns out that the steady state of the economy is given by the following values:

$$\begin{bmatrix} \bar{p}_t \\ \bar{y}_t \end{bmatrix} = -\begin{bmatrix} 0 & 0.01 \\ -20 & -1.1 \end{bmatrix}^{-1} \begin{bmatrix} 0 & 0 & -0.01 \\ 0.2 & 20 & -0.1 \end{bmatrix} \begin{bmatrix} 2,100 \\ 100 \\ 2,000 \end{bmatrix} = \begin{bmatrix} 1 \\ 2,000 \end{bmatrix}$$

that is, the initial equilibrium price level (for example, at the moment $t = 0$) is $\bar{p}_0 = 1$ and the initial equilibrium production level is $\bar{y}_0 = 2,000$, which coincides with the value of the potential output. Once these values are obtained, we can use the different equations to calculate the other endogenous variables. Thus, for example, we can use equation (2.7) to calculate the value of the nominal interest rate in steady state. Substituting the corresponding values in that expression results in:

$$\bar{i}_0 = -\frac{1}{0.5}(100 - 1 - 0.05 \times 2,000) = 2$$

so, the initial steady state value of the nominal interest rate is 2. Next, we can calculate the initial equilibrium value for aggregate demand, replacing the known values in equation (2.2), which results in:

$$\bar{y}_0^d = 2,100 - 50 \times 2 = 2,000$$

since, if we assume the existence of equilibrium, the price level would be constant ($\Delta p_0 = 0$), that is $\bar{y}_0^d = 2{,}000$, equal to the initial steady state output. Finally, to verify that these values are those corresponding to the steady state, we can calculate the variations in the price level and the level of production that should be zero. In effect, if we replace the known values in equation (2.3) we would obtain:

$$\Delta p_0 = 0.01 \times (2{,}000 - 2{,}000) = 0$$

And finally, if we do the same in equation (2.4) the result would be:

$$\Delta y_0 = 0.2 \times (2{,}000 - 2{,}000) = 0$$

2.3.2. Stability analysis

When setting the value of the previous parameters we have to make sure that they meet certain conditions so that when the system suffers a disturbance, it returns to a steady state (see Appendix A regarding system stability conditions). In the particular case of this model, we will obtain a solution with global stability, so that all trajectories would be convergent to the steady state.

The stability of the system is determined by calculating $|A - \lambda I| = 0$, where A is the matrix of parameters defined above, λ represents the vector of eigenvalues and I is the identity matrix, being:

$$I = \begin{bmatrix} 1 & 0 \\ 0 & 1 \end{bmatrix} \tag{2.27}$$

In our case, we would have:

$$Det \begin{bmatrix} 0 & \mu \\ \frac{-\upsilon\beta_1}{\theta} & \upsilon\left(\beta_1\mu - \frac{\beta_1\psi}{\theta} - 1\right) \end{bmatrix} - \lambda \begin{bmatrix} 1 & 0 \\ 0 & 1 \end{bmatrix} =$$

$$Det \begin{bmatrix} 0 - \lambda & \mu \\ \frac{-\upsilon\beta_1}{\theta} & \upsilon\left(\beta_1\mu - \frac{\beta_1\psi}{\theta} - 1\right) - \lambda \end{bmatrix} = 0 \tag{2.28}$$

By calculating the roots of the coefficient matrix associated with the endogenous variables, we obtain the following expression:

$$\lambda_1, \lambda_2 = \frac{\upsilon\left(\mu\beta_1 - \frac{\beta_1\psi}{\theta} - 1\right) \pm \sqrt{\left[\upsilon\left(\mu\beta_1 - \frac{\beta_1\psi}{\theta} - 1\right)\right] - \frac{4\upsilon\beta_1\mu}{\theta}}}{2} \tag{2.29}$$

We must bear in mind that if the term $\beta_1\mu - \frac{\beta_1\psi}{\theta} - 1$ is positive, then the two roots are also positive ($\lambda_1 > 0, \lambda_2 > 0$)[2]. In this case, all trajectories are

---

[2] When calculating $|A - \lambda I| = 0$, we obtain a second-degree equation of the type: $a\lambda^2 + b\lambda + c = 0$, being its roots:

explosive, since the module plus the unit would be outside the unit circle, $|\lambda_1 + 1| > 1$ and $|\lambda_2 + 1| > 1$, therefore, this term cannot be negative, since the system shows no converge to the steady state. If, on the other hand, $\beta_1\mu - \frac{\beta_1\psi}{\theta} - 1$ is negative, then the two roots are negative ($\lambda_1 < 0, \lambda_2 < 0$), all trajectories are convergent towards the steady state, provided that the modulus of the eigenvalues plus one is less than a unit, i.e., $|\lambda_1 + 1| < 1$ and $|\lambda_2 + 1| < 1$, that is, it must be the case that $\lambda_1, \lambda_2 > -2$. Therefore, this term has to be negative, since it is the only situation in which the model can be stable. Substituting the values given in Table 2.1, we have to:

$$\beta_1\mu - \frac{\beta_1\psi}{\theta} - 1 = 50 \times 0.01 - \frac{50 \times 0.05}{0.5} - 1 = 5.5$$

so, the selected parameters meet this condition. Next, we proceed to verify if the coefficient within the square root is positive or negative:

$$\left[v\left(\beta_1\mu - \frac{\beta_1\psi}{\theta} - 1\right)\right]^2 - \frac{4v\beta_1\mu}{\theta} = 0$$

Substituting the calibrated values of the parameters, we obtain that:

$$-1.1^2 - 0.8 > 0$$

so, the eigenvalues are going to be real numbers. Finally, if we calculate the value of the roots we obtain:

$$\lambda_1 = \frac{v\left(\beta_1\mu - \frac{\beta_1\psi}{\theta} - 1\right) + \sqrt{\left[v\left(\beta_1\mu - \frac{\beta_1\psi}{\theta} - 1\right)^2 - \frac{4v\beta_1\mu}{\theta}\right]}}{2} = -0.23$$

$$\lambda_1 = \frac{v\left(\beta_1\mu - \frac{\beta_1\psi}{\theta} - 1\right) - \sqrt{\left[v\left(\beta_1\mu - \frac{\beta_1\psi}{\theta} - 1\right)^2 - \frac{4v\beta_1\mu}{\theta}\right]}}{2} = -0.87$$

$$\lambda_1, \lambda_2 = \frac{-b \pm \sqrt{b^2 - 4ac}}{2a}.$$

The sign of the two roots will depend, on the one hand, on the sign of the coefficient immediately before the square root ($-b$) and, on the other hand, the sign of the term $4ac$. Thus, we can verify that the first term within the square root is simply the square of coefficient outside the square root (b^2). Therefore, if the second term of the square root were zero ($c = 0$), then, when solved the square root, we would have:

$$\lambda_1, \lambda_2 = \frac{-b \pm \sqrt{b^2}}{2a} = \frac{-b \pm b}{2a}$$

so, it would turn out that one of the roots would be null: $\lambda_1 = -b/a$; $\lambda_2 = 0$. Therefore, the key is in the sign of the second term inside the square root, which is what will tell us if in solving the square root, the result is greater or less than the coefficient before it. If the sign of the term $4ac$ is positive, the result of solving this square root is lower than the coefficient before it and the opposite would happen if the sign of the term $4ac$ were negative.

as we can see, they are both negative and greater than -2, so this system shows global stability and the modules of the roots plus the corresponding units are 0.77 and 0.13, which are both less than one, so that the system shows global stability (see Appendix A).

2.4. Numerical solution

Once the values of the exogenous variables and the parameters have been defined, we can proceed to the numerical resolution of the model. Figure 2.1 shows the Excel sheet of the model, corresponding to the file **"ICM-2.xls"**, where are collected the different sets of information we need to numerically solve the model: definition of the variables, calibrated values of the parameters, values of the exogenous variables and calculation of the steady state.

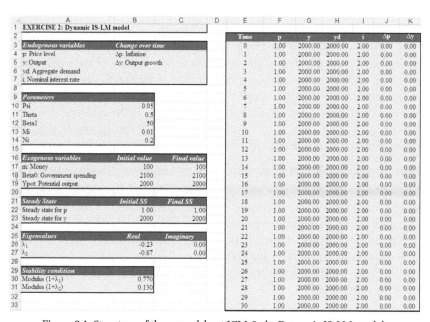

Figure 2.1. Structure of the spreadsheet ICM-2.xls: Dynamic IS-LM model.

Columns "F", "G", "H" and "I" show the value of each of the endogenous variables (prices, production, demand and nominal interest rate) at each moment of time. The calibrated values of the parameters appear in cells "B10" to "B14". The initial values of the exogenous variables appear in cells "B17", "B18" and "B19", which we have named "m_0", "Beta0_0" and "ypot_0", respectively. The initial steady-state values appear in cells "B22" and "B23", using expressions (2.24) and (2.25). Cells "C22" and "C23" show the new steady state in the case where a disturbance occurs (change in the exogenous variables). The value of the eigenvalues is given in rows 26 and 27, using expression (2.28). In cells "B26" and B27, "the real part is shown, while the imaginary part is shown in cells" C26 "and" C27 ". Finally, the root module is shown in cells "B30" and "B31".

If we place the cursor in cell "F3" this expression appears:

=(Theta*Beta0_0)/Beta1+m_0-(Psi+Theta/Beta1)*ypot_0

which is simply the expression corresponding to the initial steady-state value of the price level. Alternatively, we could simply enter the reference to cell "B22", in which we have calculated the corresponding steady-state value. The remaining rows in this column simply contain the value of the price level in the previous moment plus the change produced in that price level. Thus, cell "F4" contains the expression "=F3+J3", where "F3" refers to the price level of the previous period and "J3" to the change in the price level. This expression is copied into the remaining rows of that column.

On the other hand, if we place the cursor in cell "G3" it contains the expression: "=ypot_0", that is, the initial steady-state value of the production level that corresponds to the level of potential production. Alternatively, we can simply enter cell "B23". In cell "G4", the expression "=G3+K3" appears in which we define the production level of each period as the previous one plus the change experienced in it. Column "H" contains the aggregate demand values. If we place ourselves in cell "H3", we see that this expression appears:

=Beta0_0-Beta1*(I3-J3)

which corresponds to the aggregate demand equation of the model, in which aggregate demand depends negatively on the real interest rate, which we have defined as the difference between the nominal interest rate and inflation. This same expression appears in the following cells in this column. Column "I" contains the nominal interest rate values. Thus, cell "I3" contains the following expression:

=-1/Theta*(m_0-F3-Psi*G3)

which is the equation resulting from solving for the interest rate from the money demand equation. If we place ourselves in cell "I4", the expression that appears is:

=-1/Theta*(m_1-F4-Psi*G4)

which refers to the new amount of money from time 0. This expression is the same as that which appears in the following rows of this column.

Finally, columns "J" and "K" show the variations in prices and production levels, that is, they define the value of inflation and the growth of production in each period. In this case, we must introduce the corresponding equations that determine the behavior of both variables. If we place ourselves in cell "J3" we see that it contains the expression:

=Mi*(G3-ypot_0)

while cell "J4" contains the expression:

=Mi*(G4-ypot_1)

being this same expression the one that appears in the following cells, since it is possible that we want to analyze the effects of an alteration in the level of potential production of the economy. On the other hand, if we place ourselves in cell "K3", we see that it contains the expression:

=Ni*(H3-G3)

which corresponds to the dynamic equation of the production level. As we can see in the spreadsheet, we can enter the initial expression given by the model, since we will also calculate the corresponding value of the aggregate demand at each moment of time. If all calculations are correct, columns "J" and "K", where the change of each variable appears, must be zeros.

2.5. Shock analysis: Effects of an increase in money supply

Once we have obtained a numerical solution of the model, next we will use this solution to analyze the effects of a disturbance represented by a change in some of the exogenous variables of the model. This will allow us to calculate the value of the endogenous variables at each moment of time and, therefore, obtain their temporal dynamics. This is what is called the impulse-response analysis or dynamic transition trajectory when the disturbance gives rise to a new steady state.

In particular, we assume that at the moment $t = 1$ there is an increase in money supply, from an initial value of $m_0 = 100$ to a new value of $m_1 = 101$. This is a nominal shock affecting the equilibrium in the money market, resulting in an instantaneous change in the nominal interest rate. However, price stickiness prevents the economy to return instantaneously to the equilibrium. In this context, this disturbance will not have real effects in the long term, but in the short and medium term. To perform this exercise, we only have to change the value of cell "C17" and we will automatically obtain the results in the spreadsheet. This is because we have referenced the expressions from period 1 with respect to the new values of the exogenous variables, with the objective of automatically performing shocks analysis. Thus, in this specific case, we can analyze the effects of changes (increases or decreases) in money supply, changes in public spending and changes in the level of potential output, without the need to alter the structure of the spreadsheet. It is also possible to simulate disturbances that are combinations of changes in two or more exogenous variables simultaneously. In our case, we will focus on analyzing the effects of an increase in money supply. It is a disturbance of a nominal nature and, therefore, in the long term, it will not have real effects. This is what is known as the principle of monetary neutrality. Thus, an alteration in the amount of money, in the long term, will not affect the level of production (real variables), so we must expect that the steady state for this variable does not change. Only the nominal variables will be affected in the long term (such as the price level), so if the amount of money increases, it is expected that, in the long term, there will also be an increase in the level of prices.

However, the important element in this exercise is that this nominal disturbance will have real effects both in the short and medium term. This is due to the rigidity in the adjustment of the price level. During this period of adjustment of the initial steady state to the final, the increase in liquidity has positive effects on the level of aggregate demand of the economy, which in turn alters the level of production. Therefore, this nominal disturbance has real effects on the economy while it is in transition from the initial steady state to the final state, due to the rigidity in the adjustment of prices to its new equilibrium value. The increase in the amount of money is not instantaneously canceled by an equivalent increase in the price level. This would only happen if prices were flexible. In this case, the adjustment of the economy would be instantaneous, since the variation in the quantity of money would be transmitted instantaneously to variation in prices.

The dynamics of the transition is as follows. The increase in the amount of money in period 1 causes an instantaneous decrease in the nominal interest rate. Thus, in the simulation of the model, the nominal interest rate goes from 2 to a value of 0. As a consequence of this decrease in the interest rate, the aggregate demand increases. Thus, it goes from a value of 2,000 to a value of 2,100. This increase in aggregate demand will cause the level of production to increase in the next period, which in turn now causes an increase in the nominal interest rate. On the other hand, the increase in the level of production in period 2 will result in prices also increasing in that period. The easiest way to observe these effects is to construct a graph that represents the time path of each variable.

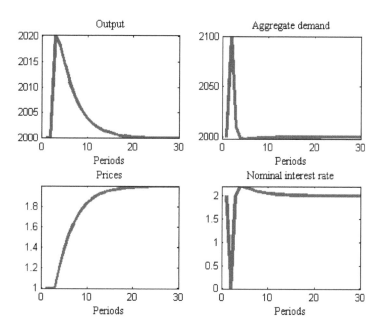

Figure 2.2. Impulse-response functions and transition dynamic: A rise in money supply.

The evolution of the different endogenous variables in their phase of transition towards the new steady state can be observed very easily through a graph that represents each variable as a function of time. Figure 2.2 shows the time path of the four endogenous variables of the model. As we can see, the price level gradually increases in time until reaching the new steady state. In this case, there are no fluctuations in the price level and the same trend follows, that is, it increases, indicating that we are always in a situation of overproduction. On the contrary, the level of production undergoes an initial increase and then decreases until reaching the new steady state. The increase in the amount of money increases the liquidity of the economy, initiating a stage of economic expansion. In this case, the level of production initially increases, indicating the existence of an excess of demand, but later decreases indicating the opposite, that is, an excess of supply. On the other hand, we see that the initial adjustment in the level of production is significant, which implies that we have assumed a value of its adjustment speed that can be excessively high. On the other hand, the behavior of aggregate demand and the interest rate show that both variables have a high level of flexibility. The nominal interest rate is a flexible variable, which decreases instantaneously in the face of the increase in the amount of money. This decrease in the nominal interest rate also implies an instantaneous decrease in the real interest rate, which in turn causes an increase in aggregate demand. However, the next increase in the level of production causes the nominal interest rate to rise again, causing the movement in the opposite direction in aggregate demand.

The most important conclusion we can draw from the analysis is that an expansion in money supply (a nominal disturbance) has real effects on the level of production of an economy due to the gradual adjustment in the price level. In the long term, the only effect is that the increase in the amount of money is transferred to a higher price level, in exactly the same amount, while the steady-state value of the rest of the variables is not altered. These effects would not occur under the assumption that prices were flexible, the adjustment being instantaneous in this case. However, if we assume that prices are rigid and do not adjust instantaneously to their new equilibrium value, then it turns out that the rest of the variables deviate from their steady state. In this specific case, the increase in the amount of money is transformed into an expansion of the economy, through the decrease in the nominal interest rate and an increase in aggregate demand.

In the long-run, we can observe that all the endogenous variables of the model, except the price level, return to their initial values. Thus, we can observe that the nominal interest rate, output and aggregate demand all return to its initial level, once the prices have been adjusted completely. All variation in money supply is transmitted to an equivalent variation in the price level in the long-run (monetary neutrality principle) but during the adjustment to the new equilibrium this nominal shock has real effects. Dynamics of the economy are different when prices are assumed totally flexible. In this case, none of the other variables would experience any variation to a change in money suply, as the price level would change instantaneously in response to that nominal shock.

2.6. Sensitivity analysis: Effects of a change in the elasticity of money demand with respect to output

Finally, we carry out a sensitivity analysis by altering some of the parameters of the model, in order to study how the dynamics that the different variables follow when faced with a certain disturbance is altered according to the value of these parameters. Specifically, we are going to study how the response of the model changes if we vary the parameter ψ, which represents the elasticity of money demand to the level of output. In particular, let's assume that the value of this parameter changes from 0.05 to 0.01, so we only have to enter the new value in cell "B10". Changing the value of this parameter also changes the value of the variables in steady state. Specifically, altering this parameter varies the steady-state value of the price level, not varying the level of steady-state production, given that we have assumed it is equal to the level of potential production. The main characteristic of this change is that now the eigenvalues of the system are complex numbers, although the property of global stability is maintained. Thus, if we calculate the value of the coefficient within the square root with the new parameters, we obtain:

$$\left[v \left(\beta_1 \mu - \frac{\beta_1 \psi}{\theta} - 1 \right)^2 - \frac{4 v \beta_1 \mu}{\theta} \right] =$$

$$\left[0.2 \times \left(50 \times 0.01 - \frac{50 \times 0.01}{0.5} - 1 \right) \right]^2 - \frac{4 \times 0.2 \times 50 \times 0.01}{0.5} = -0.71$$

that is, the resulting coefficient within the square root is negative, so the associated eigenvalues would be complex numbers. Indeed, as we can see in the spreadsheet, now the real part of the roots is -0.15, for both, while its imaginary part is 0.42 and -0.42, that is, $\lambda = -0.15 \pm 0.42i$. This means that the module plus the unit of the two roots is the same and equal to $0.95 \sqrt{(-0.15 + 1)^2 + 0.42^2} = 0.948$, which, by being less than a unit, guarantees the existence of global stability.

The dynamics that we are going to observe now, under the same disturbance (increase in the money supply from 100 to 101) is very different from the previous one. The cause of this different behavior comes from the fact that now the eigenvalues are imaginary, generating asymptotic trajectories of adjustment that lead the variables to move around the new steady state, not converging directly to it.

This variation in the value of the parameters and in that of the associated eigenvalues, causes the dynamics to be more complex than previously observed for this same disturbance, generating oscillatory movements (cyclical fluctuations) in the variables. Thus, the fact that the modules of the eigenvalues plus the unit are less than one indicates that the system converges to its new steady state. On the other hand, the existence of complex roots would indicate us that the trajectory towards the new steady state is oscillatory, with a path for the different variables that would be fluctuating around its value of steady state. Therefore, we would now be moving from one type of imbalance to another, with the variables sometimes below their steady-state value and other times above that value. Note that if the prices increase above their steady-state value, this means that we are in a situation of overproduction, while if they decrease we are in a situation of underproduction. Both situations are alternating, which causes that both the level of production and the aggregate demand and nominal interest rate are some periods above their steady-state value, while in other periods the opposite occurs.

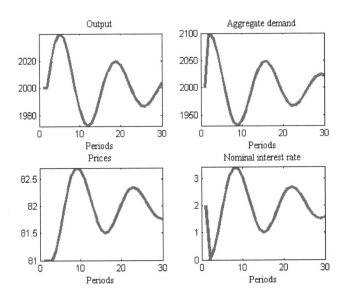

Figure 2.3. Impulse-response function and transition dynamics: Increase in money supply with $\psi = 0.01$.

In this case, the effects of the nominal shock in the short- and medium-term result in cyclical fluctuations of the endogenous variables, so that their effect on production is both positive and negative, depending on the reference period (see Figure 2.3). Thus, now the increase in the money supply initially generates an economic expansion, characterized by an increase in the level of aggregate demand and production, and a decrease in the nominal interest rate. However, after some time, the effects become negative, increasing the nominal interest rate and decreasing both the aggregate demand and the level of production. This is caused by oscillations in the price level, with values higher than their steady-state level. These movements are repeated over time (expansive and contraction phases), but with decreasing amplitude. In this case, we see that, after 30 periods, the adjustment to the new steady state is still incomplete, which makes the transition to the new steady state slower. It is also important to indicate that these fluctuations around the steady state are not synchronized for the different variables, which makes even more complex the response of the economy to a disturbance. Thus, during certain periods we can observe a positive relationship between two variables, while this relationship becomes negative in other periods, as a consequence of which these cyclical fluctuations do not occur at the same time for all the variables. Finally, this exercise serves to illustrate that the dynamic IS-LM model is capable of generating cyclical fluctuations caused both by technological changes (alterations in the level of potential production) and by changes in economic policy (changes in public spending or changes in the amount of money).

Exercises

1. Using the "**ICM-2.xls**" spreadsheet, study the effects of an increase in public spending, represented by β_0. Specifically, suppose that public spending increases by 100 units. To do this, change the value of cell "C18" from 2,100 to 2,200. What does the dynamic IS-LM model tell us about the effects of an expansionary fiscal policy?

2. Study what the effects of an increase in the level of potential production are. Suppose, for example, that the level of potential production happens to take a value of 2,050. Use the "**ICM-2.xls**" spreadsheet to determine the effects of this change. To do this, change the corresponding value in cell "C20".

3. Repeat the exercise carried out in the text (increase in the money supply), but assuming that the prices are more flexible. To do this, you have to increase the value of the adjustment parameter in the price equation, v. What happens as we increase the value of this parameter?

4. Using the development model, assume that the aggregate demand function depends negatively on the nominal interest rate:

$$y_t^d = \beta_0 - \beta_1 i_t$$

Solve the model and build the corresponding spreadsheet. Analyze the effects of an increase in the amount of money and compare the results with those obtained in the text. Explain why these results are obtained.

5. How would the dynamics of adjustment of the economy be if we alter the value of the parameter μ? Does the value of this parameter affect the steady-state values?

3. Exchange rate overshooting

3.1. Introduction

One of the dynamic non-micro-founded models with rational expectations most popular in macroeconomics and, in particular, in international economics, is the model of overreaction or overshooting of the exchange rate developed by Rudiger Dornbusch (1942-2002) and published in 1976.[1] This model is a dynamic extension of the Mundell-Fleming model (Robert Alexander Mundell, 1932-; John Marcus Fleming, 1911-1976), or IS-LM model for an open economy, which attempts to explain the significant fluctuations observed in nominal changes as a result of the abandonment of the Bretton Woods system by the developed countries and the beginning of a system of floating exchange rates. It is a model for a small open economy with perfect international capital mobility. The main objective of this model is to explain the high volatility of the exchange rate with respect to the variability observed in other macroeconomic variables when prices are sticky and, in particular, to describe the phenomenon of overreaction or overshooting of the nominal exchange rate to a monetary disturbance due to the different speed of adjustment existing in the market of goods and services, with respect to that of the money market.

The dynamic IS-LM model already solved numerically in the previous chapter presented an important characteristic – all the trajectories were convergent to the steady state. That is, the dynamic IS-LM model had global stability. However, in the open economy model presented in this chapter, the solution is a saddle-point, that is, with trajectories convergent to the steady state and with divergent trajectories with respect to it, in a way similar to the arms-race model that we studied in Chapter 1. For the numerical solution of this type of solution, we must take into account the existence of a stable saddle path, associated with each steady state, to which the forward looking (jump) variables that show high flexibility are adjusted in response to any shock hitting the economy. The overshooting model of the exchange rate presents a saddle point, which allows the phenomenon of the overshooting of the exchange rate as its adjustment to reach the stable saddle path to be explained. In short, the model consists in two difference equations: one dynamic equation for the nominal exchange rate (exchange rate depreciation), which is a completely flexible variable, and

---

[1] Dornbusch, R. (1976). Expectations and Exchange Rate Dynamics. Journal of Political Economy, 84(6): 1161-1176.

another dynamic equation for the price level (inflation), which we assume is a rigid variable.

The Dornbusch model basically consists of a version of the dynamic IS-LM model for an open economy. For this, we introduce the concept of a small open economy. The assumption of a small economy implies that external variables are considered as exogenous. If we do not make this assumption, then the external variables could not be considered as exogenous variables but endogenous, since they would be affected by the behavior of this economy. With the assumption of a small economy, we are making sure that our economy does not have the capacity to affect the determination of the variables of the rest of the world. We continue to consider the existence of two markets: the market for goods and services and the money market, as in the IS-LM model for a closed economy. In an open economy, we have two equilibrium relations at the international level, which will relate the domestic economy to the rest of the world. These international-equilibrium relations connect both domestic markets with their equivalents abroad. The equilibrium relationship between the national and foreign money markets is determined through the Uncovered Interest Parity (UIP), which establishes that the expectation of depreciation of the (log of) nominal exchange rate is equal to the difference between the domestic and foreign nominal interest rates. The equilibrium relationship between domestic and foreign goods and services markets is determined by the Purchasing Power Parity (PPP), which establishes that the (log of) nominal exchange rate is equal to the difference between the (log of) domestic and foreign price levels. Given the existence of rigidities in the adjustment of prices, the Purchasing Power Parity is only fulfilled in the long-run.

The rigidity in the adjustment of prices will explain the phenomenon of overshooting of the exchange rate. For instance, in the face of an increase in money supply, the exchange rate increases instantaneously to a value higher than its new steady-state value, and then progressively decreases as prices adjust to the new steady state. In effect, the increase in the amount of money immediately causes a decrease in the national interest rate, and given the UIP, there is an appreciation of the nominal exchange rate. However, in the long-run, the increase in money supply will lead to a higher price level, so the exchange rate will also be higher. In order for the decrease in the exchange rate to be compatible with a higher value in the long term, there must be an initial overshooting in the exchange rate, reaching a value higher than its new steady-state value, to subsequently decrease to reach its new steady state.

The structure of the rest of the chapter is as follows. In Section 2, we present the theoretical foundations of the exchange rate overshooting model. Section 3 shows the calibration of the model. Section 4 presents the numerical solution of the model, together with the description of the spreadsheet prepared for this purpose. Section 5 analyzes the effects of an increase in money supply, describing the phenomenon of the exchange rate overshooting. Finally, in Section 6, a sensitivity analysis is carried out, changing the value of the parameters of the model.

3.2. Exchange rate overshooting: The Dornbusch model

The exchange rate overshooting model resolves one of the most important economic puzzles in the area of open economies that occurred with the end of the Bretton Woods system and the beginning of floating exchange rate regimes. The puzzle can be states as follows: If we look at what PPP condition says, it turns out that an increase in money supply would cause an increase in the price level and therefore an increase in the nominal exchange rate in the long-run, given the relationship between the equilibrium in the domestic market of goods and services with the equilibrium in the foreign markets of goods and services. On the contrary, if we pay attention to the behavior resulting from the UIP condition, we obtain that the increase in money supply would cause a decrease in the nominal interest rate and therefore a decrease in the nominal exchange rate, given the equilibrium relationship between the domestic and foreign money markets. This effect would occur throughout the adjustment process towards the new steady state. Therefore, from UIP condition, we would obtain that the increase in the amount of money would cause a permanent decrease in the nominal exchange rate. The problem lies in how it is possible that, given an increase in the quantity of money, the nominal exchange rate has to be decreasing during the whole transition phase from the initial steady state to the new steady state, but in the long-run it has to increase with respect to its initial value. To solve this economic enigma, we will use a simple dynamic model of open economy, which will allow us to analyze what are the dynamic effects of such monetary shock on the nominal exchange rate.

The structure of the economy is given by the following four equations:

$$m_t - p_t = \psi y_t - \theta i_t \tag{3.1}$$

$$y_t^d = \beta_0 + \beta_1(s_t - p_t + p_t^*) - \beta_2 i_t \tag{3.2}$$

$$\Delta p_t = \mu(y_t - y_t^n) \tag{3.3}$$

$$\Delta s_t^e = i_t - i_t^* \tag{3.4}$$

where m is the logarithm of the amount of money, p the logarithm of the price level, y the logarithm of the level of production, i the nominal interest rate, y^d the logarithm of the level of demand, s the logarithm of the exchange rate, y^n the logarithm of the level of potential production, p^*, the logarithm of the foreign price level and i^* the foreign nominal interest rate. The symbol Δ defines the variation of the corresponding variable between two periods. s^e

represents the expected value of the exchange rate, that is, expectations about the future value of the exchange rate. Since we solve the model in a context of perfect foresight and under the assumption that expectations are rational, then we have that $s^e = s$.

The first equation (3.1) is the demand for money, where the demand for real balances depends positively on the level of production and negatively on the nominal interest rate. This equilibrium condition for the money market does not change with respect to what we would have in a closed economy. The second equation (3.2) is the aggregate demand of an open economy, which is altered with respect to the one for a closed economy since we have to consider the external demand for domestic produced goods. When we define the aggregate demand of an open economy, we need to take into account not only the internal component but also the external component (net exports). As we can see, the aggregate demand of an open economy depends positively on the real exchange rate, defined as the deviations from Purchasing Power Parity (the real exchange rate), that reflects the level of external competitiveness by prices of the economy. On the other hand, we assume that aggregate demand depends negatively on the nominal interest rate, instead of depending negatively on the real interest rate that would be the correct statement. We have made this simplification because the results will not be altered if instead of the real interest rate we consider the nominal interest rate, although we do not know this a priori. The other two equations are dynamic equations that tell us how to adjust prices, that is, the Phillips curve (equation 3.3) and the nominal exchange rate adjustment equation (3.4), which is represented by the Uncovered Interest Parity (the relationship between the equilibrium of the national and foreign money markets).

Importantly, the above system of equations contains 5 endogenous variables: domestic prices, domestic output, domestic nominal interest rate, aggregate demand and nominal exchange rate. On the other hand, we have 5 exogenous variables: money, public spending, foreign price level, potential output and foreign nominal interest rate. Although the number of exogenous variables included in the model can be any (their value is predetermined), the number of endogenous variables must coincide with the number of available equations. The model has 5 endogenous variables, but it consists of only 4 equations, so it is not identified. Given this structure of the economy, either an additional equation is missing or an endogenous variable is in excess to obtain a solution to this model. One alternative for solving this problem could be to include a new equation for the endogenous variable for which we have not specified its behavior, which is the case of domestic output. This new additional equation would be the aggregate supply. The other possibility is to simplify the model and eliminate the endogenous variable that is not determined, that is, domestic output. In order to keep things simple, we choose the second option and assume that domestic output is always equal to the domestic potential ($y_t = y_t^n$).

Structure of the overshooting model of the exchange rate	
Money market	$m_t - p_t = \psi y_t - \theta i_t$
Goods and services market	$y_t^d = \beta_0 + \beta_1(s_t - p_t + p_t^*) - \beta_2 i_t$
Adjustment of prices	$\Delta p_t = \mu(y_t - y_t^n)$
Uncovered interest rate parity	$\Delta s_t = i_t - i_t^*$
Production	$y_t = y_t^n$
Inflation	$\Delta p_t = p_{t+1} - p_t$
Rate of depreciation of the exchange rate	$\Delta s_t = s_{t+1} - s_t$

However, the above assumption implies that we need to modify both money market equilibrium condition and the price adjustment equation. As we can see, the level of production that appears in the demand for money is now the domestic potential output. On the other hand, domestic output also appeared in the price-level adjustment equation. However, if we consider that this output level is equal to the potential output, the price adjustment equation would be zero, so that the price level would be constant. Since in this case, the production of the economy is constant, the only variable that would affect prices would be the difference between aggregate demand and potential output. Therefore, we redefined the behavior of prices based on this difference, reflecting the existence of excess demand or excess supply in the market of goods and services. Another possibility would be to suppose that the aggregate demand is always equal to the production level ($y_t^d = y_t^n$), which would allow us to eliminate one of these two endogenous variables. Therefore, under these assumptions, the system of equations would be:

$$m_t - p_t = \psi y_t^n - \theta i_t \tag{3.5}$$

$$y_t^d = \beta_0 + \beta_1(s_t - p_t + p_t^*) - \beta_2 i_t \tag{3.6}$$

$$\Delta p_t = \mu(y_t^d - y_t^n) \tag{3.7}$$

$$\Delta s_t = i_t - i_t^* \tag{3.8}$$

Next, we calculate the difference equations for the reference variables, which are the domestic price level and the nominal exchange rate. Solving for the domestic nominal interest rate from equation (3.5):

$$i_t = -\frac{1}{\theta}(m_t - p_t - \psi y_t^n) \tag{3.9}$$

By substituting (3.9) in (3.6) and obtain the aggregate demand of the economy:

$$y_t^d = \beta_0 + \beta_1(s_t - p_t + p_t^*) + \frac{\beta_2}{\theta}(m_t - p_t - \psi y_t^n) \qquad (3.10)$$

and again, by substituting this equation in the expression (3.7), we obtain the dynamic equation for the domestic price level:

$$\Delta p_t = \mu\beta_0 + \mu\beta_1 s_t + \mu\beta_1 p_t^* - \mu\left(\beta_1 + \frac{\beta_2}{\theta}\right)p_t + \frac{\mu\beta_2}{\theta}m_t - \mu(\frac{\psi\beta_2}{\theta} + 1)y_t^n \qquad (3.11)$$

On the other hand, by substituting the equation (3.5) in the expression (3.8), we obtain the dynamic equation for the nominal exchange rate:

$$\Delta s_t = -\frac{1}{\theta}(m_t - p_t - \psi y_t^n) - i_t^* \qquad (3.12)$$

In matrix notation, the dynamic system resulting from expressions (3.11) and (3.12) can be written as:

$$\begin{bmatrix} \Delta p_t \\ \Delta s_t \end{bmatrix} = \underbrace{\begin{bmatrix} -\mu\left(\beta_1 + \frac{\beta_2}{\theta}\right) & \mu\beta_1 \\ \frac{1}{\theta} & 0 \end{bmatrix}}_{A} \begin{bmatrix} p_t \\ s_t \end{bmatrix} + \underbrace{\begin{bmatrix} \mu & \frac{\mu\beta_2}{\theta} & -\mu(\frac{\psi\beta_2}{\theta}+1) & 0 & \mu\beta_1 \\ 0 & -\frac{1}{\theta} & \frac{\psi}{\theta} & -1 & 0 \end{bmatrix}}_{B} \begin{bmatrix} \beta_0 \\ m_t \\ y_t^n \\ i_t^* \\ p_t^* \end{bmatrix}$$

$$(3.13)$$

where A is the matrix of coefficients associated with the endogenous variables and B is the matrix of coefficients associated with the exogenous variables.

3.3. Calibration of the model

To obtain a numerical solution of this model, we will now calibrate the parameters of the model and the exogenous variables. First, we assign numerical values to the parameters. Table 3.1 shows the selected values for the parameters of the model. These parameters reflect elasticities or the speed of adjustment. These values have been selected arbitrarily, but they have to comply with certain properties to guarantee the stability of the system and be consistent with the definition of the different variables that make up the model.

Table 3.1: Calibration of the parameters

Symbol	Definition	Value
ψ	Elasticity of money demand	0.05
θ	Semi-elasticity of the interest rate	0.5
β_1	Elasticity of y_t^d with respect to the real exchange rate	20
β_2	Elasticity of y_t^d with respect to the interest rate	0.1
μ	Speed of price adjustment	0.01

On the other hand, Table 3.2 presents the values of the exogenous variables in the initial period, where we can see that the model includes a total of 5 exogenous variables, two of them determining the value of foreign variables. This is so because, when applying the assumption of a small economy, all the variables from abroad are exogenous.

Table 3.2: Initial values of the exogenous variables

Variable	Definition	Value
m_0	Money supply	100
β_0	Autonomous component of aggregate demand	500
y_t^n	Potential output	2,000
p_0^*	Foreign price level	0
i_0^*	Foreign nominal interest rate	3

Once the value of the parameters and the exogenous variables have been determined, we can proceed to calculate the steady state and the stability conditions of the system (eigenvalues).

3.3.1. Steady state

From the dynamic system for the price level and the nominal exchange rate obtained previously and by applying the procedure described in the previous chapters, we would calculate the steady state as:

$$\begin{bmatrix} \bar{p}_t \\ \bar{s}_t \end{bmatrix} = -A^{-1}Bz_t \tag{3.14}$$

where, for this model, it results that:

$$A = \begin{bmatrix} -\mu\left(\beta_1 + \frac{\beta_2}{\theta}\right) & \mu\beta_1 \\ \frac{1}{\theta} & 0 \end{bmatrix}, B = \begin{bmatrix} \mu & \frac{\mu\beta_2}{\theta} & -\mu(\frac{\psi\beta_2}{\theta}+1) & 0 & \mu\beta_1 \\ 0 & -\frac{1}{\theta} & \frac{\psi}{\theta} & -1 & 0 \end{bmatrix}, z_t = \begin{bmatrix} \beta_0 \\ m_t \\ y_t^n \\ i_t^* \\ p_t^* \end{bmatrix} \tag{3.15}$$

being the inverse of the matrix A:

$$A^{-1} = \begin{bmatrix} 0 & \theta \\ \frac{1}{\mu\beta_1} & \frac{\beta_1\theta + \beta_2}{\beta_1} \end{bmatrix} \tag{3.16}$$

which results in:

$$-A^{-1}B = \begin{bmatrix} 0 & 1 & -\psi & \theta & 0 \\ -\frac{1}{\beta_1} & 1 & \frac{(1-\beta_1\psi)}{\beta_1} & \frac{\beta_1\theta+\beta_2}{\beta_1} & -1 \end{bmatrix} \tag{3.17}$$

Therefore, multiplying the previous matrix by the vector of exogenous variables, the value of the variables in steady state would be given by the following expressions:

$$\bar{p}_t = m_t - \psi y_t^n + \theta i_t^* \tag{3.18}$$

$$\bar{s}_t = m_t - \frac{\beta_0}{\beta_1} + \left[\frac{1-\psi\beta_1}{\beta_1}\right] y_t^n + \left[\frac{\theta\beta_1+\beta_2}{\beta_2}\right] i_t^* - p_t^* \tag{3.19}$$

By substituting the values corresponding to the parameters and the exogenous variables, we obtain that the steady-state values for the domestic price level and the nominal exchange rate are:

$$\bar{p}_t = 100 - 0.05 \times 2.000 + 0.5 \times 3 = 1.5$$

$$\bar{s}_t = 100 - \frac{500}{20} - \left[\frac{1 - 0.05 \times 20}{20}\right] \times 2.000 + \frac{0.5 \times 20 + 0.1}{0.1} \times 3 - 0 = 76.52$$

3.3.2. Stability analysis

Next, we proceed to study the stability condition of the system. As we have indicated previously, this model is characterized by the presence of a saddle point. Recall that the stability of the system is determined by calculating, $|A - \lambda I| = 0$, so we would have:

$$Det \begin{bmatrix} -\mu\left(\beta_1 + \frac{\beta_2}{\theta}\right) - \lambda & \mu\beta_1 \\ \frac{1}{\theta} & 0 - \lambda \end{bmatrix} = 0 \tag{3.20}$$

from which we obtain:

$$\lambda^2 + \lambda\left[\beta_1\mu + \frac{\beta_2\mu}{\theta}\right] - \frac{\beta_1\mu}{\theta} \tag{3.21}$$

By solving above, it turns out that the roots would be the following:

$$\lambda_1, \lambda_2 = \frac{-\left(\beta_1\mu + \frac{\beta_2\mu}{\theta}\right) \pm \sqrt{\left(\beta_1\mu + \frac{\beta_1\mu}{\theta}\right)^2 + 4\left(\frac{\beta_1\mu}{\theta}\right)}}{2} \tag{3.22}$$

As we can see, in this case, independently of the selected values of the parameters, the term that remains inside the square root is always positive, that is, the eigenvalues are always going to be real numbers. By substituting the values of Table 3.1 we obtain:

$$\lambda_1 = \frac{-\left(20 \times 0.01 + \frac{0.1 \times 0.01}{0.5}\right) - \sqrt{\left(20 \times 0.01 + \frac{0.1 \times 0.01}{0.5}\right)^2 + 4 \times \left(\frac{20 \times 0.01}{0.5}\right)}}{2} = -0.74$$

$$\lambda_1 = \frac{-\left(20 \times 0.01 + \frac{0.1 \times 0.01}{0.5}\right) + \sqrt{\left(20 \times 0.01 + \frac{0.1 \times 0.01}{0.5}\right)^2 + 4 \times \left(\frac{20 \times 0.01}{0.5}\right)}}{2} = 0.54$$

As we can see, if we add the unit to the roots, it results in a value of 0.26 (which is less than 1), and 1.54 (which is greater than the unit), so we get a solution of saddle point (see Appendix A). This means that certain trajectories are convergent towards the steady state while other trajectories are divergent. The fact that this model has as a solution a saddle point, introduces a new element to be considered in its numerical solution, since this type of solution implies the existence of a stable saddle path, to which the flexible forward-looking (jump) variable converges instantaneously, which in this case is the nominal exchange rate. Therefore, it is necessary to specify where this stable saddle path is located (which is an additional equation to the model) to be able to calculate the dynamics of the model to move from one steady state to another.

3.4. Numerical solution

Figure 3.1 shows the proposed structure of the spreadsheet corresponding to this model, "**ICM-3.xls**". In Appendix F, we have the code corresponding to this model solved in DYNARE. The structure of this spreadsheet presents some differences with respect to the previous model. In this case, we have a saddle-point solution, since one of the roots plus the unit is less than one while for the other it is greater than one. That is, the less-than-one root bring the economy to the steady state, while the root greater than one would lead the economy away from it. In this case, when a disturbance occurs, we must take into account the reaction of the nominal exchange rate, which is a completely flexible forward-looking variable, determined by the expectations about its future value. Thus, when solving the model numerically, we have to take into account that at the time a shock hits the economy, for instance, an increase in money supply, the nominal exchange rate will react instantaneously to that shock, jumping to the new stable saddle path. This instantaneous increase in the nominal exchange rate is caused by an upward adjustment of expectations about its future value.

Columns "F", "G", "H" and "I" show the value of each one of the endogenous variables (prices, nominal exchange rate, aggregate demand and nominal interest rate) in every moment of time. The calibrated values of the parameters appear in cells "B10" to "B14". The values of the exogenous variables appear in cells "B17" to "B21", which we have named "m_0", "iext_0", "Beta0_0", "pext_0" and "ypot_0", respectively. The initial steady-state values appear in cells "B24" and "B25". Cells "C24" and "C25" show the new steady state in the case where a disturbance occurs (change in the exogenous variables). The value of the eigenvalues is given in rows 28 and 29. In cells "B28" and B29 "the real part is shown, while the imaginary part is shown in cells" C28 "and" C29". Finally, the root modules are shown in cells "B32" and "B33".

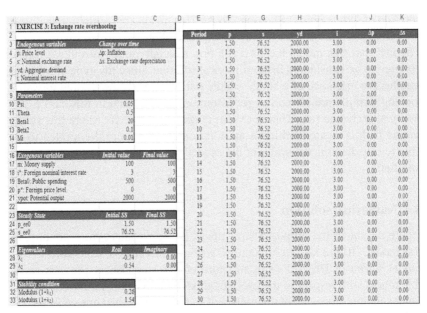

Figure 3.1. Structure of the spreadsheet "ICM-3.xls": The exchange rate overshooting model.

If we place the cursor in cell "F3" this expression appears:

=pbar_0

which is simply the expression corresponding to the initial steady-state value of the domestic price level given in cell "B24". The remaining rows in this column simply contain the value of the domestic price level in the previous moment plus the change produced in that price level. Thus, cell "F4" contains the expression "=F3+J3", where "F3" refers to the domestic price level of the previous period and "J3" to the change in the price level. This expression is copied into the remaining rows of that column.

On the other hand, if we place the cursor in cell "G3" it contains the expression:

=sbar_0

that is, the initial steady-state value of the nominal exchange rate given by cell "B25". Next, a somewhat special cell appears, the "G4", which we will define in the next section. In cell "G5", the expression "=G4+K4" appears in which we define the nominal exchange rate for each period as the previous one plus the change experienced in it. Column "H" contains the aggregate-demand values. If we place ourselves in cell "H3", we see that this expression appears:

=Beta0_0+Beta1*(G3-F3+pext_0)+(Beta2/Theta)*(m_0-F3-Psi*ypot_0)

which corresponds to the aggregate demand equation of the model (equation 3.10). This same expression appears in the following cells in this column. Column "I" contains the domestic nominal interest rate values. Thus, cell "I3" contains the following expression:

=-1/Theta*(m_0-F3-Psi*ypot_0)

which is the equation resulting from solving for the interest rate from the money-demand equation (equation 3.9). If we place ourselves in cell "I4", the expression that appears is:

=-1/Theta*(m_1-F4-Psi*ypot_1)

which refers to the new amount of money from time 1. This expression is the same one that appears in the following rows of this column.

Finally, columns "J" and "K" show the variations in domestic prices and the nominal exchange rate, that is, they define the value of inflation and the depreciation of the nominal exchange rate in each period. In this case, we must introduce the corresponding equations that determine the behavior of both variables. If we place ourselves in cell "J3" we see that it contains the expression:

=Mi*(H3-ypot_0)

while cell "J4" contains the expression:

=Mi*(H4-ypot_1)

being this same expression the one that appears in the following cells, since it is possible that we want to analyze the effects of an alteration in the level of potential output of the domestic economy. On the other hand, if we place ourselves in cell "K3", we see that it contains the expression:

=I3-iext_0

which corresponds to the dynamic equation for the nominal exchange rate (exchange rate depreciation). As we can see in the spreadsheet, we can enter the initial expression given by the model, since we will also calculate the corresponding value of the aggregate demand at each moment of time. If all calculations are correct, columns "J" and "K", where the change of each variable appears, must be zeros in the initial steady state.

3.4.1. The stable path

A key element for the numerical solution of this model is the calculation of the so-called stable saddle path, which is a stable trajectory that converges directly to the steady state. In this case, the dynamics of the economy in the adjustment from an initial steady state to another steady state when a shock occurs, is represented by an instantaneous readjustment to the new stable saddle path by the "jump" variable. Once this stable path is reached, the economy moves along it until it reaches the new steady state. This stable path can be calculated as a trajectory that is associated with the eigenvalue whose module plus 1 is less than the unit. Thus, in mathematical terms, the trajectory that defines the stable saddle path can be calculated through the following dynamic system:

$$\begin{bmatrix} \Delta p_t \\ \Delta s_t \end{bmatrix} = \lambda_1 \begin{bmatrix} p_t - \bar{p}_t \\ s_t - \bar{s}_t \end{bmatrix} \tag{3.23}$$

In general terms, we can write the stable saddle path as the solution to the following system:

$$\begin{bmatrix} \Delta p_t \\ \Delta s_t \end{bmatrix} = v_1(\lambda_1 + 1)^t a_1 + v_2(\lambda_2 + 1)^t a_2 \tag{3.24}$$

for $a_1 = 1$ and $a_2 = 0$, and where v_1 and v_2 are the eigenvectors associated to eigenvalues λ_1 and λ_2, respectively. When a disturbance occurs, the economy "jumps" to the unique stable saddle path, represented by the previous system. The model assumes that agents are rational in a context of perfect foresight and the jump to the stable path represents an adjustment in expectations.

3.4.2. Expectations readjustment: Jump to the saddle stable path

As we have indicated previously, one of the characteristics of this model is a saddle-point solution. This means that there are both trajectories that drive the economy to the steady state and trajectories that permanently distance the economy from equilibrium. In this situation, there is a stable saddle path, to which the forward-looking or jump variables move when a disturbance occurs. In the particular case of this model, the forward-looking variable is the nominal exchange rate. Therefore, when a disturbance occurs, an instantaneous readjustment occurs in the nominal exchange rate, which is caused by a readjustment in its expectations about its future value. This readjustment in expectations is instantaneously transferred to its current value. If agents in the foreign exchange market expect that in the future the exchange rate will be higher, they will readjust their expectations about the future exchange rate, which will result in an increase in the exchange rate. This readjustment in expectations cannot be calculated directly from the equations of the model since we have applied the perfect foresight assumption in such a way that the expected change in the exchange rate is equal to the current depreciation.

The key differentiating element that we have to incorporate is the computation of the corresponding value of the exchange rate at the time in which the disturbance occurs, that is, the value of cell "G4", as we assume that the shock occurs at period 1. As we have described previously, at the time in which the disturbance occurs, the exchange rate undergoes an instantaneous change as a consequence of the readjustment of expectations, jumping to the new stable saddle path. Therefore, to have a numerical solution of the model it is necessary to calculate the new value of the nominal exchange rate consistent with the new stable saddle path when a shock hits the economy. This jump in the nominal exchange rate to the new stable saddle path is what it is known as the overshooting phenomenon. To calculate the jump in the nominal exchange rate following a shock, we depart from the dynamic equation of the exchange rate:

$$\Delta s_t = -\frac{1}{\theta}(m_t - p_t - \psi \bar{y}_t) - i_t^* \tag{3.25}$$

In parallel, we can define the stable trajectory that will follow the nominal exchange rate associated with the stable root (λ_1), given by:

$$\Delta s_t = \lambda_1(s_t - \bar{s}_t) \tag{3.26}$$

As we can see, both equations result in the variation with respect to the time of the nominal exchange rate, so we can equalize both equations at the time in which the disturbance occurs ($t = 1$):

$$\lambda_1(s_t - \bar{s}_1) = -\frac{1}{\theta}(m_1 - p_1 - \psi \bar{y}_1) - i_1^* \tag{3.27}$$

Solving for the value of the exchange rate results in the following value for the nominal exchange rate:

$$s_1 = \frac{-(m_1 - p_1 - \psi \bar{y}_1)}{\theta \lambda_1} - \frac{i_1^*}{\lambda_1} + \bar{s}_1 \tag{3.28}$$

an expression that is introduced in cell "G4", such that this cell would contain the expression:

=-(m_1-F4-Psi*ypot_1)/(Theta*Lambda1)-iext_1/Lambda1+sbar_1

Cell "G5" would contain the expression:

=G4+K4

indicating that the value corresponding to the exchange rate in a period would be that of the previous period plus its variation. This expression is the one that appears in the following rows of the column. Note that the results would be equivalent if we introduce the expression:

=Lambda1*(G4-sbar_1)

which represents the movements of the exchange rate along the stable path, being a proportion of the difference between the value of the exchange rate and its value of steady state, as indicated by expression (3.26).

Finally, column "J" contains the adjustment equation for the price level, whereas column "K" contains the adjustment equation for the nominal exchange rate. If we place ourselves in cell "K3", we see that the expression that appears is:

=I3-iext_0

that is, the difference between the national interest rate and the foreign interest rate representing the Uncovered Interest Parity.

3.5. Shock analysis: Effects of an increase in money supply

We will now use the previously-solved model to calculate the effects of an increase in money supply and illustrate the phenomenon of overshooting of the exchange rate in the face of this disturbance.

From the expression (3.28) above, we obtain that the variation of the exchange rate with respect to the change in money supply (this allows knowing the adjustment in the expectations and the impact effect of the change) is given by:

$$\Delta s_1 = \frac{-1}{\theta \lambda_1}(m_1 - m_0) + (\bar{s}_1 - \bar{s}_0) \tag{3.29}$$

where the subscript of time 0 refers to the initial state and the index 1 refers to the final state. Given the relationship between the nominal exchange rate and the quantity of money (they move exactly in the same amount in the long term, as we can see in the definition of the nominal exchange rate in steady state, given by the expression 3.15), it turns out that:

$$(\bar{s}_1 - \bar{s}_0) = (m_1 - m_0) \tag{3.30}$$

By substituting in the previous expression we have:

$$\Delta s_1 = \frac{-1}{\theta \lambda_1}(m_1 - m_0) + (m_1 - m_0) > (m_1 - m_0) \tag{3.31}$$

As we can see, the variation in the nominal exchange rate is positive and higher than the unit, given that $|\lambda_1 + 1| < 1$, indicating that a certain variation in the amount of money causes an instantaneous increase more than proportional to the nominal exchange rate. This instantaneous change is precisely what we call overshooting (or overreaction) of the nominal exchange rate.

To numerically compute the effects of the previous disturbance, let's assume that the amount of money goes from a value of 100, in period 0, to a value of 101 in period 1. For this, we only have to change the corresponding value in cell "C18" in the spreadsheet and we will immediately observe the new steady-state values, as well as the dynamic trajectory for each of the variables. As we can see, the exchange rate increases instantaneously, just as the interest rate decreases and aggregate demand increases. In this particular example, the exchange rate has gone from having a value of 76.52 to increase to 80.21, to subsequently decrease until it reaches a value of 77.52, a point higher than the initial value given that the amount of money has also increased one point and the purchasing power parity is fulfilled in the long term. In effect, we can verify that since the amount of money has increased by one unit, the previous expression results in:

$$\Delta s_1 = \frac{-1}{\theta \lambda_1} + 1 \tag{3.32}$$

and substituting the values corresponding to λ_1 and θ, results in:

$$\Delta s_1 = \frac{-1}{0.5 \times (-0.74 =} + 1 = 3.70$$

If we add this amount to the initial value for the exchange rate, 76.52, we obtain a value of 80.22, which corresponds exactly to the value reached by the exchange rate at the time when the increase in the amount of money is produced.

Figure 3.2 shows the dynamics of the endogenous variables before this disturbance. First, before the increase in the amount of money prices begin to increase gradually, until reaching their new level of equilibrium, higher by one point than the initial (exactly to the same extent that increases the amount of money). The exchange rate experiences an initial increase, reaching a value well above its steady-state value. This is a consequence of the readjustment of expectations about the rate of depreciation of the exchange rate. The increase in the amount of money will cause a long-term increase in the exchange rate, which translates into an increase in expectations of depreciation and, therefore, its instantaneous increase. Once this impact effect occurs, then the exchange rate takes the opposite direction, decreasing progressively until reaching the new steady state.

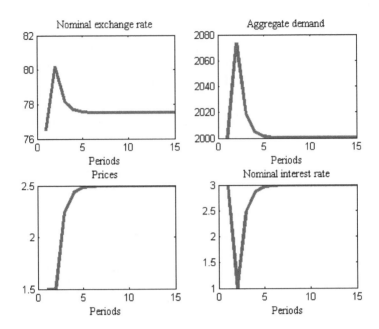

Figure 3.2. The exchange rate overshooting: Effects of an increase in money supply.

Aggregate demand also experiences an initial increase to subsequently decrease to its initial steady-state value. This is because the disturbance we are studying is nominal, so it has no real effects in the long term. Thus, the level of aggregate demand will be the same as before the disturbance. However, the increase in the exchange rate causes an increase in external competitiveness by prices, increasing aggregate demand, an effect that is eliminated as prices increase. Given that in the long term, prices will increase in the same way as the nominal exchange rate increases, this means that in the long term the level of external competitiveness by prices of the economy returns to its initial value, so that the steady state of aggregate demand does not change.

The nominal interest rate initially decreases to the increase in the amount of money proportionally, to be gradually increased later. This movement in the medium term of the nominal interest rate is similar to that experienced by the price level. Thus, as prices increase, the equilibrium in the money market causes an increase in the nominal interest rate, readjusting downward the expectations of depreciation of the nominal exchange rate.

In summary, in the long-run, we observe that both the price level and the nominal exchange rate increase by the same amount as the amount of money does (Purchasing Power Parity condition holds). On the other hand, we observe that both the aggregate demand and the nominal interest rate return to the same value that they initially had, once the adjustment in the price level has taken place.

3.6. Sensitivity Analysis: Effects of a change in the speed of adjustment in the price level

Finally, we can perform a sensitivity analysis to study how the phenomenon of the overshooting of the exchange rate is affected by the value of the parameters. Thus, we can change the different parameters of the model, both those that represent elasticities and those of speed of adjustment, and study how changes in these parameters affect the behavior of the exchange rate in the short term. In particular, let us suppose that the parameter that represents the speed of adjustment of prices, μ, goes from taking a value of 0.01 to a value of 0.001. That is, we assume that prices adjust more slowly. To do this, we only have to change the value corresponding to this parameter in cell "B14", maintaining the same disturbance that we have previously analyzed.

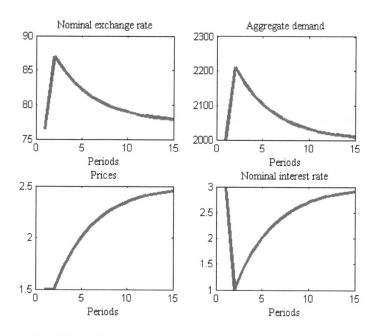

Figure 3.3. Sensibility analysis. Response to an increase in money supply with $\mu = 0.001$.

Figure 3.3 shows the impulse-response function of the different variables of the model before the same disturbance analyzed in the previous section. As we can see, the phenomenon of the overshooting of the exchange rate continues to take place due to the increase in the amount of money, initially increasing above its new steady-state value. As we can see, the new steady-state value is not altered, being similar to the one obtained in the previous example. This is because the parameter whose value we are altering is a parameter that represents the speed of adjustment in prices, it does not affect the steady state of this economy, so that the effects in the long term do not change. The steady state would change if we alter another parameter that affects the determination of the balance in the money market as well as in the goods and services market. In general terms, we obtain the same dynamic response for the different variables, but now we can see that the transition to the new steady state is slower. This is due to the fact that prices now adjust more slowly upwards, which also means that the rest of the variables experience a smoother behavior in their adjustment.

Exercises

1. Using the "**ICM-3.xls**" spreadsheet, study the effects of an increase in public spending, represented by β_0. Specifically, suppose that public spending increases by 100 units. Does the phenomenon of overshooting of the exchange rate occur in this case?

2. Suppose that a technological change occurs and increases the level of potential production (for example by 5%). Use the "**ICM-3.xls**" spreadsheet to study the effects of this disturbance on the economy. What is the transition dynamic to the new steady state?

3. What effects does an increase in the parameter θ have? As this parameter is higher, what is the phenomenon of overshooting of the exchange rate?

4. Solve and build the corresponding spreadsheet for the proposed model but now defining the aggregate demand as a function of the real interest rate.

5. Solve and construct the corresponding spreadsheet eliminating the assumption that the production level is exogenous and introducing an equation that determines the aggregate supply of the economy.

Part II: Introduction to Macroeconomic Dynamic General Equilibrium

4. The consumption-saving optimal decision

4.1. Introduction

One of the fundamental problems in economics with important implications for macroeconomic modeling is the optimal choice of consumption-savings by households. This decision taken by households is a fundamental piece in the construction of the micro-based dynamic general equilibrium models that are used in current macroeconomic analysis. These models consider households or families as one of the economic agents in an economy. These agents make decisions on some control variables to maximize their objective function, which is what we call the utility function. This utility function can depend on a wide set of variables, the main one of which is consumption. In the neoclassical framework it is assumed that these agents are rational and that they maximize their utility function throughout their life cycle. We also assume that the capital markets are perfect, that is, the savings of the agent can be positive (credit position) or negative (debit position), in each moment of time, with no-liquidity constraints. From this decision problem, we simultaneously determine two of the most relevant macroeconomic variables to explain the behavior of an economy: the level of consumption, which is the main component of aggregate demand in quantitative terms, and the level of savings, which will determine the level of investment and, therefore, the process of capital accumulation and future output.

This chapter focuses on the basic problem faced by a representative household when determining their level of optimal consumption throughout their life cycle, which result in the first block that integrates any micro-based macroeconomic model and gives rise to one of the main equations of the model: the optimal path of consumption, which is equivalent to the optimal savings decision. The objective function that this agent maximizes is the utility function, and we assume that this utility is instantaneous and only depends on the level of consumption of the period, so it is additively separable over time. In this way, we obtain the consumption-savings decision of this economic agent, a decision that has an intertemporal character, since through the saving decision the agent can separate its consumption profile from its income profile period by period, determining its levels of future consumption based on a current saving decision. For this, we will numerically solve a simple problem in discrete time, in which the objective of the consumer is to maximize their level of utility or happiness throughout their whole life that we suppose is finite, represented by an instantaneous utility function that depends only on the level of consumption in each period, subject to the budget constraint. That is to say, the individual maximizes the sum of discounted utility for each period of their life cycle, where the weight to future utility is lower compared to current utility. An important aspect of this problem is that the solution is not a certain level of consumption for the period in which the decision is made, but an optimal consumption path throughout the life cycle, in which the consumptions of the different periods are related to each other through savings. In other words, the solution will consist in a difference equation for marginal utility, where the optimal consumption path is a function of the interest rate, the discount factor and the curvature of the utility function.

The basic problem for this intertemporal consumer choice is a simple enough problem to be solved using a spreadsheet. While this is a dynamic-optimization problem, a spreadsheet such as Excel contains tools that are powerful enough to solve this type of problem, provided that the problem to solve is defined in discrete time, the life of the individual is finite, the number of lifespan periods is not very high and the functional form of the utility is not very complex. To solve the consumer problem computationally, we will use Excel's "Solver" tool. This tool is very easy to use, incorporating a Newton-type algorithm (see Appendix H) that allows us to solve not-too-complex problems of systems of equations.

The structure of the rest of the chapter is as follows. In Section 2, we present the basic household maximization problem in discrete time, assuming that the lifespan of this agent is finite, labor income is an exogenous variable, and the initial and final level of financial assets stocks are zero. In Section 3, we present the structure of the spreadsheet in which we will numerically solve this problem, as well as the description of the Excel "Solver" tool and the calibration of the parameters of the model. The fourth section studies how the decision of the agent changes with respect to a variation in an exogenous variable. Section 5 presents a sensitivity analysis, changing some of the parameters of the model. Finally, in Section 6, we present the solution to the problem using an alternative functional form for the instantaneous utility function.

4.2. The consumption-saving decision in discrete time and finite life

We start presenting the basic consumer problem in discrete time and its analytical solution. We suppose the existence of a consumer who lives T periods and whose utility function, which we denote by $U(\cdot)$, depends on the consumption of the period $U(C_t)$, where C_t is the consumption in period t

(that is, we assume an instantaneous utility function). This utility function fulfills a series of properties, mainly that it is a positive function of consumption, that is, its derivative with respect to consumption is positive, $U_C(C_t) > 0$, and that its second derivative with respect to consumption is negative $U_{CC}(C_t) < 0$, indicating that marginal utility is decreasing in the level of consumption. Thus, we assume that utility is a strictly increasing function, strictly concave and twice differentiable. The previous characteristics indicate that the utility function is increasing in consumption, that is, the higher the level of consumption of the individual, the higher is his level of happiness. On the other hand, the function is concave, indicating that as the consumption increases, the utility of the individual increases but each time it does so in a smaller amount.

The problem of maximization of the household is solved in an intertemporal context. This means that the household's objective is to maximize utility, not only at a certain point of time, but throughout the life cycle. Therefore, the problem that the individuals would solve consists in maximizing the discounted sum of the instantaneous utility throughout their lifespan. Household maximize discounted utility because of a human characteristic: impatience. This characteristic refers to the fact that we do not value utility equally at different periods. In fact, we value utility at the present period more than utility at any future time, that is, we are impatient, and hence, we discount the values of future utility. Although in micro-based dynamic general equilibrium macroeconomic models the general assumption is that household's lifespan is infinite (in reference to the time period they use to make economic decisions, since households are concerned about the welfare of future generations), except in the case of overlapping generations models, in our context we assume that households live is finite. This implies the introduction of a final condition for the maximization problem in which the amount of accumulated financial assets must be zero at the end of the lifespan, so that the utility is maximum. Finally, for the problem to be simple to solve, we assume that the utility function is additively separable over time, that is, the utility in each period only depends on the consumption made in that period, excluding the existence of consumption habits.

The maximization of the utility function is subject to a budget constraint that must be met period by period. The budget constraint is given by:

$$C_t + B_t = (1 + R_{t-1})B_{t-1} + W_t \tag{4.1}$$

where B_t is the stock of savings or amount of financial assets (which can be positive or negative) in the current period, R_{t-1} is the interest rate applied to financial assets (savings) in the previous period and that we assume is a variable that is determined exogenously and W_t is the income of the individual of the period that we also assume is exogenous. The right side of the budget constraint represents total income of the individual while the left side represents the uses (the expenses). Note that this budget constraint is a difference equation, indicating how the amount of financial assets (the stock of savings) evolves over time. Thus, the budget constraint can be rewritten as:

$$\Delta B_t = R_{t-1}B_{t-1} + W_t - C_t \tag{4.2}$$

where we define $\Delta B_t = B_t - B_{t-1}$.[1]

In this maximization problem we have to consider two additional restrictions in order to solve it. The first refers to the amount of financial assets (savings stock) that the individual has in the initial period, $t = 0$. This amount can be positive or zero. In our case, we assume that $B_{-1} = 0$, therefore, the amount of financial assets in period $t = 0$ is equivalent to the savings in that period, $B_0 = W_0 - C_0$. Second, the amount of financial assets in the final period B_T, which to obtain a maximum is required to be zero given the finite household's lifespan. That is, households, to maximize utility, selects a path of consumption and savings such that in the last period of their life cycle their stock of financial assets is zero. Therefore, we assume that $B_T = 0$.

When households make their decision of consumption-saving at a given moment of time throughout their life cycle, they do not know the future flow of income or the path corresponding to the interest rate. Nor do they know what the duration of their life cycle will be. This implies that the maximization problem is solved in expected terms, given some expectations about the income and the interest rate of future periods. As we have done in the previous chapters, we assume that the expectations are rational, and we solve the problem under the assumption that there is a perfect foresight, so that the individual knows at all times all the income flows over their life, the interest rate, and that they know the value of T. Thus, given future incomes and interest rates, which we assume are exogenous variables in this simple problem together with the number of periods of the life cycle, the agent will decide in each period how much of their wealth goes to consumption and which part is destined to savings. The budget constraint indicates that the total expenditure of the individual (the left part of the equation) has to be equal to the total income (the right part). The expenses are given by the sum of the consumption plus the stock of savings $C_t + B_t$, that is, with the available

---

[1] Alternatively, the household's budget constraint can be defined as $C_t + B_{t+1} = (1 + R_t)B_t + W_t$, by changing the time for saving and saving returns. In this case, the change in the stock of saving would be defined as $\Delta B_t = B_{t+1} - B_t$.

resources we can do two things: either we consume them in the present or we keep them to be consumed in the future. The individual's total income, which represents the available resources, is given by their exogenous labor income, by the accumulated savings up to the previous period and by interest returns on savings.

The stock of financial assets (corresponding to the accumulated volume of savings) at each moment of time can be positive or negative, indicating that the household can maintain a creditor or debtor position, respectively. In the first case, the agent is transferring present income into the future. In the second case, the agent is displacing future income to the present. Moving income from the present to the future is always possible. Just do not spend it and save it. However, transferring future income to the present is somewhat more complicated and requires the collaboration of financial markets. Here we assume that capital markets are perfect, that is, there are no restrictions on liquidity that prevent the desired future income from being brought to the present and, therefore, the individual can use the savings to separate the level of consumption of each period with respect to the income of the period without any restriction.

Finally, and as we have indicated above, a key element in the problem of utility maximization by consumers in an intertemporal context is the fact that utility is not valued equally at different moments of time. This means that individuals discount future utility, that is, a unit of future utility has a lower valuation than a unit of current utility. This discount rate depends on what we call the intertemporal subjective preference rate θ, which is a positive parameter ($\theta > 0$). This parameter indicates how much the agent assesses its future utility compared to its current utility. The higher the value of this intertemporal preference, the lower is the valuation of future utility in terms of current utility (more impatient is the agent). This means that the problem of the consumer is to maximize the sum of profits in discounted terms, where the intertemporal discount factor would be given by:

$$\beta = \frac{1}{1+\theta} \tag{4.3}$$

where $\theta > 0$ is the intertemporal subjective preference rate and, therefore, it turns out that $\beta < 1$. The value that is usually used in the macroeconomic models for the intertemporal discount rate is about $\beta = 0.97$, for the case of annual data and around $\beta = 0.99$ for the case of quarterly data. This means that the intertemporal preference rate would have a value of $\theta = 0.0309$ in the case of annual data and $\theta = 0.0101$ in the case of data with a quarterly frequency.

Structure of the basic household problem	
Utility function	$U = U(C_t)$
Budget constraint	$C_t + B_t = (1 + R_{t-1})B_{t-1} + W_t$
Initial stock of assets	$B_{-1} = 0$
Final stock of assets	$B_T = 0$

Taking into account all these elements, the problem of the consumer would be specified as follows:

$$\max_{\{c_t\}_{t=0}^T} E_t \sum_{t=0}^T \frac{U(C_t)}{(1+\theta)^t} = \max_{\{c_t\}_{t=0}^T} E_t \sum_{t=0}^T \beta^t U(C_t) \qquad (4.4)$$

subject to:

$$C_t + B_t = (1 + R_{t+1})B_{t-1} + W_t \qquad (4.5)$$

$$B_{-1} = 0 \qquad (4.6)$$

$$B_T = 0 \qquad (4.7)$$

where E_t is the mathematical expectation, that is, the expected value of the future stream of utility in discounted terms. When solving this problem, we assume perfect foresight, which means that we have information about the future value of all the variables. This means that we can directly eliminate the mathematical expectation of the problem to be maximized.

Since the objective function is concave and since the dynamic equation representing the budget constraint is linear, we can assure that the points that satisfy the Lagrange conditions are global maximums of the problem. From the resolution of this problem, we obtain that the household selects an optimal plan of consumption in each one of the periods of their life. That is, while deciding the level of consumption in the period $t = 0$, the agent also decides simultaneously the level of consumption for all subsequent periods, determining their optimal consumption path, such that it would determine the path:

$$C_0^0, C_1^0, C_2^0, C_3^0, \dots C_T^0 \qquad (4.8)$$

where all levels of consumption for the different periods have been decided at time 0. Thus, given the assumption that there is no uncertainty about the value of future variables, the problem the consumer results in maximizing, in the case of a finite life, is the next discounted sum of utilities:

$$\max_{\{C_t\}_{t=0}^T} U(C_0) + \beta U(C_1) + \beta^2 U(C_2) + \beta^3 U(C_3) + \cdots + \beta^T U(C_T) \qquad (4.9)$$

To solve the consumer maximization problem, we define the following auxiliary function of Lagrange:

$$\mathcal{L} = \sum_{t=0}^{T}[\beta^t U(C_t) - \lambda_t(C_t + B_t - W_t - (1 + R_{t-1})B_{t-1}] \tag{4.10}$$

When defining the Lagrange auxiliary function, we must take into account that the budget constraint, which is a difference equation for the stock of financial assets, includes the stock of financial assets in two different periods, therefore, its incorporation into the Lagrange auxiliary function results in the following terms for t and $t + 1$:

$$\dots - \lambda_t[(C_t + B_t - W_t - (1 + R_{t-1})B_{t-1}] - $$
$$\lambda_{t+1}[(C_{t+1} + B_{t+1} - W_{t+1} - (1 + R_t)B_t] \dots \tag{4.11}$$

By solving the previous problem, we find that the conditions of first order, for $t = 0, 1, 2, \dots, T$, are the following:

$$\frac{\partial \mathcal{L}}{\partial C_t} = \beta^t U_C(C_t) - \lambda_t = 0 \tag{4.12}$$

$$\frac{\partial \mathcal{L}}{\partial B_t} = -\lambda_t + \lambda_{t+1}(1 + R_t) = 0 \tag{4.13}$$

$$\frac{\partial \mathcal{L}}{\partial \lambda_t} = C_t + B_t - W_t - (1 + R_{t-1})B_{t-1} = 0 \tag{4.14}$$

By solving for the Lagrange multiplier, λ_t, using the first first-order condition (4.12), which represents the "shadow" price of consumption (note that it is equal to the marginal utility in discounted terms), and by substituting that value in the second first-order condition (4.13), both for its value in t and for its value in $t + 1$, we obtain:

$$-\beta^t U_C(C_t) + \beta^{t+1} U_C(C_{t+1})(1 + R_t) = 0 \tag{4.15}$$

and by operating results:

$$U_C(C_t) = \beta U_C(C_{t+1})(1 + R_t) \tag{4.16}$$

an expression that indicates what is the optimal path of consumption over time, result of the comparison of the marginal utility in two periods, given some intertemporal preferences (the discount factor), a real interest rate that indicates the cost (positive or negative) to transfer income from one period to another, and the particular functional form for the utility function. Importantly, this optimal consumption path is independent on the profile of income over the life cycle.

Solution to the basic household problem	
Optimal consumption path	$U_C(C_t) = \beta U_C(C_{t+1})(1 + R_t)$
Financial assets variation	$B_t = (1 + R_{t-1})B_{t-1} + W_t L_t - C_t$

The steady state is given by that value for the level of consumption that remains constant over time. So, if $C_t = C_{t+1} = \bar{C}$, then it turns out that $U_C(\bar{C}) = \beta U_C(\bar{C})(1 + \bar{R})$, resulting in $1 = (1 + \bar{R})$, and implying that the steady-state value for the interest rate would be given by:

$$\bar{R} = \frac{1-\beta}{\beta} = \frac{1 - \frac{1}{1+\theta}}{\frac{1}{1+\theta}} = \theta \qquad (4.17)$$

that is, in a steady state, the interest rate would be equal to the intertemporal subjective preference rate. If this condition holds, then the optimal path of consumption would imply an equal level of consumption for all periods.

4.2.1. Example: logarithmic utility function

To numerically solve the household maximization problem posed above, we need to define a specific functional form for the utility function. Let's assume that the utility function has a logarithmic form, which is a functional form very used in practice for its simplicity. In this case, the problem of the consumer would be given by:

$$\max_{\{C_t\}_{t=0}^T} \sum_{t=0}^T \beta^t \ln C_t \qquad (4.18)$$

subject to budget constraint and initial and final conditions. The problem to solve, using the auxiliary Lagrange function, would be:

$$\mathcal{L} = \sum_{t=0}^T [\beta^t \ln C_t - \lambda_t (C_t + B_t - W_t - (1 + R_{t-1})B_{t-1}] \qquad (4.19)$$

First-order conditions are the following:

$$\frac{\partial \mathcal{L}}{\partial C_t} = \beta^t \frac{1}{C_t} - \lambda_t = 0 \qquad (4.20)$$

$$\frac{\partial \mathcal{L}}{\partial B_t} = -\lambda_t + \lambda_{t+1}(1 + R_t) = 0 \qquad (4.21)$$

$$\frac{\partial \mathcal{L}}{\partial \lambda_t} = C_t + B_t - W_t - (1 + R_{t-1})B_{t-1} = 0 \qquad (4.22)$$

Since the utility function is concave, the necessary conditions are also sufficient to obtain a global maximum. By solving for the value of the Lagrange multiplier from the first first-order condition (4.20) and by substituting it into the second first-order condition (4.21), we obtain:

$$\beta^t \frac{1}{C_t} = \beta^{t+1} \frac{1}{C_{t+1}}(1 + R_t) \qquad (4.23)$$

and by operating results:

$$C_{t+1} = \beta(1 + R_t)C_t \qquad (4.24)$$

indicating the relationship between the consumption level in the period $t + 1$ with the consumption in t, this ratio being determined by the preference parameter β, the real interest rate and the specific functional form used for the utility.

Solution to the household problem	
Logarithmic utility function	
Optimal consumption path	$C_{t+1} = \beta(1 + R_t)C_t$
Financial assets variation	$B_t = (1 + R_{t-1})B_{t-1} + W_t L_t - C_t$

4.3. Numerical solution

To numerically compute the above maximization problem, we will use Excel's "Solver" tool, which allows us to easily solve relatively simple problems of dynamic optimization like the one we are proposing. This tool, which is incorporated into Excel as an add-in, solves linear programming problems, as well as systems of equations, both linear and non-linear, using different methods. In Appendix G, we present how this problem would be in MATLAB, using the "fsolve" function.

The Excel file corresponding to this exercise is "**ICM-4-1.xls**". Figure 4.1 shows the structure of the file. As we can see, in this case, for the calibration of the model we only need one parameter: the intertemporal discount rate, β. We also need to determine two exogenous variables: the real interest rate, R, as well as the income level, W. Both the intertemporal discount rate and the interest rate are determining factors of the optimal consumption path, together with the particular functional form of the utility function, as we have shown analytically. In practice, the real interest rate is an endogenous variable reflecting the marginal productivity of physical capital. However, for now, let's assume that this exogenous variable remains constant. On the other hand, we must also specify the salary income of the individual in each period of their life, which we have assumed to be exogenous but in practice is also an endogenous variable representing marginal productivity of labor. In this first exercise, we will assume that the income is constant for all periods. The values we set are an intertemporal discount factor of 0.97, which appears in cell "B4", while in cell "B7" the real interest rate of 2% ($R = 00.2$) appears, and a value for the salary income of $W = 10$, which it is included as a column.

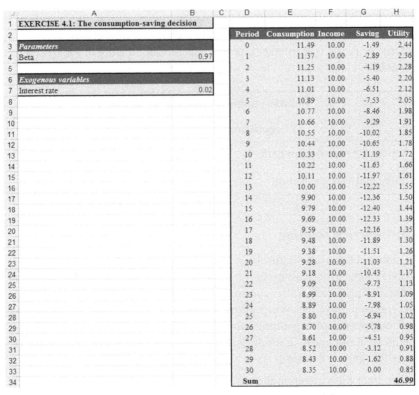

	A	B	C	D	E	F	G	H
1	EXERCISE 4.1: The consumption-saving decision							
2				Period	Consumption	Income	Saving	Utility
3	*Parameters*			0	11.49	10.00	-1.49	2.44
4	Beta	0.97		1	11.37	10.00	-2.89	2.36
5				2	11.25	10.00	-4.19	2.28
6	*Exogenous variables*			3	11.13	10.00	-5.40	2.20
7	Interest rate	0.02		4	11.01	10.00	-6.51	2.12
8				5	10.89	10.00	-7.53	2.05
9				6	10.77	10.00	-8.46	1.98
10				7	10.66	10.00	-9.29	1.91
11				8	10.55	10.00	-10.02	1.85
12				9	10.44	10.00	-10.65	1.78
13				10	10.33	10.00	-11.19	1.72
14				11	10.22	10.00	-11.63	1.66
15				12	10.11	10.00	-11.97	1.61
16				13	10.00	10.00	-12.22	1.55
17				14	9.90	10.00	-12.36	1.50
18				15	9.79	10.00	-12.40	1.44
19				16	9.69	10.00	-12.33	1.39
20				17	9.59	10.00	-12.16	1.35
21				18	9.48	10.00	-11.89	1.30
22				19	9.38	10.00	-11.51	1.26
23				20	9.28	10.00	-11.03	1.21
24				21	9.18	10.00	-10.43	1.17
25				22	9.09	10.00	-9.73	1.13
26				23	8.99	10.00	-8.91	1.09
27				24	8.89	10.00	-7.98	1.05
28				25	8.80	10.00	-6.94	1.02
29				26	8.70	10.00	-5.78	0.98
30				27	8.61	10.00	-4.51	0.95
31				28	8.52	10.00	-3.12	0.91
32				29	8.43	10.00	-1.62	0.88
33				30	8.35	10.00	0.00	0.85
34				Sum				46.99

Figure 4.1. Structure of the spreadsheet "ICM-4-1.xls".

The variables that we need to define to solve this problem are the following. The "D" column is the time index, while the "E" column will show the optimal consumption values for each period, which are the variables that we have to calculate. That is, the solution to our problem would appear in this column. Let's suppose that the household lives from period 0 to period 30 ($T = 30$). Column "F" is the exogenous (labor) income, which we assume is given and constant period to period, column "G" is the savings obtained as the difference between consumption and income of each period, and finally, column "H" shows the value for discounted utility.

To solve the exercise using Excel's "Solver" tool, we operate as follows. First, we fill with fictitious values (a guess solution) the column corresponding to consumption (column "E"). This is what is known as the "seed", and will be the initial values that the algorithm in Excel will use to obtain the solution to the problem. These initial values should be as close as possible to the final solution. The closer they are to the final solution, the easier it will be for the computer to calculate the correct solution. On the other hand, if the initial values we propose are very different from the final solution, we could find the case in which the algorithm that solves our system of equations is not able to find the correct solution. It is important to keep in mind that these fictitious values (guess solution) that we initially provide cannot be very different from the final solution. From here, and in an iterative process, the algorithm changes these initial values obtaining new solutions until reaching the final value. Appendix H shows schematically the basic operation of this type of algorithms (Newton type) to solve a system of equations.

Next, we establish the level of income of the individual in each period. In our case, we have assumed that the level of income is 10 units in each period throughout the life of the individual. Column "G" shows the savings, in terms of the stock of financial assets. The savings of the first period is simply the difference between the level of consumption and the level of income in that period. Thus, if we place the cursor in cell "G3", this expression appears:

=F3-E3

that is, wage income (column "F") minus consumption (column "E") in period 0. On the contrary, if we place ourselves in cell "G4" we see that the expression that appears is:

=(1+Rbar)*G3+F4-E4

that is, it is the income generated by the savings made up to the previous period plus the income of the period minus consumption of the period. The following rows in this column contain this same expression. That is, it is the gross yields from savings made up to the previous period plus the new savings of the period.

Finally, column "H" presents the value of the discounted utility in each period. If we place ourselves in cell "H3", the expression appears:

=Beta^D3*LN(E3)

which is the valuation of the utility in period 0, that is, the logarithm of the consumption multiplied by the intertemporal discount factor to the time index power corresponding to that period. Finally, in cell "H54" appears the sum of the discounted utilities, which is the value that we have to maximize. Once we have this information, then we go to the "Solver" tool and enter the data corresponding to the problem we want to solve. In our case, the target cell is "H34", changing the cells of the variables from "E3" to "E33" and subject to the restriction that cell "G33" must be greater than or equal to zero. Once these steps have been completed, we can execute the "Solver" tool, pressing the "Solve" button, and we will obtain the solution for the optimal consumption path in the "E" column.

To execute Excel's "Solver" to solve our maximization problem, we have to go in the main menu to "Tools" or "Data", depending on the version of Excel that we are using, and select "Solver" and the window shown in Figure 4.2 will appear. The "Solver" tool may not come incorporated directly into the Excel menu, so we probably have to install it. If the solver tool is not already installed, then we have to go to "File", "Options" and "Add-ons", to install the tool, or go to the Office Button and select "Excel Options", "Add-ons" and select "Solver" for installation, depending on the version we are using.

Figure 4.2. Excel's Solver tool menu.

When selecting "Solver", a dialogue window appears in the spreadsheet with the title "Solver Parameters". The first item that appears in the "Solver" dialog window is "Objective cell:" or "Set Objective:". This option refers to the value of the objective function of the problem that we want to solve. In our case, it will refer to the total utility of the individual throughout his life. Specifically, it would be the discounted sum of the utility obtained by the individual in each period of his life cycle.

Then, the instruction "Objective cell value:" appears in which there are three options: "Maximum", "Minimum" and "Value of:". These options refer to the type of problem we want to solve. If we want to maximize the value of the target cell, we would select "Maximum". If what we want is to minimize a certain problem, then we would select the "Minimum" option. On the contrary, if what we want is that it reaches a certain value, we would introduce this value in the option "Value of:". In our case, the problem we want to solve consists in maximizing the utility of the consumer, so we would select the option "Maximum", which is precisely the option marked by default.

Then, the instruction "By changing variable cells" appears. Here, we have to introduce the cells in which Excel will calculate the objective variable, that is, the level of consumption period by period. The spreadsheet will present the solution to the problem that we want to solve in the cells that we indicate in this section. In our specific case, we will obtain the level of consumption in each period that maximizes the total utility of the individual throughout his life. For the construction of the problem, we have previously proposed a tentative value for these cells.

Finally, the instruction "Subject to the Constraints:" appears. In this section, we must introduce the constraints to which the problem we want to solve is subject. The constraint with which our problem is going to count is that the amount of financial assets (savings) of the individual at the end of his life must be zero ($B_T = 0$).

To the right of the "Solver" dialog box appears a tab called "Options". If we click on this tab, the dialogue box shown in Figure 4.3 appears. Again, the exact format of this dialog depends on the version of Excel that we are using. This table allows to change different parameters, such as the maximum calculation time, the number of iterations, the precision, the tolerance and the convergence. It also includes other additional options. Finally, there are some options related to the estimation, calculation of derivatives and regarding the search algorithm of the solution. However, the dialog boxes of the "Solver" can be very different depending on the version of Excel that we are using. Once we have it all, we simply give the tab to "Solve" and automatically we get the solution to the problem (if Excel has not found any problem to solve it). Excel will determine the values of the level of consumption for each period such that the sum of the discounted profits is the maximum possible.

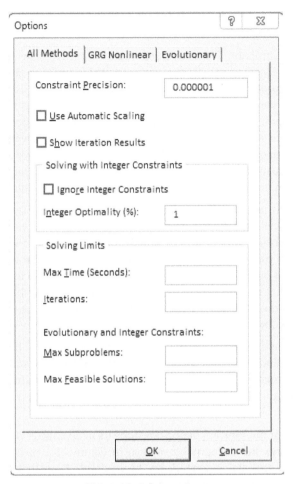

Figure 4.3. Solver options.

Figure 4.4 shows the time paths of the different variables resulting from solving the previous maximization problem. As we can see, the optimal consumption path has a negative slope, indicating that the household prefers to have a high consumption level in the first periods of its life cycle and to decrease its consumption over time. This result is a direct consequence of the values calibrated for the interest rate and the discount factor. If we compare this path of consumption with the temporal evolution of income we observe that the individual redistributes the income obtained in each period throughout his life cycle, having a level of consumption higher than his income in the initial periods, while consumption is lower than your income level in the final periods. In this way, we observe how the agent can separate its consumption decision period to period, with respect to the income obtained in said period in order to maximize its utility.

The fact that the temporary path of consumption has a negative slope is due to the calibration of the model in which the real interest rate is higher than the intertemporal preference rate. Thus, in this exercise, we have assumed that the interest rate is 2% while the intertemporal preference rate, θ, is 0.031, given that $\beta = 1/1 + \theta = 0.97$. This will cause the cost of borrowing to be reduced in relation to the discount of its future profit in utility units, so that the savings will be negative during the first periods of his life cycle. In fact, we observe that the stock of financial assets is always negative during the life cycle of this individual, that is, the agent is always indebted throughout his lifespan. The stock of savings is negative until half of their life (period 15), indicating that the agent is bringing future income to make consumption during these first periods of their life cycle higher than income. After that period, the savings become positive, decreasing the stock of debt, until reaching a zero level in the last period.

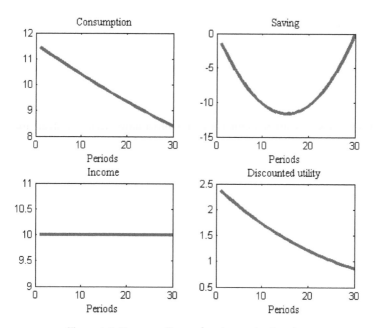

Figure 4.4. Consumption and saving optimal paths.

4.4. Shock analysis: change in income

Next, we will perform a variety of exercises to study how the consumption-savings optimal decision is altered in the face of variations in the exogenous variables. In particular, we will assume different structures for the exogenous labor income. In the first place, we assume that the exogenous labor income is not a constant but varies throughout the life cycle. Secondly, we are going to assume that the individual only obtains labor income during a part of their life (their working life is inferior to their lifespan), so during the final periods of their life cycle (retirement period), the wage income is zero. The idea of these exercises is to show that the optimal consumption decision is not affected by the individual's income structure, under the assumptions we are considering (rational agents, perfect foresight and perfect capital markets).

4.4.1. Increasing exogenous labor income over time

In the previous exercise, we assumed that the household labor income was constant in all periods of lifespan, from period 0 to period 30. However, in reality, labor income increases as work experience increases, at least up to a certain age. Therefore, we repeat the previous exercise but assuming that the labor income is represented by a growing function over time. In particular, we assume that the income of period 0 is 10 and that it increases by one unit in each period, until the end of the lifespan. This exercise is reflected in the spreadsheet named "**ICM-4-2.xls**", which has the same structure as that the previous exercise. The steps to solve this exercise are exactly the same as those described above, by introducing the same information in the "Solver" tool.

Figure 4.5 shows the time paths of the different variables with this new labor income structure. The exogenous income now presents a growing path throughout the life of the individual. This illustrates our assumption that the agent begins earning a low salary, but as they accumulate work experience over time, their salary increases. As we can see, the optimal path of consumption is again negative, similar to that obtained in the previous exercise. This is so because the structure of the income does not affect the decision of consumption of the individual. As indicated above, the consumption decision of the household is based on three elements: the real interest rate, the intertemporal preference rate and the degree of curvature of the utility function. Therefore, the optimal path of consumption is totally independent of the household's income structure, as evidenced by this numerical exercise. The value of consumption period to period is different from the previous problem, but this is because the household's global income is also different. However, its time profile remains the same.

The variable that does change in this case is savings, which accommodates to the new structure of income, such that the path of consumption is optimal. In this case, we observe how the savings of the individual during the first years of their working life are negative, that is, the individual gets into debt by consuming an amount greater than their total income, which is the result of the calibrated values for the discount factor and the real interest rate. However, although the savings decision goes in the same direction in the previous exercise, the levels of indebtedness are now much higher. This is because the individual knows that their income will be higher in the future, so the individual brings a greater amount of income from the future to the present. Obviously, this negative saving has to be compensated later with a positive saving during his last periods of life, reducing his debt position. Therefore, the change in the temporary structure of income has no effect on the intertemporal consumption-savings decision, with consumption and savings patterns similar to those obtained in the initial year, because income does not determine the optimal path of consumption period to period.

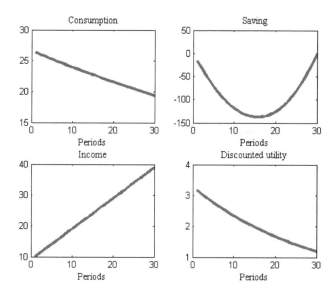

Figure 4.5. Optimal consumption-saving decision with increasing exogenous labor income.

4.4.2. Retirement period

Next, we repeat the exercise but assuming that the income is only generated during a part of the individual's life. Thus, we are going to assume that the first years of the life of the individual correspond to their working life and, therefore, they obtain an income from their work, while in the last periods the individual retires and does not obtain any income. In particular, let's assume that the income is constant and equal to 10 from period 0 to period 20, to go to take a value of 0 from period 21 to 30. This problem appears in the spreadsheet "**ICM-4-3-xls**". For solving this new problem, we proceed as before.

Figure 4.6 shows the paths of the different variables resulting from solving this maximization problem. As we can see, again, we obtain a decreasing optimal path for consumption over time, being very smooth, despite the sudden change that occurs in the individual's income from period 20. The explanation is the same that in the previous exercise: the distribution of income over the lifespan does not affect the consumption decision. However, now we obtain a different pattern in savings, as a consequence of the new structure of income. Thus, so that the consumption path is not affected, all the changes in the structure of the income are transferred to changes in the savings structure.

We obtain that the saving of the individual is positive during the first periods of their life (exactly until period 20), being negative from that moment. This means that the household accumulates assets during their working life, to later use said assets throughout their retirement period to soften their consumption profile.

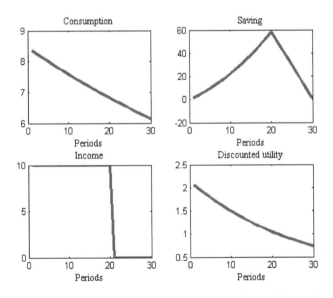

Figure 4.6. Optimal consumption-saving decision with retirement period.

The explanation for this result is simple. The household only gets (labor) income during the first periods of his life cycle (from period 0 to period 20). This means that the household must generate positive savings during this period of their life to have resources to be able to consume in the last periods of their life, once they have retired and do not obtain salary income. As we can see, the evolution of the savings stock of this agent has a pyramid shape, increasing continuously during their working life. Once the household stops working, from that moment, there is a dissaving (decreases the amount of accumulated financial assets), expending the savings that had previously generated.

4.5. Sensitivity analysis: Change in the discount factor

Next, we will analyze the effects of a change in the parameters on the optimal consumption-savings decision. This simple optimization problem has a single parameter: the intertemporal discount factor, while the interest rate and income have been assumed to be exogenous variables. Therefore, we study now how the decision of household changes according to the value of the intertemporal discount rate. So, we assume that this discount factor increases (decreases the intertemporal preference rate), passing the discount factor to take a value of 0.99. This means that the individual becomes less impatient (discount to a lesser extent the future utility). To carry out this exercise, we can use the initial sheet "**ICM-4-1.xls**" again, changing the value of cell "B4", and executing the "Solver" again, as previously specified.

Figure 4.7 shows the new path for optimal consumption and saving. Now, the optimal path of consumption has a positive slope. This means that the individual will prefer to consume less in the first periods and to increase their level of consumption as time passes. This new consumption path is determined by the new discount factor, which implies a greater concern for the future on the part of the agent. That is, the agent discounts little future utility. This variation will cause the intertemporal preference rate to be lower than the real interest rate, which results in an optimal consumption path with a positive slope. In fact, the slope of the optimal path of consumption is determined by the relationship between the interest rate and the intertemporal discount factor (or the subjective intertemporal preference rate). If the interest rate is equal to the intertemporal subjective rate, then consumption would be equal period to period (the optimal path of consumption would be a horizontal line). In fact, this is the steady-state condition for consumption, which causes it to remain constant over time. The explanation is that the returns we obtain by saving one unit of income today and consuming it tomorrow is exactly equal to the valuation of that consumption tomorrow in terms of consumption today.

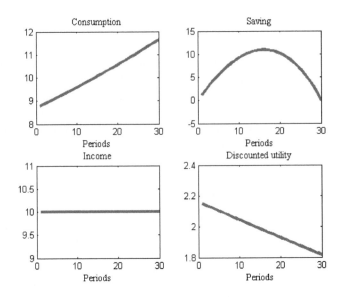

Figure 4.7. Optimal consumption-saving decision with $\beta = 0.99$.

The new optimal path of consumption reflects the fact that we are now analyzing the behavior of a household who discounted the future very little, that is, who cares a lot about it. This has important consequences in terms of the decision to save. Thus, the household will sacrifice current consumption to obtain higher levels of future consumption. As a consequence of this decision, the level of savings will be high during the first periods of the life. The explanation is the following. In this situation, the interest rate is higher than the subjective rate of intertemporal preference (given that the greater the intertemporal discount factor, the lower the subjective preference rate). This means that the returns of saving (in terms of future consumption possibilities) is higher than the discount (in terms of returns) applied to that consumption, so that the individual obtains greater utility having a higher consumption in the future than in the present.

4.6. An alternative utility function

As we have indicated previously, to obtain the numerical solution of a macroeconomic model, we need to use specific functional forms for the different functions that appear in the equations of the model. Thus, to solve the basic problem of the household, we need to specify a particular form for the utility function, which meets certain conditions. This will cause the obtained results to be conditioned by this particular functional form. Next, we repeat the previous exercise but using an alternative utility function. In particular, we will use the utility function of the CRRA type with a constant parameter of relative risk aversion. Our objective, in this case, is to study what are the effects on the consumption decision of risk aversion and how the consumer's decision varies under another functional form for its utility function. The utility function of the individual we assume has the following functional form:

$$U(C_t) = \frac{C_t^{1-\sigma}}{1-\sigma} \qquad (4.25)$$

where σ is the coefficient of relative risk aversion. If $\sigma = 1$, then the CRRA function is transformed into the logarithmic function that we used previously.

In this case, the exercise to be solved is the following:

$$\max_{\{C_t\}_{t=0}^T} \sum_{t=0}^T \beta^t \frac{C_t^{1-\sigma}}{1-\sigma} \qquad (4.26)$$

subject to the budget constraint given by (4.5) and the initial and final conditions (4.6 and 4.7). The function of auxiliary Lagrange would be given by:

$$\mathcal{L} = \sum_{t=0}^T \left[\beta^t \frac{C_t^{1-\sigma}}{1-\sigma} - \lambda_t (C_t + B_t - W_t - (1 + R_{t-1})B_{t-1}) \right] \qquad (4.27)$$

For the previous problem, the first-order conditions for $t = 0,1,2,\dots,T$, are the following:

$$\frac{\partial \mathcal{L}}{\partial C_t} = \beta^t C_t^{-\sigma} - \lambda_t = 0 \qquad (4.28)$$

$$\frac{\partial \mathcal{L}}{\partial B_t} = -\lambda_t + \lambda_{t+1}(1 + R_t) = 0 \qquad (4.29)$$

$$\frac{\partial \mathcal{L}}{\partial \lambda_t} = C_t + B_t - W_t - (1 + R_{t-1})B_{t-1} = 0 \qquad (4.30)$$

By solving for the Lagrange multiplier of the first first-order condition (4.28) and substituting it in the second first-order condition (4.29) for t and $t + 1$, we obtain:

$$\beta^t C_t^{-\sigma} = \beta^{t+1}(1 + R_t)C_{t+1}^{-\sigma} \qquad (4.31)$$

and by operating the following optimal consumption path emerges:

$$C_t^\sigma = \beta(1 + R_t)C_{t+1}^\sigma \qquad (4.32)$$

Solution to the household problem	
CRRA utility function	
Optimal consumption path	$C_t^\sigma = \beta(1 + R_t)C_{t+1}^\sigma$
Financial assets variation	$B_t = (1 + R_{t-1})B_{t-1} + W_t - C_t$

Once the problem is solved analytically, we will solve it computationally. In this case, the problem to be solved contains an additional parameter, which is the relative rate of aversion to risk. We assume that the risk-aversion parameter is high. For example, let's assume that in this case, we are assuming an individual that has a very concave utility function. The value for the rest of the parameters and exogenous variables is the same as those used in exercise 1 in order to compare the results to study how the degree of risk aversion of the individual influences them.

The problem is solved in the spreadsheet "**ICM-4-4.xls**". The value of the new parameter appears in cell "B6". To solve this new problem, we change the expression that appears in column "I". If we place the cursor in cell "I3", we see that the expression appears:

=Beta^E3*(F3^(1-Sigma)-1)/(1-Sigma)

which is the one corresponding to the new utility function. The structure of the rest of the spreadsheet is similar to those shown above, as well as the information to be introduced to the "Solver" tool.

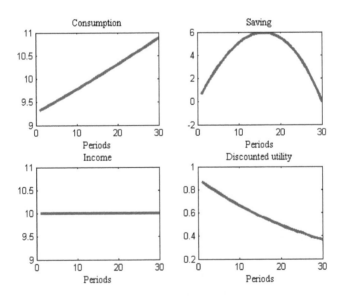

Figure 4.8. Optimal consumption-saving decision with a CRRA utility function.

Figure 4.8 shows the time paths of the relevant variables. As we can see, the optimal path of consumption has a negative slope, but now its time profile becomes more horizontal. This is because, as mentioned above, this slope depends on the difference between the subjective rate of intertemporal preference and the real interest rate. If the intertemporal preference rate is higher than the real interest rate, as is the case, then the slope is negative, this sign being independent of the risk aversion parameter. The effect of introducing the risk aversion parameter is that, the higher its value, the more horizontal the optimal path of consumption. This can easily be checked by changing the value of cell "B6" and recalculating the optimal consumption path.

The greater the aversion to risk, the more curved the utility function is and the more expensive (in terms of utility losses) are the changes in the level of consumption from one period to another. In general terms, if we are very risk-averse we do not want any change to happen period by period and that any variation in the variables (in this case, consumption) over time be as smooth as possible.

Exercises

1. Using the "**ICM-4-1.xls**" spreadsheet, study the effects of an increase in the real interest rate. In particular, suppose that the interest rate increases to 5 percent, $R = 0.05$. How is the slope of the optimal path of consumption now? What happens now with the savings? What are these changes in the optimal decision of the consumer?
2. Suppose that the interest rate is 0 percent, $R = 0.00$. What consequences does it have on the consumption-savings decision?
3. Given the parameters calibrated in the spreadsheet "**ICM-4-1.xls**", what should be the interest rate so that the level of consumption is the same for all periods? How does this value of the interest rate relate to the intertemporal preference rate?
4. Build a spreadsheet in which the individual faces restrictions on liquidity. That is, a situation in which income from the future cannot be brought, that is, cannot be indebted, with which the stock of financial assets must always be positive. Solve this problem and propose different income structures. How the consumption-saving decision is affected in this case?
5. Using the spreadsheet "**ICM-4-2.xls**", suppose that there is an increase in the retirement time in 5 periods. What are the consequences of this increase in the number of periods in which the agent is working during his life cycle?

5. The consumption-saving decision and the consumption-leisure decision

5.1. Introduction

In this chapter, we extend the analysis carried out previously and we will study jointly the consumption-savings decision and the consumption-leisure decision (labor supply). Typically, in micro-founded macroeconomic dynamic general equilibrium models, the utility function of households depends positively on two arguments: consumption and leisure, leisure being understood as the time that is not dedicated to working activities. In this context, the household gets satisfaction from both their consumption and their leisure. However, in order to consume goods and services, the household must first generate income and, therefore, she must renounce part of her leisure time and dedicate that time to production activities (working time). From this utility function, we obtain two fundamental decisions that will determine the behavior of an economy based on the households' behavior. The first is an intertemporal decision between consumption-saving as the one studied in the previous chapter, which allows us to obtain the optimal path of consumption and investment decision. The second is the consumption-leisure intratemporal decision, from which we will determine the optimal labor supply.

The fundamental idea of this utility function is that households have an endowment of available time that they can devote to different activities. The fraction of the discretionary available time that they wish to assign to working activities will give rise to the labor supply. The main characteristic of labor supply is that it is a static decision, given that the available time cannot be accumulated. That is, the decision to work or not (what fraction of the available time we will devote to work) is taken period by period, so it is a decision of a static nature. The time dedicated to work generates a disutility (loss of utility), which will be compensated by the gain of utility derived from the consumption that can be generated by the labor income. In fact, we will see that the labor supply decision corresponds to an equilibrium condition that equals the disutility of working time with the utility obtained by the generated consumption. In other words, it would be equivalent to the monetary valuation of leisure in terms of consumption, using the salary as a measure of the value of time in relation to the value of consumption. This maximization problem constitutes one of the fundamental pillars of macroeconomic dynamic general equilibrium models, from which the main variables of an economy will be determined: consumption, investment, capital stock and employment, given the prices of production factors. To solve this optimization problem numerically, we will use again the Excel "Solver" tool, as we have done in the previous chapter. The only difference is that now we have to calculate not only the optimal path of consumption but also the optimal path of the fraction of time used in working activities.

In practice, many individuals cannot decide their working time (many jobs have a fixed schedule that cannot be changed at the discretion of the worker), so their labor supply would be a dichotomous variable (working a fixed number of hours or does not work). However, at the aggregate level the variability in the number of hours worked is different to the variability of the number of workers throughout the cycle (existence of part-time work, overtime, multi-jobs, changes in the hours of work per day or per week, etc.). This leads to the incorporation of this optimal choice between leisure and working time in the construction of micro-based macroeconomic models.

The structure of the rest of the chapter is as follows. In Section 2, we present the theoretical framework, describing the household maximization problem in which the utility function depends on consumption and leisure time, resulting in the optimal path of consumption, for one side, and the labor supply, on the other. In Section 3, we present the numerical resolution of the model. Section 4 presents the effects of a change in the exogenous variables. Section 5 presents a sensitivity analysis of the model to a change in the value of the parameters. Finally, Section 6 presents the household problem using an alternative parameterization for the utility function.

5.1. The consumption-saving decision and the consumption-leisure decision

In previous chapter we assumed that consumption is the only variable that determines the level of utility of an individual. However, from an economic point of view, there are other elements that also affect the utility of households and on which they make economic decisions, including time devoted to home production, time devoted to skill acquisition activities, public goods, negative externalities as pollution, etc. In this chapter, we assume that the utility depends on two elements: Consumption, C, and Leisure, O, which is a standard definition of the households' utility function in current micro-founded macroeconomic models. Consumption refers to the amount of goods and services consumed by the household, while leisure is defined as the fraction of total discretionary available time the household does not work. Both consumption and leisure positively affect the level of happiness of the household. This means that we are assuming that the preferences are such that what the individual wants is to work as little as possible and consume as much as possible.

The instantaneous utility function of the consumer can be written as:

$$U(C, O) \tag{5.1}$$

The mathematical function $U(\cdot)$ has to fulfill the following conditions:

$$U_C(\cdot) > 0, \quad U_O(\cdot) > 0 \tag{5.2}$$

that is, the first derivative with respect to consumption and leisure is positive. This means that both variables have a positive effect on the level of happiness of the individual. The higher the level of consumption, the higher the level of utility. The higher the level of leisure, the higher the level of utility. On the contrary, the second derivative is negative, such that:

$$U_{CC}(\cdot) < 0, \quad U_{OO}(\cdot) < 0 \tag{5.3}$$

indicating that the utility function is concave. That is, as consumption increases, the level of utility increases, but each time it does so in a smaller proportion (decreasing marginal utility). We also assume that something similar happens with leisure. If we are very busy with working activities, a unit of additional leisure time is valued to a great extent. But if we have a lot of free time, it is evident that a unit of additional leisure time is not going to be valued in the same way. Finally, the utility function must also comply that:

$$U_{CO}(\cdot) > 0 \tag{5.4}$$

that is, the cross-derivative between consumption and leisure is positive, indicating that we can substitute consumption for leisure (and vice versa).

From the previous specifications, the problem of intertemporal maximization of the individual would be given by:

$$\max_{\{C_t, O_t\}_{t=0}^T} E_t \sum_{t=0}^T \beta^t U(C_t, O_t) \tag{5.5}$$

where β is the intertemporal discount factor and E_t is the mathematical expectation, subject to the budget constraint and the restriction of available time. As we have done in the previous chapter, we assume perfect foresight, so we can directly eliminate the mathematical expectation, given that we know today the future flow of the different variables.

In this household maximization problem, we have an additional restriction corresponding to the time allocation. It is usually considered that the discretionary time allocation of an individual is 16 hours a day (8 hours are excluded from the 24 that have each day because they are supposed to be used for sleep), while they are usually considered 6 working days per week. In our case, the total available to make discretionary decisions is normalized to 1. Therefore, this means that leisure can be defined as:

$$O_t = 1 - L_t \tag{5.6}$$

where L_t is the fraction of available time spent working. Therefore, the introduction of leisure in the utility function allows to determine what will be the level of labor income of the individual, obtaining the labor supply given a salary (per unit of time) that we consider exogenous. In this case, the individual not only decides what their level of consumption will be period by period, but also determines how many hours they will dedicate to work. In general terms, the macroeconomic models consider that approximately 1/3 of the available time is dedicated to work ($L_t = 0.33$), so the remaining 2/3 of the available time is dedicated to other activities other than work, which is what here we define as leisure. Although the number of hours worked per year is very different between countries (we have economies such as Germany, where average working time is around 1,300-1,400 hours a year, compared to economies such as the United States, where average working time is around 1,800 hours a year), we can assume that the average working day a week is 40 hours. If we assume a week of 7 days, multiplied by 16 hours, this would give us that the total available time is 112 hours, so by dividing 40 by 112, we would obtain a percentage of working time (the measure of employment that is usually used in the macroeconomic models), of 0.36.

The intertemporal budget constraint is given by:

$$C_t + B_t = W_t L_t + (1 + R_{t-1})B_{t-1} \tag{5.7}$$

where W_t is the salary per unit of time, R_t is the interest rate and B_t is the stock of assets, so we would maximize the sum of discounted utility subject to the budget constraint (5.6) and subject to the time restriction given by (5.6), that we will enter directly into the utility function, along with the initial and final constraints, $B_{-1} = 0$ and $B_T = 0$. As before, consumers maximize the weighted sum of their expected utility subject to the budget constraint. The intertemporal budget constraint will indicate both uses and available resources. In this problem, the resources available from households come from the rental of their endowments production factors (labor), and returns on savings. Thus, we assume that households are the owners of the productive factors of the economy. These productive factors are, on the one hand, working time, from which the amount of labor will be determined. The second productive factor is capital, which is generated through the saving process. Given the price of productive factors, consumers will decide how much productive factors (how much capital and how much work) they will rent to firms. In this problem, we are not considering the existence of a productive sector, so households save in the form of financial assets.

Structure of the household problem	
Utility function	$U = U(C_t, O_t)$
Budget constraint	$C_t + B_t = (1 + R_{t-1})B_{t-1} + W_t L_t$
Initial stock of assets	$B_{-1} = 0$
Final stock of assets	$B_T = 0$
Time restriction	$L_t + O_t = 1$

Given the restriction of available time, replacing the leisure function with the utility function, the problem to be maximized by the consumer can be defined as:

$$\max_{\{C_t, O_t\}_{t=0}^T} E_t \sum_{t=0}^T \beta^t U(C_t, 1 - L_t) \tag{5.8}$$

which is the usual way in which the utility function of the individual is defined when leisure is included[1]. The auxiliary Lagrange function corresponding to our problem would be given by:

$$\mathcal{L} = \sum_{t=0}^T [\beta^t U(C_t, 1 - L_t) - \lambda_t (C_t + B_t - W_t L_t - (1 + R_{t-1})B_{t-1})] \tag{5.9}$$

The first-order conditions of the consumer's problem, for $t = 0, 1, 2, \ldots, T$, are given by:

$$\frac{\partial L}{\partial C_t} = \beta^t U_C(C_t, 1 - L_t) - \lambda_t = 0 \tag{5.10}$$

$$\frac{\partial L}{\partial L_t} = \beta^t U_L(C_t, 1 - L_t) + \lambda_t W_t = 0 \tag{5.11}$$

$$\frac{\partial L}{\partial B_t} = \lambda_{t+1}(1 + R_t) - \lambda_t = 0 \tag{5.12}$$

$$\frac{\partial L}{\partial \lambda_t} = C_t + B_t - W_t L_t - (1 + R_{t-1})B_{t-1} = 0 \tag{5.13}$$

From the first-order condition (5.10) it results that:

$$\lambda_t = \beta^t U_C(C_t, 1 - L_t) \tag{5.14}$$

that is, the Lagrange parameter is the shadow price of the last consumed unit, being equivalent to the marginal utility of the individual as we obtain in the problem without leisure. On the other hand, the first-order condition (5.11) indicates that the Lagrange multiplier can also be defined in terms of the disutility generated by working, such that:

$$\lambda_t = -\frac{\beta^t U_L(C_t, 1 - L_t)}{W_t} \tag{5.15}$$

---

[1] However, we must indicate that both specifications for the utility function are different.

By equating the two previous expressions, we obtain the condition that equals the marginal substitution ratio between consumption and leisure to the opportunity cost of an additional unit of leisure, given by:

$$U_C(C_t, 1 - L_t)W_t = -U_L(C_t, 1 - L_t) \tag{5.16}$$

This equilibrium condition represents the individual's work decision (optimal labor supply). On the other hand, by substituting in the first-order condition (5.12) we obtain that:

$$\beta(1 + R_t)U_C(C_{t+1}, 1 - L_{t+1}) = U_C(C_t, 1 - L_t) \tag{5.17}$$

equilibrium condition that represents the optimal path of consumption, in which the marginal utility of consumption today is equal to the marginal utility of next period consumption weighted by the interest rate and the intertemporal preference rate, a condition that is the same as the one that we would get in the basic problem without leisure.

Solution to the household problem	
Consumption optimal path	$\beta(1 + R_t)U_C(C_{t+1}, 1 - L_{t+1}) = U_C(C_t, 1 - L_t)$
Stock of financial assets	$B_t = (1 + R_{t-1})B_{t-1} + W_t L_t - C_t$
Labor supply	$U_C(C_t, 1 - L_t)W_t = -U_L(C_t, 1 - L_t)$

5.2.1. Example: Logarithmic utility function

Next, we define a specific functional form for the utility function with the aim of obtaining explicit optimality conditions that can be computed numerically. To parameterize the utility function, we assume a logarithmic function in both arguments. In practice, we have a wide variety of utility functions that meet the established conditions, although the simplest and one of the most used in macroeconomic models is the logarithmic function. Specifically, we will use the following specification:

$$U(C_t, 1 - L_t) = \gamma \, lnC_t + (1 - \gamma) \, ln(1 - L_t) \tag{5.18}$$

where $\gamma \in (0,1)$ represents the proportion of consumption over total income, indicating how consumption and leisure weight in the utility of the individual.

This utility function is separable over time, which facilitates the calculations since the utility in each period only depends on the consumption and leisure levels of that period. On the other hand, it is a separable utility function between consumption and leisure. This means that the marginal utility of consumption only depends on consumption and not leisure, while the disutility of work is only a function of working time and not consumption.

In this context, the problem to solve would be:

$$\max_{\{C_t, O_t\}_{t=0}^T} E_t \sum_{t=0}^T \beta^t [\gamma \, lnC_t + (1-\gamma) \, ln(1-L_t)] \tag{5.19}$$

subject to the intertemporal budget constraint:

$$C_t + B_t = W_t L_t + (1 + R_{t-1})B_{t-1} \tag{5.20}$$

together with the initial and final conditions for the stock of assets. To solve this problem, we build the associated Lagrangian auxiliary function given by:

$$\mathcal{L} = \sum_{t=0}^T [\beta^t [\gamma \, lnC_t + (1-\gamma) \, ln(1-L_t)] - \lambda_t (C_t + B_t - W_t L_t - (1 + R_{t-1})B_{t-1})]$$
$$\tag{5.21}$$

The first-order conditions, for $t = 0,1,2,\dots,T$, are given by:

$$\frac{\partial \mathcal{L}}{\partial C_t} = \beta^t \frac{\gamma}{C_t} - \lambda_t = 0 \tag{5.22}$$

$$\frac{\partial \mathcal{L}}{\partial L_t} = -\beta^t \frac{(1-\gamma)}{1-L_t} + \lambda_t W_t = 0 \tag{5.23}$$

$$\frac{\partial \mathcal{L}}{\partial B_t} = -\lambda_t + \lambda_{t+1}(1 + R_t) = 0 \tag{5.24}$$

$$\frac{\partial \mathcal{L}}{\partial \lambda_t} = C_t + B_t - W_t L_t - (1 + R_{t-1})B_{t-1} = 0 \tag{5.25}$$

From the first-order condition (5.22) it turns out that:

$$\lambda_t = \beta^t \gamma C_t^{-1} \tag{5.26}$$

that is, the Lagrange parameter is the discounted value of the shadow price of the last unit consumed, being equivalent to the marginal utility of consumption, as we obtained in the problem without leisure resolved previously. By substituting the value of the Lagrange multiplier in the first-order condition with respect to the stock of financial assets (5.24), we obtain the optimal path of consumption given by:

$$C_{t+1} = \beta(1 + R_t)C_t \tag{5.27}$$

On the other hand, the first-order condition (5.23) indicates that the Lagrange's multiplier must also be equal to:

$$\lambda_t = \frac{\beta^t (1-\gamma)}{(1-L_t)W_t} \tag{5.28}$$

Finally, the condition that equals the marginal substitution ratio between consumption and leisure to the opportunity cost of an additional leisure unit is given by:

$$(1-\gamma)C_t = \gamma(1-L_t)W_t \tag{5.29}$$

which is the equilibrium condition that represents the labor supply. This equilibrium condition determines the labor supply (the proportion of hours available that the individual will dedicate to work) based on the cost of leisure (measured through the salary per unit of time), the weight of leisure with respect to consumption in the utility function and the marginal utility of consumption.

Solution to the household problem	
Logarithmic utility function in consumption and leisure	
Optimal consumption path	$C_{t+1} = \beta(1 + R_t)C_t$
Financial assets variation	$B_t = (1 + R_{t-1})B_{t-1} + W_t L_t - C_t$
Labor supply	$(1 - \gamma)C_t = \gamma(1 - L_t)W_t$

5.3. Numerical solution

To numerically compute the previous problem, we will use the Excel "Solver" tool, similar to what we did in the previous chapter. In this case, we use this tool to calculate the optimal values of both the consumption and the proportion of time that the agent will dedicate to working activities. The file where we have solved this problem is called "**ICM-5-1.xls**" and its structure is shown in Figure 5.1. In Appendix I, we present the code of this optimization problem in MATLAB using the "fsolve" function.

As we can see, in this case, we need to calibrate two parameters: the intertemporal discount rate, β, and the weight to consumption in the utility function, γ. In addition, we have two exogenous variables: the real interest rate and the salary per unit of time. The values we have set are an intertemporal discount factor of 0.97, a value that appears in cell "B4" and a weight for consumption in the utility function of 40%, a value that appears in cell "B5". Additionally, we will assume that the real interest rate is 2%, which corresponds to cell "B8", and a salary per unit of time of 30. Note that these values will cause the optimal consumption path to decrease over time (see Chapter 4), as we will see below. In fact, from the expression (5.27), we obtain that the condition of steady state implies that:

$$\beta(1 + \bar{R}) = 1 \tag{5.30}$$

so that the consumption is constant period to period. This means that in steady state it has to be fulfilled that:

$$\bar{R} = \frac{1}{\beta} - 1 \tag{5.31}$$

If the interest rate is greater than $1/\beta - 1$, then the optimal path of consumption is increasing over time, being decreasing in the opposite case. In our example, the interest rate is 0.02, whereas $1/\beta - 1 = 0.031$ so the resulting optimal path will be decreasing in time.

	A	B	C	D	E	F	G	H	I
1	EXERCISE 5.1: The consumption-leisure decision								
2				Period	Consumption	Labor	Income	Saving	Utility
3	*Parameters*			0	13.92	0.31	9.32	-4.60	0.83
4	Beta	0.97		1	13.76	0.32	9.54	-8.92	0.79
5	Gamma	0.4		2	13.60	0.33	9.75	-12.95	0.76
6				3	13.45	0.33	9.97	-16.69	0.73
7	*Exogenous variables*			4	13.29	0.34	10.18	-20.13	0.70
8	Interest rate	0.02		5	13.14	0.35	10.39	-23.28	0.67
9				6	12.99	0.35	10.60	-26.14	0.64
10				7	12.84	0.36	10.81	-28.70	0.61
11				8	12.70	0.37	11.01	-30.96	0.58
12				9	12.55	0.37	11.21	-32.92	0.56
13				10	12.41	0.38	11.41	-34.58	0.53
14				11	12.27	0.39	11.61	-35.93	0.51
15				12	12.13	0.39	11.80	-36.97	0.48
16				13	11.99	0.40	12.00	-37.71	0.46
17				14	11.85	0.41	12.19	-38.13	0.44
18				15	11.72	0.41	12.38	-38.24	0.42
19				16	11.59	0.42	12.56	-38.03	0.40
20				17	11.46	0.42	12.75	-37.50	0.38
21				18	11.33	0.43	12.93	-36.65	0.37
22				19	11.20	0.44	13.11	-35.47	0.35
23				20	11.07	0.44	13.29	-33.96	0.33
24				21	10.95	0.45	13.47	-32.12	0.32
25				22	10.82	0.45	13.64	-29.94	0.30
26				23	10.70	0.46	13.81	-27.43	0.29
27				24	10.58	0.47	13.99	-24.57	0.27
28				25	10.46	0.47	14.16	-21.36	0.26
29				26	10.34	0.48	14.33	-17.81	0.25
30				27	10.22	0.48	14.49	-13.90	0.23
31				28	10.11	0.49	14.66	-9.63	0.22
32				29	9.99	0.49	14.82	-5.00	0.21
33				30	9.88	0.50	14.98	0.00	0.20
34				Sum					14.09

Figure 5.1. Spreadsheet "ICM-5-1.xls". Consumption-saving and consumption-leisure optimal decisions.

The rest of the information we need appears in columns "D" through "I". Column "D" represents the time, while column "E" will present the consumption values, which together with column "F", that is the labor supply, are the variables that we have to calculate to solve the optimization problem. "G" is labor income, which is obtained by multiplying the salary per unit of time, which is assumed exogenous, by the working time optimal decision, column "H" is the savings obtained as the difference between consumption and income of each period and finally column "I" shows the satisfaction of the individual based on consumption in updated terms. The values that we have to introduce in columns "E" and "F" to solve this problem, are values that we assume are close to the final solution, and constitute the initial values of the maximization algorithm that the "Solver" tool will apply.

Savings are calculated in the following way. Saving in the first period is simply calculated as the difference between the level of consumption and the level of income in that period. Thus, if we place the cursor in cell "H3", we see that the expression appears:

=G3-E3

that is, the wage income (column "G") minus consumption (column "E") in period 0.

On the contrary, if we place ourselves in cell "H4", we see that the expression that appears is:

=(1+R_0)*H3+G4-E4

that is, the gross returns to savings made up to the previous period plus the income of the period less the consumption of the period. The following rows in this column contain this same expression. That is, the gross returns of the savings made up to the previous period plus the new savings of the period.

Finally, column "I" presents the valuation of the discounted utility in each period. If we place the cursor in cell "I3", the expression appears:

=Beta^D3*(Gamma*LN(E3)+(1-Gamma)*LN(F3))

which is the valuation of the utility in period 0, that is, the logarithm of the consumption multiplied by the intertemporal discount factor raised to the time index corresponding to that period. Finally, in cell "I34" appears the sum of the discounted utilities, which is the value that we have to maximize.

To solve the exercise using the Excel Solver tool, we operate as follows. First of all, we fill with fictitious values (a guess solution) the column corresponding to consumption and the one corresponding to labor. For example, we can give a value of 0.35 to labor (this supposes that 35% of the available time is dedicated to working activities), and we suppose that the consumption is equal to the income. As in the previous chapter, to execute this Excel tool, we have to go to "Tools" and select "Solver". The first element that appears in the window is "Objective cell:". This option refers to the value of the objective function of the problem that we want to solve. In our case, it refers to the total utility of the individual throughout their life. Specifically, it would be the discounted sum of the utility obtained by the individual in each period of their life, and would be given in cell "I34".

Then, the instruction "By Changing Variable Cells" appears. Here we have to introduce the cells in which Excel will calculate the objective variables, that is, the level of consumption and the level of working time, period by period. In the cells that we indicate in this section is where the spreadsheet will present the solution to the problem that we want to solve. In our specific case, we will obtain the level of consumption in each period that maximizes the total utility of the household throughout their life, as well as the job offer (the proportion of time dedicated to work) in each period. The expression we would have to enter is "$F3:G33$". Finally, the instruction "Subject to the constraints:" appears. In this section, we must introduce the restrictions to which the problem we want to solve is subject. This constraint is the quantity of assets (savings) of the agent at the end of their life must be zero.

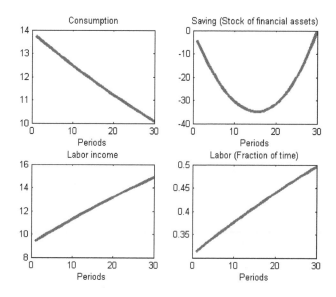

Figure 5.2. The optimal consumption-saving and labor supply decisions.

Figure 5.2 shows the time paths of the different variables. We have assumed that the salary per unit of time is exogenous and that it takes a value of 30 for all the periods. The labor income of the household in each period will be given by multiplying the salary per unit of time, by the time dedicated to work (the labor supply). When solving this maximization problem, we obtain that the optimal path of consumption has a negative slope, indicating that the agent prefers to have a high level of consumption in the first periods of their life cycle and to decrease their consumption over time. As we have indicated previously, the fact that the temporary path of consumption has a negative slope is due to the fact that the real interest rate is higher than the intertemporal rate of preference. Thus, in this exercise, we have assumed that the interest rate is 2% while the intertemporal preference rate, θ, is 0.031, given that $\beta = 1/(1 + \theta) = 0.97$. This will cause the cost of borrowing to be relatively low, while it is not profitable to save (in terms of profits) during the first part of its life cycle. Thus, the individual gets into debt (its consumption is greater than income) during the first part of their life cycle, so that the stock of financial assets is negative during this first stage, while during the second part, the savings are positive to return the borrowed order, undoing their debtor position to end with a zero stock of financial assets, as imposed by the final condition on the maximization problem.

On the other hand, we see that the labor supply is increasing over time. This means that at the beginning of their life cycle, the individual prefers to have high levels of leisure. However, as time progresses, the individual would work more hours reducing their leisure time, so their labor income is also a growing function over time (although we have assumed the salary per unit of time is constant). Again, this result depends on the relationship between the interest rate and the intertemporal discount factor. When the interest rate is very low, the returns of saving is also very low, so there are fewer incentives to work to generate a higher labor income. On the contrary, when the interest rate is high, there are incentives to offer more work to generate higher labor income, since their savings also generate higher returns that compensate for the loss of utility due to the less time spent on leisure. Therefore, the difference between the interest rate and the intertemporal discount factor will also be fundamental to determine the slope of the temporary path of the labor supply throughout the life cycle of the agent.

5.4. Shock analysis: Change in exogenous variables (change in salary)

In the previous section, we have assumed that the exogenous salary per unit of time is constant during his working life, from period 0 to period 30. However, in reality, as we have indicated above, the salary income of workerss increases as working experience increases, at least until a certain age. Therefore, now we repeat the previous exercise but assuming that the salary shows a growing temporal profile, with the objective of studying its implications regarding the labor supply. In particular, we are going to assume that the income for period 0 is 30 and that it increases by one unit in each period. We have built this exercise in the "**ICM-5-2.xls**" spreadsheet, with a structure similar to that of the previous exercise.

To solve this new exercise, we introduce the new values for the salary and then execute the "Solver" tool again, which instantly recalculates the optimal consumption path and the optimal labor supply. Figure 5.3 shows the time paths of the different variables. In this exercise, the wage income per unit of time now presents a growing path throughout the working life of the individual.

This means that the individual begins to work with a low salary, but as they accumulate work experience, their salary increases.

As we can see, the optimal path of consumption is again negative, similar to that obtained in the case of a constant salary. This is so because the structure of the income does not affect the decision of consumption of the individual. The consumption decision of the individual is based on three elements: the real interest rate, the intertemporal preference rate and the degree of curvature of the utility function. Therefore, the optimal path of consumption is totally independent of the individual's income structure, as evidenced by this numerical exercise, since we assume that the capital markets are perfect and that, therefore, individuals can completely separate the profile of the consumption of the temporary profile of their income. To obtain these different paths between consumption and income, the agent makes use of savings. In this case, we observe that the savings of the individual during the first years of their working life is negative, that is, the individual gets into debt by consuming a quantity greater than their income. This is because the individual knows that their income will be higher in the future, so the individual brings income from the future to the present. Obviously, this negative saving has to be compensated later with a positive saving during their working life.

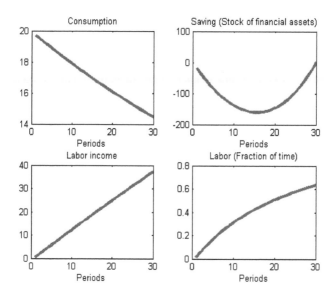

Figure 5.3. Optimal consumption-saving and consumption-leisure with increasing labor income.

The variable that presents the greatest change is the labor supply. As expected, a change in the salary structure will affect the labor supply of the individual period by period. In particular, with this income structure, the agent initially starts offering very little work (practically zero), increasing their labor supply as the salary increases (at very high values). That is, the variability in the labor supply is very high throughout the life cycle. In this case, the labor supply throughout the life cycle of the individual depends on two factors: the difference between the interest rate and the intertemporal discount rate and the temporary path of the salary per unit of time. Thus, even in the case where the interest rate is very high, the individual will prefer to work fewer hours at the beginning of their life cycle and to increase this number of hours because the salary is a growing function of time. This means that the household in taken the optimal labor supply decision is comparing three variables: the present salary versus the future salary, the profitability of savings and the intertemporal discount rate. Thus, the higher the interest rate, the flatter the labor supply would be in this case and only for relatively high-interest rate values, the labor supply would have a decreasing time profile.

5.5. Sensitivity analysis: Change in parameters

Next, we analyze the effects of a change in some of the parameters of the model. In our model, we have two parameters: the intertemporal preference rate of individuals and the relative weight of consumption versus leisure in the utility function. We want to study the effects of an alteration in the temporary discount factor. For this, we can use the initial spreadsheet "**ICM-5-1.xls**". In particular, we are going to suppose that there is a decrease in the intertemporal preference rate, θ, such as the discount factor, β, increases to a value of 0.99. To do this, we simply have to change the value assigned to cell "B4" to this new value and run the "Solver" tool again.

Figure 5.4 shows the time paths of the different solution variables to the model. Again, we assume that the salary per unit of time is exogenous and remains constant for all periods. As a consequence of the increase in the discount factor, we observe that the optimal consumption path now has a positive slope. This means that the household will prefer to consume less in the first periods and to increase their level of consumption as time passes. This new consumption path is determined by the new discount factor, which implies a greater concern for the future on the part of the agent. That is, the agent discounted very little the future utility, indicating that it is more patient. This variation will cause the intertemporal preference rate to be lower than the real interest rate, which results in an optimal consumption path with increasing slope.

The new optimal path of consumption reflects the fact that we are now analyzing the behavior of a household who discounted the future very little, that is, who cares a lot about it. This is going to have important consequences in terms of their savings decision. Thus, the household will sacrifice current consumption to obtain higher levels of future consumption, that is, it shifts income from the first periods to future periods. As a result of this decision, their level of savings will be positive during the first periods of their life cycle, maintaining a creditor position during the same. Thus, the agent accumulates financial assets for approximately half of their life cycle, and later disaccumulates them, until reaching the final condition of an asset stock equal to zero at the end of their life cycle.

With regard to the labor supply, we now obtain that the time that the agent will spend working at the beginning of his life cycle is very high, showing a decreasing trend over time. Therefore, now the labor supply has a negative slope with respect to time. This is because the household discounts the future very little, so it maximizes its level of utility by working hard at the beginning to obtain a high salary income in the first periods. In the future, the household will work less, thus decreasing their labor income. This path of labor supply is related to the optimal path of consumption. Thus, the household maximizes the discounted value of their utility by increasing their future consumption instead of the present, for which she carries out a positive saving plan during their life cycle. This positive saving conditions that the labor supply is maximum at the beginning of the life cycle and will gradually decrease over time.

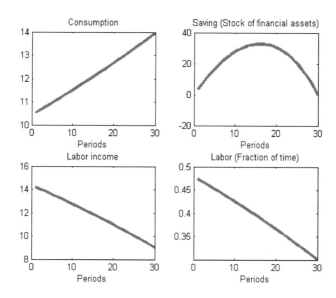

Figure 5.4. Optimal consumption-saving and labor supply decisions with $\beta = 0.99$.

5.6. An alternative utility function

Finally, we will repeat the previous exercise but using an alternative utility function. Specifically, we will use a utility function which is a combination of a CRRA type with a constant parameter of relative risk aversion for the case of consumption and a component that depends negatively on the worked hours in terms of Frisch's elasticity, which is a common way of introducing working time into the utility function. Our objective, in this case, is to study what are the effects on the decision of consumption-saving and consumption-leisure of the risk aversion parameter and variations in Frisch's elasticity. Frisch's elasticity measures the substitution effect of a change in the salary on the number of hours worked.

In this case, the exercise to solve consists in maximizing the following utility function:

$$\max_{\{C_t, L_t\}_{t=0}^T} \sum_{t=0}^T \beta^t \left(\frac{C_t^{1-\sigma}}{1-\sigma} - \gamma \frac{L_t^{1+1/\phi}}{1+1/\phi} \right) \tag{5.32}$$

where the risk aversion parameter is $\sigma > 0$, the parameter $\phi > 0$ represents the so-called Frisch elasticity of the labor supply and where the parameter $\gamma > 0$ denotes the willingness to work. The corresponding Lagrange auxiliary function is:

$$\mathcal{L} = \sum_{t=0}^T \left[\beta^t \left[\frac{C_t^{1-\sigma}}{1-\sigma} - \gamma \frac{L_t^{1+1/\phi}}{1+1/\phi} \right] - \lambda_t (C_t + B_t - W_t L_t - (1+R_{t-1})B_{t-1}) \right] \tag{5.33}$$

By solving the previous problem, we find that first-order conditions, for $t = 0, 1, 2, \dots, T$, are the following:

$$\frac{\partial \mathcal{L}}{\partial C_t} = \beta^t C_t^{-\sigma} - \lambda_t = 0 \tag{5.34}$$

$$\frac{\partial \mathcal{L}}{\partial L_t} = -\beta^t \gamma L_t^{1/\phi} + \lambda_t W_t = 0 \tag{5.35}$$

$$\frac{\partial \mathcal{L}}{\partial B_t} = -\lambda_t + \lambda_{t+1}(1+R_t) = 0 \tag{5.36}$$

$$\frac{\partial \mathcal{L}}{\partial \lambda_t} = C_t + B_t - W_t L_t - (1+R_{t-1})B_{t-1} = 0 \tag{5.37}$$

Solving for the Lagrange multiplier in the first first-order condition (5.34) and substituting it in the third first-order condition (5.36) we obtain:

$$\beta^t C_t^{-\sigma} = \beta^{t+1}(1+R_t)C_{t+1}^{-\sigma} \tag{5.38}$$

and operating the following optimal consumption path:

$$C_{t+1}^\sigma = \beta(1+R_t)C_t^\sigma \tag{5.39}$$

This optimal path of consumption is similar to that obtained previously, with the only difference that now the curvature of the utility function (measured by the parameter) is different. It also turns out to be the alike equation as that derived from a household problem where utility only depends on consumption and its functional form is a CRRA. This is because in this utility function preferences on consumption are separable from leisure. On the other hand, by replacing the Lagrange multiplier in the second first-order condition (5.35), the labor supply is given by:

$$\gamma L_t^{1/\phi} = W_t C_t^{-\sigma} \qquad (5.40)$$

Solution to the consumer problem CRRA utility function and Frisch elasticity	
Optimal consumption path	$C_{t+1}^{\sigma} = \beta(1 + R_t)C_t^{\sigma}$
Financial assets variation	$B_t = (1 + R_{t-1})B_{t-1} + W_t L_t - C_t$
Optimal labor supply	$\gamma L_t^{1/\phi} = W_t C_t^{-\sigma}$

Once the problem is solved analytically, we proceed solve it computationally. In this case, we need to define the value assigned to the four parameters of the model. The higher the aversion to risk parameter, the more concave is the marginal utility derived from consumption. The values that we use to solve this problem are $\beta = 0.97$, $\sigma = 2$, $\gamma = 3$ and $\phi = 0.5$. On the other hand, we assume that the interest rate is 2% ($R_t = 0.02$) and that the salary per unit of time is 30 ($W_t = 30$).

The problem is solved in the spreadsheet "**ICM-5-3.xls**", which has a structure similar to the previous ones. The intertemporal discount factor appears in cell "B4", the risk aversion parameter is reflected in cell "B5", the weighting parameter of the hours worked in cell "B6" and the parameter representing Frisch's elasticity in cell "B7". On the other hand, the interest rate is entered in cell "B10".

The variables appear in cells "D-I". In column "D" we have entered the time index. In columns "E" and "F", we will obtain the solution of the problem for consumption and the number of worked hours. Previously, we have to introduce tentative solution values in these two columns. Column "G" shows the labor income, while column "H" shows the stock of financial assets (savings), in the same way as we have done previously. Finally, in column "I" we enter the utility in discounted terms. Thus, if we place the cursor in cell "I3", we see that this expression appears:

```
=Beta^D3*((E3^(1-Sigma)-1)/(1-Sigma)-
Gamma*((F3^(1+(1/Phi)))/(1+(1/Phi))))
```

which is the one corresponding to the (discounted) new utility function. The sum of the discounted utilities appears in cell "I33". To solve it, we only have to execute the "Solver" tool as before.

Figure 5.5 shows the time paths of the relevant variables. The main result we observe is that the stock of financial assets is relatively small throughout the life cycle of the agent, which is indicating that the level of consumption period to period is not very different from their level of income. Given the parameters of the model, the agent maximizes their level of well-being through a decreasing path of consumption, which leads them to have a debt position during their life cycle, with consumption greater than their income during the first part of their vital cycle, to subsequently have a level of consumption lower than their income. The main result is that now the optimal consumption path is very flat, that is, the variations in consumption from one period to another are very small. The agent continues to separate the temporary profile of consumption from their temporary income profile, but the greater aversion to risk makes changes in consumption from one period to another very smooth, although their consumption profile maintains a negative path in time.

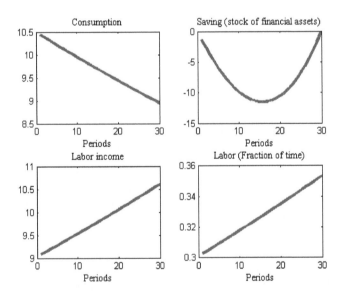

Figure 5.5. Optimal consumption-saving and labor supply decisions with a CRRA utility function.

For the labor supply we also obtain a similar result. The fraction of time devoted to work shows an increasing trend throughout the life cycle, although the variations are not very high. The agent prefers to work less at the beginning of their life cycle and borrow to finance their consumption. As time progresses, the individual increases their job offer to increase their income and finance their debt position without the consumption undergoing important changes over time.

Exercises

1. Using the "**ICM-5-1.xls**" spreadsheet, study the effects of an increase in the real interest rate. In particular, suppose that the interest rate increases to 5 percent, $R = 0.05$. How is the slope of the optimal path of consumption now? What happens with labor supply?
2. Analyze the effects of a change in the parameter γ, using the "**ICM-5-1.xls**" spreadsheet.
3. Suppose that the interest rate is 0 percent, $R = 0.00$. What consequences does it have on the consumption-savings decision and the consumption-leisure decision?
4. Suppose that the utility function of the individual is the following:

    $$U(C_t, L_t) = lnC_t - \gamma \frac{L_t^{1+1/\phi}}{1+1/\phi}$$

    Solve the problem of the consumer by building the spreadsheet corresponding to this problem.
5. Suppose that there is a maximum limit to work for which the fraction of work time cannot be greater than 50% of the available time. Use the spreadsheet "**ICM-5-2.xls**" and evaluate what the effects of this limit are (Hint: for this, you have to introduce an additional restriction in the problem to be solved such that the column corresponding to the employment cannot be higher than 0.5: "$G$3:$G$33<=0.5").

6. The government and the fiscal policy

6.1. Introduction

Apart from households and firms, decisions by other economic agents can also be incorporated into micro-based macroeconomic models. This is the case of the government. However, in the majority of models, the government decisions have no microeconomic foundation. Usually, the government enters in macroeconomic models exogenously, through the different variables representing fiscal policy instruments. In this framework, the government decides a certain level of public expenditure and its structure, which is financed through public revenues obtained through the setting of taxes. Both public spending and tax rates are exogenous variables, so the basic structure of the model is not altered, as no additional endogenous variables are considered. However, public spending and tax rates can be distortionary instruments, as these exogenous variables can alter the optimal decision of economic agents and the resulting macroeconomic equilibrium. This means that even when public expenditure equals fiscal revenues (that is, under the existence of a balanced public budget and, therefore, in a situation in which the government returns via transfers of public goods the same amount to the economic agents that it collects via taxes), the resulting macroeconomic equilibrium will be affected by both public spending and the taxes, since the decisions taken by the different economic agents are conditioned by these exogenous variables. The difference between public revenues and expenditures is financed through the issuance of debt, these being the elements, together with the interest rate of public debt, which define the government's budget constraint.

In the majority of micro-founded macroeconomic models, the role of the government associated with the household's maximization problem is usually introduced, not affecting in most cases the problem of maximizing profits of firms (given that it is usually assumed that there is perfect competition, so its benefits are zero), except in the case a social security system is considered. On the side of public revenues, different types of taxes are introduced, which can be both of a fixed amount (lump-sum taxes), taxes on the generation of income (direct taxes), and taxes on expenditure on final goods and services (indirect taxes). Lump-sum taxes have the characteristic that they are non-distortionary taxes, that is, they do not affect the optimal decision of economic agents. This is so because the burden of the tax cannot be altered in any way as the tax is fixed and independent of what decisions the different economic agents make. On the other hand, both direct and indirect taxes are distorting taxes, affecting the optimal decision of households. The distortion comes from the fact that the government introduces a tax rate on a certain tax base. This tax base can be altered by economic agents, through changes in their decisions that will determine the final amount to be paid for the tax. With regard to public spending, in most cases, it is assumed that they are represented by a lump-sum transfer to households and that, therefore, they have no effect on the decisions of the agent since it is a fixed amount. In this case, this lump-sum transfer would enter as an additional (fixed) income into the household's budget constraint of the individual. However, there are some models that pay greater attention to the different types of public expenditure and different fiscal policies on the expenditure side, including the provision of goods produced by the public sector, public employment and public wages, the consumption of intermediate goods by the government, etc. In this case, public spending would have distorting effects on the decision of the other economic agents in the economy.

In this chapter, we carry out different exercises regarding the household's decisions but taking into account the taxation by the government. Taxes are considered exogenous variables since they constitute economic (fiscal) policy instruments, so the structure of the household's maximization problem (in terms of the endogenous variables to be solved) is not altered. In this context, households take taxes as additional information for taking optimal decisions. First, we solve again the basic household maximization problem with a utility function depending on consumption but introducing a lump-sum tax. For instance, we can introduce a labor income tax on the wage income, which we consider exogenous. Since in this case the tax base is exogenous (it is given) as no labor decisions are taken into account, the tax rate is non-distorting (the amount to be paid is pre-fixed independently on the household's decisions). Secondly, in Section 3, we will analyze the household maximization problem in terms of consumption-savings and consumption-leisure decisions, considering the existence of three tax rates: taxes on consumption, taxes on labor income and taxes on savings returns, which constitute the tax menu usually considered in micro-based macroeconomic models. In this context, the labor income tax is distortionary. Finally, in Section 4, we solve the household maximization problem but considering the existence of social security contributions. The objective of all these exercises is to study the effects caused by changes in fiscal policy via taxes on household' decisions. For the numerical solution of these exercises, we use the "Solver" tool of the Excel spreadsheet, as in the previous chapters.

6.1. Non-distorsionary taxes

First, the basic household's maximization problem is considered but introducing a tax on the wage income, which is supposed to be exogenous.

This means that this is a lump-sum tax and, therefore, does not have distorting effects on household's optimal decisions. This is because the tax base on which the tax applies is given, so the individual cannot alter it to affect the amount of taxes to be paid to the government. In practice, there is a great variety of lump-sum taxes (this is the case of a poll tax or fees), but which quantitatively represent a relatively small fraction of total fiscal revenues. The key characteristic of lump-sum taxation is that it does not alter the optimal decision by economic agents and, therefore, changes in these taxes have no consequences on the economy, and simply imply a change in the government's fiscal revenues (a transfer from household to the government).

Let's assume that the household's utility function is logarithmic and only depends on consumption. Therefore, the problem to be maximized is given by:

$$\max_{\{C_t\}_{t=0}^T} \Sigma_{t=0}^T \beta^t \ln C_t \tag{6.1}$$

where C_t is the consumption and β is the discount factor, subject to the budget constraint:

$$C_t + B_t = (1 - \tau_t^w)W_t + (1 + R_{t-1})B_{t-1} + G_t \tag{6.2}$$

where B_t is the stock of financial assets, τ_t^w is the tax rate on the wage income, W_t is the wage income that we consider exogenous, and R_t is the interest rate of the assets, which we also assume is an exogenous variable. We assume that the government returns to the households all fiscal revenues via lump-sum transfers, where G_t are the transfers or public spending (balanced budget), $G_t = \tau_t^w W_t$. Alternatively, we can assume that the government does not return the fiscal revenues levied and simply destroys the fiscal revenues ($G_t = 0$) gets. In this case, the budget constraint would be simply:

$$C_t + B_t = (1 - \tau_t^w)W_t + (1 + R_{t-1})B_{t-1} \tag{6.3}$$

where the results in this case would be equivalent in terms of the optimal consumption-saving decision of the agent (although the numerical values would be different in each case).

Structure of the model: Non-distortionary taxes	
Utility function	$U = U(C_t)$
Budget constraint	$C_t + B_t = (1 - \tau_t^w)W_t + (1 + R_{t-1})B_{t-1} + G_t$
Initial stock of assets	$B_{t-1=0}$
Final stock of assets	$B_T = 0$
Government budget constraint	$G_t = \tau_t^w W_t$

To solve the previous problem we have to impose an initial condition, which is given by $B_{t-1} = 0$, and a final condition that is given by $B_T = 0$. The Lagrangian auxiliary function associated with this maximization problem is given by:

$$\mathcal{L} = \sum_{t=0}^{T}[\beta^t \ln C_t - \lambda_t(C_t + B_t - (1 - \tau_t^w)W_t - (1 + R_{t-1})B_{t-1}) - G_t] \quad (6.4)$$

The first-order conditions, for $t = 0, 1, 2, \dots, T$, are the following:

$$\frac{\partial \mathcal{L}}{\partial C_t} = \frac{\beta^t}{C_t} - \lambda_t = 0 \quad (6.5)$$

$$\frac{\partial \mathcal{L}}{\partial B_t} = -\lambda_t + \lambda_{t+1}(1 + R_t) = 0 \quad (6.6)$$

$$\frac{\partial \mathcal{L}}{\partial \lambda_t} = C_t + B_t - (1 - \tau_t^w)W_t - (1 + R_{t-1})B_{t-1} - G_t = 0 \quad (6.7)$$

By solving from the first first-order condition (6.5) and substituting it in the second first-order condition (6.6) we obtain:

$$\beta^t \frac{1}{C_t} = \beta^{t+1} \frac{1}{C_{t+1}}(1 + R_t) \quad (6.8)$$

and operating results:

$$C_{t+1} = \beta(1 + R_t)C_t \quad (6.9)$$

resulting in an expression that determines the optimal consumption decision and in which there is no trace of the tax. Thus, we can observe that the optimal consumption path over time (the intertemporal consumption-saving decision) remains the same as we obtained without government, so the tax does not affect this optimal consumption tax. This is because the tax applied on an exogenous variable, and therefore, households do not have any chance of change the amount of payable taxes (the tax base cannot be altered), so this tax is equivalent to a lump-sum tax.

Solution to the problem of the consumer with taxes Non-distorting taxes. Logarithmic utility function	
Optimal consumption path	$C_{t+1} = \beta(1 + R_t)C_t$
Financial assets	$B_t = (1 + R_{t-1})B_{t-1} + (1 - \tau_t^w)W_t + G_t - C_t$

6.2.1. Numerical solution

Next, we proceed to numerically solve the previous maximization problem. For this, we will use the "Solver" tool of Excel, just as we have done in the previous chapters. In fact, the problem we are solving here is identical to that solved in Chapter 4. The only difference is the introduction of an additional exogenous variable; the tax rate. We assume that the government does not return to households what is collected through taxes, that is, $G_t = 0$.

	A	B	C	D	Period	Consumption	Labor income	Taxes	Saving	Utility
1	EXERCISE 6.1: Non-distortionary tax									
2					0	4.82	10.00	4.00	1.18	1.57
3	*Parameters*				1	4.91	10.00	4.00	2.32	1.54
4	Beta	0.97			2	5.01	10.00	4.00	3.43	1.52
5					3	5.09	10.00	4.00	4.51	1.49
6	*Exogenous variables*				4	5.19	10.00	4.00	5.55	1.46
7	Real interest rate	0.05			5	5.28	10.00	4.00	6.54	1.43
8	Labor income tax	0.4			6	5.39	10.00	4.00	7.48	1.40
9					7	5.49	10.00	4.00	8.37	1.38
10					8	5.59	10.00	4.00	9.20	1.35
11					9	5.69	10.00	4.00	9.97	1.32
12					10	5.79	10.00	4.00	10.68	1.30
13					11	5.90	10.00	4.00	11.32	1.27
14					12	6.00	10.00	4.00	11.88	1.24
15					13	6.12	10.00	4.00	12.36	1.22
16					14	6.23	10.00	4.00	12.74	1.19
17					15	6.35	10.00	4.00	13.03	1.17
18					16	6.47	10.00	4.00	13.21	1.15
19					17	6.59	10.00	4.00	13.27	1.12
20					18	6.72	10.00	4.00	13.22	1.10
21					19	6.84	10.00	4.00	13.04	1.08
22					20	6.96	10.00	4.00	12.73	1.06
23					21	7.09	10.00	4.00	12.28	1.03
24					22	7.22	10.00	4.00	11.68	1.01
25					23	7.35	10.00	4.00	10.92	0.99
26					24	7.48	10.00	4.00	9.98	0.97
27					25	7.62	10.00	4.00	8.87	0.95
28					26	7.76	10.00	4.00	7.55	0.93
29					27	7.90	10.00	4.00	6.03	0.91
30					28	8.06	10.00	4.00	4.27	0.89
31					29	8.22	10.00	4.00	2.27	0.87
32					30	8.38	10.00	4.00	0.00	0.85
33					Sum					36.75

Figure 6.1. Structure of the spreadsheet "ICM-6-1.xls". Household maximization problem with no distortionary taxes.

The spreadsheet in which we have solved this problem is **"ICM-6-1.xls"**, whose structure is shown in Figure 6.1, being similar to those used in chapter 4. First, we define the parameters of the model. Since the utility function is logarithmic, only one parameter have to be calibrated: the intertemporal discount rate, β. The value assigned to this parameter is 0.97, and it is reflected in cell "B4". Additionally, the problem comprises three exogenous variables: the interest rate, the wage income and the tax rate. The value for the interest rate is 0.05 that appears in cell "B7", while we have assumed a tax rate of 40% ($\tau_t^w = 0.4$), introduced in cell "B8". Regarding the wage income, we have assumed that it takes a value of 10 in each period. Instead of introducing it as a single value for all periods, we have introduced it as a column with the same value for all periods to facilitate simulations with different structures for wage income.

Columns "D" through "I" show the rest of the information we need to solve this problem. Column "D" is the time index. In column "E", the solution to the problem appears in terms of the optimal level of consumption period to period.

As we have seen before, in order to obtain this solution, first of all, we have to introduce some values (guess solution) as "seed" of the algorithm, values that is advisable not to be very different from the final planned solution. Column "F" shows the wage income, which we consider as given, while column "G" shows the taxes that the individual has to pay, which is obtained by multiplying the income by the tax rate. Then, column "H" calculates the stock of savings (accumulated financial assets plus their profitability). For the first period, savings is the difference between disposable income (total income minus taxes) and consumption. If we place the cursor in cell "H3", the expression that appears is:

=F3-E3-G3

If we place the cursor in cell "H4", the expression that appears is:

=(1+R_0)*H3+F4-E4-G4

This same expression appears in the following cells in this same column. Finally, in column "I", we present the values of the discounted utility. Thus, in cell "I3", we can observe the expression:

=Beta^D3*LN(E3)

The sum of the discounted utilities is calculated in cell "I34", which will be the target cell to be maximized in the "Solver" tool. The solution to the problem is obtained by executing the "Solver", once we have defined the target cell to be maximized (the "I34"), the final condition ("$H$33=0"), and the cells to change with the solution ("$E$3:$E$33"), similar to how it has been carried out in the previous chapters.

6.2.2. Change in the tax rate

Next, we proceed to study a fiscal policy reform consisting in a change in the tax rate to observe to what extent the decision of consumption-optimal savings of the individual is altered by a change in fiscal policy. Figure 6.2 shows the consumption-savings decision before (dashed line) and after the variation in the tax (solid line). To do this, we only have to change the value of cell "B8". Suppose, for example, that there is an increase in the tax rate on exogenous income and it becomes 45%. If we change the value of this cell to 0.45 and execute the "Solver" again, we will observe that the optimal path of consumption (and the one corresponding to saving) remains the same. The result with the new tax is reflected by the solid line in Figure 6.2. Thus, changes in this tax rate have no consequence on the optimal decisions of the consumer, so it does not generate distortions. The optimal path of consumption and savings are shown in Figure 6.2.

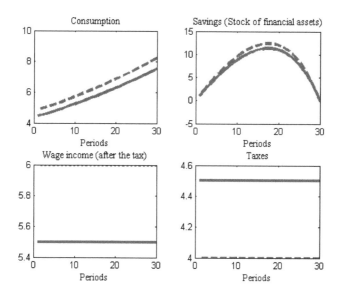

Figure 6.2. Optimal consumption-saving decision with a lump-sum tax. Dash line: Initial solution. Solid line: Solution after increasing the tax rate to 0.45.

In the numerical solution of this exercise, we have assumed that the government does not return the collected amount to the consumer. This means that as the tax rate increases, the disposable income is reduced, so that the consumption and savings levels are lower, the higher the tax. If the government returns the proceeds, as we have stated analytically, then the levels of consumption and savings would be the same for any tax rate, given that the disposable income would always be equal to the total income, regardless of the level of the tax.3

This exercise shows that fiscal policy is ineffective if it does not have distorting effects on the decisions of the rest of the agents that intervene in the economy. This is what is known as the Principle of Ricardian Equivalence (David Ricardo, 1772-1823) or the irrelevance theorem in the way in which an increase is financed (via taxes or via public debt) in public spending. The Principle of Ricardian Equivalence is only fulfilled under the assumptions we are using in this basic consumer problem.

6.3. Distortionary taxes

Next, we consider the existence of distortionary taxes on the consumer problem. In micro-based macroeconomic models, the existence of two types of taxes is usually considered: taxes on expenditures and taxes on income. The tax on spending is an indirect tax, which is applied on consumption. This tax assumes that the agents pay an overprice for each consumed unit. The most important tax within the indirect taxes is the Value-Added Tax (VAT). In general, we will denoted this tax plus other taxes that also apply to the final price of goods and services as excise taxes, as the consumption tax. The second type of tax is a direct rate on the income. Given that households have two sources to generate income, labor and capital, we will distinguish between a tax applied to labor income and another tax rate applied to capital income, or to the returns of financial assets, such as the case of the basic household problem that we are solving.

As we can see, these taxes are going to alter the budget constraint of the individual. Indirect taxes are applied on the part of the expense, while direct taxes are applied on the part of the income. In this case, the household's budget constraint can be written as:

$$(1 + \tau_t^c)C_t + B_t = (1 - \tau_t^w)W_tL_t + [(1 - \tau_t^r)R_{t-1}]B_{t-1} + G_t \qquad (6.10)$$

where B_t is the stock of financial assets, τ_t^c is the tax rate on consumption, τ_t^w is the tax rate on labor income and τ_t^r is the tax rate on capital income (financial assets returns). The budget constraint indicates that the spending on consumption, including the overprice introduced by the consumption tax, together with net investment, cannot exceed the sum of net labor income plus and net capital income. These taxes are distorting, since they will affect the economic decisions of households. This is because the tax base of each tax can be altered by the agent, thus changing the total amount of taxes to be paid to the government. That is, the government is the one that determines the tax rate, but before this exogenous variable, consumers can alter their decisions, thereby changing the tax base, either by altering their labor supply or altering the amount of savings, and affecting the amount to pay to the government. This means that changes in the government's tax policy will lead to changes in consumption-saving decisions and in the quantity of productive factors, capital and labor, so in this case, fiscal policy would be effective, affecting macroeconomic equilibrium, thus, not fulfilling the Ricardian Equivalence Principle.

On the other hand, the government makes an expenditure, G_t ,which is carried out in the form of lump-sum transfers received by the individual and is also assumed to be an exogenous variable. Note that the transfers enter as a constant (a certain amount of money) in the budget constraint of the government, so it will not have any influence on the decisions of it. If public spending is carried out in the form of public goods or salaries for public employees, then, in this case, public spending would also be distortionary. Therefore, we see that the introduction of the government changes the budget constraint of the individual, so four new variables appear, but they are assumed exogenous, so that the structure of the household maximization problem is not affected, but in which the optimal decision that maximizes the utility will be affected by the decisions that the government makes regarding these variables.

Finally, we assume that period by period, the budget constraint of the government is met. Therefore, the transfers that consumers receive are:

$$G_t = \tau_t^c C_t + \tau_t^l W_t L_t + \tau_t^Y R_{t-1} B_{t-1} \tag{6.11}$$

Then, we will proceed to solve the problem of the consumer, assuming that the utility depends on consumption and leisure. The problem to be maximized by the individual would be:

$$\max_{\{C_t L_t\}_{t=0}^T} \sum_{t=0}^T \beta^t \left(\gamma \ln C_t \right) + (1 - \gamma) \ln(1 - L_t) \tag{6.12}$$

Subject to the budget constraint defined above:

$$(1 + \tau_t^c)C_t + B_t = (1 - \tau_t^w)W_t L_t + (1 - \tau_t^r)R_{t-1}B_{t-1} + G_t \tag{6.13}$$

and the initial and final conditions for the stock of financial assets.

Structure of the model: distortionary taxes	
Utility function	$U = U(C_t, O_t)$
Household budget constraint	$(1 + \tau_t^c)C_t + B_t = (1 - \tau_t^w)W_t L_t + (1 - \tau_t^r)R_{t-1}B_{t-1} + G_t$
Initial stock of assets	$B_{t-1} = 0$
Final stock of assets	$B_T = 0$
Government budget constraint	$G_t = \tau_t^c C_t + \tau_t^w W_t L_t + \tau_t^r R_{t-1}B_{t-1}$

The corresponding Lagrange auxiliary function would be:

$$\mathcal{L} = \sum_{t=0}^T \beta^t \left[\gamma \ln C_t + (1 - \gamma) \ln(1 - L_t) \right]$$
$$- \lambda_t [(1 + \tau_t^c)C_t + B_t - (1 - \tau_t^w)W_t L_t - (1 - \tau_t^r)B_{t-1}R_{t-1} - G_t] \tag{6.14}$$

By solving the previous maximization problem, we find that first-order conditions, for $t = 0, 1, 2, \dots, T$, are the following:

$$\frac{\partial \mathcal{L}}{\partial C_t} = \frac{\gamma B^t}{C_t} - \lambda_t(1 + \tau_t^c) = 0 \tag{6.15}$$

$$\frac{\partial \mathcal{L}}{\partial B_t} = -\lambda_t + \lambda_{t+1}(1 - \tau_t^r)R_t = 0 \tag{6.16}$$

$$\frac{\partial \mathcal{L}}{\partial L_t} = -\frac{\beta^t(1-\gamma)}{1-L_t} + \lambda_t(1 - \tau_t^r)W_t = 0 \tag{6.17}$$

$$\frac{\partial \mathcal{L}}{\partial \lambda_t} = (1 + \tau_t^c)C_t + B_t - (1 - \tau_t^w)W_t L_t - (1 - \tau_t^r)R_{t-1}B_{t-1} = 0 \tag{6.18}$$

By solving the first first-order condition (6.15) and substituting it in the second first-order condition (6.16) we obtain:

$$\beta^t \frac{1}{(1+\tau_t^c)C_t} = \beta^{t+1} \frac{(1-\tau_t^r)R_t}{(1+\tau_{t+1}^c)C_{t+1}} \tag{6.19}$$

and by operating results that:

$$(1 + \tau_{t+1}^c)C_{t+1} = \beta[(1 - \tau_t^r)R_t(1 + \tau_t^c)C_t] \tag{6.20}$$

As we can see, the optimal consumption path depends both on the tax on the income generated by the financial assets and on the variations in the consumption tax. Thus, if the tax on consumption remains constant period to period (that is $\tau_{t+1}^c = \tau_t^c$), then the optimal consumption path would be:

$$C_{t+1} = \beta[(1 - \tau_t^r)R_t C_t] \tag{6.21}$$

so, in this case, it would only be influenced by the income tax on financial assets. This means that once the government sets a certain tax rate on consumption, if it does not change over time, it does not influence the optimal consumption decision. On the other hand, if the consumption tax is altered at any moment of time, there will be a readjustment in the optimal path of consumption. Thus, if the government increases the tax on labor income in the period $t + 1$ with respect to the existing in t, this will mean a lower marginal utility of consumption tomorrow compared to today, so the individual will readjust their level of consumption, increasing their consumption today and decreasing their consumption tomorrow. Note that a change in τ_t^r is equivalent to a variation in the return on financial assets (a change in the interest rate).

On the other hand, labor supply is obtained by substituting the first-order condition (6.15) in (6.17), obtaining:

$$\frac{1-\gamma}{\gamma}(1 + \tau_t^c)C_t = (1 - \tau_t^w)W_t(1 - L_t) \tag{6.22}$$

As we can see, the labor supply is negatively affected by both the consumption tax and the tax rate on the income generated by this factor. Thus, the higher the tax rate on labor income, the lower the net wage income received by the household and, therefore, the lower the labor supply. This result is consequence of the fact that the tax reduces the net salary, which in turn implies a lower utility in terms of consumption for each unit of time dedicated to working activities. The tax on wages (an increase in it) causes that the disutility of the last unit of time that we dedicate to work is less than the utility that we would obtain if this unit of time is dedicated to leisure, so that the individual reduces his labor supply. On the other hand, the labor supply also depends on the consumption tax. Consuming is now more expensive because you have to pay an overprice, which reduces the profitability of working (in terms of utility) with respect to the profitability of leisure, thus decreasing labor supply.

Solution to the problem of the consumer with taxes Logarithmic utility function	
Optimal consumption path	$(1 + \tau^c_{t+1})C_{t+1} = \beta[(1 - \tau^r_t)R_t](1 + \tau^c_t)C_t$
Financial assets	$B_t = (1 - \tau^r_t)R_{t-1}B_{t-1} + (1 - \tau^w_t)W_t$ $+ G_t - (1 + \tau^c_t)C_t$
Optimal labor supply	$(1 - \gamma)(1 + \tau^c_t)C_t = \gamma(1 - \tau^w_t)W_t(1 - L_t)$

Although these three tax types are distorting, in the exercise that we are solving, both the salary per unit of time and the interest rate are exogenous variables and, therefore, are not affected by the decisions of the individuals. In a dynamic general equilibrium macroeconomic model, these variables (the price of productive factors) are determined endogenously, so they are also altered by the decisions of economic agents in response to the taxes. On the contrary, in the model that we are solving, both the salary and the interest rate are exogenous variables and, therefore, constant to changes in taxes.

6.3.1. Numerical solution

Next, we proceed to the numerical solution of this problem. Figure 6.3 shows the structure of the spreadsheet "**ICM-6-2.xls**", similar to the previous one, but extended to consider the labor supply decisions and the three distortionary tax rates. For the resolution of this household maximization problem, we use again the tool "Solver" of Excel. The parameters that we need to define are the discount rate and the weight of consumption in the utility function. We assume that the discount rate is 0.97, and that the weight of consumption is 0.4. On the other hand, we have to define the exogenous variables that correspond to the price of the productive factors, the salary and the interest rate, and the three tax rates. Interest rate is fixed to 5% and the wage per unit of time to 100. For the tax rates, we assume that the consumption tax is 15%, the tax on labor income is of 35% and the capital income tax of 25%. Appendix J shows the corresponding problem solved in MATLAB, using the "fsolve" function.

Period	Consumption	Labor	Labor income	Total taxes	Consumption tax	Labor income tax	Capital income tax	Saving	Utility
0	20.27	0.45	44.63	18.73	3.04	15.62	0.07	5.70	0.85
1	20.51	0.44	44.29	18.72	3.08	15.50	0.14	11.12	0.83
2	20.75	0.44	43.91	18.68	3.11	15.37	0.20	16.22	0.81
3	20.98	0.44	43.61	18.67	3.15	15.26	0.26	21.04	0.80
4	21.21	0.43	43.21	18.62	3.18	15.12	0.32	25.52	0.78
5	21.44	0.43	42.82	18.58	3.22	14.99	0.37	29.65	0.76
6	21.67	0.42	42.49	18.54	3.25	14.87	0.42	33.46	0.75
7	21.89	0.42	42.14	18.49	3.28	14.75	0.46	36.94	0.73
8	22.10	0.42	41.77	18.44	3.31	14.62	0.50	40.06	0.72
9	22.31	0.41	41.38	18.36	3.35	14.48	0.54	42.81	0.70
10	22.51	0.41	40.99	18.29	3.38	14.35	0.56	45.17	0.69
11	22.70	0.41	40.61	18.21	3.41	14.21	0.59	47.15	0.67
12	22.89	0.40	40.24	18.13	3.43	14.08	0.61	48.75	0.65
13	23.07	0.40	39.88	18.04	3.46	13.96	0.62	49.97	0.64
14	23.25	0.40	39.51	17.95	3.49	13.83	0.63	50.79	0.62
15	23.41	0.39	39.12	17.85	3.51	13.69	0.64	51.19	0.61
16	23.57	0.39	38.73	17.73	3.54	13.55	0.64	51.18	0.60
17	23.73	0.38	38.32	17.60	3.56	13.41	0.63	50.72	0.58
18	23.88	0.38	37.91	17.47	3.58	13.27	0.62	49.80	0.57
19	24.02	0.38	37.51	17.34	3.60	13.13	0.61	48.43	0.55
20	24.15	0.37	37.11	17.19	3.62	12.99	0.58	46.60	0.54
21	24.28	0.37	36.73	17.05	3.64	12.85	0.55	44.30	0.53
22	24.40	0.36	36.35	16.90	3.66	12.72	0.52	41.52	0.52
23	24.52	0.36	35.96	16.74	3.68	12.58	0.48	38.25	0.50
24	24.63	0.36	35.55	16.57	3.69	12.44	0.43	34.48	0.49
25	24.73	0.35	35.13	16.38	3.71	12.29	0.38	30.16	0.48
26	24.83	0.35	34.69	16.18	3.72	12.14	0.32	25.29	0.47
27	24.92	0.34	34.25	15.97	3.74	11.99	0.25	19.84	0.45
28	25.01	0.34	33.83	15.76	3.75	11.84	0.17	13.81	0.44
29	25.09	0.33	33.43	15.55	3.76	11.70	0.09	7.20	0.43
30	25.17	0.33	33.05	15.34	3.78	11.57	0.00	0.06	0.42
Sum									19.19

Parameter block (columns A–C):

EXERCISE 6.2: Distortionary taxation

Parameters	
Beta	0.97
Gamma	0.40

Exogenous variables	
Real interest rate	0.05
Consumption tax rate	0.15
Labor income tax rate	0.35
Capital income tax rate	0.25
Salary	100

Figure 6.3. Structure of the spreadsheet "ICM-6-2.xls". Household maximization problem with distortionary taxes.

In column "E" we calculate the level of consumption period by period, while in column "F" we calculate the level of employment, which are the variables for which we are solving the problem. Initially, we would introduce in these two columns tentative values of the final solution, to start the execution of "Solver". Column "G" shows the gross labor income simply obtained by multiplying the salary per unit of time that is exogenous by the time spent working. In this particular example, we have assumed that the salary per unit of time is 100 and that it remains constant for all periods of the individual's life cycle. Column "H" shows the total tax collection from the three considered taxes, being the sum of the columns "I", "J" and "K". The "L" column shows savings (the stock of financial assets). This level of savings is calculated as follows. In the first period (period 0), it is simply the difference between the net income from taxes and the consumption that the individual makes. In the second and subsequent periods, it would be the difference between the net income of taxes and consumption in the period plus the savings of the previous period plus the profitability associated with said savings. The expression that appears in cell "L3" is:

=(1-Tauw)*G3-(1+Tauc)*E3

this is the net labor income of the period minus consumption, taxes included. On the other hand, the expression that appears in cell "L4" is:

=(1+Rbar*(1-Tauk))*L3+(1-Tauw)*G4-(1+Tauc)*E4

expression that we copy in the following rows of this column. Finally, column "M" shows the level of the household discounted utility in each period of their life.

The sum of the discounted utilities is calculated in cell "M34", which will be the target cell to be maximized in the "Solver" tool. The solution to the problem is obtained by executing the "Solver", once we have defined the target cell to be maximized (the "M34"), the final condition ("$L$33=0"), and the cells to change with the solution ("$E$3:$F$33"), similar to how it has been carried out in the previous chapters.

Figure 6.4 shows the time paths of the relevant variables. First, the consumption path is increasing, so the individual decides to increase consumption as time progresses. The slope of this consumption path depends on the discount rate and the real interest rate, together with the form of the agent's utility function, which in this case is logarithmic. The income is assumed to be exogenous, the individual having a level of income (before taxes) of 10 in period 0 and increasing that income by one unit until period 26, when the individual retires and their income goes to zero. The income tax has the same form since we have assumed that it is proportional to the income. Finally, the savings of the agent will have the standard form. In this case, the individual will save during the first periods of their life until the moment of retirement, after which the savings are negative, consuming the individual the financial assets that they have accumulated throughout their working life.

6.3.2. Change in the tax rate saving returns

Suppose now that the government increases the tax on capital income, from 25% to 30%. We assume that the government does not return fiscal revenues, so this tax increase implies a decrease in the disposable income of the individual. The result of maximizing household's discounted utility before (dash line) and after the tax change (solid line) is shown in Figure 6.4. As we have indicated, this tax is equivalent to a variation in the returns of financial assets, which will alter the household consumption-savings decision. Thus, we can observe how the volume of savings decreases as a result of the increase in this tax, although it remains positive during the first part of the life cycle. This change in the path of savings is due to the fact that the optimal path of consumption is now more horizontal. Given the discount factor and the change in the net returns of savings, the agent prefers to smooth their consumption level to a greater extent throughout their life cycle. This means that the level of consumption in the first periods is higher than before the fiscal policy change, while the level of consumption is lower than in the last periods of the life cycle.

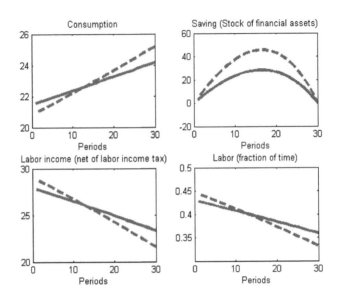

Figure 6.4. Optimal consumption-saving and labor supply decisions with distortionary taxes. Effects of an increase in the capital income tax (solid line).

Labor supply is also affected by the change in this tax. As we have derived analytically previously, labor supply is affected by both the tax rate on consumption and the tax rate on labor income. However, in the context of the theoretical model that we are analyzing, in a partial equilibrium setup, both the gross returns of saving and gross wages are exogenous variables, which are not altered by the decisions of the agent. This means that changes in these two tax rates only cause changes in the consumption-savings decision, without altering the labor supply. However, in this exercise, we observed that the job offer is indeed affected by the change in income tax on financial assets. Thus, the labor supply, which has a negative slope over time, becomes more horizontal as a result of the increase in the capital income tax. This means that the agent would work less time in the first periods of their life cycle, but more time in the final periods, in order to make their salary income profile more stable over time.

6.4. Social security

In this section, we solve again the household maximization problem, but considering the existence of a social security system, which assumes that the individual will receive a pension once he retires and stops working. Thus, we will assume that the individual only works during a fraction of their life cycle, with the last periods being in a retirement situation. As during this last part of their life cycle they do not obtain wage income, the income obtained will come from a social security system, which implies the existence of a compulsory payment during the employee's working life to a pension fund or directly to the government, from which will be generated rights on a future pension. For this, we consider the existence of a tax on the salary income in the form of social security contributions. This supposes the existence of a compulsory saving, which it is determined by the government.

In practice, there are two different social security systems: the pay-as-you-go system and the capitalization system. In the pay-as-you-go social security system, there is an intergenerational income transfer, between the agents who are working and those who are retired at each moment of time. That is to say, at a given moment the workers are paying the pensions of those who are retired, with the promise that when they are retired their pension will be paid by the agents who will be working at that moment. This is the social security system that most countries have implemented. This means that the sustainability of the system depends on the population dynamics and the level of employment that exists in the future.

On the contrary, the capitalization system assumes that it is the individual himself who pays his own pension when he is retired. In this case, the government imposes an obligation to deposit a certain amount in a pension fund in each period. This pension fund will generate a return. When the individual retires, he obtains as a pension the contributed amounts plus the returns on that compulsory saving. At first glance, it would be equivalent to a private pension fund, with the important difference that in the case of a private pension fund the contributions are voluntary, whereas in the social security system of capitalization the contributions are obligatory. In this exercise, we are going to assume that the social security regime is capitalization. This means that the amount collected through social security contributions goes to a pension fund, which generates a return given by the real interest rate.

To study the implications of a social security system, it would be more appropriate to use a model of overlapping generations. In this type of models, it is assumed that agents live for two periods, in the first they are young and they work and in the second they are old and they are retired. In each moment of time, there are two generations: young and old, young people today being the old people of tomorrow. However, this analysis can also be done with the standard structure that we are using of an agent with a finite life cycle.

Again, we are going to consider that the problem of the consumer is to maximize the following utility function (with no leisure):

$$\max_{\{C_t\}_{t=0}^T} \sum_{t=0}^T \beta^t \ln C_t \qquad (6.23)$$

subject to the following budget constraint of the individual:

$$C_t + B_t = (1 - \tau_t^{ss})W_t + (1 + R_{t-1})B_{t-1} + D_t \qquad (6.24)$$

where τ_t^{ss} is the tax rate of social security contributions and where D_t is the retirement pension received by the individual. This pension would only be positive when the individual's salary was zero, that is, when the individual has left work and is retired. In practice, the agent would face two different budgetary restrictions throughout his life cycle, depending on whether he is working or retired. Thus, if we assume that the retirement time is t^*, for $t = 0$ up to $t^* - 1$, the budget constraint would be:

$$C_t + B_t = (1 - \tau_t^{ss})W_t + (1 + R_{t-1})B_{t-1} + D_t \qquad (6.25)$$

while for the period $t = t^*$ up to T, the budget constraint would be:

$$C_t + B_t = R_{t-1}B_{t-1} + D_t \qquad (6.26)$$

given that $L_t = 0$ from $t = t^*$.

Structure of the model: Social Security	
Utility function	$U = U(C_t)$
Budget constraint	$C_t + B_t = (1 - \tau_t^{ss})W_t + [1 + R_{t-1}]B_{t-1} + D_t$
Initial stock of assets	$B_{t-1} = 0$
Final stock of assets	$B_T = 0$
Initial pension fund	$D_{t-1} = 0$
Social Security	$D_t = [1 + R_{t-1}]D_{t-1} + \tau_t^{ss}W_t$

The problem to solve would be given by the following auxiliary function of Lagrange:

$$\mathcal{L} = \sum_{t=0}^{T}[\beta^t \ln C_t - \lambda_t(C_t + B_t - (1 - \tau_t^{ss})W_t - (1 + R_{t-1})B_{t-1} - D_t)] \quad (6.27)$$

taking into account the initial and final conditions. The retirement pension is an exogenous variable that is decided by the government.

By solving the previous problem, we find that the conditions of first order, for $t = 0, 1, 2, ..., T$, are the following:

$$\frac{\partial \mathcal{L}}{\partial C_t} = \frac{\beta^t}{C_t} - \lambda_t = 0 \qquad (6.28)$$

$$\frac{\partial \mathcal{L}}{\partial B_t} = -\lambda_t + \lambda_{t+1}(1 + R_{t+1}) = 0 \qquad (6.29)$$

$$\frac{\partial \mathcal{L}}{\partial \lambda_t} = C_t + B_t - (1 - \tau_t^{ss})W_t - (1 + R_{t-1})B_{t-1} - D_t = 0 \qquad (6.30)$$

By solving from the first-order condition (6.28) and substituting it in the second first-order condition (6.29) we obtain:

$$\beta^t \frac{1}{C_t} = \beta^{t+1} \frac{1}{C_{t+1}} (1 + R_{t+1}) \tag{6.31}$$

and by operating it results that:

$$C_{t+1} = \beta(1 + R_{t+1})C_t \tag{6.32}$$

As we can see, the optimal path of consumption of the individual is totally independent of both the social security contribution tax and the amount of the pension once he is retired. The explanation is simple. In a context of perfect foresight, where the agent knows all the future variables, the social security contributions are perfect substitutes for private savings. This means that if the government changes social security contributions, agents react by altering their private saving decision, in order to maintain their consumption at their optimum level. However, if leisure is considered in the utility function, changes in the social security contributions would be distortionary, as the social security tax will affect the optimal labor supply decision.

Solution to the problem of the consumer with social security Logarithmic utility function	
Optimal consumption path	$C_{t+1} = \beta(1 + R_t)C_t$
Financial assets	$B_t = (1 + R_{t-1})B_{t-1} + (1 - \tau_t^{ss})W_t + D_t - C_t$

6.4.1. Numerical solution

Next, we proceed to the numerical resolution of the previous exercise. Figure 6.5 shows the spreadsheet "**ICM-6-3.xls**", in which we have solved the previous problem. For this, as previously, we have to give values to the parameters and exogenous variables of the model. The model has only one parameter: the discount rate. Additionally, the model has four exogenous variables: real interest rate, wage income, type of social security contributions and retirement pension.

Let's assume that $\beta = 0.97$ appears in cell "B4". The interest rate is fixed to be 5% ($R = 0.05$) and the tax rate for social security is 36% ($\tau_t^{ss} = 0.36$), which are in cells "B7" and "B8", respectively. On the other hand, we have to decide how the individual receives his pension. Once the individual retires, they have access to the pension fund. We can make two assumptions. That the individual charges in full the amount of the pension fund at the moment of retirement, or that the pension fund is distributed in some way throughout the remaining life of the individual. In our case, we are going to choose the first option. Thus, we observe that when the agent retires, with the used data, the pension fund has a total of 246.3 consumption units.

EXERCISE 6.3: Social Security system

Parameters
Beta: 0.97

Exogenous variables
Real interest rate: 0.05
Social Security Contributions (SSCs) tax rate: 0.36

Time	Consumption	Wage	Pension	SSCs	Pension Fund	Saving	Total Saving	Utility
0	12.06	10.00	0.00	3.60	3.60	-5.66	-2.06	1.08
1	12.29	11.00	0.00	3.96	7.74	-11.19	-3.45	1.06
2	12.49	12.00	0.00	4.32	12.45	-16.56	-4.11	1.03
3	12.75	13.00	0.00	4.68	17.75	-21.81	-4.07	1.01
4	12.99	14.00	0.00	5.04	23.68	-26.93	-3.26	0.99
5	13.22	15.00	0.00	5.40	30.26	-31.90	-1.64	0.96
6	13.45	16.00	0.00	5.76	37.53	-36.70	0.83	0.94
7	13.69	17.00	0.00	6.12	45.53	-41.35	4.18	0.92
8	13.95	18.00	0.00	6.48	54.29	-45.85	8.44	0.90
9	14.22	19.00	0.00	6.84	63.84	-50.20	13.65	0.88
10	14.49	20.00	0.00	7.20	74.23	-54.40	19.84	0.86
11	14.76	21.00	0.00	7.56	85.50	-58.44	27.07	0.84
12	15.04	22.00	0.00	7.92	97.70	-62.32	35.38	0.82
13	15.31	23.00	0.00	8.28	110.87	-66.03	44.83	0.80
14	15.59	24.00	0.00	8.64	125.05	-69.56	55.49	0.78
15	15.87	25.00	0.00	9.00	140.30	-72.91	67.39	0.76
16	16.15	26.00	0.00	9.36	156.68	-76.06	80.61	0.74
17	16.44	27.00	0.00	9.72	174.23	-79.03	95.20	0.72
18	16.75	28.00	0.00	10.08	193.02	-81.81	111.21	0.71
19	17.06	29.00	0.00	10.44	213.11	-84.40	128.71	0.69
20	17.38	30.00	0.00	10.80	234.57	-86.80	147.77	0.67
21	17.71	0.00	246.30	0.00	0.00	137.44	137.44	0.66
22	18.05	0.00	0.00	0.00	0.00	126.26	126.26	0.64
23	18.40	0.00	0.00	0.00	0.00	114.17	114.17	0.63
24	18.75	0.00	0.00	0.00	0.00	101.13	101.13	0.61
25	19.10	0.00	0.00	0.00	0.00	87.08	87.08	0.60
26	19.46	0.00	0.00	0.00	0.00	71.98	71.98	0.58
27	19.81	0.00	0.00	0.00	0.00	55.78	55.78	0.57
28	20.15	0.00	0.00	0.00	0.00	38.41	38.41	0.56
29	20.49	0.00	0.00	0.00	0.00	19.84	19.84	0.54
30	20.83	0.00	0.00	0.00	0.00	0.00	0.00	0.53
Sum								24.06

Figure 6.5. Structure of the spreadsheet "ICM-6-3.xls". Social Security system.

Figure 6.6 shows the time path of the relevant variables (dash line). In the first place, we observe that the consumption path continues to have a positive slope. This is so, because as we have seen previously, the optimal path of consumption of the individual is not affected either by social security contributions or by the way in which pensions are received. This means that a social security system of capitalization has no effect on the individual's decisions regarding consumption period by period. This is due to the fact that social security contributions imply the existence of forced saving, which is a perfect substitute for voluntary savings. Therefore, changes in the social security system only cause changes in the voluntary savings of the individual, without affecting their level of consumption. The optimal path of savings is now different as a result of the social security scheme. As we can see, the savings now are negative, and of a very high amount, during the working life of the agent. This is because the individual is replacing voluntary savings with the mandatory savings derived from social security contributions. Given the optimal path of consumption that the individual wants to follow, social security contributions represent a very large volume of savings, which will compensate through changes in voluntary savings. At the time of retirement, there is a balance in the stock of financial assets, because we are assuming that the individual receives all the pension once and only devotes a small fraction of it to consumption in that period. As of this moment, the stock of financial assets is decreasing (the agent is consuming the pension received, until in the final period, the stock of financial assets is zero.) The pension fund shows the contributions that the individual makes period by period during their working time, together with the profitability that is generated. This fund is increased until the moment in which the retirement takes place. From that moment, and given the assumption that we have made, the pension fund is null. In summary, in this social security system, we see that the compulsory savings of the system are a perfect substitute for the private savings, indicating that given a certain level of mandatory savings, the individual will adjust their private savings so that the path of consumption is the one that maximizes their welfare.

6.4.2. Change in social security contributions

Suppose now that the government increases the social security contributions. For example, let's assume that quotes increase up to 40%. What implications does this change have on the agent's decisions? The results are shown in Figure 6.6, by the continuous line. As we can see, the optimal path of consumption of the individual remains the same, since it is not affected by this tax in terms of social security contributions. However, now the level of savings (voluntary) is different, adjusting to the new level of mandatory savings. Thus, while the pension fund increases with respect to the previous situation, voluntary savings decrease, so that given the new disposable income, the social security contributions' net, the level of consumption will be the same. What we are observing in this exercise is a perfect substitution between voluntary savings and forced savings derived from a social security system. Given the assumption that the return on both financial assets is the same, both types of savings are perfectly substitutes.

Different would be the case of a pay-as-you-go social security system, where contributions to social security go directly to pay the pensions of those who are retired, and the future pension of an agent who is in his working life depends on the contributions to the system made by future workers. In this type of system, the future pension will depend on the population dynamics and the evolution of labor productivity, so that voluntary savings would not be a substitute for social security contributions.

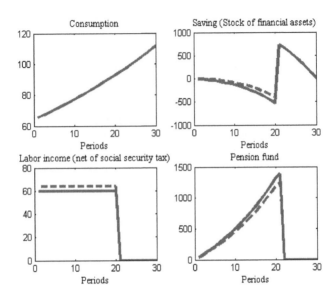

Figure 6.6. Optimal consumption-saving decision with social security system. Effects of an increase in social security contributions (solid line).

Exercises

1. Using the "**ICM-6-2.xls**" spreadsheet, study the effects of an increase in the consumption tax to 20%. How the optimal household decisions are affected by this tax change?

2. Analyze the effects of a change in the parameter γ, using the "**ICM-6-2.xls**" spreadsheet. How the different fiscal revenues change? How is the sensitivity of the optimal decisions by the households to the tax rates depending on the value of this parameter.

3. Suppose that the interest rate changes to a 3 percent, $R = 0.03$. What consequences does it have on the distortionary effects of taxation on the consumption-savings decision and the consumption-leisure decision?

4. Using the "**ICM-6-2.xls**" spreadsheet, study the effects of a decline in the labor income tax.

5. Using the "**ICM-6-3.xls**" spreadsheet, study how changes in the discount factor affects the incidence of the social security system on the household consumption-saving optimal decision.

6. Introduce the optimal labor supply decision into the household's utility function and study how are the distortionary effects on labor supply by the social security system.

7. The firm and the investment decision: The Tobin's Q model

7.1. Introduction

Another fundamental economic agent that is included in dynamic general equilibrium models is the firm. Firms, together with households, make up the two main economic agents which determine the behavior of an economy through in micro-based macroeconomic models. The firms represent the productive sector of the economy, that is, they are the economic agents that produce the final goods that are consumed or invested, by taking decisions about the demand of productive factors. To produce the final good, firms use a certain number of productive factors, given a technology function, which allows their transformation into final production. We consider the existence of two types of productive factors: physical capital and labor. Physical capital arises as a consequence of consumers savings decisions. In its simplest and traditional version, this saving is supposed to be equal to investment, which is transformed directly into physical capital, and in general it is assumed that the owner of the capital stock is the household, who rent production factors to the firms. On the other hand, the labor factor is derived from the time endowment of households. Households have an initial discretionary time endowment that can be used either for leisure activities or for working activities. Labor is just the time that households rent to firms. In the standard framework, firms rent productive factors to the households, which we assume are the owners of them, receiving a return. This makes the decision problem of firms very simple, since it is the households who make the decisions of labor supply and investment. This is the treatment that is given to firms in the majority of micro-based dynamic macroeconomic models, in which the existence of perfect competition is assumed. If the existence of imperfect competition (monopolistic competition) is introduced, the problem of the companies is more complex since they have some market power to influence the price of the produced goods.

In studying optimal decisions by the firms, we assume that their objective function is profits maximization, subject to the technological restriction that is defined by the production function. Thus, the behavior of firms will be represented by an optimization problem in which a vector of quantities (demand) of productive factors is determined, given their prices and, through the technological function, determines the level of production of the economy. The key variable we analyze in this chapter is the investment decision. Along with consumption, investment is the other fundamental variable of an economic system. As we have seen in the study of households decisions, they determine the level of optimal savings in each period, savings that we assume are transformed directly into investment and physical capital. Investment is important since it determines both the level of employment and the possibilities of growth of the economy. In the classical analysis, firms do not own the capital whose accumulation process is determined by savings, which is the instrument that consumers use to determine their optimal consumption path. In this sense, saving is simply production not consumed, so that investment decisions are derived directly from savings decisions. This is the assumption generally adopted by most micro-based models. However, this means that we cannot adequately define an investment function for physical capital, or define what are its determinants independently of the optimal saving decision in the form of financial assets.

In this chapter, we analyze the investment from the point of view of the firms. Thus, we assume that firms own their physical capital and, therefore, are the ones that make investment decisions using consumer savings as a source of financing. In this case, we would distinguish between consumers, on the one hand, and entrepreneurs, on the other, the latter being the owners of the firms and, therefore, the owner of the physical capital, representing the economic agent that makes the investment decisions. By using this alternative specification, we can separate the saving decision from the investment decision and thus, obtain the investment demand in a dynamic environment, since the investment decision today, will affect the future flow of profits of the firms, in a way equivalent to how consumers determine their level of savings today and their future level of consumption.

In the standard neoclassical model, the optimal capital stock is determined as a function of the relative prices of the productive factors. However, we expand this basic analysis considering the existence of adjustment costs associated with the investment process. Based on this analysis, we will develop the Tobin's Q model, which will constitute the framework of reference that we will use to describe investment decisions in an economy. In Tobin's Q model, the optimal investment rate depends on a ratio, called Q, defined as the ratio of the market value of the company to the replacement cost of installed capital. The resulting model will consist of a discrete-time system composed of two difference equations, which determine the behavior of that ratio and the stock of capital. However, these equations have a non-linear nature, so analyzing the behavior of the system directly is more complex because it cannot be written in matrix notation. In this case, we proceed in the first place to obtain a linear approximation to the non-linear equations of the same, rewriting the model in terms of the deviations of each variable with respect to its steady-state value, which will allow analyzing its behavior through the eigenvalues associated with the system and obtain the corresponding stable saddle path.

The structure of the rest of the chapter is as follows. In Section 2, we solve analytically Tobin's Q model, describing the intertemporal problem of profit maximization of the firms, the definition of the profit function to be used, as well as the description of the adjustment costs associated with the investment process. Section 3 performs the calibration of the model, as well as the calculation of its steady state. Section 4 carries out the log-linearization of the model, a necessary step to proceed with its numerical resolution. Section 5 presents the numerical resolution of the model, as well as the calculation of the readjustment in the expectations on the ratio Q. Section 6 carries out a disturbance analysis, while in Section 7 a sensitivity analysis is carried out.

7.2. Tobin's Q model

In this section, we will study the reference model that is used to analyze the determinants of investment. This is the so-called Tobin-Q model, developed by James Tobin (1918-2002) in the late 1960s[1], being a widely used model to analyze the behavior of firms in relation to investment and practical applications to fix the equilibrium value of the shares of a company, the value of a firm when it is acquired by another, or to fix the exchange rate of shares between companies in the case of a merger. This model is based on defining a ratio, which is called the Tobin's Q, which is constructed as the market value of the company with respect to the replacement cost of installed capital. That is, compare what the firm is valued with respect to what it would cost to install again all the capital available to the firm, which is equivalent to comparing the profitability of an investment with the cost of it. In this context, the investment will be a function of the value of this ratio and, in this way, any factor that affects this ratio will also affect the investment decision.

In the analysis that we will perform, we assume that firms' objective function is profits maximization, subject to the technological restriction. Thus, we will represent the behavior of the companies through an optimization problem in which a vector of quantities of productive factors (demand for them) is determined, given their prices, and through the technological function, the

---

[1] Tobin, J. (1969). A general equilibrium approach to monetary theory. *Journal of Money, Credit and Banking*, 1(1): 15-29.

determination of the level of production. In the neoclassical model, the optimal capital stock is determined based on the relative prices of the productive factors. However, we are going to expand this basic analysis considering the existence of adjustment costs associated with the investment process. Based on this analysis, we will develop the Tobin's Q model, which will constitute the frame of reference that we will use to describe investment decisions in an economy, as a dynamic system with two equations: one that describes the dynamics of the ratio Q, and another that describes the dynamics of the capital stock. As we have done in the case of the consumer, we are going to assume that all the companies are identical (the technological restriction they face is the same, this presents constant returns to scale and we assume the existence of a competitive environment), so we can use the concept of representative firm.

A differentiating element of the analysis that we are going to carry out with respect to those carried out previously regarding consumer decisions is that we now introduce the concept of physical capital (structures and equipment), K, in contrast to the financial capital generated by savings and given by the stock of financial assets, B. Although both variables, in equilibrium, would be equivalent in a model of a closed economy without government, the nature of both variables is very different, given that the stock of financial assets is a totally flexible variable, while the stock of physical capital is a very rigid variable (structures and equipment need time to be built).

7.2.1. The technology function

We begin with the definition of the technological restriction to which the process of profit maximization of the firm is subject. The aggregate production function is given by the expression:

$$Y_t = F(K_t, L_t) \tag{7.1}$$

where Y_t is output, K_t is the stock of physical capital, L_t is the level of employment and $F(\cdot)$ is a mathematical function that converts productive factors into production and that represents the technology that is applied in the productive process. This technological function fulfills the following properties:

$$F_K > 0; \ F_L > 0$$
$$F_{KK} < 0; \ F_{LL} < 0$$
$$F_{KL} > 0$$

that is, the function is increasing with respect to both productive factors. If we increase the amount of the productive factors, labor or physical capital, production increases. On the other hand, the second derivative with respect to each of the productive factors is negative, indicating that the production function is concave with respect to each productive factor, which implies that the marginal productivity is decreasing. As we increase the quantity of a productive factor, production increases but each time it does so in a smaller proportion. In addition, the production function has to be concave in K and L, so it has to be fulfilled that:

$$F_{KK}F_{LL} - (F_{KL})^2 > 0$$

On the other hand, the production function meets the Inada conditions:

$$\lim_{k \to 0} F_K = \infty; \ \lim_{K \to \infty} F_K = 0$$

$$\lim_{L \to 0} F_L = \infty; \ \lim_{L \to \infty} F_L = 0$$

that imply that if the quantity of a productive factor tends to zero, its marginal productivity tends to infinity, whereas if the quantity of productive factors tends to infinity, its productivity tends to zero. We also assume that both productive factors are needed to produce, that is, $F(0, L_t)F(K_t, 0) = 0$.

7.2.2. Firm's profits

The objective of the firm is to maximize profits for which the firm determines the demand for productive factors. Profits are defined as the difference between the total income and the total costs of the firm:

$$\Pi_t = IT_t - CT_t \tag{7.2}$$

where Π_t are profits, IT are the total revenues and CT are the total costs. Total revenues are given by the produced quantity multiplied by the price:

$$IT_t = P_t Y_t \tag{7.3}$$

On the other hand, the total costs are given by the costs of the productive factors labor and capital, calculated as the compensation to each unit of productive factor multiplied by the quantity of the factor:

$$CT_t = W_t L_t + R_t K_t \tag{7.4}$$

here W_t is the salary per unit of work and R_t is the interest rate of the physical capital stock. By normalizing the price of the final good to 1 ($P_t = 1$), the profit function can be defined as:

$$\Pi_t = Y_t - W_t L_t - R_t K_t \tag{7.5}$$

This standard definition of the firm's profits is what we would use under the assumption that the owners of both productive factors are the consumers. This is always true in the case of labor. The labor factor is derived from the endowment of time, and therefore labor supply is a decision taken by households. On the contrary, the physical capital factor can be assumed to be determined by the household, or can be assumed to be owned by the firms (or by another economic agent that can be named as capitalist). In the case where the consumers are the owners of both productive factors, the problem of maximizing profits of the companies is very simple. In this context, companies rent both factors, period by period, so the problem of profit maximization can be solved in static terms (there is no intertemporal decision on the part of the firm). Thus, the problem of profit maximization would consist in maximizing (7.5) subject to technological restriction (7.1), a problem that we can specify as:

$$\max_{K_t, L_t} \Pi_t = F(K_t, L_t) - W_t L_t - R_t K_t \tag{7.6}$$

being the first-order conditions:

$$\frac{\partial \Pi_t}{\partial K_t} = F_K(K_t, L_t) - R_t = 0 \tag{7.7}$$

$$\frac{\partial \Pi_t}{\partial L_t} = F_L(K_t, L_t) - W_t = 0 \tag{7.8}$$

from which are obtained the standard conditions that the prices of the productive factors are equal to the (value) of their marginal productivity:

$$R_t = F_K(K_t, L_t) \tag{7.9}$$

$$W_t = F_L(K_t, L_t) \tag{7.10}$$

However, in the context of Tobin's Q model, we are going to introduce a difference with respect to the previous analysis, since we will assume that the firms invest in physical capital instead of renting it period by period. This means that the physical capital is owned by the firm and hence is the firm the agent who decides how physical capital changes, that is, the investment decision. In this way, what the firm really decides is its gross investment volume period by period, which we define as:

$$I_t = K_{t+1} - (1 - \delta)K_t \tag{7.11}$$

that is, gross investment, I_t, is equal to the variation of the stock of capital plus what depreciates capital, where $\delta > 0$ is the rate of physical depreciation of capital.

In this case, we are introducing a distinction between consumers and entrepreneurs. Entrepreneurs are the owners of firms in the economy and, therefore, the owners of physical capital stock. In this way, the investment decision will be different from the saving decision. Given that the stock of physical capital is the result of investment decisions, the decision regarding this productive factor depends on the quantity of investment that entrepreneurs decide to make in each period. In this case, we obtain that the cost in each moment of time of the physical capital productive factor for the firm is the cost associated with the gross investment that is made. Under this assumption, firm's profits can be defined as:

$$\Pi_t = Y_t - W_t L_t - I_t \tag{7.12}$$

where now the production costs associated with capital are those that are derived from the investment made by the firm in each period, since the existing stock of physical capital at that time is already owned by the firm and does not have to be paid every period. Therefore, the assumption about who owns the capital gives rise to different definitions of the firm's profits function, as well as resulting in a dynamic optimization problem, since investment decisions today affect the future profits stream.

7.2.3. Investment adjustment costs

One of the problems presented by the neoclassical model is that it is assumed that there is no restriction to the stock of physical capital to change instantaneously to a disturbance. In fact, the standard neoclassical model implies that any deviation of the physical capital stock from its optimal value gives rise to an equivalent investment flow, so that any deviation of the physical capital stock from its optimum value is covered instantaneously. However, the stock of physical capital of firms is a variable that presents a high rigidity in time (it takes a while to be built), which causes that its adjustment is not so fast and much less instantaneous. One way to introduce rigidities in the process of capital accumulation is to consider the existence of adjustment costs associated with the investment. In practice, firms face the existence of a series of adjustment costs when altering their physical capital stock. In this section, we will introduce the existence of adjustment costs in the investment process. These adjustment costs are higher, the faster the company intends to adjust its physical capital stock.

The introduction of adjustment costs in the investment process has important consequences on the solution of the model, since it allows us to separate the optimality conditions for the stock of capital and for the investment. In a context without adjustment costs in the investment process, as in the neoclassical model, both conditions coincide, since the variation in the stock of capital is equivalent to the investment (net of depreciation). However, the adjustment costs introduce a distinction between the optimal condition of the capital stock and that corresponding to the investment. This differentiation will be fundamental when introducing the ratio defined by Tobin in the profit maximization problem of the firm.

We can distinguish between two types of adjustment costs: internal and external. External adjustment costs arise when firms face a perfectly elastic supply of capital, which causes the price of capital to depend on the speed at which it is desired to dispose of it. The more quickly you want to have an additional unit of capital, the higher the price will be. On the other hand, internal adjustment costs are measured in terms of production or profit losses. When new capital is incorporated, it is necessary to allocate part of the productive resources of the firm (mainly labor) to its installation. In this way, these factors are not temporarily available to produce, so there is a decrease in the level of production, with the consequent loss of profits. In reality, these adjustment costs can be very high, especially in the case of large companies.

We define the following adjustment cost function:

$$C = C(I_t, K_t) \tag{7.13}$$

where the adjustment costs depend on the volume of investment and the installed physical capital stock. This cost function fulfills a series of characteristics, such that:

$$C(0, K_t) = 0, C(I_t, 0) = 0$$
$$C_I(I_t, K_t) > 0, C_K(I_t, K_t) > 0$$
$$C_{II}(I_t, K_t) > 0, C_{KK}(I_t, K_t) > 0$$

that is, adjustment costs depend positively on both the investment and the capital stock (its first derivative with respect to these variables is positive), being zero in the case where no investment occurs, or is reversed for the first time (stock of starting capital equal to zero). On the other hand, its second derivative with respect to each argument is also positive, indicating that they grow more than proportionally, that is, it is a growing and convex function.

The existence of adjustment costs means a loss of capital or an additional cost to the price thereof, which occurs during the investment process. Thus, for every euro that is destined for investment, an amount less than a euro will be transformed into physical capital, due to the existence of these adjustment costs. That is, part of the resources destined for investment are lost in the process of transformation to physical capital. There are different ways to incorporate the existence of adjustment costs in the model. For instance, we can include these costs in the capital accumulation equation or as an additional cost in the profit function. Both forms give equivalent results. If we choose the first option, we must specify the amount of physical capital that obtain the firm per unit invested, which would also be a function of the arguments that define the function of adjustment costs, and would be given by:

$$\Psi(I_t, K_t) = I_t - C(I_t, K_t) \tag{7.14}$$

where the net investment function of adjustment costs, $\Psi(\cdot)$, depends on both the volume of investment and the stock of physical capital. In this case, the dynamic equation of accumulation of capital stock can be defined as:

$$K_{t+1} = (1 - \delta)K_t + I_t - C(I_t, K_t) = (1 - \delta)K_t + \Psi(I_t, K_t) \qquad (7.15)$$

Alternatively, we can assume that the adjustment costs are additional costs to the value of the investment and that they involve a cost in terms of production losses and, therefore, of benefits. In this case, the function of capital accumulation would be the standard, while the profit function of the firm would be:

$$\Pi_t = Y_t - W_t L_t - I_t - C(I_t, K_t) \qquad (7.16)$$

In the analysis that we develop next, we will use this last specification, obtaining the same results as if we had opted for the introduction of adjustment costs in the equation of capital accumulation. The key issue in considering adjustment costs in the investing process is that it allows the investment decision to be separated from the capital stock decision. This separation will cause that, depending on how the adjustment costs are, the investment in a period is not equal to the difference between the stock of capital and its optimum level (the one that maximizes profits). On the contrary, the presence of adjustment costs will cause that, in the event of a difference between the stock of capital of the firm and its optimum level, it will not be covered instantaneously, but rather the investment process will be delayed in the time, with the aim of balancing the adjustment costs with the profits derived from the investment.

Structure of Tobin's Q model	
Profits	$\Pi_t = Y_t - W_t L_t - I_t - C(I_t, K_t)$
Production function	$Y_t = F(K_t, L_t)$
Capital accumulation process	$K_{t+1} = (1 - \delta)K_t + I_t$
Adjustment costs	$C = C(I_t, K_t)$
Initial capital stock	$K_0 > 0$
Q ratio	$Q_t = V_t / K_t$

7.2.4. Intertemporal profit maximization

Next, we solve analytically the intertemporal profit maximization problem that firms face. If we assume that time is a discrete variable, and that the life cycle of the firm is finite (from $t = 0$ up to T),[2] the problem of maximizing intertemporal benefits would be given by:

$$\max E_t \sum_{t=0}^{T} \frac{1}{(1+R_t)^t} \Pi_t \tag{7.17}$$

subject to the technological restriction and to the restriction given by the equation of capital accumulation:

$$Y_t = F(K_t, L_t) \tag{7.18}$$

$$K_{t+1} = (1 - \delta)K_t + I_t \tag{7.19}$$

being the discount factor the real interest rate, R_t, E_t is the mathematical expectation operator, being $K_0 > 0$, and known. In addition, it is also going to fulfill that:

$$\lim_{T \to \infty} K_T = \bar{K} \tag{7.20}$$

where $\bar{K}$ is the steady-state capital stock. We use this condition as equivalent to the transversality condition to guarantee the stability of the system.[3]

That is, the company would maximize the sum of the expected future benefits stream, using as a discount factor the real interest rate, as the benefits are a monetary flow. As we assume the existence of perfect foresight and rational expectations, we can directly eliminate mathematical expectation, since this implies that we know the future value of the exogenous variables. Thus, taking into account the definition of profits, the problem to maximize can be written as:

$$\max \sum_{t=0}^{T} \frac{1}{(1+R_t)^t} [Y_t - W_t L_t - I_t - C(I_t, K_t)] \tag{7.21}$$

subject to the above restrictions. By substituting the technological constraint in the objective function we obtain the following auxiliary function of Lagrange:

$$V = \sum_{t=0}^{T} \frac{1}{(1+R_t)^t} [F(K_t, L_t) - W_t L_t - I_t - C(I_t, K_t)] - \lambda_t (K_{t+1} - I_t - (1 - \delta)K_t) \tag{7.22}$$

---

[2] In micro-based macroeconomic models, it is usual to consider that the life cycle of the different economic agents (consumers, firms, the government, etc.) is infinite.

[3] So that the model does not present an explosive behavior, it is necessary to fulfill an additional condition, which is given by the so-called condition of transversality, which in general terms can be defined as:

$$\lim_{T \to \infty} \frac{1}{(1 + R_t)^T} \lambda_T K_{T+1} = 0$$

The first-order conditions to the previous problem are the following:[4]

$$\frac{\partial V}{\partial K_{t+1}} = \frac{1}{(1+R_{t+1})^{t+1}}[F_K(K_{t+1},L_{t+1}) - C_K(I_{t+1},K_{t+1})] + \lambda_{t+1}(1-\delta) - \lambda_t = 0 \tag{7.23}$$

$$\frac{\partial V}{\partial I_t} = -\frac{1+C_I(K_t,I_t)}{(1+R_t)^t} + \lambda_t = 0 \tag{7.24}$$

$$\frac{\partial V}{\partial L_t} = \frac{F_L(K_t,L_t)-W_t}{(1+R_t)^t} = 0 \tag{7.25}$$

$$\frac{\partial V}{\partial \lambda_t} = -K_{t+1} + I_t + (1-\delta)K_t = 0 \tag{7.26}$$

From the first-order condition (7.24) we obtain the value of the Lagrange multiplier for the period t:

$$\lambda_t = \frac{1+C_I(I_t,K_t)}{(1+R_t)^t} \tag{7.27}$$

and for the period $t+1$:

$$\lambda_{t+1} = \frac{1+C_I(I_{t+1},K_{t+1})}{(1+R_{t+1})^{t+1}} \tag{7.28}$$

Given that the interest rate (the discount factor) is an exogenous variable, we assume that its value remains constant period to period, such that $R_{t+1} = R_t$. By substituting in the first-order condition (7.23), the Lagrange multiplier for period t and $t+1$, it turns out that:

$$F_K(K_{t+1},L_{t+1}) - C_K(I_{t+1},K_{t+1}) = (1+R_t)[1+C_I(I_{t+1},K_{t+1}]$$
$$-[1+C_I(I_{t+1}K_{t+1}](1-\delta) \tag{7.29}$$

an expression that equals the value of the marginal product of capital with the cost of using it, and that reflects the investment decision of the company.

Finally, directly from the first-order condition (7.25) we obtain the condition that equals the marginal productivity of labor with the salary:

$$F_L(K_t,L_t) = W_t \tag{7.30}$$

---

[4] Note that when obtaining the first-order conditions of this maximization problem we derive with respect to investment, employment and the Lagrange multiplier, at the moment t, while the derivative with respect to the stock of capital is performed at the moment $t+1$. This is because at the moment $t=0$, the stock of capital is known, so we would determine its value in the next period (the stock of capital is what is known as a predetermined variable, or state variable, because its value today was already decided in the previous period). In this way, the value of K_0 is given. Thus, the first-order conditions are calculated from $t=0$ up to T for the investment, employment and Lagrange multiplier variables, while the first-order condition for the capital stock would be calculated from $t=1$ to $T+1$.

7.2.5. The marginal q

Next, we define Tobin's Q ratio. This ratio would be calculated as the market value of the company with respect to the replacement cost of installed capital. In our case, we define this ratio in marginal terms, denoted as q.[5] That is, the q ratio would be the variation in the market value of the firms with respect to the variation in the replacement cost of capital, that is, the cost of investing an additional unit. Under certain assumptions, the q ratio is equal to the average of the Q ratio. The q ratio is defined as:

$$q_t = \lambda_t (1 + R_t)^t \qquad (7.31)$$

Therefore, we define the shadow price of capital as:

$$\lambda_t = \frac{q_t}{(1+R_t)^t} \qquad (7.32)$$

By using the definition of the Lagrange parameter obtained above, it turns out that,

$$q_t = 1 + C_I(I_t, K_t) \qquad (7.33)$$

By substituting this expression in the equilibrium condition for the stock of capital (7.29) we obtain:

$$F_K(K_{t+1}, L_{t+1}) - C_K(I_{t+1}, K_{t+1}) = (1 + R_t)q_t - q_{t+1}(1 - \delta) \qquad (7.34)$$

From the previous expression, we obtain the following equation that indicates the dynamics of the marginal q:

$$q_{t+1} = \frac{(1+R_t)q_t - F_K(K_{t+1}, L_{t+1}) + C_K(I_{t+1}, K_{t+1})}{1-\delta} \qquad (7.35)$$

The previous expression tells us that now the marginal productivity of capital is equal to an expression in which appears the cost of capital use but also the function of net investment of adjustment costs. Thus, if there were no adjustment costs then $C_K(I_{t+1}, K_{t+1}) = 0$, so the equilibrium condition would be:

$$q_{t+1} = \frac{(1+R_t)q_t - F_K(K_{t+1}, L_{t+1})}{1-\delta} \qquad (7.36)$$

With adjustment costs, the cost of capital use is higher depending on how the adjustment costs are based on the capital stock. The greater the $C_K(I_t, K_t)$, the greater the marginal productivity of capital has to be, that is, the smaller the capital stock. This means that although the stock of capital of a firm in a period is less than optimal, the firm does not make an investment in that

---

[5] Hayashi, F. (1982). Tobin's marginal q and average q: A neoclassical interpretation. Econometrica, 50(1): 213-224.

period to fully cover the difference, since the adjustment cost can be very important, carrying out its investments gradually over time.

Therefore, Tobin's Q model can be summarized in a system of two dynamic equations, one for the stock of capital and another for the q ratio, given by:

$$q_t = 1 + C_I(I_t, K_t) \tag{7.37}$$

$$(1 - \delta)q_{t+1} + F_K(K_{t+1}, L_{t+1}) = (1 + R_t)q_t + C_K(I_{t+1}, K_{t+1}) \tag{7.38}$$

plus the static condition that determines the level of employment. If we assume that employment remains fixed, we can solve Tobin's Q model in terms of the capital stock and the q ratio. The stock of capital is a state variable, which is predetermined by the decisions made in the previous period, while the q ratio is a full flexible forward-looking variable, which is subject to changes in expectations, and which adjusts instantaneously to disturbances.

7.3. Functional forms and calibration of the model

To solve the previous model numerically, we need to define specific functional forms, both for the technology and for the adjustment costs. First, let's normalize the employment level to 1 ($L_t = 1$). In this way, the production function would be given by:

$$Y_t = F(K_t) = K_t^\alpha \tag{7.39}$$

where the level of employment we assume is fixed and where $0 < \alpha < 1$. This is because the decision regarding labor supply are taken by the households and not by the firm. Hence, we consider a technological function as a function of the stock of capital and where α is the elasticity of the level of output with respect to the physical capital stock.

Next, we have to specify a functional form for the adjustment costs. In practice, adjustment costs can have a wide variety of functional forms. One of the most commonly used functional forms for adjustment costs, and which is also what we are going to adopt here, is the following:

$$C(I_t, K_t) = \frac{\phi}{2} \left(\frac{I_t - \delta K_t}{K_t} \right)^2 K_t \tag{7.40}$$

representing a function of quadratic adjustment costs that depends both on the investment and the stock of capital, and where $\phi > 0$ is a parameter that would indicate how sensitive the investment is with respect to the value of the q ratio. In this specific case we would have:

$$C_I(I_t, K_t) = \phi \left(\frac{I_t - \delta K_t}{K_t} \right) \tag{7.41}$$

$$C_K(I_t, K_t) = \frac{\phi}{2} \left(\frac{I_t - \delta K_t}{K_t} \right)^2 - \phi \left(\frac{I_t - \delta K_t}{K_t} \right) \frac{I_t}{K_t} \tag{7.42}$$

In the analysis to be done next, we use the adjustment cost function given by (7.40). By using this functional form and its derivatives with respect to investment and capital stock, as well as the production function defined above, and by introducing them into the model equations (7.37 and 7.38), it results that:

$$q_t = 1 + \phi \left(\frac{I_t - \delta K_t}{K_t} \right) \tag{7.43}$$

$$(1 - \delta)q_{t+1} = (1 + R_t)q_t - \alpha K_{t+1}^{\alpha-1} + \frac{\phi}{2} \left(\frac{I_{t+1} - \delta K_{t+1}}{K_{t+1}} \right)^2 \phi \left(\frac{I_{t+1} - \delta K_{t+1}}{K_{t+1}} \right) \frac{I_{t+1}}{K_t + 1} \tag{7.44}$$

From these expressions, we will obtain the two difference equations that determine this model. From the equation of capital accumulation, it turns out that:

$$I_t - \delta K_t = K_{t+1} - K_t \tag{7.45}$$

By defining $\Delta K_t = K_{t+1} - K_t$, and substituting in the expression (7.43), we obtain directly the capital accumulation equation:

$$q_t - 1 = \phi \frac{\Delta K_t}{K_t} \tag{7.46}$$

and by solving for the capital stock change, it results that:

$$\Delta K_t = (q_t - 1) \frac{K_t}{\phi} \tag{7.47}$$

On the other hand, by operating on the expression (7.44) and defining $\Delta q_t = q_{t+1} - q_t$, we obtain that:

$$q_{t+1} = \frac{(1+R_t)}{(1-\delta)} q_t - \frac{\alpha}{(1-\delta)} K_{t+1}^{\alpha-1} + \frac{\phi}{2(1-\delta)} \left(\frac{I_{t+1} - \delta K_{t+1}}{K_{t+1}} \right)^2 - \frac{\phi}{(1-\delta)} \left(\frac{I_{t+1} - \delta K_{t+1}}{K_{t+1}} \right) \frac{I_{t+1}}{K_{t+1}} \tag{7.48}$$

By adding and subtracting in the left part of this expression:

$$q_{t+1} - q_t + q_t = \frac{(1+R_t)}{(1-\delta)} q_t - \frac{\alpha}{(1-\delta)} K_{t+1}^{\alpha-1} + \frac{\phi}{2(1-\delta)} \left(\frac{I_{t+1} - \delta K_{t+1}}{K_{t+1}} \right)^2$$
$$- \frac{\phi}{(1-\delta)} \left(\frac{I_{t+1} - \delta K_{t+1}}{K_{t+1}} \right) \frac{I_{t+1}}{K_{t+1}} \tag{7.49}$$

and by rearranging the terms, it results that:

$$\Delta q_t = \frac{(R_t + \delta)q_t - \alpha K_{t+1}^{\alpha-1} + \frac{\phi}{2} \left(\frac{I_{t+1} - \delta K_{t+1}}{K_{t+1}} \right)^2 - \phi \left(\frac{I_{t+1} - \delta K_{t+1}}{K_{t+1}} \right) \frac{I_{t+1}}{K_{t+1}}}{(1-\delta)} \tag{7.50}$$

Given these functional forms for the production function and for the adjustment cost function, the calibration of the parameters of the model are the following: α, which is the technological parameter that determines the elasticity of the production level with respect to the stock of capital is assumed to be 0.35. The physical depreciation rate of capital is assumed to be 6 percent per year ($\delta = 0.06$). The adjustment cost parameter is assumed takes a value of 10, ($\phi = 10$). Finally, the model has a variable that we have assumed to be exogenous, the real interest rate. Let's assume that $R_t = 0.04$, that is 4% per year.

Table 7.1: Calibration of the parameters

Symbol	Definition	Value
α	Production-capital elasticity	0.35
δ	Depreciation rate	0.06
ϕ	Parameter adjustment costs	10.0

7.3.1. Steady state

Next, we will proceed to calculate the steady state. To simplify the notation, we are going to eliminate the time subscript of the steady-state variables. However, we must bear in mind that the steady state can be altered from one period to another, depending on the disturbances suffered by the system. The dynamic equation for the capital stock (the investment rule), in steady state, would be given by:

$$\Delta K_t = (\bar{q} - 1)\frac{\bar{K}}{\phi} = 0 \tag{7.51}$$

Since in the steady state the previous equation must be equal to zero, this supposes that the value of the q ratio in steady state has to be equal to the unit:

$$\bar{q} = 1 \tag{7.52}$$

In fact, in a steady state it turns out that $C_I(\cdot) = 0$, because it turns out that $\bar{q} = 1$. On the other hand, the dynamic equation for the q, in steady state would be given by:

$$\Delta q_t = \frac{(R_t+\delta)\bar{q}-\alpha\bar{K}^{\alpha-1}}{(1-\delta)}=0 \tag{7.53}$$

since in steady state $\bar{I}_t = \delta\bar{K}_t$. Therefore, for the previous expression to be zero, the denominator must be null, so we would have to:

$$\alpha\bar{K}^{\alpha-1} = R_t + \delta \tag{7.54}$$

resulting that the stock of capital in steady state would be given by:

$$\bar{K} = \left(\frac{R_t+\delta}{\alpha}\right)^{\frac{1}{\alpha-1}} \tag{7.55}$$

By substituting the calibrated values for the parameters and for the exogenous variable, we would have that the value of capital stock in steady state is:

$$\bar{K}_t = \left(\frac{0.04+0.06}{0.35}\right)^{\frac{1}{0.65}} = 6.87$$

7.4. Linearization of Tobin's Q model

Tobin's Q model, even in its simplest version as described here, presents an added difficulty with respect to the non-micro-based models studied previously, due to the fact that the resulting dynamic equations are non-linear. The presence of non-linear dynamic equations is common in micro-based macroeconomic models, which is an additional difficulty for their numerical resolution. This difficulty stems from the fact that the type of solution we are going to find for these models is of the saddle-point type, so we need to calculate the stable path and the change that must occur in the variable that "jumps" up to said stable path for the system to converge to its steady state. As it happened in the Dornbusch model of overshooting of the exchange rate, if we have a saddle point it is necessary to have the value of the eigenvalues of the system to calculate the impact effect of a disturbance on the variable that depends on the expectations and adjusts instantaneously. That is, we have to calculate the stable saddle path, which is easier if we are working with a dynamic system composed of linear equations.

The fact that the equations are non-linear, makes it difficult to calculate the eigenvalues of the system, without which it is not possible to calculate the stable path to determine the dynamics of the different variables. The simplest way to proceed, and that is the strategy we use here, is to obtain a linear approximation to the original non-linear equations of the model, which facilitates the calculation of the eigenvalues by applying the same procedure that we used previously. This is precisely the standard method that is carried out in macroeconomic analysis: to solve a linear approximation to the original non-linear system. Thus, once we have obtained the dynamic equations of a certain non-linear macroeconomic model, we proceed to linearize it around its steady state, in order to analyze the dynamics of the variables. This assumes that we define the variables as deviations from the steady state. Obviously, this procedure is only valid if the economy is always very close to the steady state (the error that is made in the linear approximation would be small), which would be guaranteed if the disturbances suffered by an economy are not of a high amount.

In this section, we redefine the model in linear terms. From the problem solved previously, we obtain the following two difference equations:

$$\Delta K_t = (q_t - 1)\frac{K_t}{\phi} \tag{7.56}$$

$$\Delta q_t = \frac{(R_t+\delta)q_t - \alpha K_{t+1}^{\alpha-1} + \frac{\phi}{2}\left(\frac{I_{t+1}-\delta K_{t+1}}{K_{t+1}}\right)^2 - \phi\left(\frac{I_{t+1}-\delta K_{t+1}}{K_{t+1}}\right)\frac{I_{t+1}}{K_{t+1}}}{(1-\delta)} \tag{7.57}$$

where we have defined $\Delta q_t = q_{t+1} - q_t$, and where $\Delta K_t = K_{t+1} - K_t$. The problem that we encounter is that both equations are non-linear, so we cannot write the problem in matrix notation and study the characteristics of the coefficient matrix associated with the endogenous variables directly. To apply the procedure described in prevous chapters, we must first transform these equations to be linear (a linear approximation to them).

To obtain the log-linearization of our system of equations, we will express the variables of the model as the log-linear deviation with respect to its steady-state values. The log-linear deviation of a variable, x_t, with respect to its steady-state value, $\bar{x}_t$, we will define as $\hat{x}_t$, where $\hat{x}_t = \ln x_t - \ln \bar{x}_t$. To construct the equations in log-linear form, we will follow three basic rules, as indicated in Uhlig (1999).[6] These basic rules are the following:

1. Each one of the variables can be defined as:

$$x_t \approx \bar{x}_t \exp(\hat{x}_t) \approx \bar{x}_t(1 + \hat{x}_t) \tag{7.58}$$

2. When two variables are multiplying, then:

$$x_t z_t \approx \bar{x}_t(1 + \hat{x}_t)\bar{z}_t(1 + \hat{z}_t) \approx \bar{x}_t\bar{z}_t(1 + \hat{x}_t + \hat{z}_t) \tag{7.59}$$

that is, we assume that the product of two deviations with respect to its steady states, $\hat{x}_t\hat{z}_t$, is a very small number and approximately equal to zero.

3. The third rule refers to the powers, such that:

$$x_t^a \approx \bar{x}_t^a(1 + \hat{x}_t)^a \approx \bar{x}_t^a(1 + a\hat{x}_t) \tag{7.60}$$

Log-linearization of the dynamic equation for the capital stock

First, we proceed to log-linearize the first dynamic equation, corresponding to the variations in the stock of capital. Let's write the starting equation again:

$$K_{t+1} - K_t = (q_t - 1)\frac{K_t}{\phi} \tag{7.61}$$

or equivalently:

$$K_{t+1} - K_t = q_t\frac{K_t}{\phi} - \frac{K_t}{\phi} \tag{7.62}$$

By applying the log-linearization rule (rules 1 and 2) we obtain:

$$\bar{K}_{t+1}(1 + \hat{k}_{t+1}) - \bar{K}_t(1 + \hat{k}_t) = \frac{1}{\phi}\bar{q}_t\bar{K}_t(1 + \hat{q}_t + \hat{k}_t) - \frac{1}{\phi}\bar{K}_t(1 + \hat{k}_t) \tag{7.63}$$

---

[6] Uhlig, H. (1999). A tookit for analyzing non-linear dynamic stochastic models easily, in R. Marimon y A. Scott (Eds.), Computational Methods for the Study of Dynamic Economies. Oxford University Press.

or equivalently, by eliminating the time subscripts for the steady-state variables (given that $(\bar{K}_{t+1} = \bar{K}_t = \bar{K})$,

$$\bar{K} + \bar{K}\hat{k}_{t+1} - \bar{K} - \bar{K}\hat{k}_t = \frac{1}{\phi}\bar{q}\bar{K} + \frac{1}{\phi}\bar{q}\bar{K}\hat{q}_t + \frac{1}{\phi}\bar{q}\bar{K}\hat{k}_t - \frac{1}{\phi}\bar{K} - \frac{1}{\phi}\bar{K}\hat{k}_t \quad (7.64)$$

and by simplifying and given that $\bar{q}_t = 1$, it turns out that:

$$\hat{k}_{t+1} - \hat{k}_t = \frac{1}{\phi} + \frac{1}{\phi}\hat{q}_t + \frac{1}{\phi}\hat{k}_t - \frac{1}{\phi} - \frac{1}{\phi}\hat{k}_t \quad (7.65)$$

or equivalently:

$$\hat{k}_{t+1} - \hat{k}_t = \frac{1}{\phi}\hat{q}_t \quad (7.66)$$

so, we finally get the following linear approximation to the variations in the stock of capital (in terms of its deviations from its steady state):

$$\Delta\hat{k}_t = \frac{1}{\phi}\hat{q}_t \quad (7.67)$$

This equation indicates that a positive deviation of the ratio from its steady-state value implies an increase in the deviation of the stock of capital with respect to its steady state.

Log-linearization of the dynamic equation for the ratio q

Next, we proceed to apply the same procedure to the second dynamic equation of the model. We can write this dynamic equation as:

$$(1 - \delta)q_{t+1} = (1 + R_t)q_t - \alpha K_{t+1}^{\alpha-1} + \frac{\phi}{2}\left(\frac{I_{t+1}}{K_{t+1}} - \delta\right)^2 - \phi\left(\frac{I_{t+1}}{K_{t+1}} - \delta\right)\frac{I_{t+1}}{K_{t+1}}$$

$$(7.68)$$

In steady state, that expression would be:

$$(1 - \delta)\bar{q} = (1 + \bar{R}) - \alpha\bar{K}_t^{\alpha-1} \quad (7.69)$$

since in steady state $\bar{I}_t = \delta\bar{K}_t$. On the other hand, from the expression (7.43) we obtain that the investment ratio with respect to the stock of capital is given by:

$$\frac{I_t}{K_t} = \frac{1}{\phi}(q_t - 1) + \delta \quad (7.70)$$

By substituting this expression in the dynamic equation (7.68), it results:

$$(1 - \delta)q_{t+1} = (1 + R_t)q_t - \alpha K_{t+1}^{\alpha-1} - \frac{1}{2\phi}\left(\frac{1}{\phi}(q_{t+1} - 1)\right)^2$$

$$-\phi\left(\frac{1}{\phi}(q_{t+1} - 1)\right)\left(\frac{1}{\phi}(q_{t+1} - 1) + \delta\right) \quad (7.71)$$

By operating and simplifying, we come to:

$$(1-\delta)q_{t+1} = (1+R_t)q_t - \alpha K_{t+1}^{\alpha-1} - \frac{1}{2\phi}(q_{t+1}-1)^2 - \delta(q_{t+1}-1) \qquad (7.72)$$

By applying the log-linearization rules to the previous expression, it results that:

$$(1-\delta)\bar{q}(1+\hat{q}_{t+1}) = (1+R)\bar{q}(1+\hat{q}_t) - \alpha\bar{K}^{\alpha-1}(1+(\alpha-1)\hat{k}_{t+1}) -$$
$$\frac{1}{2\phi}\bar{q}^2(1+2\hat{q}_{t+1}) - \frac{1}{2\phi} + \frac{1}{\phi}\bar{q}(1+\hat{q}_{t+1}) - \delta\bar{q}(1+\hat{q}_{t+1}) + \delta \qquad (7.73)$$

Since the steady-state value of the q ratio is equal to 1, $(\bar{q}=1)$, we can write:

$$(1-\delta)(1+\hat{q}_{t+1}) = (1+R)(1+\hat{q}_t) - \alpha\bar{K}^{\alpha-1}(1+(\alpha-1)\hat{k}_{t+1})$$
$$-\frac{1}{2\phi}(1+2\hat{q}_{t+1}) - \frac{1}{2\phi} + \frac{1}{\phi}(1+\hat{q}_{t+1}) - \delta(1+\hat{q}_{t+1}) + \delta \qquad (7.74)$$

and by operating:

$$1+\hat{q}_{t+1} - \delta - \delta\hat{q}_{t+1} = (1+\hat{q}_t + R_t + \hat{q}_t R_t) - \alpha\bar{K}^{\alpha-1}(1+(\alpha-1)\hat{k}_{t+1}) - \delta\hat{q}_{t+1} \qquad (7.75)$$

or equivalently,

$$(1-\delta) + \hat{q}_{t+1} = (1+R_t) + (1+R_t)\hat{q}_t - \alpha\bar{K}^{\alpha-1} - \alpha\bar{K}^{\alpha-1}(\alpha-1)\hat{k}_{t+1} \qquad (7.76)$$

By using the expression of steady state (7.69) and canceling terms, we arrive at:

$$\hat{q}_{t+1} = (1+R_t)\hat{q}_t - \alpha\bar{K}^{\alpha-1}(\alpha-1)\hat{k}_{t+1} \qquad (7.77)$$

and by using the definition of the stock of capital in steady state and readjusting terms, we have:

$$\hat{q}_{t+1} = (1+R_t)\hat{q}_t - (\alpha-1)(R_t+\delta)\hat{k}_{t+1} \qquad (7.78)$$

On the other hand, from the expression (7.66), we obtain that:

$$\hat{k}_{t+1} = \hat{k}_t + \frac{1}{\phi}\hat{q}_t \qquad (7.79)$$

and by replacing in the previous expression results that:

$$\hat{q}_{t+1} = (1+R_t)\hat{q}_t - (\alpha-1)(R_t+\delta)\left(\hat{k}_t + \frac{1}{\phi}\hat{q}_t\right) \qquad (7.80)$$

Since we are interested in obtaining expression in terms of the variations in $\hat{q}_t$, that we define as $\Delta\hat{q}_t = \hat{q}_{t+1} - \hat{q}_t$, by operating, we would obtain:

$$\Delta\hat{q}_t = \frac{R_t\phi - (\alpha-1)(R_t+\delta)}{\phi}\hat{q}_t - (\alpha-1)(R_t+\delta)\hat{k}_t \qquad (7.81)$$

finally obtaining the following log-linear approximation to the dynamic equation for the q ratio as a function of the deviations of the two variables with respect to their steady-state value. This expression indicates that the changes in the q ratio depend positively on their deviations with respect to their steady state and positively on the deviations of the stock of capital with respect to their value of steady state (given the assumption that $\alpha < 1$). Thus, if the value of the debt is very high, its effect is that said ratio continues to increase. On the other hand, if the deviation of the stock of capital with respect to its steady state is positive, indicating that the stock of capital is higher than its steady-state value, then the effect on the ratio is also positive.

Therefore, in matrix notation, the model of Tobin's Q (log-)linearized in terms of deviations from the steady state can be defined through the following dynamic system:

$$\begin{bmatrix} \Delta \hat{q}_t \\ \Delta \hat{k}_t \end{bmatrix} = \begin{bmatrix} \dfrac{R_t \phi - (\alpha-1)(R_t + \delta)}{\phi} & -(\alpha-1)(R_t+\delta) \\ \dfrac{1}{\phi} & 0 \end{bmatrix} \begin{bmatrix} \hat{q}_t \\ \hat{k}_t \end{bmatrix} \tag{7.82}$$

where A is the matrix of coefficients associated with the deviations of each variable with respect to its steady-state value.[7] Using the calibrated values for the parameters and the exogenous variables, the system would be:

$$\begin{bmatrix} \Delta \hat{q}_t \\ \Delta \hat{k}_t \end{bmatrix} = \begin{bmatrix} \dfrac{0.4 + 0.65x0.1}{10} & 0.65x0.1 \\ 0.1 & 0 \end{bmatrix} \begin{bmatrix} \hat{q}_t \\ \hat{k}_t \end{bmatrix}$$

7.4.1. System stability

Once the model is linearized, we can then calculate the roots (eigenvalues) associated with the coefficient matrix to study the stability conditions of the dynamic system. For this, we calculate:

$$Det \begin{bmatrix} \dfrac{R_t \phi - (\alpha-1)(R_t+\delta)}{\phi} - \lambda & -(\alpha-1)(R_t+\delta) \\ \dfrac{1}{\phi} & 0 - \lambda \end{bmatrix} = 0 \tag{7.83}$$

---

[7] The general structure of a macroeconomic model, whether micro-based or not, once linearized is given by:

$$\Delta x_t = A x_t + B z_t$$

This specification can also be written as a dynamic system in terms of deviations from the steady state. Thus, in a steady state, the previous system would be given by:

$$0 = A \bar{x}_t + B z_t$$

and by clearing,

$$-A \bar{x}_t = B z_t$$

By substituting in the initial system results that:

$$\Delta x_t = A x_t - A \bar{x}_t = A(x_t - \bar{x}_t)$$

which is the specification in terms of which we solve this model.

The corresponding second-degree equation would be:

$$\lambda^2 - \frac{R_t\phi-(\alpha-1)(R_t+\delta)}{\phi}\lambda + \frac{(\alpha-1)(R_t+\delta)}{\phi} \qquad (7.84)$$

Therefore, by solving the previous equation, the two roots would be given by:

$$\lambda_1,\lambda_2 = \frac{\frac{R_t\phi-(\alpha-1)(R_t+\delta)}{\phi} \pm \sqrt{\left(\frac{R_t\phi-(\alpha-1)(R_t+\delta)}{\phi}\right)^2 - 4\frac{(\alpha-1)(R_t+\delta)}{\phi}}}{2} \qquad (7.85)$$

As we can see, both roots are going to be real, given that $\alpha < 1$, and therefore, the sign inside the square root is positive. Only complex roots could be given when the returns to capital were increasing ($\alpha > 1$), although we do not consider plausible this possibility at the aggregate level. On the other hand, when solving the square root, we observe that one root is positive while the other is going to be negative. In effect, if we substitute the values of the parameters and the exogenous variable, it results that:

$$\lambda_1 = \frac{0.0465 - \sqrt{0.0465^2 - 4x0.0065}}{2} = -0.0607$$

$$\lambda_2 = \frac{0.0465 + \sqrt{0.0465^2 - 4x0.0065}}{2} = 0.1072$$

being the modules of the eigenvalues plus the unit, 0.94 and 1.11, respectively, so the solution will be a saddle point, and therefore, both convergent and divergent trajectories exist with respect to the steady state.

7.4.2. Stable saddle path

Once we have calculated the eigenvalues, considering λ_1 as the eigenvalue such that it fulfills the condition $|\lambda_1 + 1| < 1$, we obtain the existence of a saddle point. In this case, there is a unique trajectory that leads directly to the steady state, which we call the stable saddle path. In mathematical terms, this stable saddle path can be defined as:

$$\begin{bmatrix} \Delta\hat{q}_t \\ \Delta\hat{k}_t \end{bmatrix} = \lambda_1 \begin{bmatrix} \hat{q}_t \\ \hat{k}_t \end{bmatrix} \qquad (7.86)$$

The adjustment procedure to a disturbance is similar to the one studied in the Dornbusch model (Chapter 3). When a disturbance occurs, the economy follows the stable saddle path from the next period in which the disturbance occurs until it reaches the steady state. In fact, this is going to be the fundamental characteristic of the micro-based macroeconomic models of dynamic general equilibrium, as we will see later. The only piece of information that we lack is how the economy adjusts instantaneously, when a disturbance occurs, from the initial steady state to the stable saddle path. That is, what is the "jump" that must be produced in q in order to reach the new stable saddle path from which the economy adjusts to its new steady state.

7.4.3. Instant readjustment of the ratio q

As we have seen in Chapter 3, in which the numerical resolution of the overshooting model of the exchange rate was studied, Tobin's Q model also presents a saddle-point solution. This means that we need to determine the amount of the instantaneous readjustment of the q ratio before a certain disturbance, which will move the economy from the initial steady state to the stable saddle path calculated previously. The reduced form of the Tobin's Q model contains two endogenous variables, the stock of capital and the q ratio. While the capital stock is a rigid variable due to its characteristics (changing the stock of capital is a process that takes time; time-to-built), the q ratio is a totally flexible (jump) variable, determined by the market value of the firm, which is also highly conditioned by expectations about future profits.

The procedure to calculate the readjustment in expectations is similar to the one done previously. For this, we start with the equation that describes the dynamic behavior of the q ratio with respect to its steady state:

$$\Delta \hat{q}_t = \frac{R_t \phi - (\alpha-1)(R_t+\delta)}{\phi} \hat{q}_t - (\alpha - 1)(R_t + \delta)\hat{k}_t \tag{7.87}$$

Equivalently, we can define the following stable trajectory:

$$\Delta \hat{q}_t = \lambda_1 \hat{q}_t \tag{7.88}$$

Matching both expressions at the time the disturbance occurs ($t = 1$) results in:

$$\frac{R_t \phi - (\alpha-1)(R_t+\delta)}{\phi} \hat{q}_1 - (\alpha - 1)(R_t + \delta)\hat{k}_1 = \lambda_1 \hat{q}_1 \tag{7.89}$$

and by solving for the deviations of the q ratio from its steady-state value, it results:

$$\hat{q}_1 = \frac{(\alpha-1)(R_t+\delta)}{\frac{R_t \phi - (\alpha-1)(R_t+\delta)}{\phi} - \lambda_1} \hat{k}_1 \tag{7.90}$$

expression that is equivalent to the "jump" that must be produced in the q ratio (for this reason, this variable type is called a "jump" variable), to reach the new stable saddle path, since in the initial steady state the deviation was zero.

7.5. Numerical solution

Once we have solved the model analytically, we will proceed to its numerical solution. The spreadsheet on which we have solved this model is called "**ICM-**

7.xls". In appendix K, we present the code corresponding to this model developed in DYNARE.

Figure 7.1 shows the structure of this spreadsheet. In this case, we have calculated three types of endogenous variables: variables in levels (q, K), variables in terms of logarithmic deviations with respect to the steady state $(\hat{q}, \hat{k})$, and time variations of the logarithmic deviations with respect to the steady state, $(\Delta\hat{q}, \Delta\hat{k})$.

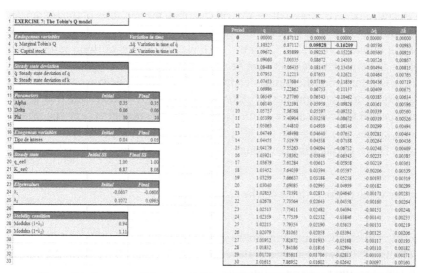

Period	q	K	q̂	k̂	Δq̂	Δk̂
0	1.00000	6.87112	0.00000	0.00000	0.00000	0.00000
1	1.10327	6.87112	0.09828	-0.16209	-0.00596	0.00983
2	1.09672	6.93899	0.09232	-0.15226	-0.00580	0.00923
3	1.09060	7.00335	0.08672	-0.14303	-0.00526	0.00867
4	1.08488	7.06435	0.08147	-0.13436	-0.00494	0.00815
5	1.07953	7.12213	0.07653	-0.12621	-0.00464	0.00785
6	1.07453	7.17684	0.07189	-0.11856	-0.00436	0.00719
7	1.06986	7.22862	0.06753	-0.11137	-0.00409	0.00675
8	1.06549	7.27780	0.06343	-0.10462	-0.00385	0.00634
9	1.06140	7.32391	0.05959	-0.09828	-0.00361	0.00596
10	1.05757	7.36768	0.05597	-0.09232	-0.00339	0.00560
11	1.05399	7.40904	0.05258	-0.08672	-0.00319	0.00526
12	1.05063	7.44810	0.04939	-0.08146	-0.00299	0.00494
13	1.04749	7.48498	0.04640	-0.07652	-0.00281	0.00464
14	1.04455	7.51979	0.04358	-0.07188	-0.00264	0.00436
15	1.04179	7.55263	0.04094	-0.06752	-0.00248	0.00409
16	1.03921	7.58362	0.03846	-0.06343	-0.00233	0.00385
17	1.03679	7.61284	0.03613	-0.05958	-0.00219	0.00361
18	1.03452	7.64039	0.03594	-0.05597	-0.00206	0.00339
19	1.03239	7.66637	0.03188	-0.05258	-0.00193	0.00319
20	1.03040	7.69085	0.02995	-0.04939	-0.00182	0.00299
21	1.02853	7.71391	0.02813	-0.04640	-0.00171	0.00281
22	1.02678	7.73564	0.02643	-0.04358	-0.00160	0.00264
23	1.02513	7.75611	0.02482	-0.04094	-0.00151	0.00248
24	1.02359	7.77539	0.02352	-0.03846	-0.00141	0.00233
25	1.02215	7.79354	0.02190	-0.03613	-0.00133	0.00219
26	1.02079	7.81063	0.02058	-0.03394	-0.00125	0.00206
27	1.01952	7.82672	0.01933	-0.03188	-0.00117	0.00193
28	1.01832	7.84186	0.01816	-0.02994	-0.00110	0.00182
29	1.01720	7.85611	0.01706	-0.02813	-0.00103	0.00171
30	1.01615	7.86952	0.01602	-0.02642	-0.00097	0.00160

Figure 7.1. Structure of the spreadsheet "ICM-7.xls". The Tobin's Q model.

Cells "B12-B14" show the initial values of the parameters. In cell "B12" the initial value of the parameter is presented, cell that we call "Alpha_0". We also include in cell "C12" the final value for this parameter, to be used in the sensitivity analysis, in case we are interested in studying the behavior of the model before a change in the value of this parameter. We call this final value "Alpha_1". Similarly, cell "B13" shows the value of the depreciation rate of the initial capital (called "Delta_0"), while in cell "B14" the value assigned to the parameter of the adjustment cost function is presented (which we have called "Phi_0"). Next, we show the values of the exogenous variable, which in the case of this model is the interest rate, both in the initial moment and in the final moment, in order to perform perturbation analysis. These values appear in cells "B17" and "C17" and their final values in cells "C13" and "C14", cells that we call "R_0" and "R_1".

The steady-state values, both with the initial values of the parameters and exogenous variable, and with the final values appear in cells "B20", "C20", "B21" and "C21". These cells are called "qbar_0" and "qbar_1" for the initial and final steady states of the q ratio, and "kbar_0" and "kbar_1", for the initial and final steady states of the capital stock. As initially, both the final and initial values of parameters and exogenous variables are the same, also the steady state shows the same values in both situations. Finally, the eigenvalues appear in cells "B24" and "B25" for the initial situation and in cells "C24" and "C25" for the final situation, while the module of the eigenvalues plus the unit are calculated in cells "B28" and "B29" for the initial situation and "C28" and "C29" for the final.

Below are the columns where we will calculate the variables of the model. In column "H", the time index is included. Columns "I" to "N" show the values of the different variables. Column "I" shows the values of the q ratio. If we place the cursor in cell "I3", we see that the expression "=qbar_0" appears, since we start from the initial steady state. If we place the cursor in cell "I4", the expression that appears is "=EXP (K4+LN(qbar_1))", indicating that in the next period the value of the q ratio is the value of its deviation from the steady state, values that appear in the "K" column, plus the new steady state for the q ratio. This is because the deviations from the steady state are defined as:

$$\hat{q}_t = q_t - \bar{q}$$

so the value of the variable can be calculated as:

$$q_t = \hat{q}_t + \bar{q}$$

This same expression appears in the following cells in this column. Next, column "J" shows the values of the capital stock. Again, if we place the cursor in cell "J3", the expression that appears is "=kbar_0", which corresponds to the value in the initial steady state of the capital stock. If we place the cursor in cell "J4", the expression that appears is "=EXP(L4+LN(kbar_1))". This expression calculates the stock of capital in this period, such as cell "L4", in which the deviation of the stock of capital appears with respect to its steady state, plus the logarithm of value of the new steady state for the stock of capital.

The "K" and "L" columns show the deviations with respect to the steady state of the q ratio and capital stock, respectively. Cell "K5" (and the following) of column "K" includes the expression "=L4+N4", in which we calculate the value of the variable as its value in the previous period plus the change produced in it. In cell "L3" we find the expression:

=LN(J3)-LN(kbar_0)

that is, the difference between the value of the stock of capital at the moment in which the disturbance occurs, which is equal to its initial steady state and the new steady-state value. Cell "L4" and the following calculate the value of the variable as the value of the previous period plus the change produced in the variable.

The two key cells in the analysis of this model are "L4" and "M4". In cell "L4", the expression that appears is:

=LN(kbar_0)-LN(kbar_1)

that would calculate the difference between the initial steady state and the new steady state when a disturbance occurs. That is, the deviation of the stock of capital from its new steady-state value.

If we place the cursor in cell "M3", the expression that appears is:

=((R_0*Phi_0-(Alpha_0-1)*(R_0+Delta_0))/Phi_0)*K3

-((R_0+Delta_0)*(Alpha_0-1))*L3

which corresponds to the expression (8.81). On the other hand, in cell "M4", the expression that appears is:

=((R_1*Phi_1-(Alpha_1-1)*(R_1+Delta_1))/Phi_1)*K4

-((R_1+Delta_1)*(Alpha_1-1))*L4

which corresponds to the expression (7.90). This cell contains the readjustment of the q ratio once a disturbance occurs. As we have indicated previously, the dynamics of this model are determined by a saddle point, which means that only some of the trajectories are convergent towards the steady state. These trajectories converge to the so-called stable path, to which the q variable moves instantaneously once a disturbance has occurred. This instantaneous change is due to a readjustment in expectations about this ratio, which come from the new expectations about the future market value of the company. We can substitute this expression with the equation (7.88) and we would obtain exactly the same result. Finally, in cell "N4", we find the expression:

=(1/Phi_1)*K4

which corresponds to the equation (7.67). Again, we can replace this expression with:

$$\Delta \hat{k}_t = \lambda_1 \hat{k}_t \tag{7.92}$$

and we would get the same result.

7.6. Shock analysis: Effects of a decrease in the interest rate

Once a numerical solution of the model is obtained, we can use it to perform different types of analysis on the effect of different disturbances on the investment decision and the installed capital stock. For instance, we can alter the values of the parameters or the exogenous variables to study their influence on the speed of adjustment of the economy towards the steady state. Another interesting exercise consists in study a change in the initial condition for the capital stock and study how the economy behaves as a function of the difference between the initial capital stock and its steady-state value. In this section, specifically, we study the effects of a decrease in the interest rate (which it assumed to be an exogenous variable). To do this, we only have to change the value of cell "C17". For example, let's assume that the interest rate starts from an initial value of 0.04 and decreases to a new value of 0.03.

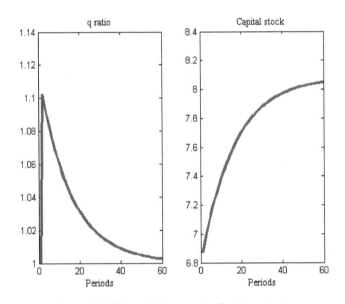

Figure 7.2. Effects of a decrease in the interest rate.

Figure 7.2 shows the dynamics of the different variables in response to this disturbance. As we can see, the decrease in the interest rate causes an instantaneous increase in the q ratio, until it reaches the new stable saddle path. This is because there is an instantaneous readjustment of expectations regarding the market value of the firm, which increases the q ratio. In fact, this effect can be observed empirically with respect to the price of the shares of companies listed on the stock exchange. When there is a decrease in the interest rate, this measure is generally accepted by the stock market with general increases in the value of the companies, reflecting the readjustment of expectations of the agents that we assume to be rational.

Thus, now the cost of capital is lower, the replacement cost of installed capital decreases and, therefore, it is profitable for the firm to invest in additional physical capital since the cost of investment including adjustment cost is lower than the increase in the market value of the firm. Then, once the increase in capital occurs, the q ratio will gradually decrease until it reaches its new steady-state equilibrium value, which is the same as initially. As regards the dynamics of the capital stock, the increase in the q ratio causes a progressive increase in the stock of capital. In fact, the stock of capital is increasing until the q ratio returns to its steady-state value. This process will result in the capital stock increasing in the long-run with respect to the initial steady state.

7.7. Sensitivity analysis: Effects of an increase in the depreciation rate

Finally, we will study how the investment responds to a change in any of the parameters of the model. In particular, we will study the sensitivity of the model to a change in the value of the parameter that determines the physical depreciation of capital, δ. The physical depreciation of the aggregate capital of the economy depends on the type of capital assets and on the characteristic of the new capital assets that are incorporated into the production process through investment. Different capital assets have different depreciation rates. For example, structures (buildings or infrastructures) have a very low physical depreciation rate in relation to the depreciation rate of equipment (machinery, vehicles, etc.). On the other hand, the investment in most technologically advanced equipment, such as hardware and software, usually have higher physical depreciation rates. Therefore, to the extent that the relative weight of each type of capital asset changes, it is expected that the physical depreciation rate of the aggregate capital of an economy will also be altered.

In particular, let's assume that the depreciation rate goes from a value of 6% to 7% per year. To perform this exercise, we simply have to change the value of cell "C13" and we will automatically obtain the new steady state as well as the transition dynamics towards it. The response of the variables to this change is shown in Figure 7.3. As we can see, the increase in the depreciation rate causes an instantaneous decrease in the q ratio. This is because now the returns on capital are lower (or equivalently its cost is higher), since it has to face a greater physical depreciation over time. As a consequence of this decrease in the q ratio, there is a decrease in the volume of investment, which together with the higher depreciation rate causes a decrease in the capital stock. The stock of capital in the new steady state is 5.93, which represents a decrease of 13.64% with respect to the stock of initial capital.

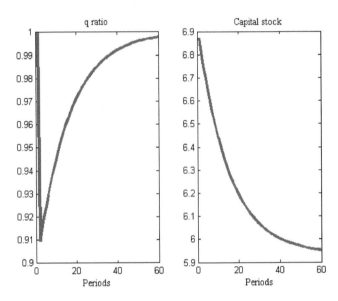

Figure 7.3. Effects of an increase in the physical capital depreciation rate, δ.

Exercises

1. Suppose that an earthquake destroys 20% of the capital stock. Using the "**ICM-7.xls**" spreadsheet, study the effects of this disturbance. (Hint: Change the initial value of the stock of capital in cell "J3" to 80% of the steady state value).

2. What effects does an increase in the parameter ϕ have on the dynamics of the economy?

3. Suppose that the adjustment-cost function only depends on the volume of investment and is given by the following function:

$$C(I_t) = \frac{\phi}{2}\left(\frac{I_t}{I_{t-1}} - 1\right)^2$$

Solve Tobin's Q model with this adjustment-cost function and build the corresponding spreadsheet. Analyze the sensitivity of the model to changes in the value of the parameter ϕ.

4. Analyze how the steady state of the economy changes with a decrease in the parameter α.

8. The basic dynamic general equilibrium model

8.1. Introduction

Current macroeconomic analysis is carried out mainly through the construction, calibration, estimation and simulation of dynamic general equilibrium models, both stochastic and deterministic. These models represent an unified theoretical framework that can be used for the study of the economy both in the short term (business cycles) and in the long term (economic growth).[1] The key characteristic of this typology of models is that they are micro-founded. That is, the behavioral equations that make up these models are derived from the microeconomic analysis of the behavior of the different economic agents interacting in the economy, as opposed to dynamic macroeconomic models with rational expectations, non-micro-based, in which the equations that represent the economy are defined directly in aggregate form.[2] This typology of micro-based models constitutes the core of macroeconomic analysis at present, being the basic tool for the realization of simulations of economic policy and for determining the dynamic effects of different disturbances on the economy. For the construction of this micro-based macroeconomic model, we set up a macroeconomic environment where both households and firms takes economic decisions. This basic framework can be extended by considering other economic agents, such as the government, the central bank, the financial sector, etc.

In this chapter, we will describe the main characteristics of the basic dynamic general equilibrium model. The model can be defined as a system of equations that represent decisions of the different agents (first-order conditions of a maximization problem), budgetary and technological restrictions, as well as national accounting identities. The basic theoretical structure of this type of models is relatively simple although it gives rise to a

---

[1] The standard denomination used to define this typology of micro-based macroeconomic models is that of Dynamic Stochastic General Equilibrium (DSGE) models.

[2] However, as shown by the approach of the New Macroeconomic Consensus, both types of models (micro-based versus non-micro-based) are equivalent, giving rise to very similar results. See, for example, Clarida, R. Galí, J. and Gertler, M. (1999). The science of monetary policy: A New Keynesian perspective. *Journal of Economic Literature*, 37: 1661-1707.

highly complex dynamic derived from general equilibrium effects and the existence of forward-looking variables, which makes the resolution of these models somewhat difficult. In fact, this typology of models does not have a closed-form solution, including the simplified version presented here, but it is only possible to solve it through graphic representations making use of phase diagrams, or through numerical methods. The latter is precisely the approach we are using in this book. The simple model that we are going to solve is reduced to a system of two difference equations, which determine the temporal dynamics of consumption and the capital stock.

The model to be solved here starts from the consideration of the behavior of the two main types of agents that exist in an economy: Households or consumers on the one hand, and firms on the other. In reality, an economy is populated by a very large number of consumers or families (millions of agents) that we are going to assume are identical in preferences. This will allow us to solve the model based on the decisions taken by a representative consumer. On the other hand, there is a large number of firms (millions of agents) that we will also assume are identical in technology in a perfect competition environment. This will allow us to solve the model based on the decisions taken by a representative firm. These agents will make decisions on a set of macroeconomic variables through the maximization of a certain objective function. We consider the model in its deterministic version, in a context of perfect foresight, although it can be extended to a stochastic environment in a simple way.

The result we obtain from the interaction of the different agents is called Dynamic General Equilibrium, given that all the variables are determined endogenously, simultaneously and in a dynamic context, or Competitive Equilibrium if we assume the existence of a market economy where the agents are free to take economic decisions in a perfect-competition environment. In this context, the functioning of the economy is as follows: consumers make decisions about how much they will consume (how much they will save and invest) and what their labor supply (working time) will be, taking as given the prices of the capital productive factor and the price of labor (wage per unit of time). On the other hand, firms decide how many productive factors they will hire, given their prices. These quantities will determine the production of the economy, given a technological constraint. The equilibrium of the model is given by a situation in which the decisions of the consumers in terms of the maximization of their utility function are compatible with the decisions of the firms in terms of profits maximization, fulfilling the feasibility restriction of the economy. Alternatively, we can suppose the existence of a central planner economy where there is an agent, the central planner, who decides the optimal quantities of each variable that maximizes social welfare, without the need for pricing of the productive factors.

In this chapter, we will study how to numerically compute the basic model of dynamic general equilibrium. For this, we are going to use two different solution strategies, which we have already used in the previous chapters. In the first place, we are going to solve the dynamic model of general equilibrium using the "Solver" tool of the Excel spreadsheet, which allows us to solve optimization problems like the one assumed by this type of models. Secondly, we proceed to linearize the equations of this model (which are non-linear), through a log-linearization process, in order to obtain a system of linear difference equations, an approximation of the original, that can be simulated numerically in the spreadsheet. The dynamics of the variables of this model will be conditioned to the existence of a saddle point, so we need to calculate the eigenvalues associated with a linear approximation to the original equations of the model to determine the stable saddle path and the jump that the forward-looking variable (the level of consumption) has to experience to reach the stable saddle path to the steady state when a shock hits the economy. Both procedures lead to similar results, but while in the first procedure we use an algorithm that is already programmed in Excel, and therefore is a black box method from which we obtain the result to our problem, in the second procedure, we simulate a system of dynamic equations numerically to obtain same results in a direct way.

The structure of the rest of the chapter is as follows. In Section 2, we analytically solve the basic model of dynamic general equilibrium without working decisions, so that the utility function of consumers will only depend on consumption. Section 3 presents the calibration of the model. Section 4 presents the numerical resolution of the model through the Solver tool. Finally, Section 5 presents the numerical resolution of the log-linearized model. In both cases, we will analyze the effects of a technological disturbance that implies an increase in the aggregate productivity of the economy.

8.2. The canonical dynamic general equilibrium model

In this section, we will analytically solve the basic model of dynamic general equilibrium with an exogenous labor supply decision. This is a deterministic version of the RBC (Real Business Cycle) model that has been extensively used in macroeconomic analysis. The model represents an economy composed of two types of economic agents: households and firms. The objective of households is the maximization of their intertemporal utility, which depends only on their level of consumption. From the maximization of this objective function, we obtain the behavior of the representative household, in terms of the consumption-savings decision, as well as the determination of the stock of capital of the economy, since we assume that the saving is equal to the investment. These decisions are taken given the relative price of capital. We assume that the firms operate in a competitive environment with the same technology, and therefore, they are identical. Thus, we analyze the behavior of a representative firm. The objective of this representative firm is to maximize profits. For this purpose, it will decide to rent a certain amount of the productive factor to the representative consumer, who is the owner of the capital stock.

The model includes as an additional variable the Total Factor Productivity (TFP), which represents aggregate productivity of the economy or neutral technological progress in the sense of Hicks. When specifying the model, TFP can be considered as an exogenous variable, and therefore, it would be a constant in the resolution of the model, or we can consider it as an endogenous variable, with the assumption that this variable follows a certain stochastic process. In the first case, we would have a deterministic model, while in the second case, the model would be stochastic. In both cases, a variation in TFP represents a technological disturbance that affects the aggregate productivity of the economy.

8.2.1. Households

The first economic agent populating the economic is the household. To analyze the behavior of the different economic agents, we will use the concept of representative agent. That is, let's assume that all agents are identical in preferences and technologies. This means that we can analyze the behavior of one of them and then add to obtain the aggregate variables. In addition, we have to make a series of assumptions about how those preferences are. The next assumption we make is that the representative agent is an optimizer, that is, it maximizes a certain objective function. In the case of households, the objective function is the utility or instantaneous happiness function. To analyze the behavior of households, we introduce another series of assumptions, which we have already seen in the chapters dedicated to the consumer-savings decision. First, let's consider that the capital markets are perfect. This means that individuals can move money from the future to the present at a cost given by the interest rate, and that there is no liquidity restriction to this movement. This assumption is fundamental for the individual to separate their consumption decisions from their income period by period. On the other hand, we also assume that the utility function is additively separable over time. This means that the utility of a period is only affected by the consumption of that period, but does not depend on the consumption of previous periods (no consumption habits).

The dynamic general equilibrium model that we solve here assumes that the utility function only depends on consumption. In this way, we eliminate the decision regarding the number of hours that individuals will spend working. This implies that the allocation of hours dedicated to work is a constant, such that $L_t = 1$. The consumer problem in this setup is slightly different from those discussed in previous Chapters, in the sense that now the budget constraint include income from physical capital. Thus, we assume that savings are equivalent to investment, which is transformed directly into physical capital at no cost through their accumulation over time, taking into account the physical depreciation suffered by the capital.

The household's maximization problem is given by:

$$\max_{\{C_t\}_{t=0}^{T}} E_t \sum_{t=0}^{T} \beta^t U(C_t) \tag{8.1}$$

where $\beta < 1$ is the intertemporal discount factor, and $E_t(\cdot)$ is the mathematical expectation on future variables. Since we consider a context without uncertainty, that is, with perfect foresight, we can eliminate the expectation operator from the maximization problem, given that the value of all the variables in the future is known at the present time.

Households maximize the weighted sum of their profits subject to the budget constraint. The budget constraint will indicate both the uses and the available resources. The household's resources come from the rent of their endowments of productive factors to the firms. This means that we assume that consumers are the owners of the productive factors of the economy. These productive factors are on the one hand the time, from which the amount of work will be determined. The second productive factor is capital, which is generated through the savings process, that is, the part of production that is not consumed. Given the price of productive factors, consumers will decide how much productive factors (how much capital and how much work) they will rent to companies.

The fact that consumers are the owners of the productive factor implies that they are also the owners of the firms. Since we assume the existence of a competitive environment with a technology that presents constant returns to scale, the benefits of the representative firm are zero. In a non-competitive environment, if the representative firm obtains positive profits, they should be included in the household's budget constraint.

Let's assume that the utility function of the individual has the following form:

$$U(C_t) = \ln(C_t) \tag{8.2}$$

where C_t is the consumption. The restriction facing the economy is given by:

$$C_t + I_t = Y_t \tag{8.3}$$

where I_t is investment and Y_t is final output.[3] The investment is accumulated in the form of physical capital, K_t, from the following process:

$$K_{t+1} = (1 - \delta)K_t + I_t \tag{8.4}$$

where $\delta > 0$ is the rate of physical depreciation of capital, that is, part of the gross investment made in a period has the objective of replacing the capital that depreciates in that period and the rest (net investment) is transformed into new capital in the following period. In reality, the capital is composed of a great variety of asset types that have different characteristics and that, therefore, present different depreciation rates. Thus, we find capital assets that present very low depreciation rates, such as non-residential buildings (structures). However, there are other types of capital assets (equipment) with very high depreciation rates, such as computer programs or computers. Another additional assumption we are making is that we can convert the produced and not consumed units into investment in the economy and, therefore, in physical capital. This means that all the variables of the model are defined in terms of consumption units.

The budget constraint is given by:

$$C_t + I_t = W_t L_t + R_t K_t \tag{8.5}$$

where W_t is the salary per unit of time and R_t is the return on capital. The expression (8.4) implies that the investment can be defined as:

$$I_t = K_{t+1} - (1 - \delta)K_t \tag{8.6}$$

so, in this case, the budget constraint of the individual would be:

$$C_t + K_{t+1} - (1 - \delta)K_t = W_t L_t + R_t K_t \tag{8.7}$$

or equivalently:

$$C_t + K_{t+1} = W_t L_t + (R_t + 1 - \delta)K_t \tag{8.8}$$

Finally, we need to determine the stock of initial capital, K_0, as well as the stock of final capital, K_{T+1}, in the case in which the life cycle of the agents is finite. In the context in which we are going to numerically solve this model, we can consider either a finite life cycle (for the case in which we use the

---

[3] This would be the constraint subject to which the utility of consumers would be maximized in the case of a centralized planning system.

Solver tool in Excel), or an infinite life cycle, for the case in which we compute numerically a linear approximation to the model.

The consumer problem, in this case, would be defined as:

$$\max_{\{C_t\}_{t=0}^{T}} \sum_{t=0}^{T} \beta^t \ln C_t \tag{8.9}$$

$s.t:$

$$C_t + K_{t+1} = W_t L_t + (R_t + 1 - \delta) K_t \tag{8.10}$$

$$K_0 > 0 \tag{8.11}$$

$$K_{T+1} = \overline{K} \tag{8.12}$$

The consumer problem can be solved, for example, through the following auxiliary function of Lagrange:

$$\mathcal{L} = \sum_{t=0}^{T} [\beta^t \ln C_t - \lambda_t (C_t + K_{t+1} - W_t L_t - (R_t + 1 - \delta) K_t)] \tag{8.13}$$

where the agents take as given the relative prices of the productive factors, that is, the salary and the real interest rate.

First-order conditions, for $t = 0, 1, 2, \ldots, T$, are given by:

$$\frac{\partial \mathcal{L}}{\partial C_t} = \beta^t \frac{1}{C_t} - \lambda_t = 0 \tag{8.14}$$

$$\frac{\partial \mathcal{L}}{\partial K_{t+1}} = \lambda_{t+1} [R_{t+1} + 1 - \delta] - \lambda_t = 0 \tag{8.15}$$

$$\frac{\partial \mathcal{L}}{\partial \lambda_t} = C_t + K_{t+1} - (R_t + 1 - \delta) K_t - W_t L_t = 0 \tag{8.16}$$

To obtain the optimal household decision, we have to calculate the value of the Lagrange parameter, which represents the shadow price of consumption, that is, how much the individual values the last unit consumed in each period. To do this, we operate in the first first-order condition (8.14) and replace it in the second first-order condition (8.15).

On the other hand, in the second first-order condition (8.15) both the Lagrange parameter appears in the period t, as in the period $t + 1$. As of the first condition of first order we have obtained that $\lambda_t = \beta^t / C_t$, this supposes that $\lambda_{t+1} = \beta^{t+1} / C_{t+1}$. By substituting, we obtain the condition that equals the marginal ratio of the consumption with that of the investment:

$$C_{t+1} = \beta [R_{t+1} + 1 - \delta] C_t \tag{8.17}$$

This equation is known as the Keynes-Ramsey rule that indicates the optimal consumption path of the individual, also known as the Lucas equation, which indicates what the decision of investment and accumulation of capital in the economy is. As we can see, this dynamic equation for consumption is exactly the same as the one obtained previously, when it was assumed that the utility function of the consumer was also logarithmic.

8.2.2. The firms

The other economic agent that we consider are firms, which represents the productive sector of the economy. The firms constitute the economic agent that is dedicated to the production the goods and services that households will wither consume or save and transform into physical capital. For this, they rent the productive factors (labor and capital) to the households, who are the owners of them. The price of these productive factors is determined by the technology.

We assume that firms maximize profits, subject to the technological restriction. As we are in a competitive environment, this means that the profits of the firms will be zero. Therefore, the factors will be remunerated based on their contribution to the production process. This means that all the income derived from the use of productive factors are equal to their retribution. The other assumptions we make in the case of this agent are in relation to the form of the production function. We assume that there are constant returns to scale, so if the number of factors increases by a certain amount, production increases in that proportion. This means that there are decreasing returns with respect to the capital productive factor and with respect to the productive factor of labor. All these assumptions make the role of companies in these types of models relatively limited, at least in their basic versions. Thus, the firms only decide the amount of productive factors that they rent, taking as given the prices, and given the existing technology, they obtain a certain level of production.

We assume that the function of aggregate production (technology) has the following form:

$$Y_t = A_t F(K_t, L_t) \tag{8.18}$$

where Y_t is the level of aggregate production of the economy and A_t is the total factor productivity (TFP). This production function has to fulfill the same properties: strictly increasing, strictly concave with respect to each factor and twice differentiable. A_t is a variable that represents the state of technology, TFP. TFP is in principle a non-observable variable, but it can be calculated as a residual from the production function.[4] The TFP can be interpreted as the

---

[4] The economic concept of Total Factor Productivity is similar to the concept that represents the cosmological constant in Einstein's Theory of Relativity. Although there is no certainty that such a constant exists, it is representing some unknown force that is necessary to explain the behavior of the Universe. Without such a constant, the Theory of Relativity would not work. Something similar happens with the TFP, there is no theory about it or of what are its determining factors, but is an essential component to

level of general knowledge about the productive arts available to an economy, that is, it would be reflecting a very broad concept of technology. In economic terms, it would be reflecting the aggregate productivity of the economy in the use of all its productive factors.

We assume the TFP is determined exogenously from the following process:

$$A_t = A_{t-1}^{\rho} + \varepsilon_t \tag{8.19}$$

where $\rho < 1$ is an autoregressive parameter that measures the persistence of shocks that affect the TFP, and ε_t is a disturbance term, which we can consider either stochastic and deterministic. In our case, we will consider it as an exogenous deterministic variable, whose value is zero, except at the moment in which a technological shock occurs, taking a value different from zero (positive for a shock that increases aggregate productivity and negative for a shock decreasing aggregate productivity).

The problem solved by the firm consists in maximizing profits, such that:

$$\max \Pi_t = P_t Y_t - W_t L_t - R_t K_t \tag{8.20}$$

subject to the technological restriction given by (8.18). If we assume a competitive environment then it turns out that the optimal benefits are zero, $\Pi_t = 0$. As we can see, the problem for maximizing profits is static, although firms takes their decisions in a dynamic context. In fact, if we solve the problem of profit maximization in a dynamic context, the result we obtain is exactly the same, given the assumptions we are making about the ownership of capital stock.

The first-order conditions of the previous problem are:

$$\frac{\partial \Pi_t}{\partial K_t} : P_t A_t F_K(K_t, L_t) - R_t = 0 \tag{8.21}$$

$$\frac{\partial \Pi_t}{\partial L_t} : P_t A_t F_L(K_t, L_t) - W_t = 0 \tag{8.22}$$

that indicate that the value of the marginal productivity of each productive factor must be equal to its cost. As we can see, the relative price of the factors is equal to their marginal productivity, such that we obtain:

$$A_t F_K(K_t, L_t) = \frac{R_t}{P_t} \tag{8.23}$$

$$A_t F_{KL}(K_t, L_t) = \frac{W_t}{P_t} \tag{8.24}$$

---

explain the level of production of an economy, as an additional element to the amount of productive factors.

The price of the final good is normalized to 1 ($P_t = 1$), such that all the variables are measured in terms of consumption units. Thus, the only prices that appear in the model are those corresponding to the productive factors, with all the variables defined in real terms. In this way, the price of labor would be a real wage and the price of physical capital would be a real interest rate.

Just as we have parameterized the utility function of consumers, we parameterize the technology function. In particular, we assume that the production function is of the Cobb-Douglas type:

$$A_t F_K(K_t, L_t) = A_t K_t^\alpha L_t^{1-\alpha} \tag{8.25}$$

where α is the elasticity of the level of production with respect to capital. This production function is the most used in practice, and implies an that the elasticity of substitution between labor and capital is the unit, and representing an intermediate situation between a Leontief technology, in which it is not possible to substitute one productive factor for another, and a technology with perfect substitutability of the productive factors. In this case, the profits maximization would be given by:

$$\max \Pi_t = A_t K_t^\alpha L_t^{1-\alpha} - W_t L_t - R_t K_t \tag{8.26}$$

By calculating the first-order conditions with respect to capital and labor, we would obtain:

$$\frac{\partial \Pi_t}{\partial K_t}: \alpha A_t K_t^{\alpha-1} L_t^{1-\alpha} - R_t = 0 \tag{8.27}$$

$$\frac{\partial \Pi_t}{\partial L_t}: (1-\alpha) A_t K_t^\alpha L_t^{-\alpha} - W_t = 0 \tag{8.28}$$

or written otherwise:

$$R_t = \frac{\alpha A_t K_t^{\alpha-1} L_t^{1-\alpha}}{K_t} = \alpha \frac{Y_t}{K_t} \tag{8.29}$$

$$W_t = \frac{(1-\alpha) A_t K_t^\alpha L_t^{-\alpha}}{L_t} = (1-\alpha) \frac{Y_t}{L_t} \tag{8.30}$$

so that the income from labor (the labor share) would be a $1 - \alpha$ proportion of the total income and the income from the capital would be a α proportion of the total income.

8.2.3. Equilibrium of the model

Once the behavior of households and firms have been described, next we study the interaction between the two economic agents to determine the macroeconomic equilibrium. Consumers decide how much they will consume, C_t, and how much they will invest, I_t, in order to maximize their level of happiness, taking as given the prices of productive factors. On the other hand, firms will produce a certain amount of goods, Y_t, which is given based on their decision on how much capital, K_t , they will hire given the prices of productive factors.

Therefore, the competitive equilibrium of the economy is composed of the following three blocks of information:

i. A price system for W and R.

ii. A value assignment for Y, C, L and K.

iii. A feasibility restriction, $Y_t = C_t + I_t$, which indicates the possible assignments.

As we can see, the definition of equilibrium we are using implies that all markets in the economy are in equilibrium. Thus, both the labor market and the capital market, as well as the goods market, are in equilibrium. This situation is what we call general equilibrium.

Structure of the basic dynamic general equilibrium model	
Household utility function	$U = U(C_t)$
Budget constraint	$C_t + I_t = W_t L_t + R_t K_t$
Initial capital stock	$K_0 > 0$
Final capital stock	$K_T = \bar{K}$
Equation of capital accumulation	$K_{t+1} = (1 - \delta)K_t + I_t$
Production function	$Y_t = A_t F(K_t, L_t)$
Total Factor Productivity	$A_t = A_{t-1}^\rho + \varepsilon_t$

Definition of competitive equilibrium: A competitive equilibrium for our economy is a sequence of consumption, and investment by consumers, $\{C_t, I_t\}_{t=0}^T$, a sequence of capital and working hours used by firms $\{K_t, L_t\}_{t=0}^T$, and a sequence of prices $\{W_t, R_t\}_{t=0}^T$:

i. The problem of optimizing consumers is satisfied.

ii. First-order conditions for companies are met.

iii. The economy's feasibility constraint is met.

In the model that we are solving, the utility function of consumers only depends on the level of consumption. This means that we have not considered leisure as an argument of the utility function and, therefore, we cannot determine the labor supply (it is given, $L_t = 1$). Competitive equilibrium consists of finding sequences of the $\{C_t, I_t, K_t, R_t, W_t, Y_t, A_t\}_{t=0}^T$ variables such that the conditions that define equilibrium are satisfied. In summary, the model of our economy would be composed of the following seven equations:

$$C_{t+1} = \beta[R_{t+1} + 1 - \delta]C_t \tag{8.31}$$

$$R_t = \alpha \frac{Y_t}{K_t} = \frac{\alpha A_t K_t^\alpha}{K_t} = \alpha A_t K_t^{\alpha-1} \tag{8.32}$$

$$W_t = (1 - \alpha)Y_t = (1 - \alpha)A_t K_t^\alpha \tag{8.33}$$

$$Y_t = A_t K_t^\alpha \tag{8.34}$$

$$K_{t+1} = (1 - \delta)K_t + I_t \tag{8.35}$$

$$C_t + I_t = Y_t \tag{8.36}$$

$$A_t = A_{t-1}^\rho + \varepsilon_t \tag{8.37}$$

8.2.4. The dynamic system

Next, we will reduce the previous system to a system of two dynamic equations, one for consumption and another for the stock of capital, plus the equation that determines the behavior of the TFP. By substituting the expression for the interest rate (8.32) in the dynamic equation of consumption (8.31) we obtain:

$$\frac{C_{t+1}}{C_t} = \beta[\alpha A_{t+1} K_{t+1}^{\alpha-1} + 1 - \delta] \tag{8.38}$$

On the other hand, by substituting the relative price of the productive factors in the budget restriction of the individual, we obtain:

$$C_t + K_{t+1} - (\alpha A_t K_t^{\alpha-1} + 1 - \delta)K_t - (1 - \alpha)A_t K_t^\alpha = 0 \tag{8.39}$$

or equivalently:

$$C_t + K_{t+1} - K_t - \alpha A_t K_t^{\alpha-1} + \delta K_t - A_t K_t^\alpha + \alpha A_t K_t^\alpha = 0 \tag{8.40}$$

and by operating we finally arrive at:

$$C_t + K_{t+1} - (1 - \delta)K_t - A_t K_t^\alpha = 0 \tag{8.41}$$

an expression that indicates the process of capital accumulation over time, in which the capital in the next period is equal to what is produced today, minus what is consumed, plus today's capital minus its depreciation.

Therefore, the competitive solution is determined by two difference equations:

$$C_{t+1} = \beta[\alpha A_{t+1} K_{t+1}^{\alpha-1} + 1 - \delta]C_t \tag{8.42}$$

$$K_{t+1} = (1 - \delta)K_t + A_t K_t^\alpha - C_t \tag{8.43}$$

plus the equation that determines the behavior of the TFP.

Solution of the basic dynamic general equilibrium model
Logarithmic utility and Cobb-Douglas technology

Optimal consumption parth	$C_{t+1} = \beta[\alpha A_{t+1}K_{t+1}^{\alpha-1} + 1 - \delta]C_t$
Capital accumulation	$K_{t+1} = (1 - \delta)K_t + A_t K_t^\alpha - C_t$
TFP	$A_t = A_{t-1}^\rho + \varepsilon_t$

8.2.5. Steady state

Next, we calculate the steady state of the economy. For this, we start from the equation that determines the optimal path of consumption, which is given by:

$$C_{t+1} = \beta[R_{t+1} + 1 - \delta]C_t \tag{8.44}$$

By eliminating the time subscripts for the variables in the optimal consumption path, we obtain that:

$$1 = \beta(\bar{R} + 1 - \delta) \tag{8.45}$$

from which we obtain the steady-state value for the interest rate, such that:

$$\bar{R} = \frac{1-\beta+\beta\delta}{\beta} \tag{8.46}$$

On the other hand, the real interest rate is equal to the marginal productivity of capital, so the equation of the optimal steady-state consumption path can also be defined as:

$$\bar{C} = \beta(\alpha\bar{A}\bar{K}^{\alpha-1} + 1 - \delta)\bar{C} \tag{8.47}$$

By operating, it results that:

$$\beta\left(\alpha\frac{\bar{Y}}{\bar{K}} + 1 - \delta\right) = 1 \tag{8.48}$$

Solving for the steady state of the stock of capital as a function of the level of steady-state production results in:

$$\bar{K} = \frac{\alpha\beta}{1-\beta+\beta\delta}\bar{Y} \tag{8.49}$$

From the equation of capital accumulation in steady state we obtain:

$$\bar{K} = (1 - \delta)\bar{K} + \bar{I} \tag{8.50}$$

so that by operating it results:

$$\bar{I} = \delta\bar{K} \tag{8.51}$$

and using the expression (8.49) so that we can write:

$$\bar{I} = \frac{\alpha\beta\delta}{1-\beta+\beta\delta}\bar{Y} \tag{8.52}$$

In turn, from the economy's feasibility constraint, we obtain that in steady state:

$$\bar{C} = \bar{Y} - \bar{I} = \frac{1-\beta+\beta\delta-\alpha\beta\delta}{1-\beta+\beta\delta} \tag{8.53}$$

Finally, the level of steady-state production is given by:

$$\bar{Y} = \bar{A}\bar{K}^{\alpha} \tag{8.54}$$

so, by using the expression (8.49) we obtain:

$$\bar{Y} = \bar{A}\bar{K}^{\alpha} = \bar{A}^{\frac{1}{1-\alpha}}\left[\frac{\alpha\beta}{(1-\beta+\beta\delta)}\right]^{\frac{\alpha}{1-\alpha}} \tag{8.55}$$

Once obtained the value of the steady-state production, we can now substitute in the previous expressions and obtain the steady-state values for the remaining variables. Thus, if we substitute the expression (8.53) in (8.47), it follows that the value of the stock of capital in steady state is given by:

$$\bar{K} = \frac{\alpha\beta}{1-\beta+\beta\delta}\bar{A}^{\frac{1}{1-\alpha}}\left[\frac{\alpha\beta}{(1-\beta+\beta\delta)}\right]^{\frac{\alpha}{1-\alpha}} = \left(\frac{(1-\beta+\beta\delta)}{\alpha\bar{A}\beta}\right)^{\frac{1}{\alpha-1}} \tag{8.56}$$

Alternatively, the steady-state capital stock can be calculated as:

$$\bar{R} = \frac{1}{\beta} - 1 + \delta = \frac{1-\beta+\beta\delta}{\beta} \tag{8.57}$$

On the other hand, from the first-order condition of the company regarding the stock of capital we have to:

$$\alpha\bar{A}\bar{K}^{\alpha-1} = \bar{R} = \frac{1-\beta+\beta\delta}{\beta} \tag{8.58}$$

Solving for the steady-state capital stock results in:

$$\bar{K} = \left(\frac{1-\beta+\beta\delta}{\alpha\bar{A}\beta}\right)^{\frac{1}{\alpha-1}} \tag{8.59}$$

Finally, the steady-state value of the TFP is equal to 1 ($\bar{A} = 1$), since in the steady state we assume that $\varepsilon_t = 0$ and therefore:

$$\bar{A} = \bar{A}^{\rho} = 1 \tag{8.60}$$

8.3. Calibration of the model

Next, we proceed to calibrate the value of the parameters and the value of the exogenous variables of the model. The value of these parameters can be estimated or obtained through a calibration process using the information available about them. In this simple model, we only have four parameters: The technological parameter of the production function, α, the discount factor of future utility, β, the rate of depreciation of capital, δ, and the parameter that determines the persistence of aggregate productivity, ρ. In addition, the model includes a variable of exogenous disturbance, which can be considered as stochastic or deterministic, and which affects the total productivity of the factors, representing a technological shock, ε_t. In our case, we will consider as deterministic this exogenous variable, taking a value of zero, except at the moment in which the disturbance occurs, which will take a positive or negative value, representing a technological change that increases or decreases the aggregate productivity. This implies we would be considering that TFP, A_t, as an endogenous variable.

The parameter value α can be calibrated directly from national accounting. Given the production function that we are using (Cobb-Douglas), this parameter reflects the proportion of capital income over total income, while $(1 - \alpha)$ reflects wage income over total income. Considering the information offered by national accounting, approximately 65% of the total income corresponds to salary income, while the remaining 35% corresponds to capital income. Therefore, we set a value of $\alpha = 0.35$. The discount factor takes a value less than one, depending on the degree of patience of the agent with respect to the future, and its value corresponds to a certain interest rate in steady state. The value that we are going to use for this discount factor is 0.96, taking as reference an annual period. The physical depreciation rate of the capital we are going to assume is 6% per year. The parameter of persistence of the technological shocks we assume is equal to 0.80. Finally, let's suppose that the variable that represents the technological disturbance, ε_t, takes the value zero, except at the moment in which this disturbance occurs, which we assume takes a value of 0.01.

Table 8.1: Calibration of the parameters

Symbol	Definition	Value
α	Production-capital elasticity	0.35
β	Discount factor	0.96
δ	Capital depreciation rate	0.06
ρ	Persistence parameter of TFP	0.80

Table 8.2 shows the steady-state values for the model variables, using the expressions calculated above and the values calibrated for the parameters. In effect, if we calculate the steady-state value for the capital stock, it results:

$$\bar{K} = \left(\frac{1-\beta+\beta\delta}{\alpha\bar{A}\beta}\right)^{\frac{1}{\alpha-1}} = \left(\frac{1-0.96+0.96\times0.96}{0.35\times1\times0.96}\right)^{\frac{1}{0.65}} = 6.70$$

From this value, we can calculate the production level in steady state as:

$$\bar{Y} = \bar{A}\bar{K}^{\alpha} = 1 \times 6.70^{0.35} = 1.95$$

The steady-state consumption can be calculated using the expression:

$$\bar{C} = \frac{1 - \beta + \beta\delta - \alpha\beta\delta}{1 - \beta + \beta\delta}\bar{Y} =$$

$$\frac{1 - 0.96 + 0.96 \times 0.06 - 035 \times 0.96 \times 0.06}{1 - 0.96 + 0.96 \times 0.06} \times 1.95 = 1.544$$

Alternatively, we can first calculate the investment as:

$$\bar{I} = \delta\bar{K} = 0.06 \times 6.70 = 0.402$$

and the consumption would be:

$$\bar{C} = \bar{Y} - \bar{I} = 1.95 - 0.402 = 1.544$$

Finally, the interest rate (equivalent to the marginal productivity of capital) in steady state would be:

$$\bar{R} = \alpha\bar{A}\bar{K}^{\alpha-1} = \frac{1 - \beta + \beta\delta}{\beta} = \frac{1 - 0.96 + 0.96 \times 0.06}{0.96} = 0.102$$

Table 8.2: Value of steady-state variables

Variable	Definition	Value
$\bar{Y}$	Production	1.946
$\bar{C}$	Consumption	1.544
$\bar{I}$	Investment	0.402
$\bar{K}$	Physical capital stock	6.699
$\bar{R}$	Interest rate	0.102

8.4. Numerical solution with Solver

Once the model has been solved analytically and the corresponding dynamic system has been obtained, then we will solve it computationally in Excel using the "Solver" tool. In Appendix M, we present the code to solve this model in MATLAB. Figure 8.1 shows the structure of the Excel sheet where we have solved this problem, called "**ICM-8-1.xls**". As we can see, we need to define first the value of the parameters of the model, which appear in cells "B4" to "B7". From these parameters and the steady-state expressions calculated above, we can obtain the steady-state values for the model variables, which appear in cells "B10" to "B15". If we place the cursor in cell "B10", the expression that appears is:

=PTF*((1-Beta+Delta*Beta)/(Alpha*PTF*Beta))^(Alpha/(Alpha-1))

which is the one corresponding to the value of the steady-state production. Similarly, in cell "B12" we have introduced the expression corresponding to the steady-state value of the stock of capital, so the expression that appears in said cell is:

=((1-Beta+Delta*Beta)/(Alpha*PTF*Beta))^(1/(Alpha-1))

A		B	C	D	E	F	G	H	I	J	K
1	EXERCISE 8.1: Dynamic General Equilibrium model										
2				Time	TFP	Consumption	Investment	Output	Capital	R	Utility
3	*Parameters*			0	1.00000	1.544	0.402	1.946	6.699	0.102	0.434
4	Beta	0.96		1	1.00000	1.544	0.402	1.946	6.699	0.102	0.417
5	Alpha	0.35		2	1.00000	1.544	0.402	1.946	6.699	0.102	0.400
6	Delta	0.06		3	1.00000	1.544	0.402	1.946	6.699	0.102	0.384
7	Rho	0.80		4	1.00000	1.544	0.402	1.946	6.699	0.102	0.369
8				5	1.00000	1.544	0.402	1.946	6.699	0.102	0.354
9	*Steady State*			6	1.00000	1.544	0.402	1.946	6.699	0.102	0.340
10	Output	1.946		7	1.00000	1.544	0.402	1.946	6.699	0.102	0.326
11	Total Factor Productivity	1.000		8	1.00000	1.544	0.402	1.946	6.699	0.102	0.313
12	Capital Stock	6.699		9	1.00000	1.544	0.402	1.946	6.699	0.102	0.301
13	Consumption	1.544		10	1.00000	1.544	0.402	1.946	6.699	0.102	0.289
14	Investment	0.402		11	1.00000	1.544	0.402	1.946	6.699	0.102	0.277
15	Interest rate	0.102		12	1.00000	1.544	0.402	1.946	6.699	0.102	0.266
16				13	1.00000	1.544	0.402	1.946	6.699	0.102	0.255
17	*Technological shock*			14	1.00000	1.544	0.402	1.946	6.699	0.102	0.245
18	Epsilon	0		15	1.00000	1.544	0.402	1.946	6.699	0.102	0.235
19				16	1.00000	1.544	0.402	1.946	6.699	0.102	0.226
20				17	1.00000	1.544	0.402	1.946	6.698	0.102	0.217
21				18	1.00000	1.544	0.402	1.946	6.698	0.102	0.208
22				19	1.00000	1.544	0.402	1.946	6.698	0.102	0.200
23				20	1.00000	1.544	0.402	1.946	6.698	0.102	0.192
24				21	1.00000	1.544	0.402	1.946	6.698	0.102	0.184
25				22	1.00000	1.544	0.402	1.946	6.699	0.102	0.177
26				23	1.00000	1.544	0.402	1.946	6.699	0.102	0.170
27				24	1.00000	1.544	0.402	1.946	6.699	0.102	0.163
28				25	1.00000	1.544	0.402	1.946	6.699	0.102	0.157
29				26	1.00000	1.544	0.402	1.946	6.699	0.102	0.150
30				27	1.00000	1.544	0.402	1.946	6.699	0.102	0.144
31				28	1.00000	1.544	0.402	1.946	6.699	0.102	0.138
32				29	1.00000	1.544	0.402	1.946	6.699	0.102	0.133
33				30	1.00000	1.544	0.402	1.946	6.699	0.102	0.128
34				Total					6.699		7.794

Figure 8.1. Structure of the spreadsheet "ICM-8.1.xls". Solving the Dynamic General Equilibrium model with Solver.

Similarly, in cell "B13" we calculate the steady-state value of the consumption, in cell "B14" the steady-state value of the investment and in cell "B15" the steady-state value of the interest rate. Finally, in cell "B18", we assign the value of the technological change that we assume occurs in period 1, taking a zero value initially.

The variables of the model are defined in the columns "D-K", where the values corresponding to the initial steady state appear in the period 0. The column "D" is the time index, the column "E" is the TFP, while the column "F" gives us the optimal path of consumption, which is the variable that we have to calculate. Column "G" is the investment, which is simply the difference between what is produced and what is consumed, column "H" is production, column "I" is the stock of capital, column "J" is the return on capital and finally the "K" column is the discounted utility. In cell "E4", the expression

=E3^Rho+Epsilon

appears with the objective of simulating a productivity shock in period 1. In cell "E5" the introduced expression is "=E4^Rho", since we assume that the shock takes a positive or negative value at time 1 and zero in the following periods. This expression is copied to the following cells in the column.

In cell "I3", the initial capital stock appears. For its part, in cell "I4" appears the expression:

=(1-Delta)*I3+G3

where the stock of capital in each period of time is the stock of capital of the previous period, discounting the depreciation, plus the new capital that is incorporated, which is determined by savings. Finally, column "K" presents the value of the utility in discounted terms.

The sum of the discounted utilities is calculated in cell "K34", which will be the target cell to be maximized in the "Solver" tool. The solution to the problem is obtained by executing the "Solver", once we have defined the target cell to be maximized (the "K34"), the final condition ("$I$34=K0"), and the cells to change with the solution ("$F$4:$F$33"), similar to how it has been carried out in the previous chapters.

As we can now see, the optimal path of consumption that we obtain is completely horizontal, indicating that the consumption is the same period to period. This is because we are calculating its steady-state value, and in steady state the variables are constant period to period. In the previous exercises in which the optimal consumption path was calculated, the slope of the same depended on the relationship between the discount factor and the interest rate, which was assumed exogenous. However, in this general equilibrium model, the interest rate is an endogenous variable, and its equilibrium value is such that, given a discount factor, it makes the rest of the variables constant, so the optimal path of the resulting consumption is horizontal. In fact, we can verify that in a steady state, given a value of $\beta = 0.96$, corresponding to an intertemporal subjective rate of $\theta = 0.042$, the steady-state value of the interest rate is 10.2% per period. Discounting the physical depreciation rate of capital, which is 6% per period, it turns out that the net return of capital is

0.102 − 0.06 = 0.042, which is exactly equal to the value of the subjective rate of intertemporal preference.

8.4.1. Shock analysis: Neutral technological shock

Once the model is solved, we will now study the impact of a disturbance consisting of a temporary positive technological shock that increases the total productivity of the factors. This is a typical exercise that is carried out within the framework of the analysis of real cycles (Real Business Cycles) and which consists in studying how the economy reacts to a technological shock that increases the Total Factor Productivity in a transitory way. To do this, we will assume that in period 1, the exogenous variable ε_t takes a value of 0.01 ($\varepsilon_1 = 0.01$). Therefore, we would include this new value in cell "B18" and execute the "Solver" to obtain the new solution of the model. Figure 8.2 shows the results obtained in terms of the dynamics (impulse-response functions) that the different variables will follow until reaching the steady state, which is the same as we had initially, given the assumption that the effects of this technological shock are transient. In these figures, we have represented the variation of each variable with respect to its steady-state value. As we can see, the increase in the total productivity of the factors causes an instantaneous increase in the level of production, consumption and investment. Given the initial endowment of productive factors, production is now higher. When obtaining a higher level of production, the consumer allocates these greater resources both to increase their level of consumption and their level of investment, since the increase in TFP entails an increase in the price of productive factors (in this case, an increase in the profitability of capital). This higher level of investment, in turn, leads to an increase in the stock of capital, which also positively contributes to increasing the level of production.

The persistence in the response of production comes both from the persistence of the shock itself, and from the increase in the stock of capital. In Figure 8.2, we have represented the dynamics of the TFP, which shows some persistence, depending on the value of the parameter ρ. This persistence of the shock is transferred to a persistent response of the rest of the macroeconomic variables. The response of consumption show a hump-shaped response, increasing progressively during the first periods, given that fewer resources are allocated to investment. However, after a certain period, the return of production to its steady-state value also causes consumption to decrease once capital is no longer accumulated. Therefore, we observe two sources of increase in production. The first as a result of the higher level of aggregate productivity and the second as a consequence of the increase in the stock of capital.

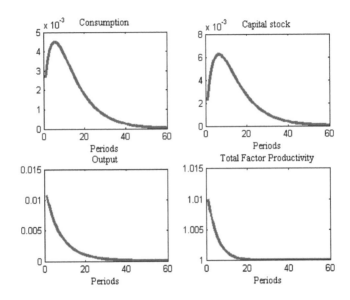

Figure 8.2. Impulse-response function to a transitory Total Factor Productivity shock.

8.5. Numerical solution of the log-linear model

In this section, we will repeat the analysis, but using the alternative approach that we have previously used to solve Tobin's Q model. To do this, we will obtain a dynamic system with two equations in linear differences, an approximation of the original non-linear equations of the model, and we will simply simulate them numerically in the spreadsheet. The solution of this dynamic linear system is a saddle-point, so it is necessary to calculate the position of the stable saddle path corresponding to the steady state. To do this, we need to previously calculate the value of the eigenvalues, a procedure that is simple when the dynamic system is linear. The only drawback associated with this method is that we have to use certain algebraic operations that can be very tedious to obtain the linear approximation of the model. To obtain the log-linearization of our system of equations, we will express the variables of the model as the logarithmic deviation with respect to its steady-state values. We will define the deviation in logarithmic terms of a variable, x_t, with respect to its value of steady state, $\bar{x}_t$, as $\hat{x}_t$, where $\hat{x}_t = \ln x_t - \ln \bar{x}_t$. To construct the equations in log-linear form, we are going to follow the three basic rules, which we have indicated in the previous chapter.

8.5.1. Log-linearization of the model

In this section, we will log-linearize the basic model of dynamic general equilibrium, to be able to solve it directly in a spreadsheet without using the "Solver" tool. The idea is to obtain a system of equations in linear differences, one for consumption and another for the stock of capital, in terms of its deviations from the steady state. The stock of capital is a state variable, whose value today was already determined in the previous period (that is why it is also called the default variable), while consumption is a variable of advanced control on which we must apply expectations, and which will change instantaneously in the face of a disturbance such that it reaches the stable path. For this, we apply the same procedure that we used in the previous chapter when log-linearizing Tobin's Q model.

Log-linearization of the production function

We will start by obtaining a linear approximation to the production function since we will need it later. The production function that we are using, given that we have normalized to 1 the level of employment, is:

$$Y_t = A_t K_t^\alpha \tag{8.61}$$

For the analysis to be as simple as possible, we assume that the Total Factor Productivity is an exogenous variable (and therefore, we assume that it is a constant). Therefore, next we will assume that the value of the TFP is a constant that we define by $\bar{A}$. By applying the first of the rules described above to the left side of the production function, it turns out that:

$$Y_t \approx \bar{Y}(1 + \hat{y}_t) \tag{8.62}$$

On the other hand, by applying the third rule to the right side of the production function, it turns out that:

$$A_t K_t^\alpha \approx \bar{A}\bar{K}^\alpha\left(1 + \hat{k}_t\right)^\alpha \approx \bar{A}\bar{K}^\alpha(1 + \alpha\hat{k}_t) \tag{8.63}$$

Therefore, the log-linearized equation for the production level is:

$$\bar{Y}(1 + \hat{y}_t) = \bar{A}\bar{K}^\alpha(1 + \alpha\hat{k}_t) \tag{8.64}$$

and operating:

$$\bar{Y} + \bar{Y}\hat{y}_t = \bar{A}\bar{K}^\alpha + \bar{A}\bar{K}^\alpha\alpha\hat{k}_t \tag{8.65}$$

By using the production function in steady state and canceling terms, it results:

$$\bar{Y}\hat{y}_t = \bar{A}\bar{K}^\alpha\alpha\hat{k}_t \tag{8.66}$$

Thus, it follows that the linear approximation to the non-linear production function (in terms of deviations from the steady state) is given by:

$$\hat{y}_t = \alpha\hat{k}_t \tag{8.67}$$

Log-linearization of the dynamic equation for the capital stock

Next, we proceed to log-linearize the dynamic equation for the capital stock, which is given by:

$$C_t + K_{t+1} - (1 - \delta)K_t = Y_t \tag{8.68}$$

By applying the rules described above, we obtain:

$$\bar{C}(1 + \hat{c}_t) + \bar{K}(1 + \hat{k}_{t+1}) - (1 - \delta)\bar{K}(1 + \hat{k}_t) = \bar{Y}(1 + \hat{y}_t) \tag{8.69}$$

For its part, this equation in steady state is given by:

$$\bar{C} + \bar{K} - (1 - \delta)\bar{K} = \bar{Y} \tag{8.70}$$

By operating, it turns out that,

$$\bar{C}\hat{c}_t + \bar{K}\hat{k}_{t+1} - (1 - \delta)\bar{K}\hat{k}_t = \bar{Y}\hat{y}_t \tag{8.71}$$

resulting in:

$$\frac{\bar{C}}{\bar{K}}\hat{c}_t + \hat{k}_{t+1} - (1 - \delta)\hat{k}_t = \frac{\bar{Y}}{\bar{K}}\hat{y}_t \tag{8.72}$$

To continue with the linearization, we need to obtain the value of the steady-state ratios that appear in the previous expression. These steady-state ratios are:

$$\frac{\bar{C}}{\bar{K}} = \frac{\frac{1-\beta+\beta\delta-\alpha\beta\delta}{(1-\beta+\beta\delta)}\bar{Y}}{\frac{\alpha\beta}{(1-\beta+\beta\delta)}\bar{Y}} = \frac{1-\beta+\beta\delta-\alpha\beta\delta}{\alpha\beta}$$

$$\frac{\bar{Y}}{\bar{K}} = \frac{\bar{Y}}{\frac{\alpha\beta}{(1-\beta+\beta\delta)}\bar{Y}} = \frac{(1-\beta+\beta\delta)}{\alpha\beta}$$

Substituting the steady-state ratios results in:

$$\frac{1-\beta+\beta\delta-\alpha\beta\delta}{\alpha\beta}\hat{c}_t + \hat{k}_{t+1} - (1 - \delta)\hat{k}_t = \frac{(1-\beta+\beta\delta)}{\alpha\beta}\hat{y}_t \tag{8.73}$$

Substituting the deviation of the production level from its steady-state value obtained previously ($\hat{y}_t = \alpha\hat{k}_t$) results in:

$$\frac{1-\beta+\beta\delta-\alpha\beta\delta}{\alpha\beta}\hat{c}_t + \hat{k}_{t+1} = (1 - \delta)\hat{k}_t + \frac{(1-\beta+\beta\delta)}{\alpha\beta}\hat{k}_t \tag{8.74}$$

Finally, by defining $\Delta\hat{k}_t = \hat{k}_{t+1} - \hat{k}_t$, we arrive at the following difference equation for the stock of capital:

$$\Delta\hat{k}_t = -\left[\frac{1-\beta+\beta\delta-\alpha\beta\delta}{\alpha\beta}\right]\hat{c}_t + \left[\frac{1-\beta}{\beta}\right]\hat{k}_t \tag{8.75}$$

Log-linearization of the dynamic equation of consumption

Next, we will proceed to log-linearize the dynamic equation of consumption. The starting equation is:

$$\frac{C_{t+1}}{C_t} = \beta \left(\alpha \frac{Y_{t+1}}{K_{t+1}} + 1 - \delta \right) \tag{8.76}$$

By applying the rules described above, we obtain:

$$\frac{\bar{C}}{\bar{C}}(1 + \hat{c}_{t+1} - \hat{c}_t) = \alpha \beta \frac{\bar{Y}}{\bar{K}}(1 + \hat{y}_{t+1} - \hat{k}_{t+1}) + \beta(1 - \delta) \tag{8.77}$$

By operating results that,

$$1 + \hat{c}_{t+1} - \hat{c}_t = \alpha \beta \frac{\bar{Y}}{\bar{K}}(\hat{y}_{t+1} - \hat{k}_{t+1}) + \alpha \beta \frac{\bar{Y}}{\bar{K}} + \beta(1 - \delta) \tag{8.78}$$

From the definition of steady state, we obtain that:

$$\frac{\bar{Y}}{\bar{K}} = \frac{1 - \beta + \beta \delta}{\alpha \beta} \tag{8.79}$$

By substituting the previous expression, it turns out that:

$$1 + \hat{c}_{t+1} - \hat{c}_t = (1 - \beta + \beta\delta)(\hat{y}_{t+1} - \hat{k}_{t+1}) + (1 - \beta + \beta\delta) + \beta(1 - \delta) \tag{8.80}$$

and operating results in:

$$\hat{c}_{t+1} - \hat{c}_t = (1 - \beta + \beta\delta)(\hat{y}_{t+1} - \hat{k}_{t+1}) \tag{8.81}$$

By using the linear approximation for the production level obtained previously ($\hat{y}_{t+1} = \alpha \hat{k}_{t+1}$) and substituting, we obtain:

$$\hat{c}_{t+1} - \hat{c}_t = (1 - \beta + \beta\delta)(\alpha - 1)\hat{k}_{t+1} \tag{8.82}$$

On the other hand, from the expression (8.74) obtained previously it, results that:

$$\hat{k}_{t+1} = \frac{1}{\beta} \hat{k}_t - \frac{1 - \beta + \beta\delta - \alpha\beta\delta}{\alpha\beta} \hat{c}_t \tag{8.83}$$

By substituting in the previous expression, we obtain that:

$$\hat{c}_{t+1} - \hat{c}_t = (1 - \beta + \beta\delta)(\alpha - 1)\left(\frac{1}{\beta} \hat{k}_t - \frac{1 - \beta + \beta\delta - \alpha\beta\delta}{\alpha\beta} \hat{c}_t \right) \tag{8.84}$$

Defining $\Delta \hat{c}_t = \hat{c}_{t+1} - \hat{c}_t$, we can write it as:

$$\Delta \hat{c}_t = \frac{(1 - \beta + \beta\delta)(\alpha - 1)}{\beta} \hat{k}_t - \frac{(1 - \beta + \beta\delta)(\alpha - 1)(1 - \beta + \beta\delta)}{\alpha\beta} \hat{c}_t \tag{8.85}$$

where the variations in consumption depend negatively on the deviations of the stock of capital with respect to its steady state (the coefficient that multiplies the deviations of the stock of capital is negative) and positively of the deviations of consumption with respect to the steady state (given that the associated coefficient is positive).

Log-linearization of the investment equation

Finally, the log-linear equation for the investment (although this equation does not need it) is given by:

$$I_t = Y_t - C_t \qquad (8.86)$$

so, applying the rules of log-linearization results in:

$$\bar{I}(1 + \hat{i}_t) = \bar{Y}(1 + \hat{y}_t) - \bar{C}(1 + \hat{c}_t) \qquad (8.87)$$

or equivalently,

$$\bar{I} + \bar{I}\hat{i}_t = \bar{Y} + \bar{Y}\hat{y}_t - \bar{C} - \bar{C}\hat{c}_t \qquad (8.88)$$

In steady state, it turns out that:

$$\bar{I} = \bar{Y} - \bar{C} \qquad (8.89)$$

so, the above expression can be simplified to:

$$\bar{I}\hat{i}_t = \bar{Y}\hat{y}_t - \bar{C}\hat{c}_t \qquad (8.90)$$

and clearing the deviations of the investment with respect to its value of steady state results in:

$$\hat{i}_t = \frac{\bar{Y}}{\bar{I}}\hat{y}_t - \frac{\bar{C}}{\bar{I}}\hat{c}_t \qquad (8.91)$$

By using the steady-state definitions, it turns out that:

$$\frac{\bar{Y}}{\bar{I}} = \frac{1 - \beta + \beta\delta}{\alpha\beta\delta} \qquad (8.92)$$

and:

$$\frac{\bar{C}}{\bar{I}} = \frac{1 - \beta + \beta\delta - \alpha\beta\delta}{\alpha\beta\delta} \qquad (8.93)$$

By substituting, we arrive at that:

$$\hat{i}_t = \frac{1 - \beta + \beta\delta}{\alpha\beta\delta}\hat{y}_t - \frac{1 - \beta + \beta\delta - \alpha\beta\delta}{\alpha\beta\delta}\hat{c}_t \qquad (8.94)$$

Discrete log-linearized system

Therefore, the dynamic general equilibrium model can be defined as a linear dynamic system in terms of the deviations of consumption and the stock of capital from its steady state. To simplify our analysis, we group parameters such that:

$$\Omega = 1 - \beta + \beta\delta \qquad (8.95)$$

$$\Phi = 1 - \beta + (1 - \alpha)\beta\delta \qquad (8.96)$$

Therefore, the log-linearized system in terms of deviations from the steady state remains, in matrix notation, as:

$$\begin{bmatrix} \Delta \hat{c}_t \\ \Delta \hat{k}_t \end{bmatrix} = \begin{bmatrix} -\dfrac{(\alpha-1)\Omega\Phi}{\alpha\beta} & \dfrac{(\alpha-1)\Omega}{\beta} \\ -\dfrac{\Phi}{\alpha\beta} & \dfrac{(1-\beta)}{\beta} \end{bmatrix} \begin{bmatrix} \hat{c}_t \\ \hat{k}_t \end{bmatrix} \tag{8.97}$$

In Appendix N, we present the equivalent system (in normal form) corresponding to the stochastic version of the model. Substituting the calibrated values results in:

$$\Omega = 1 - 0.96 + 0.96 \times 0.06 = 0.0976$$

$$\Phi = 1 - 0.96 + 0.65 \times 0.96 \times 0.06 = 0.07744$$

By substituting the calibrated values of the parameters, the dynamic system results in:

$$\begin{bmatrix} \Delta \hat{c}_t \\ \Delta \hat{k}_t \end{bmatrix} = \begin{bmatrix} 0.0146 & -0.066 \\ -0.2305 & 0.0417 \end{bmatrix} \begin{bmatrix} \hat{c}_t \\ \hat{k}_t \end{bmatrix}$$

8.5.2. Stability analysis

Once we have the model in log-linear terms, we can proceed to analyze its stability and obtain the eigenvalues associated with it. As we can see, we have transformed a system of non-linear dynamic equations into a linear dynamic system, in terms of the deviations (in logarithmic terms, that is, in percentage) of each variable with respect to the steady state. For this, we calculate:

$$Det \begin{bmatrix} -\dfrac{(\alpha-1)\Omega\Phi}{\alpha\beta} - \lambda & \dfrac{(\alpha-1)\Omega}{\beta} \\ -\dfrac{\Phi}{\alpha\beta} & \dfrac{(1-\beta)}{\beta} - \lambda \end{bmatrix} = 0 \tag{8.98}$$

From the previous system, we obtain the following equation of the second degree:

$$\lambda^2 + \left(\frac{(\alpha-1)\Omega\Phi}{\alpha\beta} - \frac{(1-\beta)}{\beta}\right)\lambda - \left(\frac{(1-\beta)}{\beta}\right)\left(\frac{(\alpha-1)\Omega\Phi}{\alpha\beta}\right) + \left(\frac{(\alpha-1)\Omega}{\beta}\right)\left(\frac{\Phi}{\alpha\beta}\right) = 0 \tag{8.99}$$

or equivalently:

$$\lambda^2 + \left(\frac{(\alpha-1)\Omega\Phi-\alpha(1-\beta)}{\alpha\beta}\right)\lambda + \frac{(\alpha-1)\Omega\Phi}{\alpha\beta} = 0 \tag{8.100}$$

By resolving, we obtain the following roots:

$$\lambda_1, \lambda_2 = \frac{-\frac{(\alpha-1)\Omega\Phi-\alpha(1-\beta)}{\alpha\beta} \pm \sqrt{\left(\frac{(\alpha-1)\Omega\Phi-\alpha(1-\beta)}{\alpha\beta}\right)^2 - 4\frac{(\alpha-1)\Omega\Phi}{\alpha\beta}}}{2} \tag{8.101}$$

being a positive root and the other negative. In effect, by substituting the values of the parameters, we obtain that:

$$\lambda_1 = \frac{0.0.56 - \sqrt{0.056^2 + 0.0585}}{2} = -0.096$$

$$\lambda_2 = \frac{0.0.56 + \sqrt{0.056^2 + 0.0585}}{2} = 0.1523$$

If we calculate the root module plus the unit, we obtain 0.91 for the first and 1.16 for the second, so the solution is a saddle point.

8.5.3. Stable saddle path

The existence of a saddle point causes the existence of a single stable path that determines the dynamics of adjustment of the economy to the steady state. As we have seen previously, in this case, there is a jump in the forward-looking variable (consumption) in the face of a disturbance, which directly leads the economy to this stable saddle path, determining the adjustment in the short term. From that initial adjustment, the economy moves along this stable saddle path, in a process of gradual adjustment (depending on the speed of adjustment of the rest of the variables), until reaching the steady state.

Once we have calculated the eigenvalues, defining λ_1 as the own value that fulfills that $|\lambda_1 + 1| < 1$, the system can be written as:

$$\begin{bmatrix} \Delta \hat{c}_t \\ \Delta \hat{k}_t \end{bmatrix} = \lambda_1 \begin{bmatrix} \hat{c}_t \\ \hat{k}_t \end{bmatrix} \tag{8.102}$$

from which we obtain the mathematical trajectories for both variables that lead us to the steady state.

8.5.4. Instant readjustment in the level of consumption

To compute the model, we need to calculate the short-term effect, that is, the variation in consumption (which is the "jumping" variable) just at the moment when a disturbance occurs. As we have seen in theoretical terms, when a disturbance occurs, the consumption is adjusted immediately until reaching the stable saddle path.

The dynamic equation obtained previously for consumption is:

$$\Delta \hat{c}_t = -\frac{(\alpha-1)\Omega\Phi}{\alpha\beta} \hat{c}_t + \frac{(\alpha-1)\Omega}{\beta} \hat{k}_t \tag{8.103}$$

On the other hand, the stable path is defined by the trajectory:

$$\Delta \hat{c}_t = \lambda_1 \hat{c}_t \tag{8.104}$$

Matching both expressions results in:

$$-\frac{(\alpha-1)\Omega\Phi}{\alpha\beta}\hat{c}_t + \frac{(\alpha-1)\Omega}{\beta}\hat{k}_t = \lambda_1\hat{c}_t \qquad (8.105)$$

By operating, we obtain the value that consumption has to take (in terms of deviations from the steady state) so that it is located in the stable saddle path and is given by:

$$\hat{c}_t = \frac{\alpha(\alpha-1)\Omega}{(\alpha-1)\Omega\Phi+\alpha\beta\lambda_1}\hat{k}_t \qquad (8.106)$$

an expression that is equivalent to the variation that has to be experienced at the time of the disturbance, since the initial deviation is zero (steady state).

8.5.5. Numerical solution of the linear approximation

The numerical resolution of the log-linearized model corresponds to the spreadsheet "**ICM-8-2.xls**". In Appendix M, we show the code to solve this same exercise using DYNARE. The structure of the spreadsheet is shown in Figure 8.3. First, we define the parameters of the model. In this exercise, we will use the same parameters as in the previous exercise – the intertemporal discount factor, the elasticity of production with respect to the stock of capital and the rate of depreciation of capital. We also calculate two parameters that are a combination of the previous ones to simplify the used expressions. The corresponding values appear in cells "B14" to "B18". In column "C", these values are reproduced, in order to perform a sensitivity analysis and study the implications of changes in the values of these parameters. Below, we present the steady-state values, rows 21 to 25, which are the same as those obtained in the previous exercise. In column "B", the steady-state values are presented with the initial values, while in column "C", these values are presented with the final values. Given that in this exercise we have considered TFP as an exogenous variable, we have introduced its initial value in cell "B25". If we want to introduce a new value to simulate a permanent technological disturbance, we would do so by changing the corresponding value in cell "C25".

Rows 28 and 29 calculate the eigenvalues associated with the dynamic system, in column "B" for the initial steady state and in column "C" for the final steady state. Given the restrictions on the parameters, the roots are going to be real, so the calculation of the imaginary part is not necessary. If we place the cursor in cell "B28", the expression that appears is:

=((-((Alpha_0-1)*OMEGA_0*PHI_0-Alpha_0*(1-Beta_0)))/(Alpha_0*Beta_0)

-ROOT((((Alpha_0-1)*OMEGA_0*PHI_0-Alpha_0*(1-
Beta_0))/(Alpha_0*Beta_0))^2

-4*((Alpha_0-1)*OMEGA_0*PHI_0)/(Alpha_0*Beta_0)))/2

which corresponds to the equation (8.101), for the first root, while in cell "B29", the equivalent expression for the other root appears. In rows 32 and 33, the module of each root plus the unit is calculated.

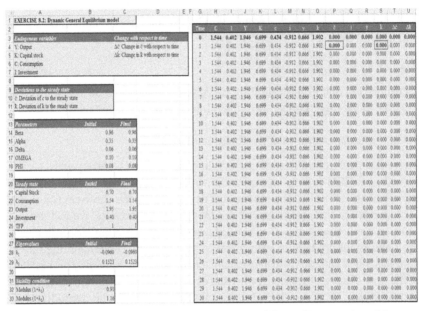

	A	B	C	D	E F	G	H	I	J	K	L	M	N	O	P	Q	R	S	T	U
1	EXERCISE 8.2: Dynamic General Equilibrium model																			
2						Time	C	i	Y	K	c	i	y	k	ê	î	ŷ	k̂	Δc	Δk
3	*Endogenous variables*		Change with respect to time			0	1.544	0.402	1.946	6.699	0.434	-0.912	0.666	1.902	0.000	0.000	0.000	0.000	0.000	0.000
4	Y. Output		Δĉ Change in ĉ with respect to time			1	1.544	0.402	1.946	6.699	0.434	-0.912	0.666	1.902	0.000	0.000	0.000	0.000	0.000	0.000
5	K. Capital stock		Δk̂ Change in k̂ with respect to time			2	1.544	0.402	1.946	6.699	0.434	-0.912	0.666	1.902	0.000	0.000	0.000	0.000	0.000	0.000
6	C. Consumption					3	1.544	0.402	1.946	6.699	0.434	-0.912	0.666	1.902	0.000	0.000	0.000	0.000	0.000	0.000
7	I. Investment					4	1.544	0.402	1.946	6.699	0.434	-0.912	0.666	1.902	0.000	0.000	0.000	0.000	0.000	0.000
8						5	1.544	0.402	1.946	6.699	0.434	-0.912	0.666	1.902	0.000	0.000	0.000	0.000	0.000	0.000
9	*Deviations to the steady state*					6	1.544	0.402	1.946	6.699	0.434	-0.912	0.666	1.902	0.000	0.000	0.000	0.000	0.000	0.000
10	ĉ Deviation of c to the steady state					7	1.544	0.402	1.946	6.699	0.434	-0.912	0.666	1.902	0.000	0.000	0.000	0.000	0.000	0.000
11	k̂ Deviation of k to the steady state					8	1.544	0.402	1.946	6.699	0.434	-0.912	0.666	1.902	0.000	0.000	0.000	0.000	0.000	0.000
12						9	1.544	0.402	1.946	6.699	0.434	-0.912	0.666	1.902	0.000	0.000	0.000	0.000	0.000	0.000
13	*Parameters*		*Initial*	*Final*		10	1.544	0.402	1.946	6.699	0.434	-0.912	0.666	1.902	0.000	0.000	0.000	0.000	0.000	0.000
14	Beta		0.96	0.96		11	1.544	0.402	1.946	6.699	0.434	-0.912	0.666	1.902	0.000	0.000	0.000	0.000	0.000	0.000
15	Alpha		0.35	0.35		12	1.544	0.402	1.946	6.699	0.434	-0.912	0.666	1.902	0.000	0.000	0.000	0.000	0.000	0.000
16	Delta		0.06	0.06		13	1.544	0.402	1.946	6.699	0.434	-0.912	0.666	1.902	0.000	0.000	0.000	0.000	0.000	0.000
17	OMEGA		0.10	0.10		14	1.544	0.402	1.946	6.699	0.434	-0.912	0.666	1.902	0.000	0.000	0.000	0.000	0.000	0.000
18	PHI		0.08	0.08		15	1.544	0.402	1.946	6.699	0.434	-0.912	0.666	1.902	0.000	0.000	0.000	0.000	0.000	0.000
19						16	1.544	0.402	1.946	6.699	0.434	-0.912	0.666	1.902	0.000	0.000	0.000	0.000	0.000	0.000
20	*Steady state*		*Initial*	*Final*		17	1.544	0.402	1.946	6.699	0.434	-0.912	0.666	1.902	0.000	0.000	0.000	0.000	0.000	0.000
21	Capital Stock		6.70	6.70		18	1.544	0.402	1.946	6.699	0.434	-0.912	0.666	1.902	0.000	0.000	0.000	0.000	0.000	0.000
22	Consumption		1.54	1.54		19	1.544	0.402	1.946	6.699	0.434	-0.912	0.666	1.902	0.000	0.000	0.000	0.000	0.000	0.000
23	Output		1.95	1.95		20	1.544	0.402	1.946	6.699	0.434	-0.912	0.666	1.902	0.000	0.000	0.000	0.000	0.000	0.000
24	Investment		0.40	0.40		21	1.544	0.402	1.946	6.699	0.434	-0.912	0.666	1.902	0.000	0.000	0.000	0.000	0.000	0.000
25	TFP		1	1		22	1.544	0.402	1.946	6.699	0.434	-0.912	0.666	1.902	0.000	0.000	0.000	0.000	0.000	0.000
26						23	1.544	0.402	1.946	6.699	0.434	-0.912	0.666	1.902	0.000	0.000	0.000	0.000	0.000	0.000
27	*Eigenvalues*		*Initial*	*Final*		24	1.544	0.402	1.946	6.699	0.434	-0.912	0.666	1.902	0.000	0.000	0.000	0.000	0.000	0.000
28	λ₁		-0.0960	-0.0960		25	1.544	0.402	1.946	6.699	0.434	-0.912	0.666	1.902	0.000	0.000	0.000	0.000	0.000	0.000
29	λ₂		0.1523	0.1523		26	1.544	0.402	1.946	6.699	0.434	-0.912	0.666	1.902	0.000	0.000	0.000	0.000	0.000	0.000
30						27	1.544	0.402	1.946	6.699	0.434	-0.912	0.666	1.902	0.000	0.000	0.000	0.000	0.000	0.000
31	*Stability condition*					28	1.544	0.402	1.946	6.699	0.434	-0.912	0.666	1.902	0.000	0.000	0.000	0.000	0.000	0.000
32	Modulus (1+λ₁)		0.91			29	1.544	0.402	1.946	6.699	0.434	-0.912	0.666	1.902	0.000	0.000	0.000	0.000	0.000	0.000
33	Modulus (1+λ₂)		1.16			30	1.544	0.402	1.946	6.699	0.434	-0.912	0.666	1.902	0.000	0.000	0.000	0.000	0.000	0.000

Figure 8.3. Structure of the spreadsheet "ICM-8-2.xls". Log-linear version of the Dynamic General Equilibrium model.

The information that results from numerically simulating this model appears in the "G-U" columns. Column "G" is the time index. The variables of the model are defined in the columns "H", the consumption, "I" corresponds to the investment, "J" the level of production, "K" the stock of capital, while the columns "L", "M", "N", and "O", present the previous variables in the same order, but in logarithms. Next, the column "P" corresponds to the logarithmic deviation of the consumption with respect to its steady-state value, the "Q" is the logarithmic deviation of the investment with respect to its steady-state value, which is simply the difference between what is produced and what is consumed, in terms of deviations. Column "R" is the logarithmic deviation of production, which depends on the deviation of the stock of capital from its steady-state value, and column "S" is the logarithmic deviation of the capital stock with respect to its steady-state value.

To determine the initial consumption, C_0 column "H", we will start from its steady-state value. To determine the consumption in period 1 (cell "H4"), we use the following expression:

=EXP(P4+LN(Css_1))

This same expression appears in the following cells. A similar expression appears in the "K" column to calculate the stock of capital from its logarithmic deviation. To determine the values corresponding to column "J", we use the expression, "=PTF_0*K_0^Alpha_0", corresponding to the initial period, while the initial expression entered in the column "I" is "=K_0*Delta_0". For the following periods, it is determined using the following expression, "=Alpha1*Q4". The only value that would change is "Q" that corresponds to the logarithmic variations of the stock of capital in each period of time with respect to the steady state.

Columns "P" to "S" show the deviations of each variable with respect to its steady state, where the key cells are "P4" and "S4". The "P" column corresponds to the logarithmic variation in consumption with respect to its steady-state value. For the initial period (zero), cell "P3", is the difference between the logarithm of the steady-state consumption and the logarithm of the same, whose result is zero. Cell "P4" contains the new value of the deviation of the consumption before a disturbance that places said variable in the new stable path. Thus, $\hat{c}_1$ is determined with the following expression:

=Alpha_1*(Alpha_1-1)*OMEGA_1/((Alpha_1-1)*OMEGA_1*PHI_1

+Alpha_1*Beta_1*Lambda1_1)*S4

which corresponds to the expression (8.106). For the successive periods, the consumption deviation is determined using the expression, "=N4+R4", that is, the consumption in the previous period plus the variation in consumption, which is the value corresponding to cell "R4". This expression is copied into the remaining rows of that column.

Column "S" contains the differences of the logarithm of the stock of capital with respect to the steady state. For the period zero it would be determined using the following expression, "=LN(K3)-LN($K$3)", it is the difference between the logarithm of the stock of capital in steady state and the same, therefore it is zero. On the other hand, to calculate this deviation in period 1, corresponding to cell "S4", it would correspond to the difference between the logarithm of the stock of capital in the steady state and the logarithm of the stock of capital in the final steady state, the expression that we use is:

=LN(K_0)-LN(Kss_1)

which corresponds to the expression (8.93). On the other hand, the column "R" calculates the deviations of the production level, using the expression "=Alpha_0*S3", which corresponds to the expression (8.68). In the following periods and until the end of the column, the expression used is, "=Alpha_1*S4".

Finally, columns "T" and "U" show the variations in the deviations of consumption and capital stock, respectively. Column "T" contains the variations of the logarithmic deviations of the consumption with respect to the steady state. If we place the courses in cell "T3", the expression that appears is:

=-(Alpha_0-1)*OMEGA_0*PHI_0/(Alpha_0*Beta_0)*P3

+(Alpha_0-1)*OMEGA_0/Beta_0*S3

which corresponds to the equation (8.86). This same expression appears in the following cells of this column but referred to the values of the final parameters. Finally, column "U" presents the value of the variations of the deviations of the stock of capital with respect to the initial steady state. In this case, the expression that appears in cell "U3" is

=-PHI_0/(Alpha_0*Beta_0)*P3+(1-Beta_0)/Beta_0*S3

which corresponds to the equation (8.76). This same expression appears in the following cells of the column but refers to the values of the parameters in the final steady state.

8.5.6. Shock analysis: Technological shock

Once the numerical solution of the model has been obtained, we carry out a disturbance analysis. In particular, we consider that there is a positive technological shock, represented by an increase in Total Factor Productivity, for example an increases of 5% in TFP, similar to the one made previously, but in this case, the technological shock is permanent. To do this, we will introduce a value of 1.05 in cell "C25". This is what is called a neutral technological shock since it increases the productivity of both the capital productive factor and the labor factor. That is, we assume that TFP increases permanently, which will lead to the existence of a new steady state.

Figure 8.4 shows the transition dynamics of the model variables towards the new steady state. TFP is greater from moment 1, staying at that level in the following periods (permanent change). This causes production to increase instantaneously in the value of the increase in aggregate productivity, although the adjustment is not instantaneous to the new steady state due to the transition dynamics that the capital stock will show. Thus, by instantly increasing production, so do consumption and investment. The increase in investment is due to the higher return on capital. This increase in investment causes the accumulation of physical capital, which in turn, will cause increases in production in addition to that initially produced by higher aggregate productivity. As production increases, so does consumption. However, these increases in production are decreasing, due to the existence of diminishing returns with respect to capital. The final result is the generation of a process of economic growth until the economy reaches the new steady state.

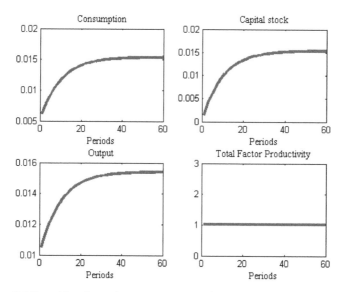

Figure 8.4. Transition dynamics to a permanent change in Total Factor Productivity.

Exercises

1. Suppose that an earthquake decreases by 20% the capital stock of the economy. Using the "**ICM-8-1.xls**" spreadsheet, study what the effects of this shock. To perform this experiment, simply enter in the spreadsheet that the initial value of the capital stock in cell "I4" is 20% lower than the corresponding steady-state value.

2. Solve the dynamic general equilibrium model assuming that the utility function of consumers is:

$$U(C_t, L_t) = \gamma \ln C_t + (1 - \gamma) \ln(1 - L_t)$$

Where $0 < \gamma < 1$. Build a spreadsheet similar to the "**ICM-8-1.xls**", which calculates both the optimal path of consumption and the optimal labor supply. What effects does a positive technological disruption have on the labor supply?

3. Repeat exercise 1, but now using the spreadsheet "**ICM-8-2.xls**". In this case, you have to enter a value of -0.2 in cell "S4". What differences do you observe regarding exercise 1?

4. Analyze the effects of an increase in the discount factor using the "**ICM-8-2.xls**" spreadsheet. What is the economic explanation of these results?

5. Build a spreadsheet similar to "**ICM-8-2.xls**", but resolving the model again under the assumption that the utility function is the one that appears in exercise 2.

Part III: Economic growth

9. The neoclassical model of exogenous growth

9.1 Introduction

Macroeconomic models aim to study the behavior of economies at the aggregate level with respect to two phenomena of special relevance: the behavior of economies in the short-run, which is determined by the existence of cyclical fluctuations in most macroeconomic variables, and the behavior of economies in the long-run, which is determined by the phenomenon of output growth. In both cases, Dynamic General Equilibrium models suppose an integrated theoretical framework from which to study both phenomena. In this chapter and the next, we will focus on numerically solving models that aim to study the second phenomenon: economic growth, which implies that over time, the output level of an economy shows an increasing trend.

In this chapter, we will numerically solve the standard neoclassical growth model with exogenous saving, developed by Robert Merton Solow (1924-)[1] and Trevor Winchester Swan (1918-1989)[2], the so-called Solow-Swan model or exogenous growth model, which is a very popular model and whose main characteristic is that it considers that saving is determined exogenously and, therefore, does not include any optimizing criteria. It is a very simple model, with a single endogenous variable to be determined, the capital stock per capita, which is determined through a predetermined saving process, which is assumed exogenous. This means that it is a dynamic, non-micro-based macroeconomic model, resulting in a very simple computational problem, since we only need to simulate the process of capital accumulation over time, given assumptions about technology. As investment is a constant fraction of output, from the determination of the capital stock we can determine the rest of the macroeconomic variables: output and consumption.

A new element that we introduce with respect to the analyses carried out previously, refers to the role played by the dynamics of the population. The

---

[1] Solow, R. M. (1956). A contribution to the theory of economic growth, Quarterly Journal of Economics, 70: 65-94.

[2] Swan, T. W. (1956). Economic growth and capital accumulation. Economic Record, 32(2): 334-361.

population and its variation over time play a fundamental role in economic-growth models since the way to compare the level of wealth between economies of different sizes is to define all the macroeconomic variables in per capita terms. Thus, the population would be the scale measure of the economies and the per capita output (output divided by population) would be a measure of wealth (or productivity if we assimilate population with employment as it is standard in economic growth models) across economies. In practice, population increases over time, so a fundamental variable in economic growth models will be the population growth rate which can be interpreted as a depreciation factor, since the population is in the denominator when level variables are converted in per capita terms. We assume that population growth rate is an exogenous variable, although there are models in which the population growth rate is determined endogenously, being an additional decision variable of the economy.

Specifically, the exogenous growth model is reduced to a dynamic equation that indicates the evolution of the capital stock per capita over time. Given the assumption of exogenous saving rate, once we have the solution for the capital stock of the economy, we can in turn determine the rest of macroeconomic variables, given a technological restriction. Despite its simplicity, this model produces a lot of interesting results. For example, the growth rate of the production level depends on the distance from the steady state: the farther an economy is from its steady state, the higher is its growth rate, a rate that decreases as we get closer to the steady state. This steady state will depend on the total factor productivity, the savings rate, the rate of physical depreciation of capital and the population growth rate. This result has important implications in terms of convergence among economies and in explaining the dramatic differences across countries in income per capita.

The structure of the rest of the chapter is as follows. In Section 2, we present the analytical solution of the Solow-Swan growth model in discrete time. Section 3 presents the calibration, while in Section 4, the numerical simulation of the model is performed. In Section 5, we conducted a disturbance exercise, consisting of a change in the exogenous saving rate. Finally, Section 6 performs a sensitivity analysis by changing one of the parameters of the model.

9.2. Neoclassical growth model in discrete time

One of the most popular macroeconomic models is the neoclassical growth model of Solow-Swan. The main reason for this is that it is a very stylized and simple model, while very intuitive to understand the dynamic behavior of an economy in the long-run. It is a non-micro-based model, so it does not include any optimality criteria, and its main assumption is that the saving rate of the economy is an exogenous variable. In this theoretical framework, the behavior of the economy over time is determined by the process of capital accumulation or neutral technological progress if we assume that the total factor productivity shows a growing trend over time. This means that it is only necessary to determine the level of capital stock of the economy to calculate the rest of the macroeconomic variables (production, consumption and investment).

9.1.1. The population

Economic growth models introduce the population and its dynamics over time as a fundamental variable when explaining the behavior of economies in the long-run. In particular, we consider that the population, which we denote as L_t, is not constant period by period, but increases with time:

$$L_t = L_0(1 + n)^t \tag{9.1}$$

where $n > 0$ is the growth rate of the population and L_0 is the population at the initial period. Thus, the population at a certain moment of time is given by:

$$L_t = L_{t-1}(1 + n) \tag{9.2}$$

The fact that the population is not constant makes the individual well-being depend as much on how the level of production evolves, as on the evolution of the population. This means that the relevant variables in this analysis are not the aggregate variables in levels but those related to the population. For this reason, the variables in economic growth models are defined in per capita terms. In addition, the population is a measure of the size of an economy, so to make comparisons across different economies at the international level, it is necessary to define all the variables in terms of per capita. The main implication of population growth is that, given that we assume that its growth rate is positive, we have to distribute the aggregate variables (consumption, stock of capital, production, etc.) among more individuals, thus representing an additional depreciation factor of the economy (additional to the physical depreciation of capital). It is usually assumed that the growth rate of the population is an exogenous variable or even a parameter of the model. However, in some theoretical developments, it is considered that it is an endogenous variable, determined through the decision of the agents. In the analysis to be done here, we consider it as a constant.

Finally, another of the simplifying assumptions commonly used in this macroeconomic model is that the concept of population and labor force are interchangeable. Thus, the level of employment of an economy is assimilated to the population, or at least it is assumed that the growth rate of both variables is equal. This causes the level of output per capita to be equivalent to labor productivity. This is the assumption we adopt in our analysis.

9.1.2. The technology

Secondly, we define the technological function, which we assume presents constant returns to scale and, therefore, diminishing returns with respect to each of the productive factors. The aggregate production function of the economy we assume is given by:

$$Y_t = A_t F(K_t, L_t) \tag{9.3}$$

where Y_t is the level of aggregate production of the economy, A_t is the total factor productivity, representing neutral-technology in the sense of Hicks, which we assume is an exogenous variable, K_t is the stock of capital and L_t is labor, which we assume is equivalent to the population. In particular, we will use a production function of the Cobb-Douglas type, which guarantees the existence of constant returns to scale and decreasing returns for each of the productive factors, being, therefore:

$$Y_t = A_t K_t^\alpha L_t^{1-\alpha} \tag{9.4}$$

where the technological parameter $(0 < \alpha < 1)$, determines the elasticity of the production level with respect to the stock of capital.

From this production function, we can identify the two elements that explain the growth of per capita output in this model: the accumulation of inputs and the neutral technological progress consisting in an increase in the total factor productivity.

9.1.3. The capital accumulation process

The central element of the neoclassical growth model is the equation of per capita capital accumulation. For this, we start from the standard equation of capital accumulation that is given by:

$$K_{t+1} = (1 - \delta)K_t + I_t \tag{9.5}$$

where I_t is the investment and $\delta > 0$ is the physical depreciation rate of capital, given $K_0 > 0$. The key element of this model is to assume that the savings rate, s_t, $(0 < s_t < 1)$, is exogenous. Therefore, this means that the investment can be defined as:

$$I_t = s_t Y_t \tag{9.6}$$

From the previous expression, we can now determine the level of consumption. In effect, the economic feasibility constraint is given by,

$$C_t + I_t = Y_t \tag{9.7}$$

so, the consumption is defined by $C_t = (1 + s_t)Y_t$. By substituting the investment in the capital accumulation equation, we obtain the following difference equation that indicates the dynamics of the capital stock:

$$C_t + K_{t+1} - (1 - \delta)K_t = Y_t \tag{9.8}$$

9.1.4. Variables in per capita terms

To take account of population growth, we rewrite the production function in terms of per capita (or per worker given the assumption that population is equal to labor). For this, what we do is multiply and divide one of the sides of the production function by the number of workers:

$$Y_t = A_t K_t^\alpha L_t^{1-\alpha} \frac{L_t}{L_t} \tag{9.9}$$

By operating, we obtain that:

$$\frac{Y_t}{L_t} = \frac{A_t K_t^\alpha L_t^{1-\alpha}}{L_t} = \frac{A_t K_t^\alpha L_t L_t^{-\alpha}}{L_t} = A_t K_t^\alpha L_t^{-\alpha} = A_t \frac{K_t^\alpha}{L_t^\alpha} = A_t \left(\frac{K_t}{L_t}\right)^\alpha \tag{9.10}$$

We define the variables in per capita terms with a lowercase letter, such that the level of production per capita of the economy is given by,

$$y_t = \frac{Y_t}{L_t} \tag{9.11}$$

Similarly, the stock of capital per capita (per worker) would be given by:

$$k_t = \frac{K_t}{L_t} \tag{9.12}$$

By substituting these definitions in the expression (9.9), we obtain the following production function in per capita terms:

$$y_t = A_t k_t^\alpha \tag{9.13}$$

This function of production is called the intensive production function, since the level of output per capita is defined as a function of a single combined productive factor, the stock of capital per capita.

Next, we proceed to obtain the capital accumulation equation in per capita terms. The equation of capital accumulation in aggregate terms, using the expression (9.8), is given by:

$$\Delta K_t = Y_t - C_t - \delta K_t \tag{9.14}$$

where we define $\Delta K_t = K_{t+1} - K_t$. Multiplying and dividing by the population in one of the sides, results in:

$$\frac{C_t + K_{t+1} - (1-\delta)K_t}{L_t} = \frac{Y_t}{L_t} \tag{9.15}$$

and operating in the above expression results in:

$$\frac{C_t}{L_t} + \frac{K_{t+1}L_{t+1}}{L_t L_{t+1}} - \frac{(1-\delta)K_t}{L_t} = \frac{Y_t}{L_t} \tag{9.16}$$

and readjusting terms and redefining the variables in per capita terms results in:

$$\frac{C_t}{L_t} + \frac{K_{t+1}}{L_{t+1}}\frac{L_{t+1}}{L_t} - \frac{(1-\delta)K_t}{L_t} = \frac{Y_t}{L_t} \tag{9.17}$$

On the other hand, considering that population dynamics are given by:

$$\frac{L_{t+1}}{L_t} = (1+n) \tag{9.18}$$

we arrived at:

$$c_t + k_{t+1}(1+n) - (1-\delta)k_t = y_t \tag{9.19}$$

Solving for the stock of capital per capita for $t+1$ results in:

$$k_{t+1} = \frac{(1-\delta)k_t + y_t - c_t}{(1+n)} \tag{9.20}$$

Substituting the definition of consumption (given that $y_t - c_t = i_t = s_t y_t$):

$$k_{t+1} = \frac{(1-\delta)k_t + s_t y_t}{(1+n)} \tag{9.21}$$

Adding and subtracting k_t in the left part of the previous expression results in:

$$k_{t+1} - k_t + k_t = \frac{(1-\delta)k_t + s_t y_t}{(1+n)} \tag{9.22}$$

or equivalently:

$$\Delta k_t = \frac{(1-\delta)k_t + s_t y_t}{(1+n)} - k_t \tag{9.23}$$

defining $\Delta k_t = k_{t+1} - k_t$. Finally, by operating in the previous expression we come to:

$$\Delta k_t = \frac{s_t y_t - (n+\delta)k_t}{(1+n)} = \frac{s_t A_t k_t^\alpha - (n+\delta)k_t}{(1+n)} \tag{9.24}$$

an expression that indicates that the variation in the per capita stock of capital depends positively on the rate of savings and the total factor productivity and negatively on the rate of physical depreciation of capital and the rate of population growth.

Structure of the neoclassical growth model	
Production function	$Y_t = A_t F(K_t, L_t)$
Equation of capital accumulation	$K_{t+1} = (1-\delta)K_t + I_t$
Initial capital stock	$K_0 > 0$
Feasibility restriction	$Y_t = C_t + I_t$
Investment	$I_t = s_t Y_t$
Population growth rate	$L_t = L_0(1+n)^t$

9.1.5. Steady state

The steady state is given by that situation in which the dynamic equation for the stock of capital per capita is zero, that is, the stock of capital per capita (and therefore the rest of the variables) is kept constant period by period. In this case, the growth rate of the model variables is all equal to zero. By equaling the expression (9.24) to zero and clearing, we obtain that the equilibrium condition is given by:

$$s_t \bar{y} = (\delta + n)\bar{k} \tag{9.25}$$

where $s_t \bar{y}$ is the saving or gross investment per worker in steady state and where $(\delta + n)$ is the effective depreciation rate of the capital stock per unit of capital per worker. That is, the capital stock per capita will be constant when the volume of savings per unit of capital per capita is equal to the capital-per-capita losses due to effective depreciation, where the effective depreciation rate is the sum of the physical depreciation rate plus the population growth. If we assume that the production function is of the Cobb-Douglas type, it follows that the steady state would be given by:

$$s_t A_t \bar{k}^\alpha = (\delta + n)\bar{k} \tag{9.26}$$

Solving for the capital stock per capita, we obtain that:

$$\bar{k}^{\alpha-1} = \frac{\delta + n}{s_t A_t} \tag{9.27}$$

being the steady state capital stock per capita:

$$\bar{k} = \left(\frac{\delta + n}{s_t A_t}\right)^{\frac{1}{\alpha-1}} \tag{9.28}$$

The steady state output per capita would therefore be:

$$\bar{y} = A_t \bar{k}^\alpha = A_t \left(\frac{\delta + n}{s_t A_t}\right)^{\frac{\alpha}{\alpha-1}} \tag{9.29}$$

Finally, the steady state per capita consumption would be given by,

$$\bar{c} = (1 + s_t)\bar{y} = (1 - s_t)A_t \left(\frac{\delta + n}{s_t A_t}\right)^{\frac{\alpha}{\alpha-1}} \tag{9.30}$$

9.2. Calibration of the model

To numerically simulate the Solow-Swan model, we need to give values to both the parameters and the exogenous variables. With a Cobb-Douglas technology, the model has three parameters: the technological parameter that determines the elasticity of production with respect to the stock of capital, α, the physical depreciation rate of capital, δ, and the population growth rate, n. The calibrated values of these parameters are defined in Table 9.1. The assigned value for α, which must be between 0 and 1, is 0.35, and would correspond to the proportion of capital income with respect to total income (it would be the gross surplus operating ratio with respect to the Gross Domestic Product), and where $1 - \alpha$ represents the labor income share (compensation to employees over GDP). The depreciation rate is assumed to be 6% per period (year), while the rate of population growth is set at 2%. Notice that here we consider the population growth rate as a parameter, but it could also be considered as an exogenous variable.

Table 9.1: Calibration of the parameters

Symbol	Definition	Value
α	Production-capital elasticity	0.35
δ	Depreciation rate	0.06
n	Population growth rate	0.02

On the other hand, it is necessary to give values to the exogenous variables: the total factor productivity, A_t, and the savings rate, s_t. The values that we use initially are given in Table 9.2, in which we have assumed a savings rate of 20% and a value for the TFP of 1.

Table 9.2: Value of exogenous variables

Variable	Definition	Value
s_t	Savings rate	0.20
A_t	Total Factor Productivity	1.00

From these values, we can calculate the steady-state value for the different variables of the model. Thus, the value of the stock of capital per capita in the initial steady state would be given by:

$$\bar{k}_0 = \left(\frac{\delta+n}{s_0 A_0}\right)^{\frac{1}{\alpha-1}} = \left(\frac{0.02+0.06}{0.20\times 1}\right)^{\frac{1}{-0.65}} = 4.095$$

This value appears in cell "B13", which we have named "kss_0", cell that contains expression (9.28). By placing the cursor in said cell, the expression appears:

=((n_0+Delta_0)/(PTF_0*s_0))^(1/(Alpha_0-1))

Similarly, the steady-state value for the production level would be:

$$\bar{y}_0 = A_0 \left(\frac{\delta + n}{s_0 A_0}\right)^{\frac{\alpha}{\alpha-1}} = 1 \times \left(\frac{0.4 + 0.06}{0.20 \times 1}\right)^{\frac{0.35}{-0.65}} = 1.6378$$

value that appears in cell "B14", named "yss_0", in which we have simply introduced the definition of the production function:

=PTF_0*kss_0^Alpha_0

The per capita consumption in steady state is calculated as:

$$\bar{c}_0 = (1 - s_0)\bar{y}_0 = 0.80 \times 56.59 = 1.310$$

If we place the cursor in cell "B15", the expression we have used is:

=yss0-(n_0+Delta0)*kss0

which is equivalent to the one used previously. Finally, cell "B16" contains the steady-state value of the investment, which can be calculated as:

$$\bar{\iota}_0 = \bar{y}_0 - \bar{c}_0 = 56.9 - 45.27 = 0.328$$

Table 9.3. shows the steady state values given the calibration of the model using values in Tables 9.1 and 9.2.

Table 9.3: Steady-state values

Variable	Definition	Value
$\bar{k}$	Stock of capital per capita	4.095
$\bar{y}$	Level of production per capita	1.638
$\bar{c}$	Consumption per capita	1.310
$\bar{\iota}$	Investment per capita	0.328

9.3. Numerical solution

Since the neoclassical exogenous growth model does not include any optimizing criteria, we can simulate numerically the equations that integrate it directly. That is, we simply have to write the corresponding equations in a spreadsheet and assign values to the parameters and exogenous variables and, starting from an initial situation, we can simulate the trajectory of the different variables over time. The spreadsheet in which we have numerically simulated this model is "**ICM-9.xls**". In Appendix O, we present the numerical resolution of the Solow-Swan model in MATLAB.

	A	B	C		Time	k	y	sy	c	Δk	gy
1	Exercise 9: The Solow-Swan model										
2					0	4.09	1.64	0.33	1.31	0.00	0.00
3	*Parameters*	*Initial*	*Final*		1	4.09	1.64	0.33	1.31	0.00	0.00
4	Alpha	0.35	0.35		2	4.09	1.64	0.33	1.31	0.00	0.00
5	Delta	0.06	0.06		3	4.09	1.64	0.33	1.31	0.00	0.00
6	n	0.02	0.02		4	4.09	1.64	0.33	1.31	0.00	0.00
7					5	4.09	1.64	0.33	1.31	0.00	0.00
8	*Exogenous variables*	*Initial*	*Final*		5	4.09	1.64	0.33	1.31	0.00	0.00
9	A	1	1		6	4.09	1.64	0.33	1.31	0.00	0.00
10	s	0.20	0.20		7	4.09	1.64	0.33	1.31	0.00	0.00
11					8	4.09	1.64	0.33	1.31	0.00	0.00
12	*Steady State*	*Initial*	*Final*		9	4.09	1.64	0.33	1.31	0.00	0.00
13	Capital stock	4.095	4.095		10	4.09	1.64	0.33	1.31	0.00	0.00
14	Output	1.638	1.638		11	4.09	1.64	0.33	1.31	0.00	0.00
15	Consumption	1.310	1.310		12	4.09	1.64	0.33	1.31	0.00	0.00
16	Investment	0.328	0.328		13	4.09	1.64	0.33	1.31	0.00	0.00
17					14	4.09	1.64	0.33	1.31	0.00	0.00
18					15	4.09	1.64	0.33	1.31	0.00	0.00
19					16	4.09	1.64	0.33	1.31	0.00	0.00
20					17	4.09	1.64	0.33	1.31	0.00	0.00
21					18	4.09	1.64	0.33	1.31	0.00	0.00
22					19	4.09	1.64	0.33	1.31	0.00	0.00
23					20	4.09	1.64	0.33	1.31	0.00	0.00
24					21	4.09	1.64	0.33	1.31	0.00	0.00
25					22	4.09	1.64	0.33	1.31	0.00	0.00
26					23	4.09	1.64	0.33	1.31	0.00	0.00
27					24	4.09	1.64	0.33	1.31	0.00	0.00
28					25	4.09	1.64	0.33	1.31	0.00	0.00
29					26	4.09	1.64	0.33	1.31	0.00	0.00
30					27	4.09	1.64	0.33	1.31	0.00	0.00
31					28	4.09	1.64	0.33	1.31	0.00	0.00
32					29	4.09	1.64	0.33	1.31	0.00	0.00
33					30	4.09	1.64	0.33	1.31	0.00	0.00
34					31	4.09	1.64	0.33	1.31	0.00	0.00
35											

Figure 9.1. Structure of the spreadsheet "ICM-9.xls". The Solow-Swan growth model.

The structure of this spreadsheet is shown in Figure 9.1. As we can see, we need to define, first of all, the value of the parameters, which appear in column "B". The calibrated values of the parameters defined in Table 9.1 appear in cells "B4", "B5" and "B6". In column "C" appear those same parameters, in order to analyze the changes in them. In cells "B9" and "B10", we have introduced the value of the exogenous variables at the initial moment. In order to perform different types of analysis based on the value of the parameters, we have introduced a new column, "C", where we can change its value and automatically calculate its effects on the variables of the economy. We have named the values in column "B" as the initial situation, with a subscript 0, while we call the values in column "C" the final situation, with a subscript 1.

Next, cells "B13" through "B16" show the steady state for the stock of capital per capita, production per capita, consumption per capita and investment per capita, with the initial values of the parameters and exogenous variables. The equivalent cells in column "C" show the corresponding steady-state values calculated with the final values for the parameters and exogenous variables.

The model information appears in columns "E" to "K". Column "E" is the time index. In the "F-K" columns, we calculate the value of the relevant variables: capital stock per capita, production level per capita, per capita savings, per capita consumption, variation in the stock of capital per capita and growth rate of the level of production per capita. Cell "F3" is the initial steady-state value, calculated above. On the other hand, in cell "F4" we find the following expression:

=(H3+(1-Delta_1)*F3)/(1+n_1)

The previous expression corresponds to equation (9.21), where the stock of capital per capita of a period is defined in terms of the stock of capital of the previous period, of the saving of the previous period (column "H") and of the rate parameters of population growth and physical depreciation rate of capital. In this way, we are numerically computing the discrete version of the model in an exact way. This same expression appears in the remaining cells of column "F". Alternatively, we can simplify this expression and introduce the following:

=F3+J3

where cell "J3" calculates the variation of the stock of capital per capita in the period. Column "G" is the level of production per capita. If we place the cursor in cell "G3" the expression that appears is:

=PTF_0*F3^Alpha_0

which is the expression corresponding to the capital intensive production function obtained previously. In cell "G4" the expression is:

=PTF_1*F4^Alpha_1

to allow the possibility of performing analysis on changes in any of the parameters of the model. Column "H" contains the saving of the economy, which is simply obtained by multiplying the savings rate by the level of production. Column "I" is per capita consumption, which is obtained as the difference between the two previous columns, that is, the difference between what is produced and what is saved. Column "J" shows the variation in the stock of capital per capita. If we place the cursor in cell "J3", the expression that appears is,

=(H3-(n_0+Delta_0)*F3)/(1+n_0)

which corresponds to the expression (9.24). This same expression appears in the following rows of this column, but referred to the values of the parameters and exogenous variables in the final situation. Finally, column "K" contains the expression for the growth rate of per capita production. To calculate the growth rate of per capita production, we must first calculate the growth rate of the capital stock per capita. To calculate the growth rate of the capital stock per capita, we simply have to multiply and divide the left side of the expression (9.24) by the capital stock per capita, such that:

$$\Delta k_t \frac{k_t}{k_t} = \frac{s_t y_t - (n+\delta)k_t}{(1+n)} \tag{9.31}$$

or equivalently:

$$g_k = \frac{\Delta k_t}{k_t} = \frac{k_{t+1} - k_t}{k_t} = \frac{s_t y_t - (n+\delta)k_t}{(1+n)k_t} \tag{9.32}$$

where g_k is the growth rate of the capital stock per capita. It is this expression that we have introduced in the "K" column. If we apply logarithms to the function of capital-intensive production (intensive expression), it results:

$$\ln y_t = \ln A_t + \alpha \ln k_t \tag{9.33}$$

and using the same expression for the period, it turns out that:

$$\ln \frac{y_{t+1}}{y_t} = \ln \frac{A_{t+1}}{A_t} + \alpha \ln \frac{k_{t+1}}{k_t} \tag{9.34}$$

and defining $g_y = \ln(y_{t+1}/y_t)$, as the growth rate of the per capita production, $g_A = \ln(A_{t+1}/A_t)$ the growth rate of the Total Factor Productivity and $g_k = \ln(k_{t+1}/k_t)$, the rate of growth of the stock of capital, results in:

$$g_y = g_A + \alpha g_k \tag{9.35}$$

If we assume that the TPF is constant ($g_A = 0$), then it turns out that the growth rate of per capita production is the fraction of the growth rate of the capital stock per capita.[3]

---

[3] This relationship between the growth rate of output and the growth rate of the stock of capital per capita is different from that which would be obtained in a steady state, in which the rate of growth of the stock of capital per capita, of per capita consumption and of the level of production per capita would be equal (in the context of this model equal to zero if the TFP is constant). This is what is called the path of balanced growth.

9.4. Shock analysis: Effects of an increase in the savings rate

Next, we will use the previous spreadsheet to study the effects of disturbances. In particular, we study the case of an increase in the savings rate. Initially, the saving rate is 20% of the total income (output), and we assume that it increases up to 25% (change in cell "C10" to a value of 0.25). First, we can observe how the steady state changes. In particular, the per capita capital stock in steady state increases to a value of 5.77, a value greater than that corresponding to the initial steady state. This result is explained by the higher savings rate. The greater the savings, the greater the capital stock in steady state, since it depends positively on the amount of resources devoted to investment. As a consequence of this increase in the steady-state value of the stock of capital per capita, the level of steady-state production also increases. In addition, we can also observe that both the steady-state values of consumption and of investment are higher than the initial steady state. This does not always have to be true for the case of consumption. Thus, the increase in the savings rate always increases both the stock of capital and the level of production in the long term. However, the effect of the increase in the saving rate on per capita consumption is indeterminate, depending on the initial and final position in relation to the golden rule. The golden rule determines the steady state that generates the highest level of well-being, that is, the highest level of per capita consumption. Thus, of all the possible steady states (one for each saving rate), there is only one for which the level of consumption is maximum. This situation is what is known as the golden steady state. If the saving rate is very low in the economy, then the stock of capital will also be reduced, as will production, leading to a low level of consumption. On the contrary, if the saving rate is very high, the stock of capital and production will also be very high. However, in this case, we will need a large amount of resources to maintain the stock of capital (replace the depreciating capital), so the volume of investment must also be very high, which also leads to low levels of consumption. These cases would indicate that the economy would be on the left and on the right, respectively, of the golden rule.

Figure 9.2 shows the transition trajectories of the model variables to the new steady state. Now, the stock of capital in the new steady state is superior to the one that existed previously. The stock of capital per capita is increasing progressively, showing a concave shape (given the assumption of decreasing marginal productivity for capital), until reaching the new value of steady state higher than the initial one. In this case, the increase in the savings rate causes an instantaneous increase in per capita savings, since it increases the savings per unit of production. Then, the savings continues to grow given that a greater amount of capital must be replaced by its depreciation. This growth is derived from the increase that occurs in the level of production per capita. Therefore, there is an impact effect caused by the increase in the savings rate and subsequently, there is an additional effect derived from the higher level of production.

Regarding the dynamics of per capita consumption, it increases in the long term. In this case, the impact effect is negative, producing an instantaneous decrease in per capita consumption. This is due to the fact that the increase in the savings rate causes a greater proportion of production to be saved, so that the part of the production that is destined for consumption decreases. As of this moment, consumption begins to recover, due to the accumulation of more capital as a result of greater savings and, therefore, the level of production increases, so that a greater quantity can be consumed again. This dynamic of transition from the per capita consumption of the initial steady state to the final steady state, shows that saving is a sacrifice (in terms of consumption) that is carried out in the short-run, but that is compensated by a higher level of consumption in the long-run.

An interesting result that we could obtain is the case in which if we compare the final per capita consumption, it is lower than the per capita consumption that existed at the beginning. That is, the increase in the savings rate of the economy does not always have to lead to a higher level of consumption in the long term. In the event that this situation occurs, this means that the level of welfare of the economy decreases as a consequence of this disturbance, which would be reflecting a situation in which the level of savings is too high, with respect to which it would maximize the level of consumption per capita. In particular, in this case, we would be located to the right of the golden rule, where the savings rate is excessively high. The fact that the savings rate is very high would imply that the per capita stock of steady-state capital is very high and, therefore, also the per capita production. However, a large amount of resources must also be allocated to maintain this stock of capital, so that the part of the production that remains to be consumed is very small, and lower than that which would exist if the saving rate were lower. This is what is called the golden rule. There is a savings rate, which is called gold saving, which results in a steady state with the highest level of consumption. If the savings rate is higher or lower than the savings rate determined by the golden rule, the resulting steady state would lead to a lower level of consumption.

Finally, the evolution of the growth rate of the economy in per capita terms is also shown. As we can see, the growth rate of the economy would increase instantaneously, as a consequence of the higher level of savings, which would cause a greater accumulation of capital. This growth rate would remain in positive values throughout the time trajectory towards the steady state, although with a lower growth rate as the economy bring closer to the steady state.

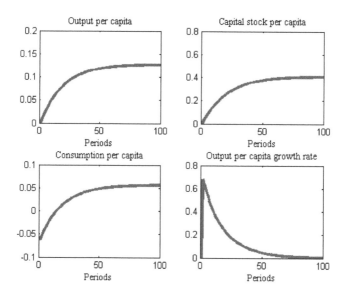

Figure 9.2. Effects of an increase in the saving rate.

9.5. Sensitivity analysis: Change in the population growth rate

Finally, we will study the sensitivity of the model facing changes in the value of the parameters. In particular, we are going to analyze the implications of a change in the population growth rate. In the model, we have assumed that the population growth rate is a constant, which is why we have assimilated it to a parameter. However, the population growth rate could also be interpreted as an exogenous variable. In fact, the only difference between a parameter and an exogenous variable is that we usually assume that the former does not change its value, while the exogenous variables can change representing a shock. The sensitivity analysis comes to eliminate, in practice, this difference.

As we have seen previously, in the Solow-Swan model, the stock of per capita capital of the steady state depends on the rate of population growth. This assumes that the growth rate of the population will determine the steady state of the economy. This is especially relevant in a context in which the population growth rate is considered an endogenous variable or an exogenous variable determined by the policies of promotion of the birth rate, the migratory policies, or policies of control of the population growth. In fact, in reality we have seen experiences, such as the case of China, of governments that use the birth rate as a policy instrument to affect economic growth. Next, we will use the developed theoretical framework to determine the implications of a change in the population growth rate.

To perform this analysis, we only have to change the value of cell "C6". In particular, let's assume that the population growth rate decreases to 0.01. Figure 9.3. shows the dynamics of transition towards the new steady state derived from this decrease in n. As we can see, there is an increase in the stock of capital per capita until reaching the new steady state, given that it depends negatively on the rate of population growth, which is an additional depreciation factor. This is due to the fact that, given the volume of initial savings, the decrease in n assumes a decrease in the rate of depreciation of the stock of capital per capita (which depends on the rate of physical depreciation of capital and the rate of growth of the population). This is because now, period by period, there is more capital per worker, given the lower growth in the number of workers. The increase in the stock of capital per capita is decreasing until reaching the new steady state, where the stock of capital per capita is higher than the initial one. This higher level of capital stock per capita also implies a higher level of per capita production and consumption per capita. The greatest volume of savings per capita is due to the fact that, although the rate of depreciation of the stock of capital per capita is now lower, the stock of capital per capita is higher. Finally, we observe how the growth rate of the economy is positive, increasing instantaneously when the decrease occurs in n, to be decreasing until reaching the new steady state (note that the effects are, qualitatively, similar to the obtained in the case of an increase in the savings rate).

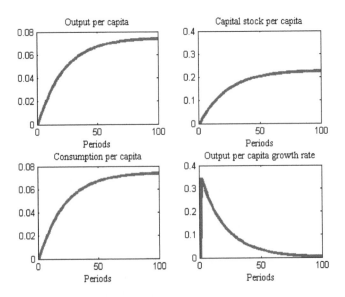

Figure 9.3. Effects of a decrease in the population growth rate.

Exercises

1. Suppose that an earthquake reduces the stock of capital by 10% (without causing population losses). Using the "**ICM-9.xls**" spreadsheet, study the effects of this disturbance (Hint: change the value of cell G4 and enter in this cell the expression "=0.9*kss0").

2. Analyze the effects of an increase in the technological parameter that determines the elasticity of the production level with respect to the stock of capital (for example, suppose that the new value of α is of 0.40). What happens if the value of α is the unit (in this case the returns on capital would be constant)? How the dynamics of the economy change in the face of this assumption? Why is this result obtained?

3. Although the physical depreciation rate of capital is assumed to be a parameter that remains constant over time, in practice its value depends on the type of capital asset in which it is invested. However, the type of capital assets changes over time. In fact, investment in capital assets related to new technologies usually have high depreciation rates. This means that the rate of physical depreciation of capital is altered over time by the different composition of capital, increasingly. Assume that the physical depreciation rate of capital increases to 8 percent per year (change the value of cell "C5" to 0.08). What consequences this increase in the physical depreciation rate of capital has on the economy? How this change affects the rate of growth of the economy?

4. Suppose that the initial savings rate, with the parameters given in the spreadsheet "**ICM-9.xls**", is 20%. Compare this situation with a savings rate of 30%. In what situation output per capita is higher? And the per capita consumption. Check now what happens with per capita consumption if the savings rate increases to 40%. What causes this behavior? In view of these results, what would be the savings rate that generates the highest level of welfare, that is, the one that generates the highest level of per capita consumption (this is what is called the gold-saving rate)? What relationship does the gold-saving rate have with the technological parameter that determines the elasticity of the production level with respect to the capital stock?

5. Study the effects of an increase in total factor productivity (TFP). For example, suppose the TFP increases to 1.05. What effects does this change have on the economy? What proportion of the level of production in the new steady state is due to the increase in the TFP and what part to the process of generated capital accumulation?

10. Ramsey's optimal growth model

10.1. Introduction

In chapter 8, we have solved a simple version of the standard Dynamic General Equilibrium model that is currently used in macroeconomic analysis. The model only includes the behavior of two economic agents: Households and firms, from whose optimizing decisions the competitive equilibrium of the economy is derived. This model has as its starting point the model developed by Frank Plumpton Ramsey (1903-1930) almost a century ago.[1] The Ramsey model, also called the optimal growth model (as opposed to the Solow-Swan model, in which there is no optimality criterion and in which the saving rate is exogenous), or named the Ramsey-Cass-Koopmans model, has become the theoretical framework of reference of modern macroeconomic analysis, not only to study the behavior of the economy in the long-run but also for the study of economic fluctuations in the short-run. As we have seen previously, we have two alternative approaches to numerically solve this type of models in a spreadsheet: through the "Solver" tool, which solves the household's optimization problem, or by obtaining a linear approximation to the model and numerically calculating the system of resulting linear difference equations. In this chapter, we will numerically solve the Ramsey model using only the second approach to avoid "black-box" shortcomings. Specifically, we will numerically compute the dynamic equations for per capita consumption and for the per capita capital stock, resulting in a system of linear difference equations in terms of the deviations of each variable with respect to its steady state, which constitute a linear approximation to the initial dynamic system that has a non-linear nature. When analytically solving the model, it results in a system of non-linear equations, which will have a saddle-point solution, so it is necessary to previously calculate the eigenvalues associated with it in order to determine the jump in the forward looking variable to reach the new stable saddle path when a disturbance hits the economy. For this, the simplest method is to first proceed to obtain a (log) linear approximation to that system. The procedure used here is similar to the one used previously in solving Tobin's Q model and the basic dynamic general equilibrium model.

---

[1] Ramsey, F. P. (1928). A mathematical theory of saving. Economic Journal, 38(152): 543-559.

The structure of the model is similar to the basic Dynamic General Equilibrium model studied in Chapter 8. Thus, we assume the existence of two agents: households and firm, which interact in a competitive environment. Households aim to maximize the discounted sum of their utility throughout their life cycle, while the firm's goal is to maximize profits period-by-period. However, the analysis to be done here presents some differences with respect to the basic model of dynamic general equilibrium studied previously. First, this model has a new exogenous variable: population growth, since demographic dynamics is a key factor to take into account when studying economic growth. We can think in the household as a family where the number of members increases over time. Secondly, we define all the variables in per capita terms, since it is the relevant measure in this context. Third, since we are not using the "Solver" tool, but rather directly calculate the linear equations approximated to those of the model, we adopt the assumption of infinite life. Finally, for the analysis to be as simple as possible, we will not consider leisure in the utility function of households, but instead we assume that labor is equal to the population.

In contrast to the result we obtained in the Solow-Swan model, the stock of steady-state capital in the Ramsey model does not depend on the rate of population growth, and instead depends on the discount factor. This is because the utility function that we maximize is that which corresponds to the family, which includes the entire population and its evolution over time, giving rise to the fact that the discount factor is not only formed by the subjective rate of intertemporal preference but also by the rate of population growth. In addition, consumption is the forward-looking variable that "jumps" when a disturbance occurs, in order to reach the new stable saddle path corresponding to the steady state, which will lead to some very different adjustment dynamics than the one previously obtained in the Solow-Swan model.

The structure of the rest of this chapter is as follows. In Section 2, we solve analytically the Ramsey's model, in its discrete-time version. Section 3 presents the parametrization and calibration of the model, as well as the calculation of the steady state. Section 4 proceeds to the log-linearization of the model, transforming the initial model in a dynamic system with two linear difference equations. Section 5 presents the numerical resolution of the model in the spreadsheet. Finally, Section 6 presents a disturbance analysis, studying the dynamic effects of a decrease in the intertemporal preference rate that reflects an increase in the desires to saving.

10.2. The Ramsey model

In this section, we will propose a very simplified Ramsey model, in discrete time and with household's infinite lifespan. We assume an economy where the growth rate of the population is positive. As in the exogenous growth model solved in the previous chapter, this forces us to redefine all the variables in per capita terms, since the rate of population growth becomes an additional factor of depreciation of the stock of accumulated assets in the economy.

10.2.2. Families

In Ramsey's model, we introduce the concept of family and the variation in the number of family members over time. In particular, we assume that the individuals that inhabit an economy belong to the same family. This is a natural way of introducing the concept of infinite life for consumers that is commonly used in micro-based macro models. In this way, individuals can have finite life and cease to exist at a particular moment in time, but the family is immortal. Using the concept of family has important connotations from the economic point of view, since we are referring to the existence of a relationship of kinship between the individuals that live in an economy, so it is to be assumed that the welfare of the future generations also affects the welfare of agents at the present time. In other words, the individuals of a generation would also be concerned with the welfare of individuals of future generations, which results in the decision-maker, the family, acting as an agent with infinite life.

In this context, the reference variable will be the level of per capita consumption (consumption of each member of the family, which we assume is the same for all individuals), given that we consider the existence of a positive population growth rate. We define the population, which we assume is equivalent to the number of workers, at the moment t as:

$$L_t = L_{t-1}(1 + n) \tag{10.1}$$

where $n > 0$ is the growth rate of the population. In general terms we would have:

$$L_t = L_0(1 + n)^t \tag{10.2}$$

where L_0 is the population at the initial moment 0 that we will normalize to 1 ($L_0 = 1$). Then, it turns out that:

$$L_t = (1 + n)^t \tag{10.3}$$

Let us assume that the population growth rate (birth rate minus mortality rate) is an exogenous constant to the economy, so we assimilate it to a parameter of the model. This could not be true and it could happen that the birth rate was also determined by the decision of the individuals, which would lead us to have to determine it as an additional variable of the model. However, as we will see below, the population growth rate is closely related to other variables that determine the behavior of the economy.

The assumption that the population is equal to the number of workers makes the per capita income equivalent to labor productivity. As in the previous chapter, we defined all the variables in terms of per capita (denoted by lowercase), simply dividing by population. Therefore, per capita consumption would be defined as:

$$c_t = \frac{C_t}{L_t} \tag{10.4}$$

When specifying the household maximization problem, we must take into account two elements when defining the variables in per capita terms. First, individuals discount the future, so we must consider the existence of an intertemporal preference rate greater than zero. Second, we must take into account that the number of members of the family unit is not constant over time, but increases at the rate defined above. This means that the problem will consist in maximizing the total utility of the family, or what is equivalent, per capita consumption.

The problem to be maximized by the family is:

$$\max_{\{c_t\}_{t=0}^{\infty}} E_t \sum_{t=0}^{T} \beta^t U(c_t) L_t \tag{10.5}$$

where $\beta \in (0,1)$ is the discount factor, which we define as,

$$\beta = \frac{1}{1+\theta} \tag{10.6}$$

being $\theta > 0$, the intertemporal subjective preference rate. As we have done previously, we assume the existence of a perfect foresight, so we can directly eliminate the mathematical expectation operator. The problem, using the expression (10.5) can be written as:

$$\max_{\{c_t\}_{t=0}^{\infty}} \sum_{t=0}^{T} \beta^t (1+n)^t U(c_t) \tag{10.7}$$

or,

$$\max_{\{c_t\}_{t=0}^{\infty}} \sum_{t=0}^{T} \left(\frac{1+n}{1+\theta}\right)^t U(c_t) \tag{10.8}$$

where the total discount factor is given by the expression:

$$\left(\frac{1+n}{1+\theta}\right)^t \tag{10.9}$$

In principle, the number within the parenthesis may be greater or less than the unit depending on the value of the population growth rate, n, in relation to the value of the intertemporal subjective rate, θ. However, this value must be less than the unit to discount future utility (if it were equal to 1, the future would not be discounted, so that the sum of profits would be infinite), implying that it must be fulfilled that $n < \theta$. That is, the growth rate of the population in an economy must be lower than the subjective rate of intertemporal preferences. Therefore, give our specification of this maximization problem, we have to impose this additional condition that $\theta > n$. This is because, on the one hand, to obtain aggregate consumption, we start with the consumption of an individual (per capita consumption) and multiply by the number of individuals that are part of our economy. On the other hand, we would be discounting the future utility in terms of the current utility as in the basic household maximization problem. Since this discount factor has to be positive, this implies that it has to happen that $\theta > n$. Let's say that the larger the family is in the future, the more we discount future utility and the greater the importance we give to the happiness of family members at the present time.

We define the budget constraint in aggregate terms as:

$$C_t + I_t = W_t L_t + R_t K_t \tag{10.10}$$

being the equation of capital accumulation:

$$K_{t+1} = (1 - \delta)K_t + I_t \tag{10.11}$$

By substituting the capital accumulation equation into the budget constraint, it can be defined as:

$$C_t + K_{t+1} = W_t L_t + (R_t + 1 - \delta)K_t \tag{10.12}$$

Now, we proceed to write the budget constraint in per capita terms, where:

$$k_t = \frac{K_t}{L_t} \tag{10.13}$$

Multiplying and dividing one of the sides of the budget constraint (10.12) by the population results in:

$$\frac{C_t}{L_t} + \frac{K_{t+1}}{L_t} = \frac{W_t L_t + (R_t + 1 - \delta)K_t}{L_t} \tag{10.14}$$

what supposes that:

$$c_t + \frac{K_{t+1}}{L_t} = W_t + (R_t + 1 - \delta)k_t \tag{10.15}$$

By multiplying and dividing by the population in $t + 1$, the second term on the left is:

$$c_t + \frac{K_{t+1}}{L_t}\frac{L_{t+1}}{L_{t+1}} = W_t + (R_t + 1 - \delta)k_t \tag{10.16}$$

or equivalently:

$$c_t + k_{t+1}\frac{L_{t+1}}{L_t} = W_t + (R_t + 1 - \delta)k_t \tag{10.17}$$

and operating, given that,

$$\frac{L_{t+1}}{L_t} = (1+n) \tag{10.18}$$

results in:

$$c_t + k_{t+1}(1+n) = W_t + (R_t + 1 - \delta)k_t \tag{10.19}$$

Structure of the Ramsey model	
Household utility function	$U = U(C_t)$
Budget constraint	$C_t + I_t = W_t L_t + R_t K_t$
Initial capital stock	$K_0 = \bar{K} > 0$
Equation of capital accumulation	$K_{t+1} = (1-\delta)K_t + I_t$
Production function	$Y_t = A_t F(K_t, L_t)$
Production growth rate	$L_t = L_{t-1}(1+n)$

Logarithmic utility function

To obtain an explicit solution to the previous problem, we are going to define a functional form for the preferences. In particular, let's assume that the utility function is logarithmic, such that:

$$U(c_t) = \ln c_t \tag{10.19}$$

The problem of the consumer would be to solve the following problem:

$$\max_{\{c_t\}_{t=0}^{\infty}} \sum_{t=0}^{T} \left(\frac{1+n}{1+\theta}\right)^t \ln c_t \tag{10.20}$$

subject to:

$$c_t + (1+n)k_{t+1} = W_t + (R_t + 1 - \delta)k_t \tag{10.21}$$

given a $k_0 > 0$.

The Lagrange auxiliary function would be:

$$\mathcal{L} = \sum_{t=0}^{T} \left(\frac{1+n}{1+\theta}\right)^t \ln c_t - \lambda_t [c_t + (1+n)k_{t+1} - W_t - (R_t + 1 - \delta)k_t] \tag{10.22}$$

First-order conditions, for $t = 0, 1, 2, \dots, T$, are the following:

$$\frac{\partial \mathcal{L}}{\partial c_t} = \left(\frac{1+n}{1+\theta}\right)^t \frac{1}{c_t} - \lambda_t = 0 \tag{10.23}$$

$$\frac{\partial \mathcal{L}}{\partial k_{t+1}} = \lambda_{t+1}(R_{t+1} + 1 - \delta) - \lambda_t(1+n) \tag{10.24}$$

$$\frac{\partial \mathcal{L}}{\partial \lambda_t} = c_t + (1+n)k_{t+1} - W_t - (R_t + 1 - \delta)k_t = 0 \tag{10.25}$$

From the first first-order condition we obtain:

$$\lambda_t = \left(\frac{1+n}{1+\theta}\right)^t \frac{1}{c_t} \tag{10.26}$$

Substituting the value of the Lagrange multiplier in t and in $t+1$, in the second condition of first order, results in:

$$\left(\frac{1+n}{1+\theta}\right)^{t+1} \frac{1}{c_{t+1}} (R_{t+1} + 1 - \delta) = (1+n)\left(\frac{1+n}{1+\theta}\right)^t \frac{1}{c_t} \tag{10.27}$$

and simplifying:

$$\frac{1}{1+\theta}\frac{1}{c_{t+1}}(R_{t+1} + 1 - \delta) = \frac{1}{c_t} \tag{10.28}$$

resulting in the following dynamic equation for per capita consumption:

$$c_{t+1} = \frac{(R_{t+1} + 1 - \delta)}{1+\theta} c_t \tag{10.29}$$

or equivalently:

$$c_{t+1} = \beta(R_{t+1} + 1 - \delta)c_t \tag{10.30}$$

As we can see, this optimal path of consumption is the same as we have previously obtained in the basic dynamic general equilibrium model, with the only difference that in this expression consumption is defined in per capita terms. In terms of aggregate consumption, this equation would be:

$$\frac{C_{t+1}}{L_{t+1}} = \beta(R_{t+1} + 1 - \delta)\frac{C_t}{L_t} \tag{10.31}$$

or equivalently, using the expression (10.18):

$$C_{t+1} = \beta(R_{t+1} + 1 - \delta)(1+n)C_t \tag{10.32}$$

where now the optimal path of aggregate consumption also depends on the rate of population growth. If we assume that the population remains constant, that is $n = 0$, then the previous expression is exactly the same as what we have obtained when solving the basic household maximization problem.

10.2.3. The firms

Next, we will analyze the behavior of firms. Since our variables of interest are defined in per capita terms, and also the household maximization problem had been solved in per capita terms, we also have to define the firm profit maximization problem in per capita terms. Since we are assuming that the owner of the productive factors is the family, the profit maximization problem is static, in which the firms maximize profits period by period, deciding the quantity of productive factors that they rent to the family at every moment of time. In general terms, companies maximize the benefits, Π_t, subject to technological restriction:

$$\max \Pi_t = Y_t - W_t L_t - R_t K_t \tag{10.33}$$

where the production function (the technological restriction) is:

$$Y_t = A_t F(K_t, L_t) \tag{10.34}$$

As we can see, we have defined the total costs as the wage costs plus the costs of capital. However, we have to define all the variables in per capita terms to be compatible with the family' maximization problem. The profit maximization problem in per capita terms would be:

$$\max \pi_t = y_t - w_t - R_t k_t \tag{10.35}$$

being the function of intensive production in capital:

$$y_t = A_t f(k_t) \tag{10.36}$$

Now, firms would maximize with respect to the stock of capital per capita, which would be the only productive factor considered since it is a combination of the two productive factors, capital and labor. The first-order condition from the maximization is given by:

$$\frac{\partial \pi}{\partial k} = A_t f_k(k_t) - R_t \tag{10.37}$$

From the previous expression, we obtain that the marginal productivity of capital per capita is equal to the interest rate:

$$A_t f_k(k_t) = R_t \tag{10.38}$$

When defining the profit maximization problem in per capita terms, the labor factor does not appear explicitly, so we do not have a first-order condition with respect to this productive factor, given that labor is equal to the population. The equilibrium wage is obtained as the difference between what is produced (total income) and the fraction of production that is destined to return the stock of capital per capita:

$$w_t = A_t f(k_t) - A_t f_k(k_t) \tag{10.39}$$

Cobb-Douglas production function

In the case where the production function is of the Cobb-Douglas type, we would have that the problem for firms in per capita terms would be:

$$\max \pi_t = A_t k_t^\alpha - w_t - R_t k_t \tag{10.40}$$

Again, only one first-order condition is derived with respect to per capita capital stock, since it is a combination of the two productive factors, capital and labor:

$$\frac{\partial \pi}{\partial k} = \alpha A_t k_t^{\alpha-1} - R_t = 0 \tag{10.41}$$

From the previous expression, we obtain that the marginal productivity of capital per capita is equal to the real interest rate:

$$\alpha A_t k_t^{\alpha-1} = R_t \qquad (10.42)$$

or what is the same, the return to capital is a proportion given by α of output:

$$R_t k_t = \alpha y_t \qquad (10.43)$$

Given that the maximization of profits is carried out in per capita terms, we do not have a first-order condition with respect to employment. In this case, the equilibrium wage would be obtained as the difference between total income and capital income, in per capita terms, as we have defined previously, and hence,

$$w_t = A_t k_t^{\alpha} - k_t \alpha A_t k_t^{\alpha-1} = A_t k_t^{\alpha} - \alpha A_t k_t^{\alpha} = (1-\alpha)y_t \qquad (10.44)$$

10.2.4. The competitive equilibrium

The competitive equilibrium is given by the vector of values for the endogenous variables in which the optimal plans of the family and the firm coincide. That is, it is defined by that situation in which the stock of capital per capita that firms want to hire is equal to the amount of financial assets per capita that households decide to accumulate. To obtain the expressions corresponding to the equilibrium of the model, we have to substitute the price of the productive factors (wage and interest rate) in the expressions that reflect the optimal decisions of the households. Thus, we obtain a system of two difference equations, which allow us to determine both the per capita consumption and the capital stock per capita. Once these two variables are determined, we can calculate the level of output per capita and the saving (investment) per capita.

We start from the dynamic equation for per capita consumption, which is given by the expression:

$$c_{t+1} = \beta(R_{t+1} + 1 - \delta)c_t \qquad (10.45)$$

Substituting the equilibrium value for the interest rate results in:

$$c_{t+1} = \beta(\alpha A_{t+1} k_{t+1}^{\alpha-1} + 1 - \delta)c_t \qquad (10.46)$$

On the other hand, the dynamic equation for the stock of capital per capita is obtained from the budgetary restriction of the individual. By substituting the equilibrium values for the interest rate and salary:

$$c_t + (1+n)k_{t+1} = A_t k_t^{\alpha} - \alpha A_t k_t^{\alpha} + (\alpha A_t k_t^{\alpha-1} + 1 - \delta)k_t \qquad (10.47)$$

and by rearranging terms we would arrive at:

$$c_t + (1+n)k_{t+1} = A_t k_t^{\alpha} + (1-\delta)k_t \qquad (10.48)$$

so we would obtain a dynamic system composed of two non-linear difference equations, one for per capita consumption and another for the stock of capital per capita.

10.2.5. Steady state

The steady state is defined as that situation in which all the variables of the economy are constant over time. Since we assume that the total productivity of the factors is an exogenous variable, we consider it constant, so we are going to eliminate the time subscript. Starting from the dynamic condition for per capita consumption, in steady state we obtain:

$$1 = \beta\left(\alpha \bar{A}\bar{k}^{\alpha-1} + 1 - \delta\right) \tag{10.49}$$

from which we obtain that the stock of per capita capital in steady state is:

$$\bar{k} = \left(\frac{1-\beta+\beta\delta}{\alpha A \beta}\right)^{\frac{1}{\alpha-1}} \tag{10.50}$$

From the dynamic condition for the stock of per capita capital in steady state, it results:

$$\bar{c} + (1+n)\bar{k} = (1-\alpha)A\bar{k}^{\alpha} + \alpha A\bar{k}^{\alpha} + (1-\delta)\bar{k} \tag{10.51}$$

And by operating results that:

$$\bar{c} = A\bar{k}^{\alpha} - (n+\delta)\bar{k} \tag{10.52}$$

So the per capita consumption in steady state would be given by:

$$\bar{c} = A\left(\frac{1-\beta+\beta\delta}{\alpha A \beta}\right)^{\frac{\alpha}{\alpha-1}} - (n+\delta)\left(\frac{1-\beta+\beta\delta}{\alpha A \beta}\right)^{\frac{1}{\alpha-1}} \tag{10.53}$$

10.3. Calibration of the model

Before proceeding with the resolution and numerical simulation of the model, it is necessary to calibrate the value of the model parameters. The value of these parameters can be estimated or simply calibrated using the information available about them. In this simple model we have four parameters: The technological parameter of the production function, α, the discount factor of future utility, β, the rate of depreciation of capital, δ, and the rate of population growth, n. The values that we are going to use for these parameters appear in Table 10.1. The technological parameter that determines the elasticity of the production level with respect to the stock of capital is set at 0.35, which corresponds approximately to the proportion of labor income over total income, given that from the Cobb-Douglas production function that we are using it turns out that:

$$\alpha = \frac{R_t K_t}{Y_t} \tag{10.54}$$

that is, the proportion of capital income over total income, which in national accounts, is around 35%. We have assumed the discount factor is equal to 0.97, which implies that the annual steady-state interest rate is of 9.09% (this type includes 6% of capital depreciation, so the real return is of 3.09%), given that in steady state we obtain that:

$$\bar{R} = \frac{1}{\beta} - 1 + \delta \tag{10.55}$$

We assume the physical depreciation rate of capital is 6% per year, which is a standard value used in macroeconomic models.

Table 10.1: Calibration of parameters

Symbol	Definition	Value
α	Production-capital elasticity	0.35
β	Discount factor	0.97
δ	Depreciation rate	0.06

Additionally, the model includes as exogenous variables the aggregate productivity or Total Factor Productivity, A_t, and the population growth rate. The steady-state value that we will consider the TFP is normalized to one. Finally, let's assume that the population growth rate is 2% ($n = 0.02$). Note that with these calibrated values the condition that $\theta > n$ is met. In fact, $\theta = 1/\beta - 1 = 0.0309$, which is greater than the calibrated value for the population growth rate of 0.02.

Table 10.2 shows the steady-state values for the model variables, using the expressions obtained previously. In effect, if we use the calibrated value of the parameters, we substitute them in the expression for the stock of capital per capita, it results:

$$\bar{k} = \left(\frac{1-\beta+\beta\delta}{\alpha A\beta}\right)^{\frac{1}{\alpha-1}} = \left(\frac{1-0.97+0.97\times0.06}{0.35\times1\times0.97}\right)^{\frac{1}{-0.65}} = 7.954$$

Next, we can calculate the steady-state production level since:

$$\bar{y} = A\bar{k}^\alpha = 1 \times 7.954^{0.35} = 2.066$$

Similarly, steady state real interest rate would be given by:

$$\bar{R} = \alpha A\bar{k}^{\alpha-1} = 0.35 \times 1 \times 7.954^{-0.65} = 0.0909$$

The consumption in steady state would be given by:

$$\bar{c} = A\bar{k}^\alpha - (n+\delta)\bar{k} = 2.066 - (0.02 + 0.06) \times 7.954 = 1.430$$

so the investment in steady state would be:

$$\bar{\iota} = \bar{y} - \bar{c} = A\bar{k}^\alpha - A\bar{k}^\alpha - (n + \delta)\bar{k} = (n + \delta)\bar{k} = (0.02 + 0.06) \times 7.954 = 0.636$$

Table 10.2: Value of steady-state variables

Variable	Definition	Value
$\bar{y}$	Production per capita	2.066
$\bar{c}$	Consumption per capita	1.430
$\bar{\iota}$	Investment per capita	0.636
$\bar{k}$	Stock of capital per capita	7.954
$\bar{R}$	Interest rate	0.091

10.4. Linearization of the model

Next, we proceed to the log-linearization of the model, a task that may be tedious, but necessary to proceed with its numerical resolution.

Log-linearization of the production level equation

First, we log-linearize the production function in per capita terms. To simplify our analysis, we assume that TFP is an exogenous variable and therefore a constant, so we ignore the time subscript for TFP. The equation corresponding to the level of production is given by:

$$y_t = Ak_t^\alpha \tag{10.55}$$

Applying the rules of log-linearization results in:

$$\bar{y}(1 + \hat{y}_t) = A\bar{k}^\alpha(1 + \alpha\hat{k}_t) \tag{10.56}$$

or equivalently:

$$\bar{y} + y\hat{y}_t = A\bar{k}^\alpha + \alpha A\hat{k}_t\bar{k}^\alpha \tag{10.57}$$

In steady state we would have to $\bar{y} = A\bar{k}^\alpha$, so it turns out:

$$y\hat{y}_t = \alpha A\hat{k}_t\bar{k}^\alpha \tag{10.58}$$

and by operating, again using the definition of steady state, we finally arrive at:

$$\hat{y}_t = \alpha\hat{k}_t \tag{10.59}$$

where $\hat{y}_t = \ln Y_t - \ln \bar{Y}$.

Log-linearization of the dynamic equation of the capital stock per capita

Next, we proceed to log-linearize the dynamic equation for the stock of capital per capita:

$$c_t + k_{t+1}(1+n) = (1-\delta)k_t + y_t \tag{10.60}$$

Applying the rules of log-linearization results in:

$$\bar{c}(1+\hat{c}_t) + \bar{k}(1+n)\left(1+\hat{k}_{t+1}\right) = (1-\delta)\bar{k}\left(1+\hat{k}_t\right) + \bar{y}(1+\hat{y}_t) \tag{10.61}$$

Using the definition of steady state:

$$\bar{c} + \bar{k}(1+n) = (1-\delta)\bar{k} + \bar{y} \tag{10.62}$$

and operating results:

$$\bar{c}\hat{c}_t + \bar{k}(1+n)\hat{k}_{t+1} = (1-\delta)\bar{k}\hat{k}_t + \bar{y}\hat{y}_t \tag{10.63}$$

Reordering terms:

$$\frac{\bar{c}}{\bar{k}}\hat{c}_t + (1+n)\hat{k}_t = (1-\delta)\hat{k}_t + \frac{\bar{y}}{\bar{k}}\hat{y}_t \tag{10.64}$$

Using the steady state values for consumption, capital and output, it turns out that:

$$\frac{\bar{c}}{\bar{k}} = \frac{A\left(\frac{1-\beta+\beta\delta}{\alpha A\beta}\right)^{\frac{\alpha}{\alpha-1}} - (n+\delta)\left(\frac{1-\beta+\beta\delta}{\alpha A\beta}\right)^{\frac{1}{\alpha-1}}}{\left(\frac{1-\beta+\beta\delta}{\alpha A\beta}\right)^{\frac{1}{\alpha-1}}} \tag{10.65}$$

and:

$$\frac{\bar{y}}{\bar{k}} = \left(\frac{1-\beta+\beta\delta}{\alpha\beta}\right) \tag{10.66}$$

By substituting the values of steady state, we obtain:

$$\left[\frac{1-\beta+\beta\delta}{\alpha\beta} - (n+\delta)\right]\hat{c}_t + (1+n)\hat{k}_{t+1} = (1-\delta)\hat{k}_t + \left(\frac{1-\beta+\beta\delta}{\alpha\beta}\right)\hat{k}_t \tag{10.67}$$

Operating:

$$\left[\frac{1-\beta+\beta\delta}{\alpha\beta} - (n+\delta)\right]\hat{c}_t + (1+n)\hat{k}_{t+1} = \frac{1}{\beta}\hat{k}_t \tag{10.68}$$

Operating again:

$$(1+n)\hat{k}_{t+1} = \frac{1}{\beta}\hat{k}_t - \left[\frac{1-\beta+\beta\delta}{\alpha\beta} - (n+\delta)\right]\hat{c}_t \tag{10.69}$$

or equivalently,

$$\hat{k}_{t+1} = \frac{1}{\beta(1+n)}\hat{k}_t - \left[\frac{1-\beta+\beta\delta}{\alpha\beta(1+n)} - \frac{(n+\delta)}{(1+n)}\right]\hat{c}_t \tag{10.70}$$

By adding and subtracting $\hat{k}_t$ in the above expression, we obtain:

$$\hat{k}_{t+1} - \hat{k}_t + \hat{k}_t = \frac{1}{\beta(1+n)}\hat{k}_t - \left[\frac{1-\beta+\beta\delta}{\alpha\beta} - (n+\delta)\right]\hat{c}_t \tag{10.71}$$

and by defining $\Delta\hat{k}_t = \hat{k}_{t+1} - \hat{k}_t$, we finally arrive at the log-linearized dynamic equation for the stock of capital per capita:

$$\Delta\hat{k}_t = \frac{1-\beta(1+n)}{\beta(1+n)}\hat{k}_t - \left[\frac{1-\beta+\beta\delta-\alpha\beta(n+\delta)}{\alpha\beta}\right]\hat{c}_t \tag{10.72}$$

Note that if we assume that the population is constant $(n = 0)$, this equation would be the same as that obtained in the basic dynamic general equilibrium model solved in Chapter 8.

Log-linearization of the dynamic equation of consumption per capita

Next, we proceed to log-linearize the dynamic equation for per capita consumption, whose expression is given by:

$$c_{t+1} = \beta(\alpha A k_{t+1}^{\alpha-1} + 1 - \delta)c_t \tag{10.73}$$

By applying the above rules results that:

$$\bar{c}(1 + \hat{c}_{t+1}) = \beta(1-\delta)\bar{c}(1+\hat{c}_t) + \beta\alpha A\bar{k}^{\alpha-1}\bar{c}(1+(\alpha-1)\hat{k}_{t+1}+\hat{c}_t) \tag{10.74}$$

By operating, we obtain:

$$\bar{c} + \bar{c}\hat{c}_{t+1} = \beta(1-\delta)\bar{c} + (1-\delta)\bar{c}\hat{c}_t + \beta\alpha A\bar{k}^{\alpha-1}\bar{c}$$

$$+\beta\alpha A\bar{k}^{\alpha-1}\bar{c}(\alpha-1)\hat{k}_{t+1} + \beta\alpha A\bar{k}^{\alpha-1}\bar{c}\hat{c}_t \tag{10.75}$$

Using the definition of said equation in steady state,

$$\bar{c} = \beta(1-\delta)\bar{c} + \beta\alpha A\bar{k}^{\alpha-1}\bar{c} \tag{10.76}$$

and by operating, it results that:

$$\bar{c}\hat{c}_{t+1} = (1-\delta)\bar{c}\hat{c}_t + \beta\alpha A\bar{k}^{\alpha-1}\bar{c}((\alpha-1)\hat{k}_{t+1}+\hat{c}_t) \tag{10.77}$$

or equivalently

$$\hat{c}_{t+1} = \beta(1-\delta)\hat{c}_t + \beta\alpha A\bar{k}^{\alpha-1}((\alpha-1)\hat{k}_{t+1}+\hat{c}_t) \tag{10.78}$$

and replacing the steady-state value for the capital stock per capita results in:

$$\hat{c}_{t+1} = \beta(1-\delta)\hat{c}_t + (1-\beta+\beta\delta)((\alpha-1)\hat{k}_{t+1}+\hat{c}_t) \tag{10.79}$$

and operating:

$$\hat{c}_{t+1} = \hat{c}_t + (1-\beta+\beta\delta)(\alpha-1)\hat{k}_{t+1} \tag{10.80}$$

From the expression (10.70), we obtain that:

$$\hat{k}_{t+1} = \frac{1}{\beta(1+n)}\hat{k}_t - \left[\frac{1-\beta+\beta\delta-\alpha\beta(\delta+n)}{\alpha\beta(1+n)}\right]\hat{c}_t \tag{10.81}$$

and by substituting it results that:

$$\hat{c}_{t+1} = \hat{c}_t + (1-\beta+\beta\delta)(\alpha-1)\left[\frac{1}{\beta(1+n)}\hat{k}_t - \left[\frac{1-\beta+\beta\delta-\alpha\beta(\delta+n)}{\alpha\beta(1+n)}\right]\hat{c}_t\right] \tag{10.82}$$

Defining

$$\Omega = 1 - \beta + \beta\delta$$

and

$$\Gamma = 1 - \beta + \beta\delta - \alpha\beta(\delta + n)$$

results in:

$$\Delta\hat{c}_t = \frac{(\alpha-1)\Omega}{\beta(1+n)}\hat{k}_t - \frac{(\alpha-1)\Omega\Gamma}{\alpha\beta(1+n)}\hat{c}_t \tag{10.83}$$

This expression indicates that variations in per capita consumption (in terms of their deviations from their steady state) depend negatively (α is less than one and β is less than one), deviations from the stock of capital per capita with respect to its steady-state value and positively of the deviations of per capita consumption with respect to its steady state. That is, if the stock of capital per capita is below its steady-state value ($\hat{k}_t$ is a negative number), then the variation of per capita consumption must be positive. Note that if we assume that the population is constant ($n = 0$), this expression is exactly the same as that obtained in Chapter 8 for the linear approximation to the dynamic equation of consumption in the basic general equilibrium model.

Log-linearization of the investment equation

Finally, the log-linear equation for the investment is given by:

$$i_t = y_t - c_t \tag{10.84}$$

so applying the rules of log-linearization results in:

$$\bar{\imath}(1 + \hat{\imath}_t) = \bar{y}(1 + \hat{y}_t) - \bar{c}(1 + \hat{c}_t) \tag{10.85}$$

or equivalently

$$\bar{\imath} + \bar{\imath}\hat{\imath}_t = \bar{y} + \bar{y}\hat{y}_t - \bar{c} - \bar{c}\hat{c}_t \tag{10.86}$$

In steady state it turns out that:

$$\bar{\imath} = \bar{y} - \bar{c} \tag{10.87}$$

so the above expression can be simplified to:

$$\bar{\imath}\hat{\imath}_t = \bar{y}\hat{y}_t - \bar{c}\hat{c}_t \tag{10.88}$$

and clearing the deviations of the investment with respect to its value of steady state results in:

$$\hat{\imath}_t = \frac{\bar{y}}{\bar{\imath}}\hat{y}_t - \frac{\bar{c}}{\bar{\imath}}\hat{c}_t \tag{10.89}$$

Using the steady-state definitions it turns out that:

$$\frac{\bar{y}}{\bar{\imath}} = \frac{1-\beta+\beta\delta}{\alpha\beta(n+\delta)} \tag{10.90}$$

And

$$\frac{\bar{c}}{\bar{\iota}} = \frac{1-\beta+\beta\delta-\alpha\beta\delta}{\alpha\beta(n+\delta)} \tag{10.91}$$

By substituting we arrive at:

$$\hat{\iota}_t = \frac{1-\beta+\beta\delta}{\alpha\beta(n+\delta)}\hat{y}_t - \frac{1-\beta+\beta\delta-\alpha\beta\delta}{\alpha\beta(n+\delta)}\hat{c}_t \tag{10.92}$$

Discrete log-linearized system

Therefore, the Ramsey model can be defined through the following discrete linear dynamic system:

$$\begin{bmatrix} \Delta\hat{c}_t \\ \Delta\hat{k}_t \end{bmatrix} = \begin{bmatrix} -\frac{(\alpha-1)\Omega\Gamma}{\alpha\beta(1+n)} & \frac{(\alpha-1)\Omega}{\beta(1+n)} \\ -\frac{\Gamma}{\alpha\beta(1+n)} & \frac{1-\beta(1+n)}{\beta(1+n)} \end{bmatrix} \begin{bmatrix} \hat{c}_t \\ \hat{k}_t \end{bmatrix} \tag{10.93}$$

In this version of the Ramsey model, we have four fundamental macroeconomic variables: consumption, investment, capital stock and production. From the previous dynamic system, we extract all trajectories associated with consumption and capital stock. Once these values are obtained, from the production function, we obtain output and from the economy's feasibility constraint we obtain investment.

By substituting the calibrated values for the parameters, we obtain that:

$$\Omega = 1 - 0.97 + 0.97 \times 0.06 = 0.0882$$

$$\Gamma = 1 - 0.97 + 0.97 \times -0.35 \times 0.97 \times 0.08 = 0.061$$

so the Ramsey model would be given by the following system of two linear difference equations:

$$\begin{bmatrix} \Delta\hat{c}_t \\ \Delta\hat{k}_t \end{bmatrix} = \begin{bmatrix} 0.01 & -0.0579 \\ -0.176 & 0.0107 \end{bmatrix} \begin{bmatrix} \hat{c}_t \\ \hat{k}_t \end{bmatrix}$$

From this system, we can simulate the future values of both consumption and capital stock. Thus, knowing the values of these variables at period t (their deviations from their steady state), we can calculate the variation that these variables will experience in that period, which in turn gives us its value in the following period, given that $\Delta\hat{c}_t = \hat{c}_{t+1} - \hat{c}_t$, so it turns out that $\hat{c}_{t+1} = \Delta\hat{c}_t + \hat{c}_t$. For the stock of capital, it would be equivalent. Thus, the model says, for example, that if the consumption deviation with respect to its steady-state value today is 5% ($\hat{c}_t = 0.05$), and the deviation of the stock of capital is 10% ($\hat{k}_t = 0.10$), then it turns out that $\hat{c}_{t+1} = \Delta\hat{c}_t + \hat{c}_t = 0.01 \times 0.05 - 0.057 \times 0.10 + 0.05 = 0.045$, while $\hat{k}_{t+1} = \Delta\hat{k}_t + \hat{k}_t = -0.176 \times 0.05 + 0.0107 \times 0.10 + 0.10 = 0.092$.

10.4.2. Stability analysis

Next, we perform the stability analysis to calculate the value of the eigenvalues associated with this model. This model will have a saddle-point solution, which implies that one of the roots will be positive and the other will be negative. To calculate the value of the eigenvalues associated with this model, we solve

$$Det \begin{bmatrix} -\frac{(\alpha-1)\Omega\Gamma}{\alpha\beta(1+n)} - \lambda & \frac{(\alpha-1)\Omega}{\beta(1+n)} \\ -\frac{\Gamma}{\alpha\beta(1+n)} & \frac{1-\beta(1+n)}{\beta(1+n)} - \lambda \end{bmatrix} = 0 \tag{10.94}$$

giving rise to the following equation of the second degree:

$$\lambda^2 + \left[\frac{(\alpha-1)\Omega\Gamma}{\alpha\beta(1+n)} - \frac{1-\beta(1+n)}{\beta(1+n)}\right]\lambda + \frac{(\alpha-1)\Omega\Gamma}{\alpha\beta(1+n)} - \left(\frac{(\alpha-1)\Omega\Gamma}{\alpha\beta(1+n)}\right)\left(\frac{1-\beta(1+n)}{\beta(1+n)}\right) = 0 \tag{10.95}$$

or equivalently

$$\lambda^2 + \left[\frac{(\alpha-1)\Omega\Gamma-\alpha+\alpha\beta(1+n)}{\alpha\beta(1+n)}\right]\lambda + \frac{(\alpha-1)\Omega\Gamma}{\alpha\beta(1+n)} = 0 \tag{10.96}$$

By calculating its roots results that:

$$\lambda_1, \lambda_2 = \frac{-\left[\frac{(\alpha-1)\Omega\Gamma-\alpha+\alpha\beta(1+n)}{\alpha\beta(1+n)}\right]\pm\sqrt{\left[\frac{(\alpha-1)\Omega\Gamma-\alpha+\alpha\beta(1+n)}{\alpha\beta(1+n)}\right]^2 - 4\frac{(\alpha-1)\Omega\Gamma}{\alpha\beta(1+n)}}}{2} \tag{10.97}$$

Using the calibrated values of the parameters, it results in:

$$\lambda_1 = \frac{0.021-\sqrt{0.021^2+0.04}}{2} = -0.091$$

$$\lambda_2 = \frac{0.021+\sqrt{0.021^2+0.04}}{2} = 0.111$$

so the module of the eigenvalues plus the unit would be 0.91 and 1.11, respectively, so that the model has as a saddle point solution.

10.4.3. The stable saddle path

As we have calculated in the previous section, the trajectories of the variables are determined by the existence of a saddle point. That means that there is a single stable path that converges to the steady state. Thus, when a disturbance occurs, the economy adjusts instantaneously until reaching this stable path. The variable "jumping" will be the forward looking variable (consumption), whose value will be adjusted instantaneously to a value compatible with the new stable saddle path, along which the economy will move until reaching the new steady state. This stable saddle path will be associated with the stable eigenvalue, the one whose module plus one is less than a unit. For the calibrated model we are solving, the stable saddle path would be represented by:

$$\begin{bmatrix} \Delta\hat{c}_t \\ \Delta\hat{k}_t \end{bmatrix} = \lambda_1 \begin{bmatrix} \hat{c}_t \\ \hat{k}_t \end{bmatrix} = -0.091 \begin{bmatrix} \hat{c}_t \\ \hat{k}_t \end{bmatrix}$$

Thus, using the same values as in the previous example, if we assume that the deviation of the consumption with respect to its steady-state value is 5% and that of the stock of capital is 10%, then we would have that the deviations in the next period would be from 0.05-0.091 = 0.044 and 0.10-0.091 = 0.092, respectively. As we can verify, these values are the same as those calculated previously, so this trajectory verifies the stable saddle path of the system.

10.4.4. Instant readjustment in consumption

As we have seen in previous exercises, when the trajectories of the system variables are determined by a saddle-point solution, then it becomes necessary to resort to another additional equation to be able to solve the model. This additional equation is what we call the stable saddle path. The stable saddle path would indicate the trajectory that takes us directly to the steady state, being a trajectory to which the forward looking (jump) variable is instantaneously adjusted. In the case of the Ramsey model, we are solving the model in terms of two variables: per capita consumption and the stock of capital per capita. While consumption is a forward-looking variable, which can be adjusted instantaneously in a new economic environment (is a flexible variable), the stock of capital is a rigid variable, since it implies the change in a physical variable that cannot be realized instantaneously, but rather needs time for its adjustment. To calculate the adjustment that has to occur in per capita consumption, we start from its dynamic equation:

$$\Delta \hat{c}_t = \frac{(\alpha-1)\Omega}{\beta(1+n)} \hat{k}_t - \frac{(\alpha-1)\Omega\Gamma}{\alpha\beta(1+n)} \hat{c}_t \tag{10.98}$$

On the other hand, the stable path would be defined by the following trajectory,

$$\Delta \hat{c}_t = \lambda_1 \hat{c}_t \tag{10.99}$$

Matching both expressions results in:

$$\frac{(\alpha-1)\Omega}{\beta(1+n)} \hat{k}_t - \frac{(\alpha-1)\Omega\Gamma}{\alpha\beta(1+n)} \hat{c}_t = \lambda_1 \hat{c}_t \tag{10.100}$$

Solving for the derivation of per capita consumption, we obtain that the new value of the deviations of consumption at the moment in which the disturbance occurs is given by:

$$\hat{c}_t = \frac{\alpha(\alpha-1)\Omega}{(\alpha-1)\Omega\Gamma+\alpha\beta(1+n)\lambda_1} \hat{k}_t \tag{10.101}$$

where value coincides with the readjustment that must occur in this variable, since the deviation from the steady state is zero before the disturbance occurs.

10.5. Numerical solution

Figure 10.1 shows the Excel spreadsheet corresponding to the proposed model, called "**ICM-10.xls**". By solving numerically, the previous linear dynamical system, we can obtain the optimal trajectories of consumption, investment, capital stock and output, following any disturbance, from what we can predict the future behavior of the economy by simply simulating numerically the discrete dynamic system in terms of which this model is defined. The equivalent code in DYNARE is shown in Appendix P.

EXERCISE 10: The Ramsey model

Parameters	Initial	Final
Beta	0.97	0.96
Alpha	0.35	0.35
Delta	0.06	0.06
OMEGA	0.088	0.088
GAMMA	0.061	0.061

Exogenous variables	Initial	Final
A	1	1
n	0.02	0.02

Steady State	Initial	Final
Capital stock	7.954	8.080
Output	2.066	2.070
Consumption	1.430	1.431
Investment	0.636	0.646

Eigenvalues	Initial	Final
λ_1	-0.091	-0.095
λ_2	0.111	0.105

Stability condition	
Modulus (1-λ1)	0.91
Modulus (1-λ2)	1.10

Time	C	I	Y	K	c	i	y	k						
0	1.430	0.636	2.066	7.954	0.358	-0.452	0.726	2.074	0.000	0.000	0.000	0.000	0.000	0.000
1	1.419	0.647	2.066	7.954	0.350	-0.435	0.726	2.074	-0.009	0.003	-0.006	-0.016	0.001	0.001
2	1.420	0.647	2.067	7.966	0.351	-0.435	0.726	2.075	-0.008	0.003	-0.005	-0.014	0.001	0.001
3	1.421	0.647	2.068	7.976	0.352	-0.435	0.727	2.076	-0.007	0.003	-0.005	-0.013	0.001	0.001
4	1.422	0.647	2.069	7.986	0.352	-0.435	0.727	2.078	-0.006	0.002	-0.004	-0.012	0.001	0.001
5	1.423	0.647	2.070	7.995	0.353	-0.435	0.728	2.079	-0.006	0.002	-0.004	-0.011	0.001	0.001
6	1.424	0.647	2.071	8.003	0.353	-0.436	0.728	2.080	-0.005	0.002	-0.003	-0.010	0.000	0.001
7	1.425	0.647	2.071	8.010	0.354	-0.436	0.728	2.081	-0.005	0.002	-0.003	-0.009	0.000	0.001
8	1.425	0.647	2.072	8.017	0.354	-0.436	0.729	2.082	-0.004	0.002	-0.003	-0.008	0.000	0.001
9	1.426	0.647	2.073	8.023	0.355	-0.436	0.729	2.082	-0.004	0.001	-0.002	-0.007	0.000	0.001
10	1.426	0.647	2.073	8.028	0.355	-0.436	0.729	2.083	-0.004	0.001	-0.002	-0.006	0.000	0.001
11	1.427	0.647	2.074	8.033	0.355	-0.436	0.729	2.084	-0.003	0.001	-0.002	-0.006	0.000	0.001
12	1.427	0.647	2.074	8.038	0.356	-0.436	0.729	2.084	-0.003	0.001	-0.002	-0.005	0.000	0.001
13	1.428	0.647	2.074	8.042	0.356	-0.436	0.730	2.085	-0.003	0.001	-0.001	-0.005	0.000	0.000
14	1.428	0.647	2.075	8.045	0.356	-0.436	0.730	2.085	-0.002	0.001	-0.001	-0.004	0.000	0.000
15	1.428	0.647	2.075	8.049	0.356	-0.436	0.730	2.086	-0.002	0.001	-0.001	-0.004	0.000	0.000
16	1.429	0.647	2.075	8.052	0.357	-0.436	0.730	2.086	-0.002	0.001	-0.001	-0.004	0.000	0.000
17	1.429	0.647	2.075	8.054	0.357	-0.436	0.730	2.086	-0.002	0.001	-0.001	-0.003	0.000	0.000
18	1.429	0.647	2.076	8.057	0.357	-0.436	0.730	2.087	-0.002	0.001	-0.001	-0.003	0.000	0.000
19	1.429	0.647	2.076	8.059	0.357	-0.436	0.730	2.087	-0.001	0.001	-0.001	-0.003	0.000	0.000
20	1.430	0.647	2.076	8.061	0.357	-0.436	0.730	2.087	-0.001	0.000	-0.001	-0.002	0.000	0.000
21	1.430	0.647	2.076	8.063	0.357	-0.436	0.731	2.087	-0.001	0.000	-0.001	-0.002	0.000	0.000
22	1.430	0.647	2.076	8.065	0.358	-0.436	0.731	2.088	-0.001	0.000	-0.001	-0.002	0.000	0.000
23	1.430	0.647	2.076	8.066	0.358	-0.436	0.731	2.088	-0.001	0.000	-0.001	-0.002	0.000	0.000
24	1.430	0.646	2.077	8.067	0.358	-0.436	0.731	2.088	-0.001	0.000	-0.001	-0.002	0.000	0.000
25	1.430	0.646	2.077	8.069	0.358	-0.436	0.731	2.088	-0.001	0.000	-0.001	-0.001	0.000	0.000
26	1.430	0.646	2.077	8.070	0.358	-0.436	0.731	2.088	-0.001	0.000	0.000	-0.001	0.000	0.000
27	1.430	0.646	2.077	8.071	0.358	-0.436	0.731	2.088	-0.001	0.000	0.000	-0.001	0.000	0.000
28	1.431	0.646	2.077	8.072	0.358	-0.436	0.731	2.088	-0.001	0.000	0.000	-0.001	0.000	0.000
29	1.431	0.646	2.077	8.072	0.358	-0.436	0.731	2.088	-0.001	0.000	0.000	-0.001	0.000	0.000
30	1.431	0.646	2.077	8.073	0.358	-0.436	0.731	2.089	0.000	0.000	0.000	-0.001	0.000	0.000

Figure 10.1. Structure of the spreadsheet "ICM.10.xls": The Ramsey model.

The structure of this spreadsheet is as follows. In cells "B4" to "B8" appear the calibrated values of the parameters that define the initial steady state: the intertemporal discount rate, "Beta_0", the technological parameter of the stock of capital, "Alpha_0" and the depreciation physical rate of capital, "Delta_0". We also calculate the value of the combinations of parameters that will be useful to simplify the expressions in cells "B7" and "B8", which we have named "OMEGA_0" and "GAMMA_0". In column "C", these same parameters appear, in order to be able to perform direct simulations of changes in their value (sensitivity analysis). Initially, these values are the same in the initial state as in the final state, then the value of the exogenous variables is determined in cell "B11" for total factor productivity and cell "B12" for the population growth rate. The name assigned to these cells is "PTF_0" and "n_0", respectively. The same as the case of the parameters in column "B", the values of the initial steady state are entered and in column "C" the new values in the case in which you want to perform a disturbance analysis. Then, in cells "B15" to "B18", we have the values of the initial steady state for the stock of capital, production, consumption and investment. If we place the cursor in cell "B15", the expression we find is:

$$=(OMEGA\_0/(Alpha\_0*PTF\_0*Beta\_0))\wedge(1/(Alpha\_0-1))$$

expression that corresponds to the steady-state value for the stock of capital, given by (10.51). Cell "B16" contains the steady-state value of the production level, through the expression:

$$=PTF\_0*kss\_0\wedge Alpha\_0$$

which is simply the aggregate production function of the economy. If we place the cursor in cell "B17", we obtain the steady-state value for consumption, which we calculate using the following expression:

$$=yss\_0-(n\_0+Delta\_0)*kss\_0$$

Finally, cell "B18" contains the steady-state value of the investment, which we simply calculate as the difference between production and consumption. In cells "C15" to "C18", we obtain the steady-state values for these variables in the final situation, whose expressions are equivalent to the previous ones but are referenced to the values of the parameters at the final moment.

The eigenvalues associated with this system are calculated in cells "B21" and "B22". If we place the cursor in cell "B21", the expression that appears is:

$$=(-(((Alpha\_0-1)*OMEGA\_0*GAMMA\_0-Alpha\_0+Alpha\_0*Beta\_0*(1+n\_0))$$
$$/(Alpha\_0*Beta\_0*(1+n\_0)))$$
$$-ROOT((((Alpha\_0-1)*OMEGA\_0*GAMMA\_0-Alpha\_0$$
$$+Alpha\_0*Beta\_0*(1+n\_0))/(Alpha\_0*Beta\_0*(1+n\_0)))\wedge2$$
$$-4*(Alpha\_0-1)*OMEGA\_0*GAMMA\_0/(Alpha\_0*Beta\_0*(1+n\_0))))/2$$

which corresponds to the negative root of the expression (10.101). We find an equivalent expression, but for the positive root, in cell "B22". These eigenvalues correspond to the parameters that define the initial steady state. Cells "C21" and "C22" calculate the eigenvalues corresponding to the parameters that determine the final steady state. Finally, cells "B25" and "B26" show the module of each eigenvalue plus the unit, in order to determine the stability of the system.

The variables of the model are calculated in columns "E" to "S". In column "E", the time index is shown. In columns "F" to "I", the value of the variables in levels is calculated. The values of these variables in period 0 correspond to the initial steady state. In column "F", we have calculated the consumption for each period. If we place the cursor in cell "F3", the expression that appears is "=css_0", which is the consumption in the initial steady state. The expression that appears in cell "F4" is

$$=EXP(N4+LN(css\_1))$$

Columns "J" to "M" simply calculate the logarithm of the variables, while columns "N" to "Q" calculate the deviation of each variable with respect to its steady-state value. The key cells to numerically solve the model are the "N4" and the "Q4". If we place the cursor in cell "N4", the expression that appears is

$$=(Alpha\_1*(Alpha\_1-1)*OMEGA\_1/((Alpha\_1-1)*OMEGA\_1*GAMMA\_1$$
$$+Alpha\_1*Beta\_1*(1+n\_1)*Lambda1\_1))*Q4$$

that corresponds to the expression (10.101) and that calculates the jump that per capita consumption must take to reach the stable path. The rest of the cells in this column are simply calculated as the consumption value in the previous period plus the change in that period. Thus, for example, the expression in cell "N5" is "=N4+R4". For its part, cell "Q4" introduces the deviation that occurs in the stock of capital per capita with respect to its new steady-state value, so the expression corresponding to this cell is

$$=LN(kss\_0)-LN(kss\_1)$$

Finally, in the columns "R" and "S", the variations in the variables are calculated. The expression entered in cell "R3" is

$$=-((Alpha\_0-1)*OMEGA\_0*GAMMA\_0/(Alpha\_0*Beta\_0*(1+n\_0)))*N3$$
$$+((Alpha\_0-1)*OMEGA\_0/(Beta\_0*(1+n\_0)))*Q3$$

expression that corresponds to the dynamic equation of per capita consumption (10.87). This same expression appears in the following cells, but referred to the values of the parameters and exogenous variables in the new steady state. The expression entered in cell "S3" is

$$=-GAMMA\_0/(Alpha\_0*Beta\_0*(1+n\_0))*N3$$
$$+((1-Beta\_0*(1+n\_0))/(Beta\_0*(1+n\_0)))*Q3$$

expression that corresponds to the dynamic equation of the stock of capital per capita given by (10.72).

10.6. Shock analysis: Permanent change in Total Factor Productivity

Once obtained the numerical solution of the model, from the discrete dynamic system obtained previously, we can perform different simulation exercises of the economy. Thus, we can change the value of the exogenous variables and observe how the different variables of the model respond to this change. In Chapter 8, we studied the effect of a technological shock that involved an increase in TFP. In this section, we will repeat this analysis in the context of the Ramsey model. To do this, we only have to change the value of cell "C11" in spreadsheet "**ICM-10.xls**". In particular, we are going to assume that there is a decrease in the population growth rate, and its value goes from 1 to 1.05. Simply changing this value, we automatically obtain in the spreadsheet the new steady state as well as the transition dynamics to it for the different variables of the model.

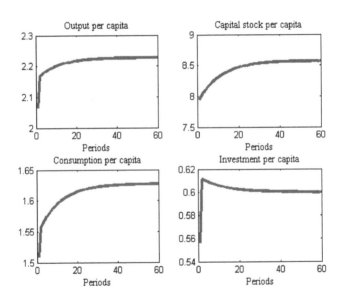

Figure 10.2. Effects of a permanent increase in Total Factor Productivity.

Figure 10.2 shows the adjustment path for the variables of the model before this disturbance. Since this increase in the TFP has a permanent character, the steady state for the different variables of the model is greater than the initial one. The increase in TFP causes an instantaneous increase in the level of production per capita, given the higher aggregate productivity of the economy. As a result of this increase in production, both consumption and investment also increase instantaneously. This means that one part of the newly generated income is dedicated to consumption and another part to investment. This increase in investment causes more capital to accumulate, which in turn generates an additional positive effect on production. Thus, the increase in initial aggregate productivity leads to a process of capital accumulation until reaching the new steady state, which in turn generates higher levels of production. In this process of adjustment, the investment decreases slightly until reaching its new steady state, while consumption shows a growing path during the transition to the new steady state.

10.7. Sensitivity analysis: Change in the intertemporal discount rate

Finally, we study the effects of a change in one of the parameters to check the sensibility of the Ramsey model to this change. In particular, we will analyze the effects of a change in the intertemporal discount rate. For this, we simply have to change the value of cell "C4". So, for example, instead of assuming that the discount factor is 0.97, let's assume that it increases to 0.98. The discount factor is a parameter of preferences, which reflects the sacrifice that the agent is willing to make in terms of present consumption with respect to future consumption. Thus, this parameter, which basically reflects the degree of patience of the agents, being a key determinant of the saving rate of an economy. In fact, the disturbance that we are simulating, consisting of an increase in this discount rate, can be interpreted as an increase in the desire to save, since the increase in the discount factor makes it willing to sacrifice a greater proportion of consumption today to obtain a higher level of future consumption (agents become more patient).

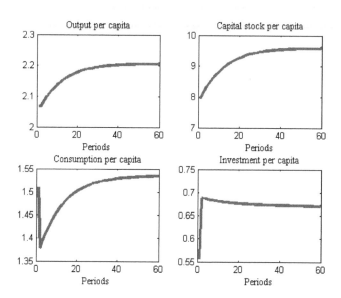

Figure 10.3. Effects of an increase in the discount factor.

Figure 10.3 shows the adjustment transition to the new steady state. As we can see, the increase in the discount factor produces an instantaneous decrease in per capita consumption (an instantaneous increase in savings). This is because there is a substitution between consumption and savings today when a change in intertemporal preferences occurs. As a result of this decrease in consumption, there is an increase in investment, which leads to a process of capital accumulation. The stock of capital per capita will increase until the economy reaches the new steady state. As the stock of capital increases, so does the level of output, so that consumption begins to recover. The long-run effect is an increase in both the stock of capital and consumption in per capita terms. These effects show that an increase in the savings rate leads to a new steady state where the value of output, consumption and capital is higher. This effect will always occur because in the Ramsey model, the economy is always located below the golden rule and, therefore, increases in the savings rate have positive effects on the steady state.

Exercises

1. Starting from the calibrated model in the text, suppose there is a decrease in the population growth rate to 0.01. Using the spreadsheet "**ICM-10.xls**", study the effects of this shock (you only need to change the value of cell "C12"). Why is the adjustment of the economy to this disturbance instantaneous? What consequences does it have on the level of per capita consumption and the stock of capital per capita?

2. Suppose that there is an increase in the value of the parameter α, which means that the proportion of capital income increases over total income (thus decreasing the proportion of labor income). Suppose a new value of 0.4. What effects does this new value of this parameter have on the steady state of the economy and the dynamics towards it?

3. From the calibration of the Ramsey model made in the spreadsheet "**ICM-10.xls**", determine what is the steady state savings rate. Compare this savings rate with the technological parameter that determines the elasticity of the production level with respect to the stock of capital. What conclusions are drawn regarding the golden rule?

4. Suppose there is a natural disaster that destroys 20% of the capital stock of the economy, without affecting the population. What effects does this disturbance have both on the steady state and on the dynamics of adjustment towards it?

5. Repeat the previous exercise, but now assuming that the disaster decreases by 20% the population without affecting the stock of capital. How are now the effects of this disturbance on the economy in relation to those obtained previously?

Appendices

Appendix A: Some mathematical concepts

In the numerical resolution of the models studied in this book, we use a series of mathematical tools and techniques that are necessary to operating with systems of difference equations, as well as to solve dynamic-optimization problems. In this appendix, we include a brief review on the set of complex numbers, as well as some basic concepts in the field of linear algebra and for the resolution of difference equations. It also includes a series of basic concepts in relation to the resolution of optimization problems with restrictions.

A.1 The set of complex numbers

The set of complex numbers, denoted by C, is given by

$$C = \{z = \alpha + \beta_i : \alpha, \beta \in R\} \tag{A.1}$$

where i is the imaginary unit, such that,

$$i^2 = -1 (or\ i = \sqrt{-1}) \tag{A.2}$$

Given a complex number, z, where $z = \alpha + \beta_i$, the real number α is called the real part of z and the real number β the imaginary part of z. Complex numbers are an extension of the set of real numbers, $\mathbb{R}$, since any real number can be considered to be a complex number with an imaginary null part, that is, with $\beta = 0$. So, $\mathbb{R} \subset \mathbb{C}$. From the set of complex numbers, any algebraic equation has a solution. In particular, the solutions of the quadratic equation, $ax^2 + bx + c$, in the case that $b^2 - 4ac < 0$, would not be real and would be given by:

$$x \frac{-b \pm i\sqrt{-(b^2 - 4ac)}}{2a} = \frac{-b}{2a} \pm \frac{\sqrt{-(b^2 - 4ac)}}{2a} i$$

which are called conjugated complexes, since they have the same real part and opposite imaginary part. Given the complex number $z = \alpha + \beta_i$, we can also express it as:

$$z = \rho(cos\ \theta + i\ sin\ \theta) \tag{A.3}$$

what is known as polar representation of the complex number, where $\rho = \sqrt{\alpha^2 + \beta^2}$ is called the module and $\theta = arc\ tangent\ (\alpha/\beta)$ is called the argument of z. From this polar representation, the power k of z, is given by

$$z^k = \rho^k(cos\ \theta k + i\ sin\ \theta k) \tag{A.4}$$

for all $k = 1, 2, 3 \ldots$.

A.2 Matrices

Definition 1. *Let us say that a number λ is a proper value of a square matrix $A(n \times n)$, if there is a v nonzero vector such that*

$$Av = \lambda v \tag{A.5}$$

The vector v is known as the eigenvector A associated with the eigenvalue λ.

The equation (A.5) is equivalent to the homogeneous system $(A - \lambda I)v = 0$ having a non-zero solution. For this, a necessary and sufficient condition is that the determinant of the coefficient matrix is null, that is, $|A - \lambda I| = 0$. Therefore, to determine the eigenvalues of a matrix, we must solve the equation $|A - \lambda I| = 0$ called the characteristic equation of the matrix A. Subsequently, for each different λ_r eigenvalue, solving the homogeneous system $(A - \lambda_r I)v = 0$, we obtain the set of eigenvectors associated with λ_r.

Properties:

1. The sum of the eigenvalues of A is equal to its trace (sum of the elements of its main diagonal).

2. The product of the eigenvalues of A is equal to its determinant.

3. The eigenvalues of a diagonal matrix are equal to the elements of the main diagonal.

4. If λ is a proper value of A, then λ^k is an eigenvalue of A^k, for every $n \in \mathbb{N}$, with the same associated eigenvectors.

5. $\lambda = 0$ is the eigenvalue of $A \Leftrightarrow |A| = 0 \Leftrightarrow A$ is not invertible (A is a singular matrix).

6. The eigenvectors associated with different eigenvalues are linearly independent.

Definition 2. *A matrix A ($n \times n$) is diagonalizable if there exist an invertible matrix $P(n \times n)$ and a diagonal matrix D ($n \times n$) such that $D = P^{-1}AP$.*

Theorem 3. *A matrix A ($n \times n$) is diagonalizable if and only if A has n linearly independent eigenvectors (base of $\mathbb{R}^n$). In that case,*

$$P^{-1}AP = D = \begin{bmatrix} \lambda_1 & \cdots & 0 \\ \vdots & \ddots & \vdots \\ 0 & \cdots & \lambda_n \end{bmatrix} \tag{A.6}$$

where P is the matrix whose columns are the eigenvectors $v_1, v_2, \ldots, v_n$ and $\lambda_1, \lambda_2, \ldots, \lambda_n$

are the eigenvalues of A and form the main diagonal of the D matrix. We can also define the A matrix as $A = PDP^{-1}$.

Keep in mind that if the matrix A $(n \times n)$ has different eigenvalues, then there will be a set of n linearly independent eigenvectors, and, consequently, the matrix will be diagonalizable. Also, if the A matrix $(n \times n)$ is diagonalizable, then its powers can be calculated easily, since,

$$A^k = PD^kP^{-1} \tag{A.7}$$

where D^k is a diagonal matrix, whose elements of the main diagonal are the $k - th$ powers $(k = 1, 2, 3 \dots)$ of the elements of the diagonal matrix D (the eigenvalues of A).

Proposition 4. *If λ is an eigenvalue of a matrix A $(n \times n)$, then $\lambda + 1$ is an eigenvalue of the matrix $A + 1$ with the same set of associated eigenvectors, where I $(n \times n)$ is the identity matrix.*

Proof 5. If λ is an eigenvalue of the matrix A $(n \times n)$, then there is a nonzero vector such that

$$\lambda v = Av$$

On the other hand,

$$(\lambda + 1)v = \lambda v + v = Av + v = (A + I)v$$

with which $\lambda + 1$ is an eigenvalue of $A + I$ with the same set of associated eigenvectors.

Based on this proposition, if a matrix $A(n \times n)$ is diagonalizable, so will the matrix $A + I$, and we will have

$$(A + I)^k = P(D + I)^k P^{-1} \tag{A.8}$$

where $(D + I)^k$ is a diagonal matrix, whose elements of the main diagonal are the k-th powers $(k = 1,2,3 \dots)$ of the elements of the diagonal matrix $D + I$ (the eigenvalues of $A + I$) and P is the matrix whose columns are the corresponding $v_1, v_2, \dots, v_n$ eigenvectors.

In the case that the A matrix is not diagonalizable, it can be decomposed using the canonical form of Jordan, which generalizes the process of diagonalization, such that:

$$J = P^{-1}AP \quad \text{or} \quad A = PJP^{-1}$$

where J is the diagonal matrix by blocks.

A.3 Resolution of systems of difference equations

If we consider time as a discrete variable that can take values $T = 0, 1, 2, ...,$ then a function that depends on this variable $X: \mathbb{N} \to \mathbb{R}^n$ is a succession of vectors $X(0), X(1), X(2), ...$

Definition 6. *A first order system of difference equations is an expression of the form*

$$\Delta X(t) = f(X(t), t) \tag{A.9}$$

or if we take into account that $\Delta X_{t+1} = X_{t+1} - X_t$*, it could be expressed as*

$$X_{t+1} = g(X_t, t) \tag{A.10}$$

which is known as the normal form of the system of difference equations.

If the variable t does not appear explicitly, it is said that the system is autonomous.

A first order system of difference equations with n equations and n unknowns variables is said to be linear when it can be written as:

$$\Delta X_{t+1} = A_t X_t + b_t \tag{A.11}$$

where

$$X_t = \begin{bmatrix} x_{1,t} \\ ... \\ x_{n,t} \end{bmatrix}$$

is the vector of unknowns variables,

$$A_t = \begin{bmatrix} a_{11,t} & \cdots & a_{1n,t} \\ \vdots & \ddots & \vdots \\ a_{n1,t} & \cdots & a_{nn,t} \end{bmatrix}$$

the coefficient matrix, and

$$b_t = \begin{bmatrix} b_{1,t} \\ ... \\ b_{n,t} \end{bmatrix}$$

the vector of independent terms, equivalent to the exogenous variables multiplied by their respective coefficients.

If the coefficient matrix is invariant with time $A_t = A$, (for every t), then the dynamic system (A.11) will be,

$$\Delta X_{t+1} = A X_t + b_t \tag{A.12}$$

or, if we take into account that $\Delta X_{t+1} = X_{t+1} - X_t$, the normal form of the system (A.12) would be,

$$X_{t+1} = \hat{A} X_t + b_t \tag{A.13}$$

where $\hat{A} = A + I$, with I the identity matrix $(n \times n)$.

Starting from initial conditions, X_0, the system of linear difference equations has a unique solution. To determine it, we give values to t, $t = 0, 1, 2, \dots$, in (A.13) and we will have

$$X_1 = \hat{A}X_0 + b_0 = (A + I)X_0 + b_0$$

$$X_2 = \hat{A}X_1 + b_1 = \hat{A}^2X_0 + \hat{A}b_0 + b_1 = (A + I)^2 X_0 + (A + I)b_0 + b_1$$

$$\vdots$$

In general,

$$X_t = \hat{A}X_{t-1} + b_{t-1} = \hat{A}^t X_0 + \sum_{t=0}^{t-1} \hat{A}^{t-i-1} b_i =$$

$$(A + I)^t X_0 + \sum_{t=0}^{t-1}(A + I)^{t-i-1} b_i$$

Therefore, the problem of determining the solution of the system is related to the problem of determining the successive powers of a matrix. If the coefficient matrix of the system (A or, $\hat{A}$ if the system is in normal form) is diagonalizable, such powers can be easily calculated from the expression (A.7) or (A.8).

Consider that the vector of independent terms is constant, so that the linear system can be written,

$$\Delta X_{t+1} = AX_t + b \tag{A.14}$$

or, in a normal way,

$$X_{t+1} = \hat{A}X_t + b \tag{A.15}$$

Definition 7. *Given the system (A.14), we will say that the state vector $\bar{X}$ is a steady state or equilibrium solution whenever the system starts in that state and remains there indefinitely, that is, $\bar{X}$ is a steady state of the system if it is its constant solution. Therefore, it has to be verified, if the matrix A is invertible*

$$0 = A\bar{X} + b \Rightarrow \bar{X} = -(A)^{-1}b \tag{A.16}$$

or, if we start from the system in a normal way (A.15) and the matrix $(I - \hat{A})$ is invertible

$$\bar{X} = A\bar{X} + b \Rightarrow \bar{X} = -(A)^{-1}b \tag{A.17}$$

Definition 8. *The $\bar{X}$ steady state will say that it is stable if any solution of the system that starts from close initial conditions remains close to $\bar{X}$.*

Definition 9. *The $\bar{X}$ steady state will say that it is asymptotically stable if any solution of the system with close initial conditions tends to said steady state with the passage of time.*

From these definitions, it follows that if a steady state is asymptotically stable it is stable. However, if it is stable it does not have to be asymptotically stable. We say in this last case that the steady state is marginally stable. If a steady state is not stable, nor asymptotically stable, we say it is unstable.

Starting from the system in normal form (A.14) and applying the expression (A.13), we obtain that the solution with initial condition is given by

$$X_t = \hat{A}^t X_0 + \left(I + \hat{A} + \hat{A}^2 + \cdots + \hat{A}^{t-1}\right) b$$

However,

$$\left(I + \hat{A} + \hat{A}^2 + \cdots + \hat{A}^{t-1}\right)\left(I + \hat{A}\right) = \left(I + \hat{A}^t\right)$$

With which

$$X_t = \hat{A}^t X_0 + (I + \hat{A}^t)(I + \hat{A})^{-1} b$$

and taking into account (A.15)

$$X_t = \hat{A}^t(X_0 - \bar{X}) + \bar{X} \tag{A.18}$$

From (A.18) it is observed that if the matrix $\hat{A}$ tends to the null matrix, when t tends to infinity, the trajectory X_t tends toward the steady state, which guarantees that this state is asymptotically stable. Let us suppose that the $\hat{A}$ matrix is diagonalizable, then it is verified, as we have seen in the previous section (A.6), that

$$\hat{A}^t = P \begin{bmatrix} \hat{\lambda}_1^t & \cdots & 0 \\ \vdots & \ddots & \vdots \\ 0 & \cdots & \hat{\lambda}_2^t \end{bmatrix} P^{-1}$$

where $\hat{\lambda}_i^t (i = 1, 2, \ldots n)$ are the eigenvalues of the matrix $\hat{A}$. Based on the above, the expression (A.18) can be written as

$$X_t = P \begin{bmatrix} \hat{\lambda}_1^t & \cdots & 0 \\ \vdots & \ddots & \vdots \\ 0 & \cdots & \hat{\lambda}_n^t \end{bmatrix} P^{-1}(X_0 - \bar{X}) + \bar{X}$$

and denoting

$$P^{-1}(X_0 - \bar{X}) = \begin{bmatrix} c_1 \\ \cdots \\ c_n \end{bmatrix}$$

we will have that (A.18) is equivalent to:

$$X_t = c_1 v_1 \hat{\lambda}_1^t + c_2 v_2 \hat{\lambda}_2^t + \cdots + c_n v_n \hat{\lambda}_n^t + \bar{X}$$

Consequently, asymptotic stability is equivalent to the fact that the elements of the matrix $\hat{A}^t$ tend to zero when t grows, which is equivalent to the fact that $|\hat{\lambda}_i^t| < 1$ $(i = 1, 2, \ldots, n)$, that is, a necessary and sufficient condition for asymptotic stability is that all the eigenvalues of the coefficient matrix of the normal system have a module (absolute value in the case of real numbers) less than 1. In the case where at least one eigenvalue has a module greater than 1, the $\hat{A}^t$ matrix grows with time, and the steady state is unstable.

Now, considering that $\hat{A} = A + I$ we know, that the proper values of $\hat{A}(\hat{\lambda}_i)$ and those of $A(\lambda_i)$ keep the relation $\hat{\lambda}_i = \lambda_i + 1$ (see Proposition 4) and, therefore, we can say that the necessary and sufficient condition for the steady state (A.16) to present asymptotic stability is that all the eigenvalues of the A-coefficient matrix verify $|\lambda_i + 1| < 1, (i = 1, 2, \dots, n)$.

To analyze in depth the different cases that can occur, we will assume that $n = 2$, that is, the discrete dynamic system would be formed by two difference equations and two endogenous variables. In particular, the system would be

$$\begin{bmatrix} \Delta X_{1,t} \\ \Delta x_{2,t} \end{bmatrix} = \begin{bmatrix} a_{11} & a_{12} \\ a_{21} & a_{22} \end{bmatrix} \begin{bmatrix} X_{1,t} \\ x_{2,t} \end{bmatrix} + \begin{bmatrix} b_1 \\ b_2 \end{bmatrix}$$

being the coefficient matrix

$$A = \begin{bmatrix} a_{11} & a_{12} \\ a_{21} & a_{22} \end{bmatrix}$$

If the determinant of A is nonzero, the only steady equilibrium is given by:

$$\bar{X} = \begin{bmatrix} \bar{X}_1 \\ \bar{X}_2 \end{bmatrix} = -A^{-1} \begin{bmatrix} b_1 \\ b_2 \end{bmatrix}$$

and the general solution of the system, given some initial conditions $X(0)$, can be expressed as

$$X_t = (A + I)^t (X_0 - \bar{X}) + \bar{X} \tag{A.19}$$

As we have seen previously, the stability of the steady state depends on the eigenvalues of the matrix of coefficients of the system, which will be the solution of the equation of the second degree

$$|A - \lambda I| = \left| \begin{bmatrix} a_{11} & a_{12} \\ a_{21} & a_{22} \end{bmatrix} - \begin{bmatrix} \lambda & 0 \\ 0 & \lambda \end{bmatrix} \right| =$$

$$\lambda^2 - (a_{11} + a_{22})\lambda + (a_{11}a_{22} - a_{12}a_{21}) = 0$$

or equivalently

$$\lambda^2 - tr(A)\lambda + |A| = 0$$

where $tr(A)$ and $|A|$ denote, respectively, the trace and the determinant of the matrix A.

The roots of this equation are

$$\lambda_1, \lambda_2 = \frac{(a_{11}+a_{22}) \pm \sqrt{(a_{11}+a_{22})^2 - 4(a_{11}a_{22} - a_{12}a_{21})}}{2}$$

By resolving, we can obtain real roots that are different, real, equal or complex, depending on whether the discriminant (D) is positive, null or negative (see Table A.1), with

$$D = (a_{11} + a_{22})^2 - 4(a_{11}a_{22} - a_{12}a_{21}) = [tr(A)]^2 - 4|A|$$

Table A.1: Possible solutions for system stability

Cases	Roots (eigenvalues)
I. $D > 0$	Real and different: λ_1, λ_2
II. $D = 0$	Real and equal: $\lambda_1, \lambda_2 = \lambda$
III. $D < 0$	Complex: $\alpha \pm \beta_i$

- **Case I.** If $D > 0$ then the eigenvalues λ_1, λ_2 are real and different. Then $\lambda_1 + 1$ and $\lambda_2 + 1$ will also be real and different and, consequently, the matrix $A + I$ is diagonalizable. In this case, the general solution (A.19) can be expressed as:

$$\begin{bmatrix} X_{1,t} \\ X_{2,t} \end{bmatrix} = P \begin{bmatrix} (\lambda_1 + 1)^t & 0 \\ 0 & (\lambda_2 + 1)^t \end{bmatrix} P^{-1} \begin{bmatrix} X_{1,0} - \bar{X}_1 \\ X_{2,0} - \bar{X}_2 \end{bmatrix} + \begin{bmatrix} \bar{X}_1 \\ \bar{X}_2 \end{bmatrix}$$

In addition, we can distinguish the following situations:

a) If it is verified that $\lambda_1 + 1 < 1$ and $\lambda_2 + 1 < 1$ then $(\lambda_1 + 1)^t$ and $(\lambda_2 + 1)^t$ tend to zero when t tends to infinity and therefore $X(t)$ tends to the steady state $\bar{X}$, for any initial condition $X(0)$ and there is asymptotic stability. The figure that is generated is known as *a stable node.*

b) If $\lambda_1 + 1 > 1$ and $\lambda_2 + 1 > 1$ then $(\lambda_1 + 1)^t$ and $(\lambda_2 + 1)^t$ tend to infinity when t does and, therefore, $X(t)$ moves away from the steady state $\bar{X}$ and there is instability. The figure that is generated is known as an *unstable node.*

c) If $|\lambda_1 + 1| < 1$ and $|\lambda_2 + 1| > 1$ then $(\lambda_1 + 1)^t$ tends to zero when t tends to infinity, while $(\lambda_2 + 1)^t$ tends to infinity. Consequently $X(t)$ moves away from the steady state $\bar{X}$, for any initial $X(0)$ condition except the trajectory that verifies $X_{2,0} = \bar{X}_2$ and $X_{1,0} \neq \bar{X}_1$ that it will be a linear combination of $(\lambda_1 + 1)^t$ and, therefore, this trajectory tends toward the steady state. The figure that is generated is known as *saddle point.*

d) A case similar to that of c) is if $|\lambda_1 + 1| > 1$ and $|\lambda_2 + 1| < 1$.

e) If $|\lambda_1 + 1| = 1$ and $|\lambda_2 + 1| < 1$ then $X(t)$ neither moves away nor approaches the steady state since $(\lambda_1 + 1)^t$ is maintained or oscillates between -1 and 1, while $(\lambda_2 + 1)^t$ tends to zero, and we will say that the steady state is marginally stable. However, there is a trajectory that tends to the steady state, which would be one that starts from initial conditions that cancel the behavior of $(\lambda_1 + 1)^t$. On the other hand, if $|\lambda_1 + 1| = 1$ and $|\lambda_2 + 1| > 1$ then $(\lambda_2 + 1)^t$ tends to infinity when t does and the steady state is unstable.

- **Case II.** If $D = 0$ then $\lambda_1 = \lambda_2 = \lambda$ and, therefore, $(\lambda_1 + 1) = (\lambda_2 + 1) = (\lambda + 1)$ so we would have real and equal roots. We will distinguish two situations, depending on whether the starting matrix is diagonal or not.

  a) If the starting matrix is diagonal, then the system is given by
  $$\begin{bmatrix} \Delta X_{1,t} \\ \Delta X_{2,t} \end{bmatrix} = \begin{bmatrix} a_{11} & 0 \\ 0 & a_{22} \end{bmatrix} \begin{bmatrix} \Delta X_{1,t} \\ \Delta X_{2,t} \end{bmatrix} + \begin{bmatrix} b_1 \\ b_2 \end{bmatrix}$$
  and it has to be fulfilled that $\lambda = a_{11} = a_{22}$. Consequently, the solution (A.17) will be given by
  $$\begin{bmatrix} X_{1,t} \\ X_{2,t} \end{bmatrix} = \begin{bmatrix} (\lambda_1 + 1)^t & 0 \\ 0 & (\lambda_2 + 1)^t \end{bmatrix} \begin{bmatrix} X_{1,0} - \bar{X}_1 \\ X_{2,0} - \bar{X}_2 \end{bmatrix} + \begin{bmatrix} \bar{X}_1 \\ \bar{X}_2 \end{bmatrix}$$
  Therefore, if $|\lambda + 1| < 1$, the solution trajectory tends to the steady state and is asymptotically stable, while if $|\lambda + 1| > 1$ the solution trajectory moves away from the steady state and is unstable. Now, if $|\lambda + 1| = 1$ the steady state is stable, since the solution trajectories that start close to it will remain close to it.

  b) If the starting matrix is not diagonal, then it will not be diagonalizable, but we can find a quasi-diagonal matrix, called Jordan's canonical form, so that the solution (A.17) can be expressed as
  $$\begin{bmatrix} X_{1,t} \\ X_{2,t} \end{bmatrix} = Q \begin{bmatrix} (\lambda_1 + 1)^t & 0 \\ 0 & (\lambda_2 + 1)^t \end{bmatrix} Q^{-1} \begin{bmatrix} X_{1,0} - \bar{X}_1 \\ X_{2,0} - \bar{X}_2 \end{bmatrix} + \begin{bmatrix} \bar{X}_1 \\ \bar{X}_2 \end{bmatrix}$$
  Therefore, if $|\lambda + 1| < 1$ the solution trajectory tends to the steady state and it is asymptotically stable, while if $|\lambda + 1| \geq 1$ the solution trajectory moves away from the steady state and is unstable.

- **Case III.** If $D < 0$ then the eigenvalues are complex conjugates, that is $\lambda = \alpha \pm \beta_i$. The matrix of the system is diagonalizable, and the solution path,
$$\begin{bmatrix} X_{1,t} \\ X_{2,t} \end{bmatrix} = P \begin{bmatrix} (\lambda_1 + 1)^t & 0 \\ 0 & (\lambda_2 + 1)^t \end{bmatrix} P^{-1} \begin{bmatrix} X_{1,0} - \bar{X}_1 \\ X_{2,0} - \bar{X}_2 \end{bmatrix} + \begin{bmatrix} \bar{X}_1 \\ \bar{X}_2 \end{bmatrix}$$
which will depend on the behavior of $\lambda + 1 = (\alpha + 1) \pm \beta_i$ and taking into account (A.4) we get,
$$\begin{bmatrix} X_{1,t} \\ X_{2,t} \end{bmatrix} = P \begin{bmatrix} \rho^t(\cos \theta t + i \sin \theta t) & 0 \\ 0 & \rho^t(\cos \theta t - i \sin \theta t) \end{bmatrix} P^{-1} \begin{bmatrix} X_{1,0} - \bar{X}_1 \\ X_{2,0} - \bar{X}_2 \end{bmatrix} + \begin{bmatrix} \bar{X}_1 \\ \bar{X}_2 \end{bmatrix}$$
where $\rho = \sqrt{(\alpha + 1)^2 + \beta^2}$ is the module of the complex number $\lambda + 1$ and θ is its argument. We will have different situations depending on the value of the module since the terms $(\cos \theta t \pm i \sin \theta t)$ are limited.

a) If $\rho < 1$, then ρ^t tends to zero when t tends to infinity and the solution path $X(t)$ tends towards the steady state, for any $X(0)$ initial condition, there is asymptotic stability. The figure that is generated is called *stable focus*.

b) If $\rho > 1$, then ρ^t tends toward infinity when t does and the solution trajectory $X(t)$ moves away from the steady state, for any initial condition $X(0)$. The steady state is unstable. The resulting figure is called an *unstable focus*.

c) If $\rho = 1$, the steady state is marginally stable because if the solution path $X(t)$ begins near it, it will stay close to it. The figure that is generated is known as *center*.

A.4 Optimization with restrictions

Micro-based macroeconomic models are based on the behavior at the microeconomic level of the different considered agents. Thus, the macroeconomic variables are derived from the optimizing behavior of both households and firms. These agents obtain their decisions on the control variables from a dynamic maximization problem subject to certain restrictions. In this appendix, we present some important concepts regarding this form of macroeconomic modeling.

Definition 10. *It is said that a* $K \subset \mathbb{R}^n$ *set is convex, if the segment that joins any two points of the set is contained in it, that is,*

$$(x_1,...,x_n), (y_1,...,y_n) \in K \Rightarrow \mu \cdot (x_1,...,x_n) + (1 - \mu)(y_1,...,y_n) \in K$$

with $0 \leq \mu \leq 1$.

Definition 11. *A function* $f \colon S \subset \mathbb{R}^n \to \mathbb{R}$ *is said to be convex if for any pair of* $(x_1,...,x_n), (y_1,...,y_n) \in S$ *and any scalar with* $0 \leq \mu \leq 1$ *is fulfilled that*

$$f((\mu(x_1,...,x_n) + (1 - \mu)(y_1,...,y_n)) = \mu f(x_1,...,x_n) + (1 - \mu)f(y_1,...,y_n) \qquad (A.20)$$

Similarly, a function is concave if the relationship (A.18) with inverse inequality is met, that is, f is concave if $(-f)$ is convex. Note that all linear function is concave and convex at the same time.

We can characterize the convexity/concavity of twice differentiable functions through the Hessian matrix that contains the second-order partial derivatives of the function, so that the element i,j of Hf is $\delta^2 f/\delta x_i \delta x_j$. In addition, if these derivatives are continuous, the Hessian is a symmetric matrix.

A function f is convex (concave) if and only if its Hessian matrix is positive (negative) semidefinite everywhere in S, and strictly convex (concave) if and only if its Hessian matrix is definite. These concepts have an important role in optimization with restrictions since they will allow us to establish sufficient global conditions.

The general formulation of an optimization problem with constraints is as follows

$$\max F(x_{1,\dots,}x_n) \tag{A.21}$$

subject to:

$$g_1(x_{1,\dots,}x_n) = b_1 \quad h_1(x_{1,\dots,}x_n) \le d_1$$

$$g_2(x_{1,\dots,}x_n) = b_2 \quad h_2(x_{1,\dots,}x_n) \le d_2$$

$$\vdots \qquad\qquad \vdots$$

$$g_m(x_{1,\dots,}x_n) = b_m \quad h_p(x_{1,\dots,}x_n) \le d_p$$

where $m \le n$ and the functions F, $g_j (j = 1, 2, \dots, m), h_i (i = 1, 2, \dots, p)$ are real continuous functions and are supposed to have second continuous partial derivatives. We must bear in mind that if the problem were $\text{Min}\,F$ would be equivalent to $\text{Max}(-F)$.

Admissible solution is called the one that verifies all the restrictions of the problem. *Optimal solution* is called the admissible solution in which the maximum value of the F function is reached.

An inequality constraint $h_i(x_{1,\dots,}x_n) \le d_i$ is said to be active at an admissible $(\bar{x}_1, \dots, \bar{x}_n)$ point if it is verified as equality, that is, $h_i(\bar{x}_1, \dots, \bar{x}_n) = d_i$ and the constraint is inactive at the point if $h_i(\bar{x}_1, \dots, \bar{x}_n) < d_i$. Logically, any equality constraint is active at any admissible point. Keep in mind that if a constraint is inactive at one point, there will always be some neighborhood of the point where the constraint is verified, while this is not always the case when the restriction is active. Therefore, the restrictions that are inactive at one point do have no influence in the neighborhood of the point, and by analyzing the properties of a local maximum, we can focus our attention on the constraints that are active at it. Consequently, if it were known in advance what constraints are active in the solution of (A.21), that solution would be a local maximum point of the defined problem, ignoring inactive constraints and treating all active constraints as equality constraints.[1] Therefore, the problem could be addressed as if it only had equality constraints.

---

[1] Bazaraa, M.S., and Sherali, H.D., and Shetty, C.M. (2006). *Nonlinear Programming: Theory and Algorithms*, 3rd Edition. Wiley Interscience: New Jersey.

Consequently, we will focus on a problem that has only equality restrictions, whose general formulation is:

$$\max F(x_{1,\dots,}x_n) \tag{A.22}$$

subject to:

$$g_1(x_{1,\dots,}x_n) = b_1$$

$$g_2(x_{1,\dots,}x_n) = b_2$$

$$\vdots$$

$$g_m(x_{1,\dots,}x_n) = b_m$$

To solve (A.22), we define the associated Lagrange function:

$$\mathcal{L}(x_1, \dots, x_n, \lambda_1, \dots, \lambda_m) = F(x_1, \dots, x_n) - \lambda_1(g_1(x_{1,\dots,}x_n) - b_1 -$$

$$\dots - \lambda_m(g_m(x_{1,\dots,}x_n) - b_m \tag{A.23}$$

where $\lambda_1, \dots, \lambda_m$ are additional variables (one for each restriction), known as Lagrange multipliers.

From (A.23) we determine $x_1, \dots, x_n$ and $\lambda_1, \dots, \lambda_m$ that verify the following $n + m$ conditions (known as necessary first-order conditions):

$$\frac{\partial \mathcal{L}}{\partial x_1} : \frac{\partial F}{\partial x_1} - \lambda_1 \frac{\partial g_1}{\partial x_1} - \dots - \lambda_m \frac{\partial g_m}{\partial x_1} = 0$$

$$\vdots$$

$$\frac{\partial \mathcal{L}}{\partial x_n} : \frac{\partial F}{\partial x_n} - \lambda_1 \frac{\partial g_1}{\partial x_n} - \dots - \lambda_m \frac{\partial g_m}{\partial x_n} = 0$$

$$\frac{\partial \mathcal{L}}{\partial \lambda_1} : -(g_1(x_1, \dots, x_n) - b_1 = 0$$

$$\vdots$$

$$\frac{\partial \mathcal{L}}{\partial \lambda_m} : -(g_m(x_1, \dots, x_n) - b_m = 0$$

If the functions g_j ($j = 1, 2, \dots, m$) are linear and the F function is concave, then all the points that verify the necessary conditions are solutions to the problem (A.22). If these conditions are not satisficed, we must apply the following sufficient local condition.

The point that satisfies the first-order conditions is a local solution for (A.23) if the last $n - m$ leading principal inors of the following matrix, evaluated at that point, alternate in sign, where the last minor has the sign as $(-1)^n$,

$$\begin{bmatrix} 0 & J_g \\ J_g^T & H_{x,y}L \end{bmatrix} = \begin{bmatrix} 0 & \cdots & 0 & \dfrac{\delta g_1}{\delta x_1} & \cdots & \dfrac{\delta g_1}{\delta x_n} \\ \vdots & \ddots & \vdots & \vdots & \ddots & \vdots \\ 0 & \cdots & 0 & \dfrac{\delta g_m}{\delta x_1} & \cdots & \dfrac{\delta g_m}{\delta x_n} \\ \dfrac{\delta g_1}{\delta x_1} & \cdots & \dfrac{\delta g_m}{\delta x_1} & \dfrac{\delta^2 L}{\delta x_1^2} & \cdots & \dfrac{\delta^2 L}{\delta x_1 \delta x_n} \\ \vdots & \ddots & \vdots & \vdots & \ddots & \vdots \\ \dfrac{\delta g_1}{\delta x_n} & \cdots & \dfrac{\delta g_m}{\delta x_n} & \dfrac{\delta^2 L}{\delta x_n \delta x_1} & \cdots & \dfrac{\delta^2 L}{\delta x_n^2} \end{bmatrix}$$

Appendix B: An example of a dynamic system in MATLAB

The dynamic systems in discrete time that we have solved numerically in a spreadsheet can also be computed using any other software that allows numerical calculation, and can even be solved by hand, using paper and pencil, although this is a more tedious task. In practice, we have a wide variety of computer programs, applications and programming languages that can perform numerical calculations easily. Given the values for the parameters and for the exogenous variables, it is possible to numerically simulate a set of endogenous variables, using the corresponding discrete dynamic system. Here is how a simple program in MATLAB would be, to solve the model presented in Chapter 1. MATLAB (MATrix LABoratory) is a program widely used in economics and has a large number of "toolboxes" of econometrics and computational macroeconomics that make it a very useful tool for macroeconomic analysis. Programming the simple models that we are solving here in MATLAB is a relatively simple task since we practically only have to replicate the different components and equations that we have used in the design or the corresponding spreadsheet. The most important difference between the two is that while in the spreadsheet we copy an expression in different cells and the value of the same appears in each cell, in MATLAB we have to perform this procedure through a loop.

The code shown below numerically calculates the model equations that we have used in Chapter 1, the steady state, as well as the eigenvalues associated with it. It also makes a representation of the corresponding phase diagram, as well as the path to the steady state based on an initial disequilibrium situation. To simulate a shock, we simply have to change the value of the corresponding exogenous variable.

```
% ********************************************
% An Introduction to Computational Macroeconomics
% A. Bongers, T. Gómez and J. L. Torres (2019)
% An example of a dynamic system in MATLAB
% Richardson's arms race model
% File: m1.m
% ********************************************
clear all
% Periods
T = 30;
```

```
% Model parameters
Alpha = 0.50;
Beta  = 0.25;
Gamma = 0.25;
Delta = 0.50;
Theta = 1.00;
Ita   = 1.00;
% Value of exogenous variables
z1 = 1;
z2 = 1;
% Matrices
A=[-Alpha Beta; Gamma -Delta];
B=[Theta 0; 0 Ita];
z=[z1; z2];
% Steady state
EE = -A^(-1)*B*z;
x1(1) = EE(1);
x2(1) = EE(2);
dx1(1) = 0;
dx2(1) = 0;
% Eigenvalues
v=eig(A);
Lambda1=v(1);
Lambda2=v(2);
% Shocks
%z1 = 2;
%Alpha = 0.7;
% Dynamics
for i=1:T-1;
 x1(i+1)  = x1(i)+dx1(i);
 x2(i+1)  = x2(i)+dx2(i);
 dx1(i+1) = -Alpha*x1(i+1)+Beta*x2(i+1)+Theta*z1;
 dx2(i+1) = Gamma*x1(i+1)-Delta*x2(i+1)+Ita*z2;
end;
% Graphics
j=1:T;
subplot(1,2,1)
plot(j,x1,'Color',[0.25 0.25 0.25],'linewidth',3.5)
title('Variable x1')
xlabel('Periods')
subplot(1,2,2)
plot(j,x2,'Color',[0.25 0.25 0.25],'linewidth',3.5)
title('Variable x2')
xlabel('Periods')
% Phase diagram
syms x1 x2;
[x1 x2]=meshgrid(0:1:10, 0:1:10);
dx1  =  -Alpha*x1+Beta*x2+Theta*z1;
dx2  =  Gamma*x1-Delta*x2+Ita*z2;
figure;
```

```
quiver(x1,x2,dx1,dx2);
title(Phase Diagram: Richardson Model')
xlabel('Variable x1')
ylabel('Variable x2')
hold on
grid on
plot(EE(1),EE(2),'o','Color',[0 0 0])
% Trajectory
figure
quiver(x1,x2,dx1,dx2);
title(Richardson Model: Trajectory to the Steady State')
xlabel('Variable x1')
ylabel('Variable x2')
hold on
%grid on
y=[10; 8];
n=20;
d=@(x1,x2) [-Alpha*x1+Beta*x2+Theta*z1; Gamma*x1-Delta*x2+Ita*z2];
for i=1:n
 yy = y+d(y(1),y(2));
 plot([y(1),yy(1)],[y(2),yy(2)],'o-','Color',[0 0 0])
 y=yy;
end
```

Figure B.1 shows the representation of the phase diagram corresponding to this model. MATLAB has a command, "quiver", for the graphic representation of phase diagrams. This command allows a graphical representation to be made using arrows representing the speed and the direction of adjustment of the variables. The tip of the arrows indicates the direction in which both variables move. As we can see in the graph, for this calibrated model all the arrows lead us to the steady state, which is located at the point (4.4), given the initial values of the exogenous variables and the parameters. Given the calibration of the parameters we are using, the system shows global stability, so any initial value for the endogenous variables other than the steady state is associated with a path that leads both variables to their steady state. The size of each arrow indicates the change that occurs in the variables period by period.

Figure B.2 shows how the path to the steady state would be if the initial value of the endogenous variables is outside the steady state. In particular, in this graph, we have represented an initial situation at point ($x_1 = 10, x_2 = 8$). As we can see, given the values of the parameters, the trajectory that the variables follow takes us directly towards the steady state. The circles in the adjustment path show the evolution in the values of the variables period by period. At the beginning, the changes are very big, decreasing as we approach the steady state.

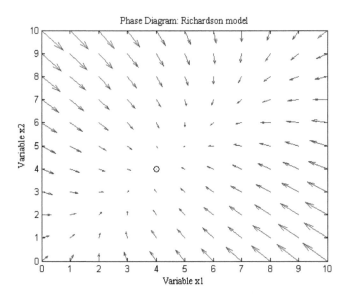

Figure B1. Phase diagram of the Richardson's model (Global stability)

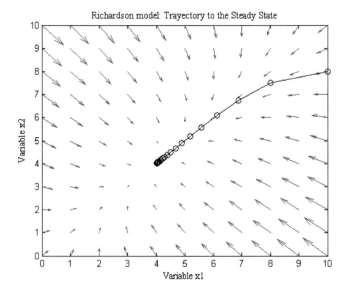

Figure B.2. Example of transitional dynamic in the Richardson's model

Appendix C: The arms race model in DYNARE

In this appendix, we present Richardson's arms race model in DYNARE. One of the most used tools in the current macroeconomic analysis, mainly when working with micro-based macroeconomic models, is the DYNARE (DYNAmic Rational Expectations) pre-processor. DYNARE is a tool, which can be used with both MATLAB and Octave, designed primarily for the resolution, simulation and estimation of micro-based or non-micro-based macroeconomic models, in which agents make predictions about future variables using rational expectations, although it is also possible to incorporate other alternative-expectations schemes. The used language is very simple, being only necessary to learn a small number of commands to solve and simulate a model, although it also has a large number of options that allow more complex analysis.

While DYNARE is designed for numerical resolution of macroeconomic models, their structure is similar to Richardson's model. In particular, we are going to solve this model assuming that the parameter values are such that the solution has a saddle point. This means that there is only a small set of trajectories that take us to the steady state. In addition, when a disturbance occurs, one of the variables has to be adjusted until the stable path is reached, a path that will take the system towards the new steady state. For this, an instantaneous readjustment must take place in the value of one of the endogenous variables until the stable path is reached. DYNARE automatically calculates both the stable path and the instantaneous adjustment that must occur in the variable in the event of a disturbance. The code presented here reproduces the exercise performed in Chapter 1, under a calibration that results in a saddle point. We have defined the changes in the variables in the same way as in the spreadsheet, such that

$$\Delta x_{1,t} = x_{1,t+1} - x_{1,t}$$

$$\Delta x_{2,t} = x_{2,t+1} - x_{2,t}$$

with the aim of indicating that it is the variable that will experience the instantaneous readjustment towards the stable path. With this, we are telling DYNARE that this would be the advanced variable or "jump" variable. From this node, we make the exercise equivalent to the one performed in the spreadsheet "**ICM-1-2.xls**".

```
% **************************************************
% An Introduction to Computational Macroeconomics
% A. Bongers, T. Gómez and J. L. Torres (2019)
% An example of a dynamic system in DYNARE
% Richardson's arms race model
% File: m1d.mod
% **************************************************
// Endogenous variables
var x1 x2 dx1 dx2;
// Exogenous variables
varexo z1, z2;
// Parameters
parameters Alpha, Beta, Gamma, Delta, Theta, Ita;
Alpha = 0.25;
Beta  = 0.5;
Gamma = 0.5;
Delta = 0.25;
Theta = 1.0;
Ita   = 1.0;
// Model equations
model;
 x1(+1) = x1+dx1;
 x2     = x2(-1)+dx2(-1);
 dx1    = -Alpha*x1+Beta*x2+Theta*z1;
 dx2    = Gamma*x1-Delta*x2+Ita*z2;
end;
// Initial values
initval;
 x1  = 4;
 x2  = 4;
 dx1 = 0;
 dx2 = 0;
 z1  = -1;
 z2  = -1;
end;
// Calculation of the initial steady state
steady;
check;
// End values
endval;
 x1  = 4;
 x2  = 4;
 dx1 = 0;
 dx2 = 0;
 z1  = -0.5;
 z2  = -1;
end;
// Calculation of the final steady state
steady;
// Disturbance analysis
```

```
shocks;
 var z1;
 periods 0;
 values 0;
end;
// Deterministic simulation
simul(periods=30);
// Graphics
T=30;
j=1:T;
figure;
subplot(1,2,1)
plot(j,x1(1:T),'Color',[0.5 0.5 0.5],'linewidth',2.5)
title('Armament stock country 1')
xlabel('Periods')
subplot(1,2,2)
plot(j,x2(1:T),'Color',[0.5 0.5 0.5],'linewidth',2.5)
title('Armament stock country 2')
xlabel('Periods')
```

Appendix D: The dynamic IS-LM model in MATLAB

Below, we present what a simple program in MATLAB would be like to solve the dynamic IS-LM model presented in Chapter 2. Being a model that presents global stability, all trajectories are convergent to the steady state when a disturbance occurs. The program also calculates the corresponding phase diagram, as well as the trajectory that the economy follows when there is a monetary disturbance towards a new steady state. The calibration of the parameters we use in this example gives rise to imaginary roots.

```
% ************************************************
% An Introduction to Computational Macroeconomics
% A. Bongers, T. Gómez and J. L. Torres (2019)
% Dynamic IS-LM model in MATLAB
% File: m2.m
% ************************************************
clear all
% Periods
T = 30;
% Exogenous variables
Beta0 = 2100;
m0    = 100;
ypot0 = 2000;
% Parameters
Theta = 0.5;
Psi   = 0.01;
Beta1 = 50;
Mi    = 0.01;
Ni    = 0.2;
%Matrices
A=[0 Mi;-Ni*Beta1/Theta Ni*(Beta1*Mi-Beta1*Psi/Theta-1)];
B=[0 0 -Mi; Ni Ni*Beta1/Theta -Ni*Beta1*Mi];
Z=[Beta0 m0 ypot0];
%Steady state
pbar  = (Theta*Beta0)/Beta1+m0-(Psi+Theta/Beta1)*ypot0;
ybar  = ypot0;
dp(1) = 0;
dy(1) = 0;
p(1)  = pbar;
y(1)  = ybar;
i(1)  = -(1/Theta)*(m0-p(1)-Psi*y(1));
yd(1) = Beta0-Beta1*(i(1)-dp(1));
```

```
% Proper values
v=eig(A);
Lambda1=v(1);
Lambda2=v(2);
% Disturbance
m1= 101;
% Dynamics
for j=1:T;
 y(j+1)   = y(j)+dy(j);
 p(j+1)   = p(j)+dp(j);
 dp(j+1)  = Mi*(y(j+1)-ybar);
 i(j+1)   = -(1/Theta)*(m1-p(j+1)-Psi*y(j+1));
 yd(j+1)  = Beta0-Beta1*(i(j+1)-dp(j+1));
 dy(j+1)  = Ni*(yd(j+1)-y(j+1));
end;
% Graphics
j=1:T+1;
subplot(2,2,1)
plot(j,y,'Color',[0.25 0.25 0.25],'linewidth',3.5)
xlabel('Periods')
title('Production')
subplot(2,2,2)
plot(j,yd,'Color',[0.25 0.25 0.25],'linewidth',3.5)
xlabel('Periods')
title('Aggregate Demand')
subplot(2,2,3)
plot(j,p,'Color',[0.25 0.25 0.25],'linewidth',3.5)
xlabel('Periods')
title('Prices')
subplot(2,2,4)
plot(j,i,'Color',[0.25 0.25 0.25],'linewidth',3.5)
xlabel('Periods')
title('Nominal interest rate')
% Phase Diagram
syms p y;
ymin=1980;
ymax=2040;
pmin=80;
pmax=84;
[y p]=meshgrid(ymin:(ymax-ymin)/20:ymax,pmin:(pmax-pmin)/20:pmax);
dp=Mi*(y-ypot0);
dy=Ni*(Beta0-Beta1*(-(1/Theta)*(m0-p-Psi*y)-Mi*(y-ypot0))-y);
figure;
quiver(y,p,dy,dp);
title('Phase Diagram: Dynamic IS-LM Model')
xlabel('Production level')
ylabel('Prices')
hold on
plot(ybar,pbar,'o','Color',[0 0 0])
% Trajectory towards steady state
```

```
dp=Mi*(y-ypot0);
dy=Ni*(Beta0-Beta1*(-(1/Theta)*(m1-p-Psi*y)-Mi*(y-ypot0))-y);
figure
quiver(y,p,dy,dp);
title('Dynamic IS-LM Model: Trajectory to the new Steady State')
xlabel('Production level')
ylabel('Prices')
hold on
m=[ybar; pbar];
n=100;
d=@(y,p)  [Ni*(Beta0-Beta1*(-(1/Theta)*(m1-p-Psi*y))-Mi*(y-ypot0)-
    y); Mi*(y-ypot0)];
for i=1:n
 mprima = m+d(m(1),m(2));
 plot([m(1),mprima(1)],[m(2),mprima(2)],'o-','Color',[0 0 0])
 m=mprima;
end
```

Figure C.1 shows the phase diagram corresponding to the dynamic IS-LM models, built using the "quiver" command in MATLAB. The circle points to the steady-state point, while the arrows indicate the movement of each variable outside the steady state. As we can see, regardless of the initial position in which we find ourselves, the direction in which both variables move points to the steady state, given that this model presents global stability. Thus, if we are in a position above and to the left of the steady state, the level of production would decrease, but so would the price level, until reaching a position below the steady state, in which the arrows point to the right, indicating that in this situation the level of production would increase. The resulting phase diagram shows arrows that are very horizontal. This is because, given the calibration of this model, the prices are very rigid, so they adjust very slowly.

To appreciate more clearly how the movements of the variables are in the phase diagram of this model, Figure C.2 shows the trajectory of the economy in the face of an increase in the amount of money. The initial steady state is at point $(\bar{p}_0 = 81, \bar{y}_0 = 2000)$

Given the increase in the amount of money, the new steady state of the economy is placed at point $(\bar{p}_0 = 82, \bar{y}_0 = 2000)$, as can be seen by analyzing this disturbance in the corresponding spreadsheet. Given the existence of complex roots for the values of the selected parameters, the transition path from the initial steady state to the end is asymptotic, resulting in a series of cyclic fluctuations in which both the level of production and prices fluctuate around its new steady-state value. As we can see in this figure, initially, there is an increase in the level of production, also gradually increasing the price level, until reaching a point where while prices continue to increase, the level of production decreases, moving up and toward the left. This movement occurs until prices begin to decrease again, moving, in this case, down and to the left. Subsequently, production begins to increase again, while prices continue to decline, so the direction would be to the right and down. From this moment, the trajectories of the variables are repeated again, but with values closer to the new steady state. These trajectories continue to repeat until we reach the new steady state.

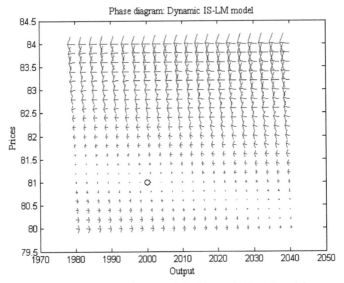

Figure C.1. Phase diagram of the Dynamic IS-LM model.

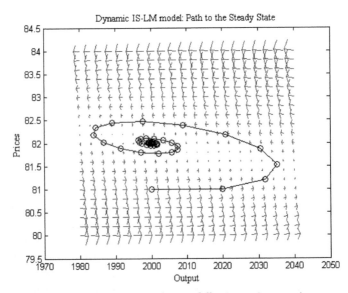

Figure C.2. Trajectory to the new steady state following an increase in money supply.

Appendix E: The dynamic IS-LM model in DYNARE

Here is how the code in Dynare would be to solve the dynamic IS-LM model presented in Chapter 2:

```
% *************************************************
% An Introduction to Computational Macroeconomics
% A. Bongers, T. Gómez and J. L. Torres (2019)
% Dynamic IS-LM model in DYNARE
% File: m2d.mod
% *************************************************
// Endogenous variables
var p y yd i dy dp;
// Exogenous variables
varexo m, beta0, ybar0;
// Parameters
parameters psi, theta, beta1, mi, ni;
theta = 0.5;
psi   = 0.05;
beta1 = 50;
mi    = 0.01;
ni    = 0.2;
// Model equations
model;
m-p=psi*y-theta*i;
yd=beta0-beta1*(i-dp);
dp=mi*(y-ybar0);
dy=ni*(yd-y);
dp(-1)=p-p(-1);
dy(-1)=y-y(-1);
end;
// Initial values
initval;
y  = ybar0;
yd = y;
p  = 1;
i  = 1;
dy = 0;
dp = 0;
m  = 100;
beta0 = 2100;
ybar0 = 2000;
end;
```

```
// Calculation of steady state
steady;
check;
// End values
endval;
y   = ybar0;
yd = y;
p   = 1;
i   = 1;
dy = 0;
dp = 0;
m   = 101;
beta0 = 2100;
ybar0 = 2000;
end;
steady;
shocks;
 var m;
 periods 0;
 values 0;
end;
simul(periods=30);
// Graphics
T=31;
j=1:T;
subplot(2,2,1)
plot(j,y,'Color',[0.25 0.25 0.25],'linewidth',3.5)
xlabel('Periods')
title('Production')
subplot(2,2,2)
plot(j,yd,'Color',[0.25 0.25 0.25],'linewidth',3.5)
xlabel('Periods')
title('Aggregate Demand')
subplot(2,2,3)
plot(j,p,'Color',[0.25 0.25 0.25],'linewidth',3.5)
xlabel('Periods')
title('Prices')
subplot(2,2,4)
plot(j,i,'Color',[0.25 0.25 0.25],'linewidth',3.5)
xlabel('Periods')
title('Nominal interest rate')
```

Appendix F: The overshooting model of the exchange rate in DYNARE

Next, we present what the Dornbusch nominal exchange rate overshooting model would be like to be solved through DYNARE. As we can see, we only need the equations of the model for resolution, without the need to indicate the instantaneous readjustment of the nominal exchange rate in the event of a disturbance. This is because DYNARE allows us to meet the rational expectations that we assume determine the behavior of the nominal exchange rate. For the model to be equivalent to the one solved in the "**ICM-3.xls**" spreadsheet, we have assumed that there is only one advanced variable (the nominal exchange rate).

```
% ************************************************
% An Introduction to Computational Macroeconomics
% A. Bongers, T. Gómez and J. L. Torres (2019)
% Exchange rate overshooting model in DYNARE
% File: m3d.mod
% ************************************************
//Endogenous variables
var p s yd i dp ds;
// Exogenous variables
varexo m, beta0, ypot, pstar, istar;
// Parameters
parameters psi, theta, beta1, beta2, mi;
// Calibration
theta = 0.5;
psi   = 0.05;
beta1 = 20;
beta2 = 0.1;
mi    = 0.001;
// Model equations
model;
  m-p     = psi*ypot-theta*i;
  yd      = beta0+beta1*(s-p+pstar)-beta2*i;
  dp      = mi*(yd-ypot);
  ds      = i-istar;
  dp(-1)  = p-p(-1);
  ds      = s(+1)-s;
end;
// Initial values
initval;
  yd = ypot0;
```

```
p  = 1;
s  = 10;
i  = 3;
dp = 0;
ds = 0;
m  = 100;
beta0 = 500;
ypot  = 2000;
pstar = 0;
istar = 3;
end;
// Initial steady state
steady;
check;
// End values
endval;
yd = ypot0;
p  = 1;
s  = 10;
i = 3;
dp = 0;
ds = 0;
m  = 101;
beta0 = 500;
ypot  = 2000;
pstar = 0;
istar = 3;
end;
// Final steady state
steady;
// Disturbance
shocks;
 var m;
 periods 0;
 values 0;
end;
// Deterministic simulation
simul(periods=30);
// Graphics
T=15;
j=1:T;
subplot(2,2,1)
plot(j,s(1:T),'Color',[0.25 0.25 0.25],'linewidth',3.5)
xlabel('Periods')
title('Nominal exchange rate')
subplot(2,2,2)
plot(j,yd(1:T),'Color',[0.25 0.25 0.25],'linewidth',3.5)
xlabel('Periods')
title('Aggregate Demand')
subplot(2,2,3)
```

```
plot(j,p(1:T),'Color',[0.25 0.25 0.25],'linewidth',3.5)
xlabel('Periods')
title('Prices')
subplot(2,2,4)
plot(j,i(1:T),'Color',[0.25 0.25 0.25],'linewidth',3.5)
xlabel('Periods')
title('Nominal interest rate')
```

Appendix G: The consumption-saving decision in MATLAB

To solve the basic consumer problem in MATLAB, we will use the "fsolve" function. The "fsolve" function of MatLab solves systems of equations using different algorithms. For this, we have to write two programs. A main program (or script file) in which a call to the "fsolve" function is made on an equation system, and an auxiliary program (a function file), in which the system of equations is to be solved by the the algorithms included in the "fsolve" function. The procedure is similar to that used in the spreadsheet. First, we define the parameters and the exogenous variables and specify the system of equations to solve. Then we make a call to the resolution algorithm, which in the case of Excel is the "Solver" tool, which serves as the "fsolve" function in MATLAB. The code shown below corresponds to the "m4.m" file, which would be the main program, while the function file is "m4foc.m".

```
% ***********************************************
% An Introduction to Computational Macroeconomics
% A. Bongers, T. Gómez and J. L. Torres (2019)
% The consumption-saving decision
% Logarithmic utility function: U = ln (C)
% File: m4.m. Function file: m4foc.m
% ***********************************************
clear all
% Model parameters
T = 30;    % Individual's life time
beta = 0.97; % Intertemporal discount factor
% Exogenous variables
R = 0.02; % Real interest rate
for t=1:T;
 W(t) = 10;    % Salary income
end
%for t=21:T;
% W(t) = 0;
%end
par   =  T beta R W];
save par par;
% Initial values
x0   =   10*ones(size(1:T))';
% Zeros Search Algorithm
sol   =  fsolve('m4foc',x0);
% Solution
```

```
for t=1:T
 C(t)    =    sol(t);
end
for t=2:T;
  B(1)   =    W(1)-C(1);
  B(t)   =    (1+R)*B(t-1)+W(t)-C(t);
end
for t=1:T
  U(t)   =    beta^t*log(C(t));
end
% Graphics
subplot(2,2,1)
plot(C,'Color',[0.25 0.25 0.25],'linewidth',3.5)
title('Consumption')
subplot(2,2,2)
plot(B,'Color',[0.25 0.25 0.25],'linewidth',3.5)
title('Savings')
subplot(2,2,3)
plot(W,'Color',[0.25 0.25 0.25],'linewidth',3.5)
title('Income')
subplot(2,2,4)
plot(U,'Color',[0.25 0.25 0.25],'linewidth',3.5)
title('Discounted utility')



% ************************************************
% An Introduction to Computational Macroeconomics
% A. Bongers, T. Gómez and J. L. Torres (2018)
% The consumption-saving decision
% Logarithmic utility function: U = ln (C)
% File: m4foc.m. Script file m4.m
% ************************************************
function f=m4foc(x0, par)
% Loading parameters
load par
T = par(1);
beta = par(2);
R = par(3);
for i=1:T;
W(i) = par(3+i);
end;
% Assignment of variables
for t=1:T
 C(t) = x0(t);
end
% Calculation of savings
for t=2:T;
B(1) = W(1)-C(1);
B(t) = (1+R)*B(t-1)+W(t)-C(t);
```

```
end
% Terminal condition
 C(T+1) = C(T);
% Optimum consumption path
f(1) = C(2)-beta*(1+R)*C(1);
for t=2:T-1
 f(t) = C(t+1)-beta*(1+R)*C(t);
end
f(T) = C(T)-(1+R)*B(T-1);
```

Appendix H: The Newton-type algorithm

One of the existing and most used algorithms to solve a system of equations is an algorithm called Newton's method (or Newton-Raphson or Newton-Fourier method). This method was developed by Isaac Newton (1642-1727) in the year 1671 and by Joseph Raphson (1648-1715) in the year 1690, although the basis of this resolution method of systems of equations were previously developed by Persian mathematicians Sharaf al-Din al-Tusi (1135-1213) and Ghiyath al-Din Jamshid Kashani (1380-1429), and approximations to it had already been made by Heron of Alexandria (10-70) and by Hindu mathematicians around the year 300.

The basic idea is to apply an iterative algorithm, given an equation or a system of equations, to find values for the unknowns such that their value is zero and, therefore, find as a solution the value of the unknowns. Suppose we have a system composed of n equations with n unknowns: $F: R^n \rightarrow R^n$. The problem to be solved would be to find a vector $\hat{x} = (\hat{x}_1, \dots, \hat{x}_n)$ of R^n, such that its image by $F: R^n \rightarrow R^n$ is $F(\hat{x}) = 0$. To do this, we need to start from an initial solution proposal, x_0. This is called the "seed" or the proposed solution (equivalent to the values that we have to enter in Excel in the cells in which the solution to the problem to be solved is obtained when we use the "Solver" tool). For the selection of this tentative solution, we have to use all the information we have about F, since the efficiency and ability to obtain a solution of the algorithm depends on whether these initial values are near or far from the final solution. The objective is to find a solution, x, such that $F(x)$ is equal to zero. To do this, we start by developing the Taylor series of the function for a given initial value x_n:

$$F(x) = F(x_n) + F'(x_n)(x - x_n) + \frac{F''(x_n)}{2!}(x - x_n)^2 + \cdots$$

The procedure is iterative and consists of calculating the previous expression for the different resulting approximations. We would evaluate this expression for different values such that:

$$F(x_{n+1}) = F(x_n) + F'(x_n)(x_{n+1} - x_n) + \frac{F''(x_n)}{2!}(x_{n+1} - x_n)^2 + \cdots$$

The solution would be given by the value that makes Taylor's expansion equal to zero:

$$F(x_n) + F'(x_n)(x_{n+1} - x_n) + \frac{F''(x_n)}{2!}(x_{n+1} - x_n)^2 + \cdots = 0$$

If we truncate Taylor's expansion from the second term, (that is, we would be making a linear approximation) we obtain that:

$$F(x_n) + F'(x_n)(x_{n+1} - x_n) \simeq 0$$

As we approach the solution, the higher-order values of Taylor's expansion are set to zero. Clearing the obtained solution, x_{n+1}, it turns out:

$$x_{n+1} = x_n - \frac{F(x_n)}{F'(x_n)}$$

which is the expression called the Newton-Raphson formula.

The operation of the corresponding algorithm would be as follows. We begin with an initial value of x_0, which would be our solution proposal (and that obviously is difficult to be the solution except in very simple cases). We would obtain the result (a new possible solution) by applying the Newton-Raphson algorithm

$$x_1 = x_0 - \frac{F(x_0)}{F'(x_0)}$$

If $F(x_1) = 0$ the process ends, since the x_1 value would be the solution. On the contrary, if it is different from zero (in an amount that we have to determine) then we proceed to a second iteration calculating:

$$x_2 = x_1 - \frac{F(x_1)}{F'(x_1)}$$

Again, if $F(x_2)$ is different from zero, then we proceed to a third iteration calculating:

$$x_3 = x_2 - \frac{F(x_2)}{F'(x_2)}$$

and so, until we find a solution such that the value of the function is zero. However, finding absolute zero (the exact solution) for a relatively complex set of equations could take a long time (a very high level of iterations), because we must introduce a tolerance criterion in terms of a value that we consider very close to zero, which would correspond to the minimum error that we consider acceptable to consider a solution valid. This is what is called the tolerance criterion. This criterion determines how much the absolute zero solution can be diverted. In each iteration, we can calculate the error we make, which in absolute terms we define as

$$\varepsilon = |F(x_{t+1})|$$

If ε is greater than a very small value set a priori (tolerance), then the algorithm proceeds to perform a new iteration. In the case where the absolute relative error is lower than the tolerance criterion, the algorithm ends, giving the last iteration as the valid solution. Below, we will present several simple examples to illustrate the operation of this algorithm.

Example 1: In the case where the equation we want to solve is linear, the Newton-Rapson algorithm finds the solution directly, since the error you make in the first iteration is zero. Suppose we want to find zero for the following linear function: $F(x) = x - 2$

Obviously, the solution to the previous function is $x = 2$. But imagine that we do not know it and believe that its value should be 5, ($x_0 = 5$). If we apply the Newton-Raphson algorithm, then we should:

$$x_1 = x_0 - \frac{F(x_0)}{F'(x_0)} = 5 - 3 = 2$$

Evaluating the function for this solution results in:

$$F(x_0) = x_0 - 2 = 2 - 2 = 0$$

so we have already found the solution to this equation.

Example 2: Imagine that we want to solve the square root of a y number, and get that value, that we call x, but we don't know how to solve square roots by the standard procedure (or we have forgotten it because we learned it many years ago and we don't remember how it was done). No problem, because we can do it using the Newton-Raphson algorithm. This is what is known as the Babylon method or Heron's method. Since $X = \sqrt{y}$, we can also write it as $x^2 = y$. This means that we can solve and find zero for the following function: $F(x) = x^2 - y$

By applying the Newton-Raphson algorithm, we obtain that:

$$x_{i+1} = x_i - \frac{x_i^2 - y}{2x_i} = \frac{2x_i - x_i^2 - y}{2x_i} = \frac{1}{2}(x_i + \frac{y}{x_i})$$

Let's suppose that $y = 21$. We know that $4 \times 4 = 16$, and that $5 \times 5 = 25$, so the solution has to be between 4 and 5. Therefore, the seed (the initial value) that we would use would be between these two values. Let's try with $x_0 = 4.5$. If we enter a value in the previous expression, we get:

$$x_1 = \frac{1}{2}\left(x_0 + \frac{y}{x_0}\right) = 0.5 \times \left(4.5 + \frac{21}{4.5}\right) =$$

Extending the procedure to a system of equations is simple. Thus, in the case where we have a system with n equations, the approximation of the function through Taylor's first expansion to the function F is:

$$F(x) \approx F(\bar{x}) + J(\bar{x})(x - \bar{x})$$

where $J(\bar{x})$ is the Jacobian F matrix evaluated in $\bar{x}$:

$$J(\bar{x}) = \begin{bmatrix} F_{11}(\bar{x}) & \cdots & F_{1n}(\bar{x}) \\ \vdots & \ddots & \vdots \\ F_{n1}(\bar{x}) & \cdots & F_{nm}(\bar{x}) \end{bmatrix}$$

where $F_{ij} = \frac{\partial F_i(\bar{x})}{\partial x_j}$. Applying Taylor's Theorem that tells us that as $\bar{x}$ approaches value x, the major-order terms tend to zero. Since we are looking for a vector of zeros for the system $F(x)$, the previous expression can be evaluated in $\hat{x}$ and written as:

$$\hat{x} \approx \bar{x} - J(\bar{x})^{-1} F(\bar{x})$$

The algorithm would be similar to the one described above.

Example 3: Find the zeros of the following system of equations:

$$F_1(x, z) = x - 3z + 1$$

$$F_2(x, z) = 2x + z - 5$$

The Jacobian corresponding to this system of equations is:

$$J(x, z) = \begin{bmatrix} \dfrac{\partial F_1(x,z)}{\partial x} & \dfrac{\partial F_1(x,z)}{\partial z} \\ \dfrac{\partial F_2(x,z)}{\partial x} & \dfrac{\partial F_2(x,z)}{\partial z} \end{bmatrix} = \begin{bmatrix} 1 & -3 \\ 2 & 1 \end{bmatrix}$$

We are going to propose as a seed, that $x = 1$ and $z = 2$, that is obviously not the solution to the previous system. If we introduce this seed in the system of equations, we obtain that:

$$F_1(x, z) = 1 - 3 \times 2 + 1 = -1$$

$$F_2(x, z) = 2 \times 1 + 2 - 5 = -1$$

values that are different from zero, so the proposed seed is not the solution. If we apply the Newton-Raphson algorithm, we get that:

$$\begin{bmatrix} x_1 \\ z_1 \end{bmatrix} = \begin{bmatrix} 1 \\ 2 \end{bmatrix} - \begin{bmatrix} 1 & 3 \\ 2 & 1 \end{bmatrix}^{-1} \begin{bmatrix} -4 \\ -1 \end{bmatrix} = \begin{bmatrix} 2 \\ 1 \end{bmatrix}$$

If we introduce this new solution in the system of equations, we obtain:

$$F_1(2; 1) = 2 - 3 \times 1 + 1 = 0$$

$$F_2(2; 1) = 2 \times 2 + 1 - 5 = 0$$

being the solution of both equations equal to zero, so we have already found the solution to the previous system ($\bar{x} = 2, \bar{z} = 1$).

Appendix I: The consumption-saving and consumption-leisure decision in MATLAB

Next, we present the code in MATLAB to solve the consumer problem with leisure.

```
%*********************************************************
% An Introduction to Computational Macroeconomics
% A. Bongers, T. Gómez and J. L. Torres (2019)
% Consumption-saving and consumption-leisure decisions
% Utility function: U=gamma*ln(C)+(1-gamma)*ln(1-L)
% File: m5.m. Function file: m5foc.m
%*********************************************************
clear all
% Model parameters
T = 30; % Individual's life time
beta = 0.99;   % Intertemporal discount factor
gamma = 0.40; % Weight of consumption in profit
% Exogenous variables
R = 0.02;   % Real interest rate
for t=1:T;
 W(t) = 30; % Salary income
end
par  =  T beta R gamma W];
save par par;
% Initial values
x0  =  10*ones(size(1:T)), 0.3*ones(size(1:T))]';
% Zeros Search Algorithm
sol=fsolve('m5foc',x0);
% Solution
for t=1:T
   C(t)  = sol(t);
  L(t) = sol(t+T);
end
for t=2:T;
  B(1)  =  W(1)*L(1)-C(1);
  B(t)  =  (1+R)*B(t-1)+W(t)*L(t)-C(t);
end
% Graphics
subplot(2,2,1)
plot(C,'Color',[0.25 0.25 0.25],'linewidth',3.5)
title('Consumption')
xlabel('Periods')
subplot(2,2,2)
```

```
plot(B,'Color',[0.25 0.25 0.25],'linewidth',3.5)
title('Savings (Stock of financial assets)')
xlabel('Periods')
subplot(2,2,3)
plot(W.*L,'Color',[0.25 0.25 0.25],'linewidth',3.5)
title('Salary income')
xlabel('Periods')
subplot(2,2,4)
plot(L,'Color',[0.25 0.25 0.25],'linewidth',3.5)
title('Work (Time Fraction)')
xlabel('Periods')



%*****************************************************
% An Introduction to Computational Macroeconomics
% A. Bongers, T. Gómez and J. L. Torres (2019)
% Utility function: U=gamma*ln(C)+(1-gamma)*ln(1-L)
% Function file: m5foc.m. Script file: m5.m
%*****************************************************
function f=m5foc(x0,par)
% Load parameters
load par
T = par(1);
beta = par(2);
R = par(3);
gamma = par(4);
for i=1:T;
W(i) = par(4+i);
end;
% Assignment of variables
for t=1:T
 C(t) = x0(t);
 L(t) = x0(t+T);
end
% Calculation of savings
for t=2:T-1;
B(1) = W(1)*L(1)-C(1);
B(t) = (1+R)*B(t-1)+W(t)*L(t)-C(t);
end
% Optimum consumption path
f(1) = C(2)-beta*(1+R)*C(1);
f(2) = W(1)-(C(1)/((1-L(1))))*(1-gamma)/gamma;
for t=2:T-1
 f(2*t-1) = C(t+1)-beta*(1+R)*C(t);
 f(2*t) = W(t)-(C(t)/((1-L(t))))*(1-gamma)/gamma;
end
f(2*T) = C(T)-W(T)*L(T)-(1+R)*B(T-1);
f(2*T+1) = W(T)-(C(T)/((1-L(T))))*(1-gamma)/gamma;
```

Appendix J: The consumer problem with taxes in MATLAB

Introducing taxes in the consumer's problem is simple, since the tax rates are exogenous variables and, therefore, the basic structure of the problem is not altered. Below, we present a simple code in MATLAB to solve the consumer problem with three types of taxes: taxes on consumption, on salary income and on the profitability of financial assets. The main file, called "mc6.m", is as follows:

```
%**************************************************
% An Introduction to Computational Macroeconomics
% A. Bongers, T. Gómez and J. L. Torres (2019)
% Distorting taxes
% Utility function: U=gamma*ln(C)+(1-gamma)*log(1-L)
% File: m6.m. Function file: m6foc.m
%**************************************************
clear all
% Model parameters
T = 30; % Individual's life time
beta = 0.97;   % Intertemporal discount factor
gamma = 0.40; % Weight of consumption in profit
% Exogenous variables
R    = 0.05;   % Real interest rate
tauw = 0.35;
taur = 0.25;
tauc = 0.15;
for t=1:T;
 W(t) = 100; % Salary income
end
par  =  T beta R gamma tauw taur tauc W];
save par par;
% Initial values
x0  =  10*ones(size(1:T)), 0.3*ones(size(1:T))]';
% Zeros Search Algorithm
sol  =  fsolve('m6foc', x0);
% Solution
for t=1:T
   C(t)  =  sol(t);
 L(t) = sol(t+T);
end
for t=2:T;
  B(1) = (1-tauw)*W(1)*L(1)-(1+tauc)*C(1);
```

```
B(t) = (1+(1-taur)*R)*B(t-1)+(1-tauw)*W(t)*L(t)-(1+tauc)*C(t);
% G(t) = tauc*C(t)+tauw*W(t)*L(t)+taur*R*B(t-1);
end
% Change in tax rates
tauw1 = 0.30;
taur1 = 0.25;
tauc1 = 0.15;
par  = T beta R gamma tauw1 taur1 tauc1 W];
save par par;
% Initial values
x0  = 10*ones(size(1:T)), 0.3*ones(size(1:T))]';
% Zeros Search Algorithm
sol=fsolve('m6foc',x0);
% Solution
for t=1:T
 C1(t)  =  sol(t);
 L1(t)  =  sol(t+T);
end
W1=W;
for t=2:T;
 B1(1) = (1-tauw1)*W(1)*L1(1)-(1+tauc1)*C1(1);
 B1(t) = (1+(1-taur1)*R)*B1(t-1)+(1-tauw1)*W(t)*L1(t)
  -(1+tauc1)*C1(t);
end
% Graphics
i=1:T;
subplot(2,2,1)
plot(i,C,'--',i,C1,'Color',[0.25 0.25 0.25],'linewidth',3.5)
xlabel('Periods')
title('Consumption')
subplot(2,2,2)
plot(i,B,'--',i,B1,'-','Color',[0.25 0.25 0.25],'linewidth',3.5)
xlabel('Periods')
title('Savings (Stock of financial assets)')
subplot(2,2,3)
plot(i,(1-tauw).*W.*L,'--',i,(1-tauw1).*W1.*L1,
   'Color',[0.25 0.25 0.25],'linewidth',3.5)
xlabel('Periods')
title('Salary income (after taxes)')
subplot(2,2,4)
plot(i,L,'--',i,L1,'Color',[0.25 0.25 0.25],'linewidth',3.5)
xlabel('Periods')
title('Work (Time Fraction)')
```

The associated function file, called "m6foc.m" is as follows:

```
%*****************************************************
% An Introduction to Computational Macroeconomics
% A. Bongers, T. Gómez and J. L. Torres (2019)
% Distorting taxes
```

```
% Utility function: U=gamma*ln(C)+(1-gamma)*ln(1-L)
% Function file: m6foc.m. Script file: m6.m
%***************************************************
function f=m6foc(x0, par)
% Load parameters
load par
T = par(1);
beta = par(2);
R = par(3);
gamma = par(4);
tauw = par(5);
taur = par(6);
tauc = par(7);
for i=1:T;
W(i) = par(7+i);
end;
% Assignment of variables
for t=1:T
 C(t) = x0(t);
 L(t) = x0(t+T);
end
% Calculation of savings
for t=2:T;
B(1) = (1-tauw)*W(1)*L(1)-(1+tauc)*C(1);
B(t) = (1+(1-taur)*R)*B(t-1)+(1-tauw)*W(t)*L(t)-(1+tauc)*C(t);
end
% Optimum consumption path
f(1) = (1+tauc)*C(2)-beta*(1+(1-taur)*R)*(1+tauc)*C(1);
f(2) = (1-tauw)*W(1)*(1-L(1))-((1+tauc)*C(1))*(1-gamma)/gamma;
for t=2:T-1
 f(2*t-1) = (1+tauc)*C(t+1)-beta*(1+(1-taur)*R)*(1+tauc)*C(t);
 f(2*t) = (1-tauw)*W(t)*(1-L(t))-((1+tauc)*C(t))*(1-gamma)/gamma;
end
f(2*T-1) = (1+tauc)*C(T)-(1+(1-taur)*R)*B(T-1)-(1-tauw)*W(T)*L(T);
f(2*T) = (1-tauw)*W(T)*(1-L(T))-((1+tauc)*C(T))*(1-gamma)/gamma;
```

Appendix K: The Tobin Q model in DYNARE

Tobin's Q model can be solved in a very simple way using DYNARE. As we have seen in previous appendices, DYNARE is very easy to use, with a very simple language, specially designed to solve dynamic general equilibrium models. Tobin's Q model appears as an integral part of the dynamic general equilibrium model.

```
// ************************************************
// An Introduction to Computational Macroeconomics
// A. Bongers, T. Gómez and J. L. Torres (2019)
// The Tobin Q model in DYNARE
// File: m7d.mod
// ************************************************
// Endogenous variables
var q k dq dk;
// Exogenous variables
varexo R, delta;
// Parameters
parameters alpha, phi;
// Calibration
alpha = 0.35;
phi = 10;
// Defining the capital stock as the predetermined variable
predetermined_variables k;
// Model equations
model;
(1-delta)*q(+1)=(1+R)*q-alpha*k(+1)^(alpha-1)
  +phi/2*(((k(+2)-k(+1))/k(+1)))^2
  -phi*((k(+2)-k(+1))/k(+1))*(k(+2)-(1-delta)*k(+1))/k(+1);
k(+1)-k=(q-1)*k/phi;
dk=k(+1)-k;
dq=q(+1)-q;
end;
// Initial values
initval;
q = 1;
k = 10;
dk = 0;
dq = 0;
R = 0.04;
delta = 0.06;
end;
// Initial steady state
steady;
```

```
check;
// End values
// Disturbance: Disruption in the interest rate
endval;
q = 1;
k = 10;
dk = 0;
dq = 0;
R = 0.03;
delta = 0.06;
end;
// Final steady state
steady;
check;
// Deterministic simulation
simul(periods=200);
// Graphics
T=50;
j=1:T;
subplot(1,2,1)
plot(j,q(1:T),'Color',[0.25 0.25 0.25],'linewidth',3.5)
title('Ratio q')
xlabel('Periods')
subplot(1,2,2)
plot(j,k(1:T),'Color',[0.25 0.25 0.25],'linewidth',3.5)
title('Capital stock')
xlabel('Periods')
```

Appendix L: The dynamic general equilibrium model in MATLAB

This appendix presents the code to solve the dynamic general equilibrium model in MATLAB and simulate a temporary productivity disruption, which would be the equivalent to the exercise proposed in the spreadsheet "ICM-8-1-xls".

```
%****************************************************
% An Introduction to Computational Macroeconomics
% A. Bongers, T. Gómez and J. L. Torres (2019)
% Basic general equilibrium model
% Logarithmic utility function: U=ln(C)
% File: m8.m. Associated function: m8foc.m
%****************************************************
clear all
% Periods
T = 100;
% Parameter calibration
Ass = 1.00;
Alpha = 0.35;
Delta = 0.06;
Rho = 1;
Beta = 0.96;
% Steady State
Kss = ((1-Beta+Delta*Beta)/(Ass*Alpha*Beta))^(1/(Alpha-1));
Yss = Ass*Kss^Alpha;
Iss = Delta*Kss;
Css = Yss-Iss;
% Disturbance
Epsilon=0.01;
A(1)=Ass^Rho+Epsilon;
 for i=2:T;
 A(i)=A(i-1)^Rho;
 end
par =[Ass Alpha Delta Rho Beta Kss T A];
save par par;
% Initial values
x0 = [Kss*ones(size(1:T)) 0.20*Kss*ones(size(1:T))]';
% Algorithm
sol = fsolve('m8foc',x0);
% Solution
 for t=1:T;
 C(t) = sol(t);
```

```
 K(t) = sol(t+T);
 end
Y = A.*K.^Alpha;
K(T+1)=K(T);
I = K(2:T+1)-(1-Delta)*K(1:T);
T=60;
% Graphics
subplot(2,2,1)
plot((C(1:T)-Css)/Css,'Color',[0.25 0.25 0.25],'linewidth',3.5)
xlabel('Periods')
title('Consumption')
subplot(2,2,2)
plot((K(1:T)-Kss)/Kss,'Color',[0.25 0.25 0.25],'linewidth',3.5)
xlabel('Periods')
title('Capital stock')
subplot(2,2,3)
plot((Y(1:T)-Yss)/Yss,'Color',[0.25 0.25 0.25],'linewidth',3.5)
xlabel('Periods')
title('Output')
subplot(2,2,4)
plot((A(1:T)-Ass)/Ass,'Color',[0.25 0.25 0.25],'linewidth',3.5)
xlabel('Periods')
title('Total Factor Productivity')


%*****************************************************
% An Introduction to Computational Macroeconomics
% A. Bongers, T. Gómez and J. L. Torres (2019)
% Basic general equilibrium model
% Logarithmic utility function: U=ln(C)
% File: m8foc.m. Script function: m8.m
%*****************************************************
function f=m8foc(z,par)
% Loading parameters
load par
Ass   = par(1);
Alpha = par(2);
Delta = par(3);
Rho   = par(4);
Beta  = par(5);
Kss   = par(6);
T     = par(7);
for i=1:T;
A(i) = par(7+i);
end;
% Assignment of variables
for t=1:T
C(t) = z(t);
K(t) = z(t+T);
end
```

```
C(T+1) = C(T);
K0=Kss;
% Equation to solve
f(1) = C(2)-Beta*(Alpha*A(1)*K(1)^(Alpha-1)+(1-Delta))*C(1);
f(2) = C(1)+K(1)-(1-Delta)*K0-A(1)*K0^Alpha;
for t=2:T
f(2*t-1) = C(t+1)-Beta*(Alpha*A(t)*K(t)^(Alpha-1)+(1-Delta))*C(t);
f(2*t)   = C(t)+K(t)-(1-Delta)*K(t-1)-A(t)*K(t-1)^Alpha;
end
```

Appendix M: The dynamic general equilibrium model in DYNARE

In this appendix, we present the code in DYNARE to solve the basic general equilibrium model developed in Chapter 8. As we have commented previously, DYNARE is a tool specially designed to solve these types of models, both in a deterministic and stochastic environment. In practice, DYNARE solves an initial non-linear system approximation, and although this approximation does not have to be linear, as DYNARE can use higher orders in Taylor's expansion to approximate the original equations. One of the advantages of the DYNARE tool is that it allows to obtain the log-linearized dynamic equations of a dynamic general equilibrium model without having to calculate them by hand, as we had to do to build the spreadsheet "**ICM-8.2. xls**".

```
// *********************************************
// An Introduction to Computational Macroeconomics
// A. Bongers, T. Gómez and J. L. Torres (2019)
// Dynamic General Equilibrium Model in DYNARE
// File: m8d.mod
// *********************************************
// Definition of endogenous variables
var Y, C, I, K, R, A;
// Definition of exogenous variables
varexo e;
// Parameter definition
parameters alpha, beta, delta, rho;
// Calibration
alpha = 0.35;
beta = 0.96;
delta = 0.06;
rho = 0.80;
// Defining capital stock as predetermined variable
predetermined_variables K;
// Model equations
model;
1 = beta*((C/C(+1))*(R(+1)+(1-delta)));
Y = A*K^alpha;
K(+1) = (1-delta)*K+I;
Y = C+I;
R = alpha*A*K^(alpha-1);
A = A(-1)^rho+e;
end;
```

```
// Initial values
initval;
Y = 1;
C = 0.8;
K = 3.5;
I = 0.2;
R = alpha*Y/K;
A = 1;
e = 0;
end;
// Calculation of steady state
steady;
// Verification of compliance with the BK condition
check;
ybar=oo_.steady_state(1);
cbar=oo_.steady_state(2);
ibar=oo_.steady_state(3);
kbar=oo_.steady_state(4);
Rbar=oo_.steady_state(5);
Abar=oo_.steady_state(6);
shocks;
var e;
stderr 0.01;
end;
stoch_simul(order=1);
% Graphics
figure;
T=40;
j=1:T;
subplot(2,2,1)
plot(j,Y_e+ybar,'Color',[0.25 0.25 0.25],'linewidth',3.5)
xlabel('Periods')
title('Output')
subplot(2,2,2)
plot(j,K_e+kbar,'Color',[0.25 0.25 0.25],'linewidth',3.5)
xlabel('Periods')
title('Capital stock')
subplot(2,2,3)
plot(j,C_e+cbar,'Color',[0.25 0.25 0.25],'linewidth',3.5)
xlabel('Periods')
title('Consumption')
subplot(2,2,4)
plot(j,I_e+ibar,'Color',[0.25 0.25 0.25],'linewidth',3.5)
xlabel('Periods')
title('Investment')
```

Appendix N: Solution of the Dynamic Stochastic General Equilibrium (DSGE) model

In this appendix, we solve a stochastic version of the Real Business Cycle-Dynamic General Equilibrium model studied in Chapter 8. In practice, there is a wide variety of methods to solve this type of dynamic models with rational expectations, both in the case where the system to be solved is linear (a linear approximation) and non-linear. The idea of these methods is to obtain the so-called transition functions and policy functions, which consist of a recursive system in which all the variables of the model depend on the state variables. The state variables are predetermined variables, that is, their value has already been determined through economic agents' decisions in the previous period. For example, the capital stock is a state variable, since the capital stock today was decided through investment in the previous period. Therefore, at each period, we know the value of the state variable for that period. The solution to the model would be given by a recursive system for the state variables (called transition functions), and by a system in which the rest of the control variables depend on the value of the state variables (the policy functions). Tis appendix presents one of these methods for solving systems of linear equations with rational expectations. This means that we have to proceed previously to linearize the dynamic general equilibrium model whose equations are non-linear. In particular, we present the method of Blanchard and Khan.[1]

The solution to these types of models involves obtaining a recursive system in terms of the state variables. In general terms, this solution can be represented as

$$s_t = V s_{t-1} + W \varepsilon_t \tag{N.1}$$

$$v_t = Z s_t \tag{N.2}$$

where s_t is the vector of the state variables (in our case the capital stock and total factor productivity), v_t is the vector of the rest of the endogenous

---

[1] Blanchard, O. y Khan, C. M. (1980). The solution of linear difference models under rational expectations. *Econometrica*, 48(5): 1305-1311.

variables of the model, including the "jump" variable that is a forward-looking variable (in our case consumption), on which rational expectations apply, ε_t is a vector of exogenous variables that in this case we associate with the random component, and where V, W and Z are matrices that are composed of the model parameters. The first system would define the transition functions and the second the policy functions.

Next, we apply the method of Blanchard and Khan step by step. We start from the equations that define the stochastic version of the model in Chapter 8, which are the following:

$$E_t C_{t+1} = \beta \left[\alpha \frac{E_t Y_{t+1}}{K_{t+1}} + 1 - \delta \right] C_t \tag{N.3}$$

$$Y_t = A_t K_t^\alpha \tag{N.4}$$

$$K_{t+1} = (1 - \delta) K_t + I_t \tag{N.5}$$

$$Y_t = C_t + I_t \tag{N.6}$$

$$ln A_t = \rho ln A_{t-1} + \varepsilon_t \tag{N.7}$$

where we assume ε_t is a random disturbance.

Next, we get a linear approximation to it. The log-linearized model in terms of its deviations from the steady state would be the following:

$$E_t \hat{c}_{t+1} = (1 - \beta + \beta\delta)\left(E_t \hat{y}_{t+1} - \hat{k}_{t+1}\right) + \hat{c}_t \tag{N.8}$$

$$\hat{y}_t = \hat{a}_t + \alpha \hat{k}_t \tag{N.9}$$

$$\hat{k}_{t+1} = (1 - \delta)\hat{k}_t + \hat{\imath}_t \tag{N.10}$$

$$(1 - \beta + \beta\delta)\hat{y}_t = (1 - \beta + (1 - \alpha)\beta\delta)\hat{c}_t + \alpha\beta\delta \hat{\imath}_t \tag{N.11}$$

$$\hat{a}_t = \rho \hat{a}_{t-1} + \varepsilon_t \tag{N.12}$$

We divide the variables into two groups. The first group would be composed of the advanced variable (consumption) and the state variable (capital stock). The second group would be composed of the rest of the variables (the level of production and investment).

$$x_t = \begin{bmatrix} \hat{c}_t \\ \hat{k}_t \end{bmatrix}, \ z_t = \begin{bmatrix} \hat{y}_t \\ \hat{\imath}_t \end{bmatrix} \tag{N.13}$$

The model can be written in terms of the following systems of equations:

$$A z_t = B x_t + C \hat{a}_t \tag{N.14}$$

$$D x_{t+1} + F z_{t+1} = G x_t + H z_t \tag{N.15}$$

The system of log-linearized equations is therefore divided into two groups: those equations that are static and are defined at the same moment of time and those equations that contain future variables. The first system of equations would therefore be composed of:

$$\hat{y}_t = \hat{a}_t + \alpha \hat{k}_t \tag{N.16}$$

$$(1 - \beta + \beta\delta)\hat{y}_t - \alpha\beta\delta\hat{\imath}_t = (1 - \beta + (1 - \alpha)\beta\delta)\hat{c}_t \tag{N.17}$$

while the second system of equations would be composed of:

$$E_t\hat{c}_{t+1} - (1 - \beta + \beta\delta)(\hat{y}_{t+1} - \hat{k}_{t+1}) = \hat{c}_t \tag{N.18}$$

$$\hat{k}_{t+1} = (1 - \delta)\hat{k}_t + \delta\hat{\imath}_t \tag{N.19}$$

To simplify, we will define the following two parameters:

$$\Omega = 1 - \beta + \beta\delta$$

$$\Phi = 1 - \beta + (1 - \alpha)\beta\delta$$

Therefore, the systems (N.14) and (N.15), using each set of equations, can be written as:

$$\underbrace{\begin{bmatrix} 1 & 0 \\ \Omega & -\alpha\beta\delta \end{bmatrix}}_{A}\begin{bmatrix} \hat{y}_t \\ \hat{\imath}_t \end{bmatrix} = \underbrace{\begin{bmatrix} 0 & \alpha \\ \Phi & 0 \end{bmatrix}}_{B}\begin{bmatrix} \hat{c}_t \\ \hat{k}_t \end{bmatrix} + \begin{bmatrix} 1 \\ 0 \end{bmatrix}\hat{a}_t \tag{N.20}$$

And

$$\underbrace{\begin{bmatrix} 1 & \Omega \\ 0 & 1 \end{bmatrix}}_{D}\begin{bmatrix} E_t\hat{c}_{t+1} \\ \hat{k}_{t+1} \end{bmatrix} + \underbrace{\begin{bmatrix} -\Omega & 0 \\ 0 & 0 \end{bmatrix}}_{F}\begin{bmatrix} \hat{y}_{t+1} \\ \hat{\imath}_{t+1} \end{bmatrix} = \underbrace{\begin{bmatrix} 1 & 0 \\ 0 & 1-\delta \end{bmatrix}}_{G}\begin{bmatrix} \hat{c}_t \\ \hat{k}_t \end{bmatrix} + \underbrace{\begin{bmatrix} 0 & 0 \\ 0 & \delta \end{bmatrix}}_{H}\begin{bmatrix} \hat{y}_t \\ \hat{\imath}_t \end{bmatrix} \tag{N.21}$$

Clearing from the first system results in:[2]

$$\begin{bmatrix} \hat{y}_t \\ \hat{\imath}_t \end{bmatrix} = A^{-1}B\begin{bmatrix} \hat{c}_t \\ \hat{k}_t \end{bmatrix} + A^{-1}C\hat{a}_t \tag{N.22}$$

By writing this system in $t + 1$, we would obtain:

$$\begin{bmatrix} \hat{y}_{t+1} \\ \hat{\imath}_{t+1} \end{bmatrix} = A^{-1}B\begin{bmatrix} E_t\hat{c}_{t+1} \\ \hat{k}_{t+1} \end{bmatrix} + A^{-1}C\hat{a}_{t+1} \tag{N.23}$$

---

[2] Note that this procedure requires the inversion of the A matrix. However, it may happen that the A matrix is non-invertible, which would require another alternative procedure, such as Klein, who uses the QZ decomposition. Klein, P. (2000). Using a generalized Schur form to solve a multivariate linear rational expectation model. *Journal of Economic Dynamics and Control*, 24 (1): 405-423.

Replacing these two systems in the system (N.21), results in:

$$D \begin{bmatrix} E_t \hat{c}_{t+1} \\ \hat{k}_{t+1} \end{bmatrix} + FA^{-1}B \begin{bmatrix} E_t \hat{c}_{t+1} \\ \hat{k}_{t+1} \end{bmatrix} + FA^{-1}C\hat{a}_{t+1} =$$

$$G \begin{bmatrix} \hat{c}_t \\ \hat{k}_t \end{bmatrix} + HA^{-1}B \begin{bmatrix} \hat{c}_t \\ \hat{k}_t \end{bmatrix} + HA^{-1}C\hat{a}_t \tag{N.24}$$

and grouping terms results:

$$(D + FA^{-1}B) \begin{bmatrix} E_t \hat{c}_{t+1} \\ \hat{k}_{t+1} \end{bmatrix} + FA^{-1}C\hat{a}_{t+1} = (G + HA^{-1}B) \begin{bmatrix} \hat{c}_t \\ \hat{k}_t \end{bmatrix} + HA^{-1}C\hat{a}_t \tag{N.25}$$

Given that

$$\hat{a}_t = \rho \hat{a}_{t-1} + \hat{\varepsilon}_t \tag{N.26}$$

The expected value in $t + 1$ results in:

$$E_t \hat{a}_{t+1} = \rho \hat{a}_t \tag{N.27}$$

By substituting results that:

$$(D + FA^{-1}B) \begin{bmatrix} E_t \hat{c}_{t+1} \\ \hat{k}_{t+1} \end{bmatrix} + FA^{-1}C\rho\hat{a}_t = (G + HA^{-1}B) \begin{bmatrix} \hat{c}_t \\ \hat{k}_t \end{bmatrix} + HA^{-1}C\hat{a}_t \tag{N.28}$$

and by regrouping, we get:

$$(D + FA^{-1}B) \begin{bmatrix} E_t \hat{c}_{t+1} \\ \hat{k}_{t+1} \end{bmatrix} = (G + HA^{-1}B) \begin{bmatrix} \hat{c}_t \\ \hat{k}_t \end{bmatrix} + (HA^{-1}C - FA^{-1}C\rho)\hat{a}_t \tag{N.29}$$

Defining the matrices

$$J = (D + FA^{-1}B)^{-1}(G + HA^{-1}B)$$

$$M = (D + FA^{-1}B)^{-1}(HA^{-1}C - FA^{-1}C\rho)$$

we finally arrive at the following system:

$$\begin{bmatrix} E_t \hat{c}_{t+1} \\ \hat{k}_{t+1} \end{bmatrix} = J \begin{bmatrix} \hat{c}_t \\ \hat{k}_t \end{bmatrix} + M\hat{a}_t \tag{N.30}$$

Where

$$J = \begin{bmatrix} 1 - \dfrac{(\alpha-1)\Omega\Phi}{\alpha\beta} & (\alpha-1)\Omega(1 - \delta + \dfrac{\Omega}{\beta}) \\ -\dfrac{\Phi}{\alpha\beta} & 1 - \delta + \dfrac{\Omega}{\beta} \end{bmatrix}$$

and operating results in:

$$J = \begin{bmatrix} 1 - \dfrac{(\alpha-1)\Omega\Phi}{\alpha\beta} & \dfrac{(\alpha-1)\Omega}{\beta} \\ -\dfrac{\Phi}{\alpha\beta} & \dfrac{1}{\beta} \end{bmatrix}$$

matrix that is exactly the same as the matrix given by the expression (Table 8.1), if we write that system in a normal way, that is, if we add the unit to the elements of the main diagonal. For its part, the M matrix would be given by:

$$M = \begin{bmatrix} \Omega(\rho + \frac{(\alpha-1)\Omega}{\alpha\beta}) \\ \frac{\Omega}{\alpha\beta} \end{bmatrix}$$

Given the calibrated values for the parameters (Table 8.1), it turns out that the value of the matrices is:

$$A = \begin{bmatrix} 1 & 0 \\ 0.0976 & -0.0202 \end{bmatrix}, B = \begin{bmatrix} 0 & 0.35 \\ 0.07744 & 0 \end{bmatrix}$$

$$D = \begin{bmatrix} 1 & 0.0976 \\ 0 & 1 \end{bmatrix}, F = \begin{bmatrix} -0.0976 & 0 \\ 0 & 0 \end{bmatrix}, G = \begin{bmatrix} 1 & 0 \\ 0 & 0.94 \end{bmatrix}, H = \begin{bmatrix} 0 & 0 \\ 0 & 0.06 \end{bmatrix}$$

Therefore, the matrices J and M would be:

$$J = \begin{bmatrix} 1.0146 & -0.066 \\ -0.2305 & 1.0417 \end{bmatrix}, M = \begin{bmatrix} 0.0597 \\ 0.2905 \end{bmatrix}$$

As we can see, the values of the matrix J are the same that appear in the expression (8.97), if we add the unit to the elements of the main diagonal.

Next, we express the matrix J, in terms of two matrices that give us the eigenvectors and eigenvalues of the system, using Jordan's decomposition:

$$J = O^{-1}NO$$

where the matrix N would be the eigenvalues and the O^{-1} matrix would be formed by the eigenvectors,

$$N = \begin{bmatrix} \lambda_1 & 0 \\ 0 & \lambda_2 \end{bmatrix}, O = \begin{bmatrix} v_{11} & v_{12} \\ v_{21} & v_{22} \end{bmatrix}$$

Therefore, we would have:

$$\begin{bmatrix} E_t\hat{c}_{t+1} \\ \hat{k}_{t+1} \end{bmatrix} = \begin{bmatrix} v_{11} & v_{12} \\ v_{21} & v_{22} \end{bmatrix}^{-1} \begin{bmatrix} \lambda_1 & 0 \\ 0 & \lambda_2 \end{bmatrix} \begin{bmatrix} v_{11} & v_{12} \\ v_{21} & v_{22} \end{bmatrix} \begin{bmatrix} \hat{c}_t \\ \hat{k}_t \end{bmatrix} + M\hat{a}_t \tag{N.31}$$

For the solution to be unique, it is required that $|\lambda_1| < 1$ and $|\lambda_2| > 1$. This is what is known as the rank condition, or the Blanchard-Khan condition. This condition indicates that there is a unique solution if the number of eigenvalues outside the unit circle is equal to the number of non-predetermined variables (jumping variables). In the model we are solving, we only have one jumping variable, the level of consumption, so one of the roots has to be outside the unit circle for the solution to be unique.

Applying Jordan's decomposition to model values results in:

$$N = \begin{bmatrix} 0.9040 & 0 \\ 0 & 1.1523 \end{bmatrix}, O = \begin{bmatrix} 0.9282 & 0.4455 \\ -0.9282 & 0.5545 \end{bmatrix}, O^{-1} = \begin{bmatrix} 0.5974 & -0.4799 \\ 1 & 1 \end{bmatrix}$$

The previous system can be written as

$$\begin{bmatrix} v_{11} & v_{12} \\ v_{21} & v_{22} \end{bmatrix} \begin{bmatrix} E_t \hat{c}_{t+1} \\ \hat{k}_{t+1} \end{bmatrix} = \begin{bmatrix} \lambda_1 & 0 \\ 0 & \lambda_2 \end{bmatrix} \begin{bmatrix} v_{11} & v_{12} \\ v_{21} & v_{22} \end{bmatrix} \begin{bmatrix} \hat{c}_t \\ \hat{k}_t \end{bmatrix} + \begin{bmatrix} v_{11} & v_{12} \\ v_{21} & v_{22} \end{bmatrix} M \hat{a}_t \quad \text{(N.32)}$$

By operating (multiplying the matrices), we can define:

$$v_{11} E_t \hat{c}_{t+1} + v_{12} \hat{k}_{t+1} = \lambda_1 v_{11} \hat{c}_t + \lambda_1 v_{12} \hat{k}_t + (v_{11} M_{11} + v_{12} M_{21}) \hat{a}_t \quad \text{(N.33)}$$

$$v_{21} E_t \hat{c}_{t+1} + v_{22} \hat{k}_{t+1} = \lambda_2 v_{21} \hat{c}_t + \lambda_2 v_{22} \hat{k}_t + (v_{21} M_{11} + v_{22} M_{21}) \hat{a}_t \quad \text{(N.34)}$$

Since $\lambda_2 > 1$, that is, the root is explosive, we can solve the second equation forward and obtain a unique and stable solution, so we can write it as,

$$v_{21} \hat{c}_t + v_{22} \hat{k}_t = \frac{v_{21}}{\lambda_2} E_t \hat{c}_{t+1} + \frac{v_{22}}{\lambda_2} \hat{k}_{t+1} - \frac{(v_{21} M_{11} + v_{22} M_{21})}{\lambda_2} \hat{a}_t \quad \text{(N.35)}$$

In the following period, this expression would be:

$$v_{21} E_t \hat{c}_{t+1} + v_{22} \hat{k}_{t+1} = \frac{v_{21}}{\lambda_2} E_{t+1} \hat{c}_{t+2} + \frac{v_{22}}{\lambda_2} \hat{k}_{t+2} - \frac{(v_{21} M_{11} + v_{22} M_{21})}{\lambda_2} E_t \hat{a}_{t+1}$$
$$\text{(N.36)}$$

By substituting in the previous expression, we obtain:

$$v_{21} \hat{c}_t + v_{22} \hat{k}_t =$$
$$\frac{v_{21}}{\lambda_2} E_{t+1} \hat{c}_{t+2} + \frac{v_{22}}{\lambda_2} \hat{k}_{t+2} - \frac{(v_{21} M_{11} + v_{22} M_{21})}{\lambda_2} \hat{a}_t - \frac{(v_{21} M_{11} + v_{22} M_{21})}{\lambda_2} E_t \hat{a}_{t+1} \quad \text{(N.37)}$$

and solving to infinity results in:

$$v_{21} \hat{c}_t + v_{22} \hat{k}_t = - \frac{(v_{21} M_{11} + v_{22} M_{21})}{\lambda_2} \sum_{j=0}^{\infty} \left(\frac{1}{\lambda_2} \right)^j E_t \hat{a}_{t+j} =$$
$$- \frac{(v_{21} M_{11} + v_{22} M_{21})}{\lambda_2} \sum_{j=0}^{\infty} \left(\frac{1}{\lambda_2} \right)^j \hat{a}_t = \frac{(v_{21} M_{11} + v_{22} M_{21})}{\rho - \lambda_2} \hat{a}_t \quad \text{(N.38)}$$

Solving for $\hat{c}_t$ results in:

$$\hat{c}_t = \frac{(v_{21} M_{11} + v_{22} M_{21})}{v_{21}(\rho - \lambda_2)} \hat{a}_t - \frac{v_{22}}{v_{21}} \hat{k}_t \quad \text{(N.39)}$$

Therefore, we can write the following solution for $\hat{c}_t$,

$$\hat{c}_t = S_1 \hat{k}_t + S_2 \hat{a}_t \quad \text{(N.40)}$$

Where

$$S_1 = - \frac{v_{22}}{v_{21}}$$

$$S_2 = \frac{(v_{21} M_{11} + v_{22} M_{21})}{v_{21}(\rho - \lambda_2)}$$

In the case of $\hat{k}_t$, the equivalent solution would be, introducing the previous solution to $\hat{c}_t$:

$$v_{11}(S_1\hat{k}_t + S_2\hat{a}_t) + v_{12}\hat{k}_{t+1} =$$

$$\lambda_1 v_{11}S_1\hat{k}_t + \lambda_1 v_{11}S_2\hat{a}_t + \lambda_1 v_{12}\hat{k}_t + (v_{11}M_{11} + v_{12}M_{21})\hat{a}_t \qquad (N.41)$$

and by operating

$$(v_{11}S_1 + v_{12})\hat{k}_{t+1} =$$

$$\lambda_1(v_{11}S_1 + v_{12})\hat{k}_t + (\lambda_1 v_{11}S_2 + v_{11}M_{11} + v_{12}M_{21} - v_{11}S_2\rho)\hat{a}_t \qquad (N.42)$$

resulting in:

$$\hat{k}_{t+1} = \frac{\lambda_1(v_{11}S_1 + v_{12})}{(v_{11}S_1 + v_{12})}\hat{k}_t + \frac{(\lambda_1 v_{11}S_2 + v_{11}M_{11} + v_{12}M_{21} - v_{11}S_2\rho)}{(v_{11}S_1 + v_{12})}\hat{a}_t \qquad (N.43)$$

expression that we can write as

$$\hat{k}_t = S_3\hat{k}_t + S_4\hat{a}_t \qquad (N.44)$$

Where

$$S_3 = \lambda_1$$

$$S_4 = \frac{(\lambda_1 v_{11}S_2 + v_{11}M_{11} + v_{12}M_{21} - v_{11}S_2\rho)}{(v_{11}S_1 + v_{12})}$$

Finally, the policy functions for the rest of the variables are obtained by replacing them in the initial system (N.22), resulting in:

$$\begin{bmatrix} \hat{y}_t \\ \hat{\imath}_t \end{bmatrix} = A^{-1}B\begin{bmatrix} \hat{c}_t \\ \hat{k}_t \end{bmatrix} + A^{-1}C\hat{a}_t = A^{-1}B\begin{bmatrix} S_1\hat{k}_t + S_2\hat{a}_t \\ \hat{k}_t \end{bmatrix} + A^{-1}C\hat{a}_t$$

$$= A^{-1}B\begin{bmatrix} S_1 \\ 1 \end{bmatrix} + A^{-1}(BS_2 + C)\hat{a}_t \qquad (N.45)$$

Therefore, the solutions for $\hat{y}_t$ and $\hat{\imath}_t$ can be written as

$$\begin{bmatrix} \hat{y}_t \\ \hat{\imath}_t \end{bmatrix} = S_5\hat{k}_t + S_6\hat{a}_t \qquad (N.46)$$

Where

$$S_5 = A^{-1}B\begin{bmatrix} S_1 \\ 1 \end{bmatrix}$$

$$S_6 = A^{-1}B\begin{bmatrix} S_2 \\ 0 \end{bmatrix} + A^{-1}C$$

By using the values of the matrices obtained above, it turns out that:

$$S_1 = 0.5973$$

$$S_2 = 0.5118$$

$$S_3 = 0.904$$

$$S_4 = 0.2342$$

$$S_5 = \begin{bmatrix} 0.35 \\ -0.6001 \end{bmatrix}$$

$$S_6 = \begin{bmatrix} 1 \\ 2.8753 \end{bmatrix}$$

The solution to the model can be defined in terms of the following two systems:

$$\begin{bmatrix} \hat{k}_{t+1} \\ \hat{a}_{t+1} \end{bmatrix} = \begin{bmatrix} S_3 & S_4 \\ 0 & \rho \end{bmatrix} \begin{bmatrix} \hat{k}_t \\ \hat{a}_t \end{bmatrix} + \begin{bmatrix} 0 \\ 1 \end{bmatrix} \varepsilon_{t+1}$$

$$\begin{bmatrix} \hat{c}_t \\ \hat{y}_t \\ \hat{\imath}_t \end{bmatrix} = \begin{bmatrix} S_1 & S_2 \\ S_5 & S_6 \end{bmatrix} \begin{bmatrix} \hat{k}_t \\ \hat{a}_t \end{bmatrix}$$

the first with the transition functions and the second with the policy functions. The transition functions are:

$$\hat{k}_{t+1} = 0.904\hat{k}_t + 0.234\hat{a}_t$$

$$\hat{a}_{t+1} = 0.8\hat{a}_t + \varepsilon_{t+1}$$

while the policy functions are:

$$\hat{c}_t = 0.5973\hat{k}_t + 0.511\hat{a}_t$$

$$\hat{y}_t = 0.35\hat{k}_t + \hat{a}_t$$

$$\hat{\imath}_t = -0.6001\hat{k}_t + 2.87530\hat{a}_t$$

Appendix O: The neoclassical growth model in MATLAB

Next, we present what a simple code would look like to simulate the Solow-Swan growth model in MATLAB. In this case, no optimization instrument is required and we simply have to numerically simulate the dynamic equation for the capital stock per capita.

```
% **********************************************
% An Introduction to Computational Macroeconomics
% A. Bongers, T. Gómez and J. L. Torres (2019)
% The Solow-Swan growth model in MATLAB
% File: m9.m
% **********************************************
clear all
% Periods
T = 100;
% Exogenous variables
A = 1.00;
s = 0.20;
% Parameters calibration
Alpha = 0.35;
Delta = 0.06;
n     = 0.02;
% Initial Steady State
kbar  =  ((n+Delta)/(s*A))^(1/(Alpha-1));
ybar  =  A*kbar^Alpha;
cbar  =  ybar-(n+Delta)*kbar;
ibar  =  (n+Delta)*kbar;
% Disturbance
s = 0.25;
%n = 0.01;
% New Steady State
kbar1  = ((n+Delta)/(s*A))^(1/(Alpha-1));
ybar1  =  A*kbar1^Alpha;
cbar1  = ybar1-(n+Delta)*kbar1;
ibar1  = (n+Delta)*kbar1;
% Dynamics
k(1)=kbar;
for i=1:T-1;
 k(i+1) = ((1-Delta)*k(i)+s*A*k(i)^Alpha)/(1+n);
end;
% Variables
y = A*k.^Alpha;
```

```
c = (1-s)*y;
% Growth rate
gy(1) = 0;
for i=2:T;
 gy(i) = 100*(y(i)-y(i-1))/y(i-1);
end;
% Graphics
j=1:T;
subplot(2,2,1)
plot(j,(y-ybar)./ybar,'Color',[0.25 0.25 0.25],'linewidth',3.5)
xlabel('Periods')
title('Production per capita')
subplot(2,2,2)
plot(j,(k-kbar)/kbar,'Color',[0.25 0.25 0.25],'linewidth',3.5)
xlabel('Periods')
title('Capital stock per capita')
subplot(2,2,3)
plot(j,(c-cbar)/cbar,'Color',[0.25 0.25 0.25],'linewidth',3.5)
xlabel('Periods')
title('Consumption per capita')
subplot(2,2,4)
plot(j,gy,'Color',[0.25 0.25 0.25],'linewidth',3.5)
xlabel('Periods')
title('Growth rate of output per capita')
```

Appendix P: Ramsey's model in DYNARE

In this appendix, we show how Ramsey's model in DYNARE would be. The code simulates a permanent increase in total factor productivity of 5%.

```
// *************************************************
// An Introduction to Computational Macroeconomics
// A. Bongers, T. Gómez and J. L. Torres (2019)
// The Ramsey model in DYNARE
// File: m10d.mod
// *************************************************
// Definition of endogenous variables
var y, c, i, k, W, R;
// Definition of exogenous variables
varexo A;
// Parameter definition
parameters alpha, beta, delta, n;
// Parameter values
alpha = 0.35;
beta  = 0.97;
delta = 0.06;
n     = 0.01;
// Defining capital stock as predetermined (state) variable
predetermined_variables k;
// Model equations
model;
1 = beta*((c/c(+1)) *(R(+1)+(1-delta)));
y = A*k^alpha;
k(+1) = (1-delta-n)*k+i;
y = c+i;
W = (1-alpha)*y;
R = alpha*A*k^(alpha-1);
end;
// Initial values
initval;
y = 1;
c = 0.8;
k = 3.5;
i = 0.2;
W = (1-alpha)*y;
A = 1;
R = alpha*A*k^(alpha-1);
end;
// Initial Steady State
steady;
ybar0=oo_.steady_state(1);
```

```
cbar0=oo_.steady_state(2);
ibar0=oo_.steady_state(3);
kbar0=oo_.steady_state(4);
Wbar0=oo_.steady_state(5);
Rbar0=oo_.steady_state(6);
// Stability conditions
check;
// Final values
endval;
y = 1;
c = 0.8;
k = 3.5;
i = 0.2;
W = (1-alpha)*y;
A = 1.05;
R = alpha*A*(k^(alpha-1));
end;
// New Steady State
steady;
ybar1=oo_.steady_state(1);
cbar1=oo_.steady_state(2);
ibar1=oo_.steady_state(3);
kbar1=oo_.steady_state(4);
Wbar1=oo_.steady_state(5);
Rbar1=oo_.steady_state(6);
simul(periods=58);
% Graphics
T=58;
j=1:T;
subplot(2,2,1)
plot(j,y,'Color',[0.25 0.25 0.25],'linewidth',3.5)
xlabel('Periods')
title('Output per capita')
subplot(2,2,2)
plot(j,k,'Color',[0.25 0.25 0.25],'linewidth',3.5)
xlabel('Periods')
title('Capital stock per capita')
subplot(2,2,3)
plot(j,c,'Color',[0.25 0.25 0.25],'linewidth',3.5)
xlabel('Periods')
title('Consumption per capita')
subplot(2,2,4)
plot(j,i,'Color',[0.25 0.25 0.25],'linewidth',3.5)
xlabel('Periods')
title('Investment per capita')
```

Index